Precarious Identities

I0585593

This book investigates the construction of identity and the precarity of the self in the work of the Calvinist Fulke Greville (1554–1628) and the Jesuit Robert Southwell (1561–1595). For the first time, a collection of original essays unites them with the aim to explore their literary production. The essays collected here define these authors' efforts to forge themselves as literary, religious, and political subjects amid a shifting politico-religious landscape. They highlight the authors' criticism of the court and underscore similarities and differences in thought, themes, and style. Altogether, the essays in this volume demonstrate the developments in cosmology, theology, literary conventions, political ideas, and religious dogmas, and trace their influence in the oeuvre of Greville and Southwell.

Vassiliki Markidou is Assistant Professor in English Literature and Culture at National and Kapodistrian University of Athens, Greece.

Afroditi-Maria Panaghis is Emerita Professor of English at National and Kapodistrian University of Athens, Greece.

Routledge Studies in Renaissance and Early Modern Worlds of Knowledge
Series Editor: Harald E. Braun
(University of Liverpool)

This series explores Renaissance and Early Modern Worlds of Knowledge (*c*.1400–*c*.1700) in Europe, the Americas, Asia and Africa. The volumes published in this series study the individuals, communities and networks involved in making and communicating knowledge during the first age of globalization. Authors investigate the perceptions, practices and modes of behaviour which shaped Renaissance and Early Modern intellectual endeavour and examine the ways in which they reverberated in the political, cultural, social and economic sphere.

The series is interdisciplinary, comparative and global in its outlook. We welcome submissions from new as well as existing fields of Renaissance Studies, including the history of literature (including neo-Latin, European and non-European languages), science and medicine, religion, architecture, environmental and economic history, the history of the book, art history, intellectual history and the history of music. We are particularly interested in proposals that straddle disciplines and are innovative in terms of approach and methodology.

The series includes monographs, shorter works and edited collections of essays. The Society for Renaissance Studies (www.rensoc.org.uk) provides an expert editorial board, mentoring, extensive editing and support for contributors to the series, ensuring high standards of peer-reviewed scholarship. We welcome proposals from early career researchers as well as more established colleagues.

Precarious Identities

Studies in the Work of Fulke Greville and Robert Southwell

Edited by Vassiliki Markidou and Afroditi-Maria Panaghis

LONDON AND NEW YORK

First published 2020
by Routledge
2 Park Square, Milton Park, Abingdon, Oxon OX14 4RN

and by Routledge
605 Third Avenue, New York, NY 10017

First issued in paperback 2021

Routledge is an imprint of the Taylor & Francis Group, an informa business

British Library Cataloguing-in-Publication Data
A catalogue record for this book is available from the British Library

Library of Congress Cataloging-in-Publication Data
Names: Markidou, Vassiliki, editor. | Panaghis, Afroditi-Maria, 1947- editor.
Title: Precarious identities : studies in the work of Fulke Greville and Robert Southwell / edited by Vassiliki Markidou and Afroditi-Maria Panaghis.
Description: New York : Routledge Taylor & Francis Group, 2020. | Series: Routledge studies in renaissance and early modern worlds ; 9 | Includes bibliographical references and index.
Identifiers: LCCN 2019042655 (print) | LCCN 2019042656 (ebook) | ISBN 9781138697607 (hardback) | ISBN 9781315521138 (ebook) | ISBN 9781315521121 (adobe pdf) | ISBN 9781315521107 (mobi) | ISBN 9781315521114 (epub)
Subjects: LCSH: Greville, Fulke, Baron Brooke, 1554-1628–Criticism and interpretation. | Southwell, Robert, Saint, 1561?-1595–Criticism and interpretation. | Identity (Psychology) in literature. | Self in literature. | Religion and literature–England–History–16th century. | Politics and literature–England–History–16th century. | Renaissance–England.
Classification: LCC PR2216 .P74 2020 (print) | LCC PR2216 (ebook) | DDC 820.9/353–dc23
LC record available at https://lccn.loc.gov/2019042655
LC ebook record available at https://lccn.loc.gov/2019042656

ISBN 13: 978-1-03-208390-2 (pbk)
ISBN 13: 978-1-138-69760-7 (hbk)

Typeset in Sabon
by Wearset Ltd, Boldon, Tyne and Wear

Contents

Figures

Contributors

Robert Appelbaum received his PhD from the University of California, Berkeley, and is currently Professor Emeritus of English Literature at Uppsala University and Senior Professor in Arts and Communication at Malmö University. His books include *Literature and Utopian Politics in Seventeenth-Century England* (Cambridge University Press, 2002); *Aguecheek's Beef, Belch's Hiccup, and Other Gastronomic Interjections: Literature, Culture and Food Among the Early Moderns* (University of Chicago Press, 2008); *Terrorism Before the Letter: Mythography and Political Violence in England, Scotland and France, 1559–1642* (Oxford University Press, 2015); *Working the Aisles: A Life in Consumption* (Zero Books, 2014); and, most recently *The Aesthetics of Violence: Art, Fiction, Drama and Film* (Rowman & Littlefield International, 2017). He has been the recipient of numerous grants and awards, and is currently a fellow for Vetenskapsrådet, Sweden, working on a monograph to be entitled *The Renaissance Discovery of Violence, from Boccaccio to Shakespeare*.

Sarah Covington is Professor of History at the Graduate Center and Queens College of the City University of New York. She is the author of *The Trail of Martyrdom: Wounds, Flesh and Metaphor in Seventeenth-Century England* (Palgrave-Macmillan, 2009) and *The Trail of Martyrdom: Persecution and Resistance in Sixteenth-Century England* (Notre Dame, 2003), with articles appearing in *The Journal of Ecclesiastical History*, *Archiv für Reformationsgeschichte*, *Albion*, *Book History*, *Reformation*, the *Journal of Scottish Historical Studies*, *History*, and *Mortality*. She has also co-edited *Explorations in Protestant Aesthetics and the Arts* (Routledge, 2019) and *Early Modern Ireland: New Sources, Methods and Perspective* (Routledge, 2018). Her forthcoming book entitled *Remembering Oliver Cromwell in Ireland* will be published by Oxford University Press.

Brian Cummings FBA is Anniversary Professor at the University of York in the Department of English and Related Literature. His books include *The Literary Culture of the Reformation: Grammar and Grace* (Paperback,

OUP, 2007), and *Mortal Thoughts: Religion, Secularity & Identity in Shakespeare and Early Modern Culture* (OUP, 2013). With Freya Sierhuis, he co-edited the Special Issue on "Fulke Greville and the Arts," *Sidney Journal*, 35: 1–2 (April, 2017). In 2012 he gave the Clarendon Lectures at Oxford University on "Bibliophobia," and in 2014 the Shakespeare Birthday Lecture at the Folger Library. With Alexandra Walsham (Cambridge) he is leading the project "Remembering the Reformation," funded by the Arts and Humanities Research Council from 2016 to 2019.

Alison Findlay is Professor of Renaissance Drama at Lancaster University and Chair of the British Shakespeare Association. www.britishshakespeare. ws/. Her books include *Illegitimate Power* (Manchester University Press, 1994), *A Feminist Perspective on Renaissance Drama* (Blackwell, 1999), *Women in Shakespeare* (Continuum, 2010). She co-edited *Twelfth Night: A Critical Reader* (2014) and *Shakespeare and Greece* (2017), both for Arden Shakespeare. She is co-investigator on the Arts and Humanities Research Council (AHRC) "Encyclopedia of Shakespeare's Language" project at Lancaster which uses corpus linguistics to explore Shakespeare's language at multiple levels. She has published numerous essays and journal articles on Shakespeare and his contemporary male dramatists. She also researches the drama of Shakespeare's "sisters" or female contemporaries, editing and staging their work. She is a founding director of The Rose Company, which has staged Lady Jane Lumley's *Iphigenia at Aulis* (*c*.1555), co-author of *Women and Dramatic Production 1550–1700* (2000), and author of *Playing Spaces in Early Women's Drama* (2006). She produced a site-specific performance of Lady Mary Wroth's *Love's Victory* (1617–1619) at Penshurst Place in 2018 and is currently editing the manuscript for publication by Revels Plays.

Theresa M. Kenney is Associate Professor of English at the University of Dallas. She has edited and translated *Women Are Not Human: An Anonymous Treatise and Responses* (Crossroad Publishing, 1998), and co-edited and contributed to *The Christ Child in Medieval Culture: Alpha es et O!* (University of Toronto Press, 2012). She is currently working on a book called *"All Wonders in One Sight": The Christ Child Among the Elizabethan and Stuart Poets*. She has written and published extensively on Jane Austen and has also published essays on Dante, Dickens, Donne, Emily Bronte, and Arcangela Tarrabotti. She has just completed another book on Jane Austen's sense of an ending and is working on another on the Holy Grail and the Easter Liturgy. She resides with her husband and two daughters in Texas.

Vassiliki Markidou is Assistant Professor in English Literature and Culture at the Faculty of English Language and Literature, National and Kapodistrian University of Athens. She has published a number of essays and journal articles on representations of early modern religious, national, and cultural identity, with particular reference to the Ottomans, spatial and temporal palimpsests, and seventeenth- and eighteenth-century women's writing. She has co-edited *Shakespeare and Greece* (The Arden Shakespeare, 2017) and the second volume of the Anglophone electronic journal of comparative literary studies *Synthesis*, entitled *Configurations of Cultural Amnesia* (2010).

Elizabeth Mazzola teaches Medieval and Early Modern Literature at The City College of New York. She has written several articles and books on Spenser, Sidney, Shakespeare, and early modern women writers. Her most recent book, *Women and Mobility on Shakespeare's Stage*, was published by Routledge in 2017. A current project investigates *Macbeth*'s revisions of early modern ideas about authority, cruelty, and community.

Afroditi-Maria Panaghis was educated in Egypt, Greece, and the United States and is Emerita Professor of English at the National and Kapodistrian University of Athens, Greece. She has also taught at Carnegie-Mellon, U.S.A, and The American College of Greece, Deree. She is the author of *T. L. Beddoes: A Study in the Concept of Death* (University of Athens Press, 1990), *Vincent O'Sullivan: A Quest for Divine Union* (Biographical Publishing Company, 2001), *The Defeat of Death: A Reading of Sir Henry Rider Haggard's Cleopatra* (Peter Lang, 2013), many articles that cover a wide spectrum of English, American, and Continental literature, a translated novel, and poems. Presently, she is working on a book *Oscar Wilde and Vernon Lee in Dialogue* with Maria Pirgerou to be published in 2020 by Routledge.

Emily A. Ransom serves as Assistant Professor of Humanities and English at the University of Wisconsin–Green Bay, where she teaches courses in medieval and Renaissance literature, Shakespeare, the reformations, and biblical literature. Her research focuses on the intersection of religious and literary culture in the reformations, and her published articles on authors ranging from Thomas More to John Milton have appeared in *English Literary Renaissance*, *Studies in Philology*, and *Moreana*. Other past projects have included cataloguing the reliquary chapel of the Basilica of the Sacred Heart at the University of Notre Dame, serving as managing editor of *Religion and Literature*, copyediting for the Vatican and the European Union, and co-translating Ælred of Rievaulx's liturgical sermons for Cistercian Press, and she now serves as the representative of the Amici Thomae Mori for the Renaissance Society of America. In addition to her current projects on Ludolph of Saxony and Dame Gertrude More, she is coediting the projected five volumes of *The Complete Works of Robert Southwell* for Oxford University Press.

Alison Shell is Professor of Early Modern Studies in the Department of English at University College London. She is the author of *Catholicism,*

Controversy and the English Literary Imagination, 1558–1660 (Cambridge University Press, 1999), *Oral Culture and Catholicism in Early Modern England* (Cambridge University Press, 2007) and *Shakespeare and Religion* (Methuen Press, 2010). Currently she holds a Leverhulme Major Research Fellowship to work on "The Drama of the British Counter-Reformation."

Rachel White is currently a Research Associate on the Thomas Nashe Project at Newcastle University where she has worked on attributing authorship to texts connected with Nashe and is the editor of two texts attributed to him. She has also held a position as a Postdoctoral Research Assistant at the University of Leeds on a project looking at the effect of genre and style on authorship attribution. She completed her PhD at Lancaster University and her thesis was titled "Occult Poetics and the Production of English Verse, 1558–1603." Her research interests include the occult tradition, the boundaries between magic and science in the early modern period, poetry, and print of the late-sixteenth century.

Acknowledgments

We would like to thank all and each one of our contributors from the U.K., U.S.A., and Sweden for their excellent contribution as well as for their cooperation and understanding throughout the many stages this project underwent before materializing. We would also like to thank Harald E. Braun the Series Editor of Routledge Studies in Renaissance and Early Modern Worlds of Knowledge, and the History Editor Max Novick, for their invaluable advice during moments of crisis. Thanks are also due to the Senior Editor Jennifer Morrow for her useful suggestions and comments, Charlotte Parkins for her invaluable help with copy-editing and the Project Manager Claire Toal for overseeing the production of the book. Last but not least, we are grateful to the National and Kapodistrian University of Athens for funding our research in the United Kingdom at the Universities of Lancaster and Manchester, and the United States at Harvard, Tufts, and Boston Universities.

Timelines

Fulke Greville (1554–1628)

Timeline (excluding his literary production)

3 October 1554	Born at Alcester, Warwickshire; son to Fulke Greville, Warwickshire gentleman, and Anne Neville
1562	Sent to Shrewsbury School where he became lifelong friend to his schoolmate, Philip Sidney
1568	Attended Jesus College, Cambridge, though he never received a degree
1577	Entered the court of Elizabeth I together with Philip Sidney (as two of the youngest ones); aligned himself with the radical Protestant faction centered around the Earl of Leicester and Sir Francis Walsingham
1580s	Sidney and Greville's expansionist plans are thwarted by the Queen
1586	Sidney was fatally wounded at the battle of Zutphen; Greville was one of the pall-bearers at his funeral and published *Exequiae* on his friend's death
1586	MP for Warwickshire
1586	*Cælica*'s composition was already in process
1590	Greville was, to some extent, involved in the publication of Books I–III of Sidney's revised *Arcadia*
1590s	*Mustapha* and *Alaham*, his two surviving tragedies, are penned (an unauthorized edition of *Mustapha* was published in 1609 while *Alaham* was first printed as late as in 1633; Greville referred to a third tragedy on the topic of Antony and Cleopatra, which he set to fire in fear that it was too dangerous in political terms)
1598	Appointed Treasurer of the Navy (until 1604)
1601	Following the Earl of Essex's abortive coup-d'état, Greville commanded one of the group of soldiers that entered Essex House prior to his arrest
1603	Death of Elizabeth I; James I ascends to the throne

1604	Greville is made Knight of Bath in compensation for having been removed from the Treasureship of the Navy; the King grants him Warwick Castle
1 October 1614	Appointed Chancellor and Under-Treasurer of the Exchequer as well as Privy Counsellor
1621	Deprived of his offices yet rises to peerage and is invested as Baron Brooke of Beauchamp's Court
1625	Death of James I; Charles I ascends to the throne; Greville appointed once again Privy Counsellor and to Charles' inner cabinet
1627	Greville appointed the Dutch scholar Isaac Dorislaus to offer a series of lectures in political history at Cambridge University; his first lecture on Tacitus and authority led Archbishop Laud to ban the remainder of his lectures
1 September 1628	Greville was stabbed by his servant, Ralph Haywood, and died a month later

Note concerning his literary production

In the course of his life, Greville wrote and repeatedly revised the following extant works:

> *Caelica, Letter to an Honorable Lady, Mustapha, Alaham, A Dedication to Sir Philip Sidney* also known as *The Life of the Renowned Philip Sidney, A Treatise of Monarchy, An Inquisition Upon Fame and Honour, A Treatie of Warres, Treatie on Humane Learning,* and *Treatise on Religion.*

Due to this fact, there is lack of agreement among critics as regards the dating of his works. For information on Greville's life and works, see Ronald A. Rebholz, *The Life of Fulke Greville* (Oxford: Clarendon, 1971); Joan Rees, *Fulke Greville, Lord Brooke, 1554–1628: A Critical Biography* (London: Routledge, 1971); Matthew Steggle, "Fulke Greville: Life and Works" in *Sidney Journal* 19:1–2 (2001): 1–161. [*Fulke Greville: A Special Double Issue*, ed. Matthew C. Hansen and Matthew Woodcock]

Robert Southwell (1561–1595)

Timeline

| 1561 | Robert Southwell was born to Richard Southwell a gentlemen and courtier of Horsham St. Faith's, Norfolk, and Bridget Southwell |

1576–1578	Robert was sent to the continent to attend the Jesuit school at Douai and the Jesuit-run Collège de Clermont for six months in Paris where he came under the influence of the Jesuit theologian Leonard Lessius
1578	Robert walked to Rome and applied to the Jesuit novitiate at Saint Andrea
1578	*The Spiritual Exercises and Devotions*
1580–1585	Robert studied philosophy and theology at the Roman College (known today as the Gregorian University, or "the Greg") for two years, was ordained, graduated with a BA in philosophy, and was promoted to Prefect of Studies. During this time he published a newsletter in which he presented stories about the activities of the mission in England which he acquired by correspondents
1586	Father Robert sought and obtained leave to join Father Garnet on a mission to England. They landed secretly on the Kentish coast of Southeast England
1586–1592	For six years Father Robert ministered mass in London and made trips to Sussex and the north of England while he wrote poetry and prose
1587	He wrote *The Epistle of Comfort* which was printed in 1595
1589	Southwell took up residence in the house of the Countess of Arundel where he stayed for three years
1589	He wrote Epistle to his Father which was printed in 1596 together with *Short Rule of Good Life*
1591	Both *Triumph over Death, A Humble Supplication to her Maiestie*, and *Magdalens funeral teares* were written but were printed in 1595
1592	Southwell was arrested by Richard Topcliffe at the home of Richard Bellamy in the Harrow northwest of London. He was first tortured at Topcliffe's home then moved to the Gatehouse prison, where he was subjected to the torture of the "the manacles." He was starved and left covered in maggots and lice before he was moved to the Tower of London where he languished for three years
1594	Southwell was brought to trial and sentenced to be hung, drawn, and quartered
1595	Southwell was executed February 21st at Tyburn hill
1595	*Saint Peters complaint and other Poems, Mæoniæ*, and *Fourfold Meditation: Of the Foure Last Things*
1616	*Saint Peters complaint and Mary Magdalens funeral teares* Robert Southwell was beatified December 15th 1929 by Pope Pius XI, and canonized October 25th 1970 by Pope Paul VI

N.B. Information on the life and martyrdom of Robert Southwell is available in the following sources:

Challoner, Richard. *Memoirs of Missionary Priests*. London: Mark Wardle, 1803.

Foley, Henry. "The Life and Martyrdom of Father Robert Southwell." In Vol. I of *Records of the English Province of the Society of Jesus*. London: Burns and Oates, 1877.

Janelle, Pierre. *Robert Southwell, the Writer: A Study in Religious Inspiration*. London: Sheed & Ward, 1935.

Devlin, Christopher. *Life of Robert Southwell: Poet and Martyr*. New York: Farrar, Straus & Cudahy, 1956.

Brownlow, Frank W. *Robert Southwell*. Boston, Massachusetts: Twayne Publishers, 1996.

Pilarz, Scott. *Robert Southwell: Missions of Literature 1561–1595*. London & Burlington, Vermont: Ashgate, 2004.

Introduction

Vassiliki Markidou and Afroditi-Maria Panaghis

"The generall end is to fashion a gentleman or noble person in vertuous and gentle discipline. Which for that I conceived shoulde be most plausible and pleasing, beeing coloured with an historicall fiction, the which the most part of men delight to read."

Edmund Spenser[1]

Writing on the most acclaimed English literary figure a decade ago, Andrew Hadfield noted that

Analysis of the construction of identity has become hegemonic itself, and it dominates the theorized field of Renaissance studies. In so many ways this has been a beneficial and timely development that has transformed the study of Renaissance literature and made it a much more exciting field in which to work than it was twenty-five years ago before the publication of Stephen Greenblatt's *Renaissance Self-Fashioning*.[2]

Precarious Identities: Studies in the Work of Fulke Greville and Robert Southwell explores identity construction and the precarity of the self in the works of Fulke Greville (1554–1628) and Robert Southwell (1561–1595) in the context of the available theories and critical approaches. For the first time, the literary production of both the Calvinist Greville and the Jesuit Southwell, near contemporaries, placed, because of their religious beliefs, on either side of the confessional divide, will be investigated.[3] By setting a Protestant writer, courtier, and public official vis-à-vis a Catholic writer and missionary, this book attempts to showcase unexplored aspects of Greville and Southwell's vision shaped by as well as shaping their effort to forge themselves as literary, religious, and political subjects. The volume attempts to trace the shifting sands of selfhood within the protean latter half of the sixteenth-century and early seventeenth-century cultural, political, and religious landscape reflected in and in turn forming the work of the two writers. Besides mapping the precarious process of their self-fashioning and shedding light on Protestantism and Catholicism's role in molding religious and political subjectivity, this study also refers to the state's effort to define "the relationship between the temporal and spiritual domains, between politics and religion, treason and conscience, the royal prerogative and the liberties of the subject."[4] In doing so, *Precarious Identities* examines different genres (poetry, drama, and prose), devotional and hagiographical writings but also political, philosophical, theological, and historical views, the impact of scientific thinking and rationality on Greville and Southwell's work as well as their personal and intellectual connections.

Throughout the ages, identity and self-fashioning have had a prominent place in the thought of philosophers, theologians, and artists, who vied to induce and guide their readers into shaping their selves. According to Plato, for example, subjectivity meant "centering or unification of the moral self"; to Aristotle and Edmund Spenser, the acquisition of the twelve moral virtues; to Saint Augustine "conceptualized interiority" through introspection as an act of piety that leads to the divine; and to René Descartes "*Cogito ergo sum* (I am thinking therefore I am)."[5] The early modern era gave rise to diverse and numberless constructions of identity marked by two distinctive divergent, yet also convergent attitudes. First, alongside the religious reformation there was a relentless quest for the discovery of identity due to the shift that took place in the ethical visions of humanists and Protestant reformers, both of whom emphasized the relationship between the self and the expression of thoughts and emotions on the one hand and actions on the other. Hence not only did the process of self-fashioning reveal the fragmentation of the self, it also evidenced a public guise to conceal convictions or feelings in other words, to practice "honest dissimulation."[6] This realization is reflected in the early modern commonplace of the *theatrum mundi*, the world as a theatrical stage. Indeed, whoever wished to advance in court or survive amid persecution, as is the case with Greville and Southwell respectively, had to adopt roles or masks that is, act and not live the self as Michel de Montaigne notes in his *Essays*.[7] Second, the early modern era was cognizant to the fact that identity is the outcome of social, economic, religious, political, and intellectual factors. As Jean E. Howard points out, the self was viewed as "a text, not as an autonomous entity but rather as a site on which broader institutional and political forces are inscribed."[8] Hence, there was a keen awareness that "individualism is a multidimensional phenomenon, an amalgam of practices and values with no discernible center."[9] As such, the self is elusive and fluid, not a fixed entity, thus the individual is involved in a constant quest to actualize it. It is also distinguished for its "brittle and inadequate" nature, for its "explicitly layered quality, and for its sense of inwardness."[10] Since identity is shaped by external influences, "the self becomes a cultural artifact, a historical and ideological illusion generated by the economic, social, religious, and political upheavals of the renaissance."[11]

With the advent of the homocentric early modern world, and the individual's shift center stage, the need for the articulation of selfhood gained unprecedented momentum. Questions such as "who am I"; is the self "continually made and remade"; or does "the concept of self-fashioning provide an adequate description of the production of subjectivities or, more prosaically, of the discovery of the individual in the renaissance" were ever-present in the thought of writers.[12] Petrarch for example, highly influential with early modern English writers including Greville and Southwell, crafted, as Debora Shuger aptly noted, his *Rime sparse* as "an autobiography of inwardness in which the complex entanglements of transcendent and erotic desire weave the deep strata of the self."[13] In doing so, he explored the notion of the self by underscoring his relation to Laura, the past and present, self-knowledge, and the rational being, while he also explicitly linked self-fashioning to yearning for transcendence. Even more, in *The Soul's Conflict with Passion, Secretum*, he argued that by "coming to a tardy consciousness of our sins, we shall learn to know ourselves"; contended that being "true to [ourselves]" is achieved through contemplation of death and recognition of one's sinfulness; and advised that one should protect one's soul from the passions of the flesh so that after its purification it could begin unshackled to contemplate the mysteries of the Divine.[14] He also claimed in *On His Own Ignorance* that "it is better to will the good than to know the truth" and insisted that the soul must develop the virtues that lead to salvation.[15] Southwell echoed Petrarch in postulating that no matter how harsh the tribulations, suffering, or even violent death and martyrdom are; they are necessary for the purification of the soul and its redemption as well as for the construction of the religious self; while Greville rewrote with irony the Petrarchan entanglements of the sacred and the erotic, the religious and the secular, and the concomitant intense feelings of failure and self-effacement, that altogether provide an extraordinary disclosure of subjectivity. While Petrarch attempted in the aforementioned texts to delineate the contours of religious identity, Baldassare Castiglione associated self-fashioning inextricably with the field of politics and the figure of the courtier in particular. He stated that "nature herself createth and shapeth menne apt to express pleasantly and geveth them a countenaunce, gestures, a voice, and words for the pourpose to counterfeit what they luste."[16] Castiglione postulated the creation and adoption of roles or masks that is dissimulation, as a vital means of surviving and/or rising in court. Greville, caught in the ebb and flow of the Elizabethan and Jacobean courts, was apprehensive of this necessity. It is also worth noting that the practice of dissimulation, like equivocation, was meant to deceive political and/or religious enemies.[17] For example, because religious opposition was deemed political, both techniques were employed by the Jesuit missionaries including Southwell as well as many Catholics (and, it should be noted, even Puritans) of the Elizabethan and Jacobean era. In so doing, they concealed their beliefs by conforming to Protestant worship in order to avoid severe penalties and persecution for loyalty to their religion as well as counter the Protestant state's intolerance to treason.

Clearly then, the early modern era was distinguished by a heightened awareness that identity is (chiefly) fictional. As John J. Martin notes, one should take into consideration that "individualism itself is a construction, that, indeed, the human self is in many ways nothing more than a fiction, and that it is above all what might be called the renaissance representations of the self as an individual, expressive subject that require explanation."[18] Indeed, self-fashioning conveys the strategies through which politics and religion in the early modern era created the fiction of individual autonomy.[19] Greenblatt stresses the fictionality of the self and invites us "to read 'self-fashioning' as free, expressive self-making," pointing out that all human beings are "impersonators whose clear title to identity is secured by an authority irrevocably deeded to an artificial person."[20] Outlining the process of early modern self-fashioning he contends that

> in the sixteenth century there appears to be an increased self-consciousness about the fashioning of human identity as a manipulable artful process. Such self-consciousness had been widespread among the elite in the classical world, but Christianity brought a growing suspicion of man's power to shape identity. Fashioning may suggest the achievement of a less tangible shape, a consistent mode of perceiving and behaving. As we might expect, the recurrent model for this latter fashioning is Christ.[21]

Roy Porter also underlines the crucial role that transcendent longings play in the process of fashioning a religious subjectivity associated not only with the notion of *imago dei* but also with the relationship between individual and God realized through faith which means more than "the issue of the existence of God [since] faith has to do with knowing, doing, and being."[22] In the context of the doctrine of *imago dei*, sin is assumed to either have partially destroyed the image of God, though the ability to turn to Him at any time still exists, or to have totally obliterated it. In the first case, Christ's salvation of humankind is minimized while in the second, it proves the only means of its redemption.[23] Porter also argues that

> the age of faith took certain steps towards asserting the sovereignty of the inner self. Christianity's core doctrine of a unique, eternal soul inspired those brave acts of personal integrity, modeled on Christ's crucifixion, which were the stuff of martyrs; and St Augustine's *Confessions* gives a remarkable self-portrait of the soul as guilty sinner. Self-denial was the supreme good in monastic rule; saints and mystics transcended their selfishness in divine love, John of the Cross seeking the annihilation of the self.[24]

To Greville and Southwell, both trying to cope with humanity's sin and its repercussions, identity is in large measure conceptualized on the basis of the doctrine of *imago dei*; hence, while, as will be demonstrated, they are engaging in self-fashioning they are conscious of the limits and limitations of this process.

The significance of this realization for both writers as well as their oeuvre coheres with David Cressy and Lori Anne Farrell's statement that in early modern England religion permeated every aspect of life including "the pattern of the cosmos, the history and destiny of the world, and the ordering of social and domestic relationships" which were investigated in the context of the Bible and current theological ideas.[25] In fact, Christianity "provided a system for understanding, a framework for discussion, and a vocabulary for the expression of complex notions, from the governance of the self to the governance of the state."[26] At the same time however, "Biblical criticism was in a state of flux";[27] and religion, which infused public and private affairs and had the power to change the course of events and destabilize the state leading to either domestic or foreign war at any moment, became a divisive subject that "affected everyone since neither the political scene nor the social was immune from the claims of faith or the obligations of Christian duty. Everyone's life was affected by altercations in the structure and authority of the church, and by changes in religious values, beliefs, discipline, and style."[28] Consequently, both published writings and manuscripts from strictly religious ones to those that appeared to dabble with religion, were deemed sensitive and potentially dangerous material.

However, a break from religious constraints was triggered by humanism, which rejected "the theological dogma of man as a loathsome sinner required to abase himself before God, and began to take delight in man himself the apex of creation, the master of nature, the wonder of the world."[29] Against this backdrop, Porter argues that during the renaissance "the literate, gifted, elite began to liberate itself from the chains of custom, conformity and the Church, taking a fearless leap forward into self-discovery and self-fulfillment."[30] Yet, as Cynthia Marshall points out, "texts affording self-shattering served as counter forces to the development of modern subjectivity, in a longer view they enabled its continued growth by offering temporary respite from the accumulating pressures of individual selfhood."[31] Ultimately, historians "identified the seventeenth century as the great divide, the point from which rationality could serve as the foundation stone of the self-determining individual."[32] After all, undertaking a systematic questioning of religious beliefs and cultural values, though an unsettling experience, proved the only way to achieve identity. Notably, Descartes defines a new role for the self with his "proposition *cogito ergo sum*: my own consciousness is the one thing of which I can be sure, and hence the one fixed Archimedean point in the universe."[33] He thus underlines that it is "not God or nature, but the ego, the conscious self," that becomes "the source of understanding, and so of everything else."[34] As a result the essence of existing as a human identity is the possibility of being aware of our selves, in other words, being self-conscious.[35]

In the light of this short prelude on the self and its multiple and varied formations the editors of this volume contend that the proclivity for self-scrutiny as well as the deconstruction, re-construction, and presentation of multiple selves that characterize Greville and Southwell's oeuvre constitute one of the many reasons for which they have been brought together in this study. Both writers confronted the ubiquitous social, religious, and political changes that made life unpredictable; they grappled with and projected the fragile or fragmented self; and depicted diverse experiences that were often confusing and frustrating. Another ground for their joint appearance is the fact that their work reflects the fluidity of the self on the one hand, and their endeavor to formulate their numerous selves amid telling politico-religious contingencies into what Jacob Burckhardt labeled "many-sided men" on the other.[36] Indeed, both were apprehensive that their identity had to be continually made and modified, dismantled and assembled against an ephemeral, mutable setting. The intersecting political and religious spheres played a crucial role for both of them in the process of fashioning their religious subjectivity, especially since they were on opposite sides of the confessional divide. They were conscious of and highly concerned with the development of tensions in the theological understanding of the secular world of the latter sixteenth and early seventeenth century, which had begun to establish a different approach as regards the state and self-rule. Greville and Southwell are also conjoined as regards their varied reaction to the uncertain and ever-changing politico-religious scene and their employment of themes and methods to forge their conceptualization of the nation's tendency towards violence and cope with the fear of an eruption of civil war or foreign threats. They also converge in the great influence exerted on them by the scientific and philosophical ideas that prevailed during their time. Greville was highly interested in developments in the fields of cosmology and philosophy that were of major concern to an intellectual community which consisted of figures such as Giordano Bruno, Philip Sidney, and John Dee, all of whom he was associated with. As for Southwell, his education at Douai and Rome as well as his association with theologians and thinkers such as Thomas Darbyshire, Leonardus Lessius, Gregory Martin, William Allen, and Thomas Stapleton helped mold his thinking and in turn his work. Finally, both lived on the continent for a considerable stretch of time and were influenced by literary conventions, trends, and themes, as well as political ideas (Taciteanism and resistance theory), and religious dogmas (Calvinist and Jesuit) that informed their writings and intrigued their readership.

Not only similarities but also dissimilarities bring the two writers together. As already mentioned, though both religion and politics formed their life, shaped their writings, and played a vital part in the process of their self-fashioning, Greville enunciated his precarious identity primarily as a political figure, statesman, writer, and biographer, while Southwell as a preacher, writer, missionary, and martyr. On a more personal level, both posed as sinners yet, as will be demonstrated, they postulated disparate views on sin and redemption in their struggle to acquire knowledge of themselves and define their relationship with God. Their religious fashioning is interwoven with the doctrine of *imago dei*, according to which sin has changed human nature into something different than that which God created yet luckily the potential to recreate it has not been lost.[37] It was against this background that Greville and Southwell formed dissimilar religious subjectivities. Greville expressed deep anxiety as regards the destructive effect of the fall and of sin on humanity, while he was highly distraught at the idea that only the elect will be saved by divine grace, an issue that he retained resolutely unresolved. Southwell on the contrary, preached that all sinners, and not only the chosen few, could be redeemed due to God's love and mercy provided that they recognized their sinfulness and abjectness and followed a ceaseless process of amendment to prepare for the encounter with the Divine.

As will also be evidenced, Greville and Southwell led a precarious life in terms of their political selves. Both experienced state coercion since Greville's political ambitions were crushed and Southwell was arrested, tortured, and executed. The former however recurred to republicanism, and most particularly to Taciteanism, in order to criticize the Elizabethan and Jacobean courts and castigated tyranny despite his support for monarchy while the latter pledged his loyalty to his monarch, yet not only did he denounce the Elizabethan court he also challenged the courtiers with the aim to reform them. Interestingly, both writers declared that Elizabeth I had deficient counselors yet they remained loyal to her and rejected the idea of overthrowing a sitting monarch. Nonetheless, Greville reproved tyranny and appeared to support a "monarchical republic" and Southwell reproached queen and courtiers and though an ardent proponent of reconciliation held a more radical and intransigent stance. Lastly, in reference to their readership, Greville refrained throughout his life from publishing his works yet intended for them to be read posthumously, while Southwell published his writings in order to preach the redemption of the depraved Christian identity, prepare his coreligionists for martyrdom as well as comfort them and convert Protestants back to what he held to be the true religion.[38] His persistence to bridge the gap between the two communities attracted a wide reading public across denominational boundaries and led to numerous reprints of his works, especially after his execution.

The two writers are brought together in Sarah Covington's comparative overview "Calvinist Statesman, Jesuit Martyr: The Worlds of Fulke Greville and Robert Southwell," which opens the volume. Covington introduces them, underlines the theological and political controversies to which they responded, and establishes the historical framework of this project. She contends that although Greville and Southwell differ widely in terms of their religious denomination they both struggled to tackle complex political circumstances and make personal choices. She also argues that even though they belong to different sides of the confessional divide their writings merit comparison because they are informed by similar literary conventions while their creators appear to have "shared similar psychological impulses and frustrations." Covington, furthermore, stresses Greville and Southwell's fraught relationship towards the state. Even though both professed their loyalty to their monarch and avoided antagonizing state authority, the Calvinist statesman with the Tacitean humanist leanings verged on assuming an oppositional or politically ambiguous stance thus leading a precarious life while the Jesuit missionary was branded a traitor for his illegal return to England and accused of "dual allegiance." Finally, Covington underscores the crucial role of the volatile early modern theological and political landscape and their personal faith on their work and claims that both Greville and Southwell were compelled "to adopt a poetic as well as implicitly political response to the realities of the day."

Part I of the volume is devoted to the prose, poetry, and drama of Fulke Greville. It opens with Alison Findlay's chapter " 'Freedom Among the Dead': Greville's *Dedication to Sir Philip Sidney*" which argues that memorial biography is, for Greville, not just a process of writing another life, but a specifically Protestant means of mourning; and analyzes Greville's *Dedication* as a work in which the process of writing and of rewriting to "imitate or tread in the steps" of Sidney redefines Greville's own sense of self and shapes his Protestant politics, hopes, fears, and beliefs. In Chapter 2 "Reading might make us know: Vulcan's brothers and Myra's posies in Greville's *Caelica*," Elizabeth Mazzola offers a revisionist reading of the sonnet sequence. Unlike earlier readings that present the beloved in *Cælica* as cynical and desperate, Mazzola argues that Greville registers self-splitting together with an unparalleled meticulous depiction of "the beloved's charms and agency, her capacity for desire aligned with an affinity for language and wish for clarity and freedom." Thus *Cælica* enacts diversion from "the Petrarchan project" by fashioning the beloved as "a rival maker of meaning and authority" to his male speaker while bringing "maturity and honesty" to it through presenting female readers "as suitable readers and partners in love." Chapter 3 focuses on Greville's effort to map "the precarious position of humankind whose knowledge is 'never fixt' " as well as grapple with the double quest of gaining infinite knowledge and knowing God. In " 'The Mind of Man is this worlds true dimension': space, knowledge and the divine in Fulke Greville's *A Treatie of Humane Learning* and *A Treatise of Religion*," Rachel White postulates that the specific texts demonstrate Greville's deep concern with the human desire for intellectual inquiry and its conflict with divinely prescribed boundaries. She states that in an era of unprecedented developments in the knowledge of science and the workings of the world, Greville's verse treatises stress that true knowledge results in the realization of one's place in "the divine order" and in "an active participation in seeking God" not in the physical world, beset by temptations, but "within." Therefore, White claims, to Greville human beings are caught in an endless quest for self-knowledge, through which they aim at achieving reunion with the Divine and regaining what was lost with the fall. In Chapter 4 "Duality and aporia in Greville's political writings," Robert Applebaum sheds light on Greville's consistently conflicting ideas as a crucial means through which he fashioned his political writings. Through an examination of *A Treatise of Monarchy*, *A Treatie of Warres*, *An Inquisition upon Fame and Honour*, and (the contested and in his view non-Grevillian text which however displays affinities with Greville's political writings) *The Five Years of King James*, Applebaum argues that Greville's political texts are imbued with duality, a fact that constitutes an "enabling self-contradiction." Hence the tension of polarities such as monarchy and "resentment over social inequality," tyranny and "patience and the punishments of God, peace as an unqualified good and the conduct of war as a virtuous necessity," remains unresolved in Greville's political writings and it is precisely this irresolution that helps him craft "a space of articulation, of the poetry of political hope and polit-ical despair." The next two chapters focus on Greville's drama. In the fifth, entitled "Monarchy and patriarchy in Fulke Greville's *Mustapha*," Brian Cummings analyzes the ways in which Greville's first surviving tragedy is shaped by as well as reflects his complex political and religious identity. He examines the link between the play's religious politics and the anxieties of ideology in James's court and demonstrates that through his complex use of contemporary representations of the Ottoman Empire, Greville attempts to tackle the ideas of the divine right and patriarchal authority that reflect a crucial part of the history of English political thought. Finally, in Chapter 6 "'A voyce cries out, *Reuenge and Liberty*': republicanism and gender in Fulke Greville's *Alaham*," Vassiliki Markidou argues that Greville's second extant drama unravels his precarious political subjectivity and equivocal attitude towards gender conventions. She contends that *Alaham* dramatizes a strong critique of both tyranny and the idea of overthrowing a tyrannical monarch that is bound to result, in its author's view, in political upheaval, moral corruption, and excessive violence thus emphasizing the limits of republicanism while at the same time presenting the ambiguous interrela-tionship between republicanism and gender. Most of all, Markidou argues, *Alaham* rests heavily on the construction and deconstruction of identities as well as the benefits and losses entailed by this process.

Chapter 7 introduces Part II of the volume, which is devoted to Robert Southwell's poetry and prose. In "'This pompe is prizèd there': Southwell's challenge to courtly identities in 'New Prince, New Pompe'" Theresa Kenney contends that Southwell employs inversion, Christ's Incarnation, and Proleptic Passion "to correct the corrupt idea of the court" and challenge the identity of the queen and her courtiers. She argues that through the specific Nativity poem Southwell, besides glorifying the newborn Child, castigates the Elizabethan court. By adopting the role of the courtier and pilgrim, "in the corrected heavenly court of Bethlehem," he instructs the court to show humility, understanding, and tolerance as well as "re-orient[s] the queen and her court towards poverty and simplicity as expressions of magisterial authority." Kenney also declares that "New Prince, New Pompe" calls upon its readers, after having chastised them, to discard false identities founded on "false joys of wealth and political power" and embrace a Christian identity on seeing the Christ Child in the manger. In Chapter 8, "Complaint as reconciliation in the literary mission of Robert Southwell," Emily Ransom argues that Southwell's literary strategy of fashioning himself as an English complaint poet contributed to his popularity among Protestant readers. She demonstrates the significance of the English complaint mode to his literary mission, "both in terms of his poetic theory and his strategic success among Protestant readers," and "the affectivity and suspension" it provides by inviting the reader to "an Ignatian approach to human passion" essentially different from "the neo-Stoic moderation popular in contemporaneous consolation literature indicative of Calvin's commentaries of the biblical texts." She also claims that by translating the Ignatian aesthetic into English complaint, the poet provoked his Protestant readers to reconsider "human passions by re-directing them." Turning to Southwell's prose, Afroditi-Maria Panaghis, in Chapter 9, "Robert Southwell's articulation of self-fashioning," demonstrates Southwell's process of self-fashioning through the configuration and restoration to wholeness following suffering, scourging, self-annihilation, death, and dismemberment in *A Short Rule of Good Life, Fourfold Meditation: Of the Foure Last Things, Spiritual Exercises and Devotions,* and *A Humble Supplication to her Maiestie.* Panaghis presents the writer's public self that was persecuted and eventually executed alongside his private self that struggled for salvation, martyrdom, union with the divine, and glorification. Thus she demonstrates that Southwell's oeuvre records shifting subject-positions from defender to conciliator, to sinner, to preacher, to contemplative, to prisoner, to sacrifice, and finally, to martyr and saint underscoring as such the fact that the self is constantly in a response mode of change and adaptation. She also outlines the manner by which the *numinous* conflates feelings of spiritual transcendence and vacillation between pleasure and pain upon the awakening of the self to the potential union with the One. In the tenth, and final chapter of the volume, entitled "Southwell's influence: imitations, appropriations, reactions," Alison Shell argues that "the blood of martyrs can germinate unpredictably." She maintains that Southwell could not have anticipated that his works would undergo numerous publications, that he would acquire fame posthumously, and that he would influence so many poets across denominational boundaries. The popularity of his tears poetry, for instance, not only launched a turn to religion in late Elizabethan literature, it also inspired many Catholic *and* Protestant writers. Nonetheless, many of them did not admit Southwell's influence despite their appropriation of his subject-matter and style, either because of his religious denomination and the fact that he was sentenced and executed as a traitor or as "part of the ongoing Protestant mission to make over Catholic writing." Shell delineates the diverse responses that Southwell evoked by analyzing poetry written by and shaping the religious self-fashioning of Elizabeth Grymeston, William Evans, Richard Verstegan, Michael Drayton, and George Herbert.

Finally, in the conclusion, the editors outline the similarities/dissimilarities that characterize Greville and Southwell's corpus as presented by the essays; and pinpoint the arguments propounded by the contributors that map the precarity of self-fashioning within the fluid politico-religious landscape of the time during which the two writers lived and wrote.

Notes

1 Edmund Spenser, "Letter to Sir Walter Raleigh," in *The Fairie Queene disposed into twelve books, Fashioning XII. Moral Vertues* (London: Printed for William Ponsonbie, 1590).
2 Andrew Hadfield, *Shakespeare and Republicanism* (Cambridge: Cambridge UP, 2005), 11.
3 Yet, one needs to bear in mind that neither Greville's Calvinism nor Southwell's Jesuitism conformed fully to orthodoxy, as many of the volume's chapters point out.
4 Louis Montrose, *The Subject of Elizabeth: Authority, Gender and Representation* (Chicago, Il: Chicago UP, 2006), 188.
5 Charles Taylor, *Sources of the Self* (Cambridge: Cambridge UP, 2006), 120, 133. For an excellent analysis of the use of the word "self" in the early modern era, see also Nancy Sellek, *The Interpersonal Idiom in Shakespeare, Donne, and the Early Modern Culture* (Houndmills, Basingstoke: Palgrave Macmillan, 2008), esp. Chapter 1: "Properties of a 'Self': Words and Things, 1580–1690," 21–55.
6 Perez Zagorin, *Ways of Lying, Dissimulation, Persecution and Conformity in Early Modern Europe* (Cambridge, MA: Harvard UP, 1990), 156.
7 Michel de Montaigne, Chapter 9 "Of Lyers," in *The Essayes or Morall, Politike and Millitairie*, trans. John Florio, vol. 1 (London, 1603), 15.
8 Jean E. Howard, "The New Historicism in Renaissance Studies," *English Literary Renaissance*, 16 (Winter 1986): 15. See also Jacob Burckhardt, *The Civilization of the Renaissance in Italy*, trans. S. G. C. Middlemore (London: 1878).
9 Michael Mascuch, *Origins of the Individualist Self: Autobiography and Self-Identity in England, 1591–1791* (Stanford, CA: Stanford UP, 1996), 9.
10 John J. Martin, "Inventing Sincerity, Refashioning Prudence: The Discovery of the Individual in Renaissance Europe," *The American Historical Review*, 102, no. 5 (1997): 1321.
11 Ibid., 1315.
12 Ibid., 1320.
13 Debora Shuger, "Religious Backgrounds of Elizabethan Shorter Poetry," in *Approaches to Teaching Shorter Elizabethan Poetry*, eds. Patrick Cheney and Anne Lake Prescott (New York: The Modern Language Association of America, 2000), 91.

14 *Secretum,* in *Petrarch's Secretum with Introduction, Notes and Critical Anthology,* ed. Davy A. Carozza and H. James Shey (New York: Peter Lang, 1989), 81.
15 Francesco Petrarca, *On His Own Ignorance* in *The Renaissance Philosophy of Man,* eds. Ernst Cassirer, Paul Oskar Kristeller and John Herman Randall, Jr. (Chicago: Chicago UP, 1948), 105.
16 Baldassar Castiglione, 12, 107. *The Courtyer of Count Baldessar,* trans. Thomas Hoby, vol. 2 (London: Wyllyam Series 1562), (page unnumbered). He also states that "my self, persuading myself that all such qualities as I appoint to the courtier are in me. I thinke who so hath not the knowledge of the things intreated upon in this booke, how learned so eve he be, he can fullfil write them." Notwithstanding their aforementioned foci, both Petrarch and Castiligione reflect the significance and interlacing of religion and politics in the early modern era as well as their crucial function in molding the self. See also Perez Zagorin, "The Historical Significance of Lying and Dissimulation," *Social Research,* 63, no. 3 (Fall 1996): 869, 885.
17 Ibid., 866.
18 Martin, "Inventing Sincerity, Refashioning Prudence," 1311.
19 Frank Lentriccia, "Foucault's Legacy: A New Historicism?" in *New Historicism,* ed. Harold A. Veeser (London and New York: Routledge, 1989): 235.
20 Stephen Greenblatt, "Psychoanalysis and Renaissance Culture," in *The Renaissance Italy and Abroad,* ed. John J. Martin (London and New York: Routledge, 2003), 137.
21 Stephen Greenblatt, *Renaissance Self-Fashioning: From More to Shakespeare* (Chicago and London: Chicago UP, 2005), 2.
22 Roy Porter, "Introduction," in *Rewriting the Self: Histories from the Renaissance to the Present,* ed. Roy Porter (London and New York: Routledge, 1997), 2.
23 Gordon D. Kaufman, "The *Imago Dei* as Man's Historicity," *The Journal of Religion,* 36, no. 3 (July 1956), 157.
24 Porter, "Introduction," 2.
25 David Cressy and Lori Anne Farrell, *Religion and Society in Early Modern England* (New York and London: Routledge, 2005), 1.
26 Ibid., 27.
27 Brian Cummings, *The Literary Culture of the Reformation: Grammar and Grace* (Oxford: Oxford UP, 2009), 65.
28 Cressy and Farrell, *Religion and Society* , 1.
29 Porter, *Rewriting the Self,* 3.
30 Ibid.
31 Cynthia Marshall, *The Shattering of the Self: Violence, Subjectivity and Early Modern Tests* (Baltimore, MD: Johns Hopkins UP, 2002), 4.
32 Porter, *Rewriting the Self,* 3–4.
33 Ibid. See also René Descartes, "Introduction," in *Discourse on Method of Correctly Conducting one's Reason and Seeking Truth in the Sciences,* trans. Ian Maclean (Oxford: Oxford UP, 2006), 15, 73.
34 Ibid.
35 René Descartes, "Second Meditation: On the Nature of the Human Mind," in *The Method, Meditations, and Philosophy,* trans. John Veitch (Washington and London: M. Walter Dunne, 1901), 284.
36 Burckhardt, *The Civilization of the Renaissance in Italy,* 54.
37 Kaufman, "The *Imago Dei,*" 157.
38 In *The Life of Sidney,* Greville argues that he "chose not to write to them on whose foot the black Oxe had not already trod, as the Proverbe is, but to those only, that are weather-beaten in the Sea of the World, such as having lost the

sight of their Gardens, and groves, study to saile on a right course among Rocks, and quick-sands." See Fulke Greville, *The Life of the Renowned Sir Philip Sidney* (1652; reproduced by Delmar: Scholars' Facsimiles and Reprints, 1984), 134–135.

Bibliography

Burckhardt, Jacob. *The Civilization of the Renaissance in Italy*. Translated by S. G. C. Middlemore: London, 1878.

Carozza, Davy A. and H. James Shey, eds. "Secretum." In *Petrarch's Secretum with Introduction, Notes and Critical Anthology*. New York: Peter Lang, 1989.

Castiglione, Baldassar. *The Courtyer of Count Baldessar*. Translated by Thomas Hoby. Vol. 2. London: Wyllyam Series, 1562.

Cressy, David and Lori Anne Farrell. *Religion and Society in Early Modern England*. New York and London: Routledge, 2005.

Cummings, Brian. *The Literary Culture of the Reformation: Grammar and Grace*. Oxford: Oxford UP, 2009.

De Montaigne, Michel. Chapter 9 "Of Lyers." In *The Essayes or Morall, Politike and Millitairie*. Translated by John Florio. vol. 1. London, 1603.

Descartes, René. "Second Meditation: On the Nature of the Human Mind." In *The Method, Meditations, and Philosophy*. Translated by John Veitch. Washington and London: M. Walter Dunne, 1901.

Descartes, René. "Introduction" In *Discourse on Method of Correctly Conducting one's Reason and Seeking Truth in the Sciences*. Translated by Ian Maclean. Oxford: Oxford UP, 2006.

Greenblatt, Stephen. "Psychoanalysis and Renaissance Culture." In *The Renaissance Italy and Abroad*. Edited by John J. Martin. London and New York: Routledge, 2003.

Greenblatt, Stephen. *Renaissance Self-Fashioning: From More to Shakespeare*. Chicago and London: Chicago UP, 2005.

Greville, Fulke. *The Life of the Renowned Sir Philip Sidney*. 1652 reproduced by Delmar: Scholars' Facsimiles and Reprints, 1984.

Hadfield, Andrew. *Shakespeare and Republicanism*. Cambridge: Cambridge UP, 2005.

Howard, Jean E. "The New Historicism in Renaissance Studies." *English Literary Renaissance*, 16 (Winter 1986): 13–43.

Kaufman, Gordon D. "The *Imago Dei* as Man's Historicity." *The Journal of Religion*, 36, no. 3 (July 1956): 157–168.

Lentriccia, Frank. "Foucault's Legacy: A New Historicism?" In *New Historicism*. Edited by Harold A. Veeser. London and New York: Routledge, 1989.

Marshall, Cynthia. *The Shattering of the Self: Violence, Subjectivity and Early Modern Texts*. Baltimore: Johns Hopkins UP, 2002.

Martin, John J. "Inventing Sincerity, Refashioning Prudence: The Discovery of the Individual in Renaissance Europe." *The American Historical Review*, 102, no. 5, (1997): 1309–1342.

Mascuch, Michael. *Origins of the Individualist Self: Autobiography and Self-Identity in England, 1591–1791*. Stanford: Stanford UP, 1996.

Montrose, Louis. *The Subject of Elizabeth: Authority, Gender and Representation*. Chicago: Chicago UP, 2006.

Petrarca, Francesco. *On His Own Ignorance.* In *The Renaissance Philosophy of Man.* Edited by Ernst Cassirer, Paul Oscar Kristeller and John Herman Randall, Jr. Chicago: Chicago UP, 1948.

Porter, Roy. "Introduction." In *Rewriting the Self: Histories from the Renaissance to the Present.* Edited by Roy Porter. London and New York: Routledge, 1997.

Sellek, Nancy. *The Interpersonal Idiom in Shakespeare, Donne, and the Early Modern Culture.* Houndmills, Basingstoke: Palgrave Macmillan, 2008.

Shuger, Debora. "Religious Backgrounds of Elizabethan Shorter Poetry." In *Approaches to Teaching Shorter Elizabethan Poetry.* Edited by Patrick Cheney and Anne Lake Prescott. New York: The Modern Language Association of America, 2000.

Spenser, Edmund. "Letter to Sir Walter Raleigh." In *The Fairie Queene disposed into twelve books, Fashioning XII. Moral Vertues.* London: Printed for William Ponsonbie, 1590.

Taylor, Charles. *Sources of the Self.* Cambridge: Cambridge UP, 2006.

Zagorin, Perez. *Ways of Lying, Dissimulation, Persecution and Conformity in Early Modern Europe.* Cambridge, MA: Harvard UP, 1990.1

Zagorin, Perez. "The Historical Significance of Lying and Dissimulation." *Social Research*, 63, no. 3 (Fall 1996): 863–912.

Figure I.1 Sir Fulke Greville, 1st Baron Brooke (1554–1628). English poet and courtier. Portrait. *c.*1620.

Source: Portrait Gallery. Edmund Lodge [Public domain].

Figure I.2 Saint Robert Southwell, S.J. (1561–1595). Illustration from the frontispiece of Saint Peters complaint. Unknown date (XVIth or XVIIth century).

Source: www.luminarium.org/renlit/southwell.htm [Public domain].

Overview

Calvinist statesman, Jesuit martyr: the worlds of Fulke Greville and Robert Southwell

Sarah Covington

Few figures were more divergent yet so indirectly connected as Fulke Greville and Robert Southwell. Born seven years apart, both were raised in well-to-do families, Southwell's in Norfolk and Greville's in Warwickshire; both spent formative years abroad and raised themselves to prominence, even if they were each, in different ways, men of shadows, given to personal torments, and at odds with the political and religious authorities of early modern England. The two Cecils, William and Robert, were fond of neither, to put it mildly. And both died violent deaths, Southwell as a Tyburn martyr and Greville as a homicide, killed at the hands of his servant. But the likenesses, on this level, end there. Southwell entered the English College at Douai in 1576, and joined the Jesuit priesthood in 1584; returning to England by his own request in 1586, he immediately obtained fugitive status, and was eventually apprehended, tortured, and executed in 1595. Greville, as Philip Sidney's closest friend and most powerful mythographer after the poet's death, remained an active courtier, with the exception of his own years away from power from 1606 to 1614. Yet Greville was also a deeply committed international Calvinist who harbored serious reservations about the Elizabethan and Jacobean regimes and ended his days in a state of religious and political gloom. As he would famously write in the later years of his life, "I know the world and believe in God"—the latter part of the sentence hardly obviating the fallenness of the former, in his own melancholy estimation.[1]

Yet it was on the level of Greville and Southwell's poetry, each produced in an atmosphere of religious and political tumult, where the two would converge. As Brian Cummings has most notably pointed out, while confessional divisions within early modern religious cultures have long been emphasized, "the literary relationship between Calvinism and Catholicism is much more complex than meets the eye."[2] Greville could deeply diverge from Southwell, for example in his Calvinist refusal to find satisfaction through a repentance that was in any way conditional upon salvation; but in other matters, including the use of certain literary conventions, expressions of melancholic doubt, and an intimate, meditative spiritual introspection, his writings coincided with the Jesuit in striking ways. Southwell's devotional verse and often conciliatory language also appealed—and was meant to appeal—to a Protestant audience, as many of his books passed through the censors, with some judicious editing, while his poetry of tears proceeded to influence English Protestant writers hungry for an affective means in which to depict Christ's passion.[3] The circumstances in which both men found themselves were radically different, even if they shared similar psychological impulses and frustrations; in this regard, their writings deserve comparative analysis, despite the very different theological orientations that otherwise made them so different.

Greville and Southwell's problematic relationship with the state was another aspect that connected them, as this general introductory essay will briefly discuss. Most obvious was Southwell's status as a Jesuit illegally residing in England and considered a traitor for holding a different or at least unacceptably dual allegiance. But Greville was also highly ambivalent and at times even shockingly rebellious in his (or his characters') utterances, even if he was ultimately loyal to Elizabeth, James, and Charles. Both men did not necessarily seek out conflicts with the monarch, though the theological and political controversies that animated the period, and the mens' own personal faith, forced them to adopt a poetic as well as implicitly political response to the realities of the day. By exploring the historical background of Calvinist and English recusant culture, Jesuit missionary activities and a humanist-driven effort to serve the state, one may therefore gain greater insight into the driving forces that dominated their lives and work, and that made their own collisions with the state so tragic in the end.

Greville and Southwell adhered to the religion of their respective families, even if they proceeded to radically forge their own course in time. But those families' confessional affiliations could be ambiguous or flexible in the years before Elizabeth came to the throne: a not-unusual circumstance given the religious fluidity of the times.[4] For the respectable Greville family, this meant accepting the religion that also happened to benefit the family's fortunes, whether it was Protestantism under Henry VIII and Edward VI, and what appears to have been a relatively easy conformity on the part of Fulke's grandfather to Roman Catholicism under Mary. As one biographer has written, it is not out of the realm of possibility to speculate that Greville himself "was baptized a Roman Catholic, carried in the arms of his mother to a Latin Mass, and led by the hand at the age of five to an English service conducted according to the Book of Common Prayer."[5] Even so, members of Greville's maternal family remained Catholic under Elizabeth's reign, with his first cousin taking part in the Northern Rebellion, leading Greville, according to one biographer, to adopt a "virulent ant-Catholic [stance], if only to keep his own record unimpeached by association."[6]

The decade in which Greville was born proved critical, as the cause of godly Protestantism was advanced and harnessed to an international dimension, deeply shaping his thinking in the years to come.[7] Indeed, the Calvinism adopted by Greville was no less informed by continental influences than the Catholicism of Southwell, who was trained at schools abroad. Exiled under Mary I and influenced more than ever by a developing Calvinist doctrine, Protestants in Geneva, Basel, and the Rhineland territories advanced their understanding of liturgy, biblical translation, and church discipline; theologically, the question of predestination would dominate as it had not before, especially as it related to the increasingly hardened polarities of election and reprobation, or as one anonymous writer put it (with the help of John Knox, if it was not Knox himself), those who had been "ordeyned as vessels of wrathe, to damnation" and others "chosen ... as vessels of his mercie, to be saved."[8] If writers in previous decades also wrestled with the subject of election and reprobation, theirs was primarily in a form that adhered to Augustine and Luther. But with the Calvinism (or perhaps "further-Calvinism") of the exiles, whose writings continued to be published and read throughout the Elizabethan period, predestination was now on the offense, and would form the basis of a theological current that deeply impacted a generation in the decades to come.

Many of the Marian exiles returned home upon the accession of Elizabeth to assume power as bishops and other high clerics, even if tensions soon became apparent with the refusal on the part of many, following the conflicts of Edward VI's reign, to accept popish clerical attire and other ungodly practices. Equally if not more pressing was their embrace of a preaching ministry against her own more conservative vision of what a reformed church was to be. In this regard, the Elizabethan settlement, as others have stated, was not a settlement at all, but rather an opening salvo that would only grow more heated in the years ahead, much to the queen's chagrin.[9] The term "Puritan," which came to gather around these figures as a result of the ensuing disputes, was first utilized around the time Greville entered Shrewsbury School, in 1564, studying under the righteous headmaster Thomas Ashton;[10] it was Shrewsbury that would change the course of Greville's life, not least in its inculcation of Protestantism, patriotism and humanism, and above all, in giving him the opportunity to meet Philip Sidney, the friend who would dominate the rest of his days.[11] Sidney proceeded on to Oxford and Greville to Cambridge, where Calvin was "the acknowledged textbook," even if Greville's school, Jesus College, was more moderate than others.[12] Even so, Greville would have been exposed while there to attacks on episcopacy in the controversies of the late 1560s, and to the virulently anti-Catholic preachings, in particular those of Thomas Cartwright, later dismissed by the future archbishop of Canterbury John Whitgift.[13]

One should bear in mind that while the term "Puritan" continues to be debated, if not perhaps as ardently as in previous decades, it remains valuable in referring to an intense form of Reformed Protestantism, or a culture both established and dissident, and adapted by many in the early modern period. A more correct portrait would place it on a spectrum upon which many shadings and different emphases of belief resided, even if confusion can result from such terms as "conformist Calvinists," "non-conformist Calvinists," "forward Protestants," "perfect Protestants," "super-Protestants," and the "militant tendency."[14] Equally complex is the nature of Greville's own Calvinism, which altered over the years and could shift along the continuum in its own right. Though he dismissed the hottest Protestants and their "petty dividing schisms," he was known to patronize a few of them,[15] and even play host to heterodox thinkers such as Giordano Bruno, who described Greville as a "generous and humane spirit" and might have imparted a dose of philosophical skepticism to him as well.[16] But in the early years, upon entering Elizabeth's court, Greville belonged to the international Calvinist faction—the forward Protestants—who coalesced under the Earl of Leicester and Francis Walsingham.[17] This meant delegating vestments, for example, to the realm of "things indifferent," or urging the queen to undertake a more aggressive foreign policy, and one that would serve the cause of Protestants in France and the Low Countries. As with other varieties of Puritanism, issues such as unconditional predestination, free will, and atonement were also important, but it was the international cause that would preoccupy Greville—and Sidney—and frustrate them as well in the face of a queen whose resistance was based in part on a pragmatic combination of fiscal conservatism and a desire to avoid conflict with Spain.[18]

Greville's life was closely connected to that of Sidney, especially after they entered Elizabeth's court to advance themselves while practicing the civic humanist ideal of virtuous public service: an ideal as strong as Protestantism in shaping their lives and poems in the early years.[19] But the *politique* tendencies of William Cecil and the conservative foreign policy of the queen would disappoint the two friends, especially after diplomatic travels in which they encountered such figures as the Huguenot leader Philippe de Mornay, and the Lutheran Hubert Languet, who viewed Sidney as a messiah–champion succeeding where others could not in unifying the Protestants across national boundaries and confessions. Their endeavors abroad, as well as a squelched plan to join Francis Drake in a 1585 expedition to the West Indies, were failures, however, or at the very least sources of frustration and at times embarrassment, made worse by Sidney's heated opposition to the proposed match between the Queen and the Duke of Anjou in 1579.[20]

Greville was more successful in securing patronage and income than Sidney, his braver friend of more "solid and active reaches," whose political career in any case had peaked around 1577.[21] Perhaps it was unfortunate in the long run that after Sidney's death in 1586, Greville eventually moved on to the Earl of Essex, even if he did acquire the position of treasurer of the navy by the association. It was also the Essex circle that opened

Greville up to Tacitus, who served him well, if bleakly, in the increasingly disillusioned years of the 1590s.[22] As Alexandra Gajda has pointed out, Tacitus "electrified European literati in the later sixteenth century" and charged history "with serious political purpose."[23] There was also a "disguised Machiavellianism" in contemporary readings of Tacitus, not only in the classical republicanism but in images that Tacitus (and Machiavelli) presented of a fallen world yet one with "bold new men"[24] who could overturn this "decrepit age."[25] After Henry Savile's translation of the *Histories* and *Agricola* in 1591, the late-Roman chronicler of corrupt emperors proved all the more resonant, with dark parallels sometimes drawn, for example, between the queen and Tiberius. The addition of Seneca, while not new to the 1590s, provided later writers with an equally useful borrowed vocabulary through which they could express anxieties about absolutism and the parallels with imperial Rome. It should be noted that for Greville, Seneca was also important in his fashioning a life of Sidney; as Gregory A. Staley has argued, "Seneca's tragedies provided Greville with images of wit, and Seneca's biography provided an image of life, both of which served to honor Sidney as a Senecan."[26] The death of Sidney, the hero "greater within himself than the world," was in this regard inextricably connected with politics, as Greville ruminated gloomily on a world Sidney left behind, and one that served "the cautious wisdom of little monarchies to be safe in."[27]

Plays, both closet and public, were particularly pessimistic expressions of these classical tendencies, and included such works as Samuel Daniel's *Cleopatra* (1594) and Samuel Brandon's *Octavia* (1598), not to mention Jonson's somewhat later *Sejanus* (1603), all of which adopted a Tacitean as well as Senecan strain.[28] In the midst of a grim and factional decade, Greville himself began his play *Mustapha*, which presented the dilemma of a good counselor (in this instance, the character Achmat) finding himself in service to a tyrannical and corrupt—and pointedly ageing and successor-fearing—ruler. Rebellion is offered to Achmat as the solution against such leaders ("Tyrants! Why swell you thus against your Makers?"), but in the end and after some extensive internal debate, he decides that obedience to kings—the "rods or blessings of the sky"—is the sole answer, especially given the "rage of multitudes" that otherwise results.[29]

Karen Raber has described Greville as harboring a "complex and claustrophobically violent relationship" with his plays,[30] including his drama *Antony and Cleopatra*, which he burned (or "sacrificed to the fire") after Essex's rebellion.[31] He was wise to do so, given how the work could have been misconstrued in the wake of Essex's treason. Greville himself insisted that he deviated from "the Ancient" dramatists in that he did not seek to "exemplifie the disastrous miseries of mans life" or display "the wickednesse of power." Nor was he "Moderne," since he did not illustrate "Gods revenging aspect upon every particular sin" (a statement that was somewhat belied by the providentialism that does indeed appear at times in his plays). Instead, he simply sought to "trace out the high waies of ambitious Governours, and to show in the practice, that the more audacity, advantage and good successe such Soveraignties have, the more they hasten to their own desolation and ruine."[32] Greville was simply raising questions and warnings, not necessarily issuing condemnations; and none of the plays were intended for the stage in any case. Still, Greville's plays do contain assertions and judgments, often voiced through choruses. As Greville himself wrote, "the vices of former Ages being so like to these of this Age ... it will be easie to find out some affinity, or resemblance, between them."[33] In attacking favorites and factions, for example, Greville and his contemporaries were implying that the queen may have practiced a tyranny based not on usurpation but capriciousness in elevating evil counselors or presiding over a corrupt court; these criticisms also found their way into Greville's verse treatise entitled *A Treatise on Monarchy*, begun in the last years of the queen's reign and subsequently revised, as was the norm with Greville.[34] The work was not exactly original, utilizing as it did the metaphor of the body to describe the ideal state, and relying, as others did, on the writings of Bodin or Buchanan. The *Treatise* also tread familiar ground in discussing the diseases that could form in the body of the monarchical state, though it added in Greville's twist that "selfness," or selfishness, in the monarch could breed the same quality in the governed. And unlike Bodin, Greville resisted the absolutist solution, just as he rejected the kind of rebellion, or popular "rights," advocated by Buchanan.[35] Whether he believed that Elizabeth reached his ideal of being a "true" monarch was somewhat unclear, though he did praise her in letters and acknowledged her role in bringing England over to Protestantism. On the other hand, as Greville's biographer once wrote, the queen also "distrusted the ideals of his party," "virtually ignored or ruined the courtiers he most admired," and—not least"—"frustrated his own ambitions," both personally, religiously, and politically.[36]

With Essex's execution in 1601 Elizabeth, however, appeared to forgive Greville to a point despite her (or Cecil's) lingering suspicions. His fortunes therefore rose considerably for a time, even if they relied in the end on "so frail a thread." Upon the queen's own death in 1603, he was at the mercy not only of a new king but equally important, Robert Cecil, who sought to clean house; and in 1606 Greville, unsurprisingly, was gone.[37] Greville nevertheless continued to obey the new king, but he joined other Elizabethan courtiers—and there were a few–in viewing the new dispensation as one of hypocrisy, deviousness, and corruption: an age that was "slippery, not to be trusted unto." As Mervyn James once described Greville during this period, his "mind" in this way "showed a progressive disintegration of the synthesis of wisdom, honour and religion, which, under Sidney's influence, had sustained the idealism of his youth."[38]

Greville increasingly devoted himself to writing, and in his *Dedication to Sir Philip Sidney*, probably composed between 1610 and 1612 but not published until 1652, he created a didactic and glorified portrait of his friend as well as a history of the reign of Elizabeth, now transformed into "this miracle of princes."[39] But the treatise also highlighted the idealism of that time in order to cast shadows onto the present Jacobean world, and in the process sought to encourage the current prince of Wales, Henry (who would die in 1612) to take up the cause of forward Protestantism.[40] The *Life* also expressed Greville's continued preoccupation with tyranny or "precipitate absoluteness," concerns which had been evident as well in the *Arcadia* and his own *Cælica* poems, informed as the latter were by themes centering around dependence on a tyrannical mistress subject to the "self-loving creatures full of ... servile flatteries."[41]

Greville's participation in the changing political and cultural world of England actively continued through the 1620s, and included one unfortunate incident in which he nominated the Dutch classicist Isaac Dorislaus to a chair at Cambridge. Greville came to regret the decision after Dorislaus proceeded to deliver a series of lectures on Tacitus, in which the scholar asserted that political power in Rome resided with the people and not emperors whose power was illegitimate.[42] Greville's association with the nomination was also not helped by the fact that the lecture was presented in the heated environment of 1628, when the battles of the Roman civil wars were not-so-subtly invoked in parliament, with Tacitus deployed as a weapon even more directly against the king (and indeed, Dorislaus would later advise the prosecution in the trial of Charles I).[43] On the other hand, Greville, as mentioned, had always counseled obedience, despite his Tacitean bent and his awareness of resistance theories developed on the continent by Languet, Mornay, and the Marian exiles.[44] Greville was against tyrants, not kings who respected the law and commonweal; in this he was an adherent of what has been called a "monarchical republic" ideally composed of good commonwealth-men who abided by qualities of virtue. In other words, he was a "citizen concealed within [a] subject," at least until later in life, when an increasing conservatism brought him to cast off the republic of his earlier longings.[45]

David Norbrook has written that Greville simply "kept touching on ideas more radical than those to which he was officially committed"; perhaps as a result, he was constantly revising his writings, which were also "fissured by ellipses, by abrupt transitions, by sudden curtailments of dangerous lines of thought."[46] It was writing, in other words, at odds with itself—not to mention with the author and the state. But Greville's beliefs also stood at cross purposes with orthodox Calvinism, particularly in the wake of his political experience. On the one hand, he was restored to favor in 1614 and even assumed the office of treasurer of the exchequer. Yet his Calvinism grew darker through the years, especially with regard to the question of predestination, and his inner doubt brought him to grasp "the depth of mine iniquity." "What are Mens lives," he asked, "but labyrinths of error,/ Shops of deceit, and Seas of Misery?" Far from the ideals and hopes of his younger days, he died in an embittered state, murdered by a disgruntled servant; in his wake he left poems that spoke of "a God unknown," and succumbed to further despair over society, politics, and the failed promise of his and Sidney's dreams. Hoping to be buried next to Sidney's body, he resigned himself instead to a plain, black-stoned and lonely tomb in a chapel in a Warwick church, far from St. Paul's where his old friend reposed.

Greville and Southwell's paths indirectly crossed in 1595, when the Earl of Essex, in whose orbit Greville circled, found himself the unwitting dedicatee of a treatise entitled *A Conference about the Next Succession to the Crowne of England*. The work was most likely written by the Jesuit Robert Persons, who not only discussed a taboo subject, embedded directly in the title, but advocated for the right of a commonwealth to depose a monarch, oppose the heir, or propose another candidate to the throne.[47] The author helpfully suggested the daughter of Philip II of Spain as a good candidate, thus making the treatise all the more incendiary.[48] But 1595 would also witness the trial of Persons' fellow Jesuit, Robert Southwell, after years of imprisonment in the Tower and torture by the notorious Richard Topcliffe ("*homo sordidissimus*," to Henry Garnet). Answering to charges of treason, Southwell responded by saying that "I testify by God, the avenger of perjury, that I have hatched neither plans nor conspiracies against the Queen or the Kingdom; I have come only to offer aid to those desiring sacraments in the Catholic rites."[49] Shortly thereafter Southwell was executed, still professing his loyalty to the crown. His poems—his memorial—would be published anonymously and in the same year of his death, in the form of a small book entitled *St Peter's Complaint*, which reached an admiring readership of Protestants, even if that readership was strengthened in its own faith, and not converted, by the dead Jesuit.[50]

Southwell was no less imbricated in his contexts than Greville, even if those contexts led him to the farthest reaches in the other religious direction. Southwell's own family was sympathetic to Catholicism, but it too carried with it a longer history that reflected the general flux of relogous identity in early modern England, and one in which the divisions between Catholic and Protestant were neither as clear nor as categorically in line with a given piece of religious legislation. He lived as a child near the ruins of a Benedictine monastery that his own family had played no small part in dismantling during the reign of Henry VIII, and his grandfather rallied around the king in the rising of 1536; though inclined towards Catholicism, Southwell's grandfather embraced political advantage, even if he laid low during Edward's reign and returned to Catholicism under Mary. The grandfather even appeared in Foxe's *Acts and Monuments*, among the litany of Marian tormenters of the godly, ominously commenting at John Bradford's examination, "Lord God, what an arrogant and stubborne boy is this," or standing by the window during the questioning of John Rogers, whose burning he would soon after witness.[51] On the other hand, Robert's maternal relatives could be no less variable, with his uncle, Thomas Copley, undertaking the reverse trajectory of becoming Protestant under Mary and Catholic under Elizabeth.[52] The result of this flexibility, as Scott Pilarz has suggested, perhaps imbued Southwell with a sense of faith's complexities that was more shaded than the hardline views professed by his fellow co-religionists.[53]

In 1576 Southwell was sent to study at the English College in Douai, founded the decade previously by William Allen;[54] the purpose of these schools was to train young seminarians for the priesthood and also prepare them to missionize through words and actions.[55] Despite the schools' emphasis on proselytizing and upholding the old religion, a culture of martyrdom nevertheless emerged after the execution in 1577 of Cuthbert Mayne: the first of 160 martyrs who had come through Douai. On an educational level, one may compare Douai to Greville's Shrewsbury in the sense that the school exposed Southwell to a humanist program that required the reading of Cicero and Virgil, or training in rhetoric and *eloquentia perfecta*: all of which, in Southwell's case, were intended to be learned through imitation and ultimately serve spiritual ends.[56] The schools also confirmed Greville and Southwell in their respective faiths, though in Southwell's case the final resolution came to him during a kind of spiritual crisis, in which the lord "with new engines rock[ed] the ramparts of my heart," and "after long struggle I surrendered ... [humbled] beneath thy powerful hand."[57] Determined to join the Society of Jesus, Southwell continued to be rebuffed because of his youth; in another indirect intersection, while waiting for acceptance into the college in Rome, he witnessed the ravaging of the Low Countries (including Douai) by John Casimir of the Palatinate, a friend of Sidney and proponent of the forward Protestant cause.[58] By the end of the year, Southwell embarked upon Rome, where he would finally enter the novitiate, submitting to the spiritual directorship of Persons with the intention of eventually returning to England.

Greville and Southwell converged more directly when Southwell discovered the work of Sir Edward Dyer, who was mentor to Sidney, member of the Leicester circle, and friend to Greville as well. From Dyer Southwell imparted the style and structure of the lyric poem, but extended those elements further in directing them towards a sacred purpose, thereby turning poetry away from those who "discredit" their calling by writing of the "follies and feignings of love," and urging instead a poetry based on the "authority of God."[59] It was not altogether unusual for Catholics to cross confessional lines in this manner, with Dyer's "My Mind to Me a Kingdom Is" reworked by the Catholic William Byrd, who set the poem to music.[60] Nor was Southwell the only Catholic poet to apply Ignatian meditative aspects to the Elizabethan lyric, though he was certainly one of the most effective in transmuting profane into divine poetry, in applying a new kind of self-analysis to his writing, and in bringing a Catholic Reformation-inspired literature of tears to an English audience, particularly in his poetic ruminations on Mary Magdalen.[61]

Despite episodes of internal tension, Southwell's years at the English College in Rome constituted its heroic age, as it sponsored 100 English priests by 1580.[62] In 1585 Southwell wrote to Claudio Acquaviva, the Jesuit father-general, that "There is nothing I desire more … [than] that I may expend my labours at present upon the English." His request, however, was initially met with reluctance on the part of Acquaviva to release him for the job, attesting to the fact that while the 1581 martyrdom of Edmund Campion, for example, certainly helped the Catholic cause, death was not elevated above missionary efforts, especially when it came to such a valuable writer as Southwell.[63] Southwell, however, was insistent, and one year later, he joined his fellow priest Henry Garnet on a ship to England, the men going forth like "two arrows shot at the same target."[64]

Southwell's writings, which preceded his arrival and were already known to the English authorities, would in fact constitute the most important aspect of his missionary work, and in this he followed in the trail of Campion and Persons. Yet Southwell was distinct even from them, not only in his poetic gifts but in his desire to use poetry as a means to directly address the needs of an underground Catholic community enduring hardship, and to mission among Protestants as well. The fact that he was provided with a secret press by the Countess of Arundel, one of his patrons, certainly helped his cause, even if the same years saw him alienated from his religiously lapsed and debt-ridden family, bringing him to write to his father, in a rare bitter letter, that "In my own country I have lived like a foreigner, finding amongst strangers that which in my nearest blood I presumed not to seek."[65]

It was during his years on the run or in hiding that he would compose his greatest prose and poetic works, including *An Epistle of Comfort* (1587), dedicated to a now-imprisoned Earl of Arundel, as well as *Mary Magdalens funeral teares* (1591) and *A Short Rule of a Good Life* (1591–1592). It had been a strict injunction on the part of William Allen and Rome generally that missionaries were "not to meddle in affairs of state," and were to "shun all talk about the Queen and … not to countenance [such matters] in others."[66] But Southwell's late tracts, for all his outreach, could also be religiously oppositional, which meant that they were politically so as well. In 1592 the authorities succeeded in apprehending him, leading to an imprisonment that would last the next three years. "At last it has happened," Henry Garnet wrote to Acquaviva about Southwell's arrest; "and now in a broken and battered vessel we are sailing without a helmsman."[67] And it was here—before the notorious Richard Topcliffe and in the presence of William Cecil, under the full awareness of the queen—where Southwell finally encountered the state in its most coercive form. As Pilarz has written, Southwell was "hardly rushing to martyrdom," even if he might have been resigned to its eventuality.[68] But his silence in the face of torture also attested to resistance—as well as equivocation, shared with Calvinists[69]—when he replied to Topcliffe that he was a gentleman and not a Catholic priest or Jesuit, and then challenged the torturer to prove otherwise.[70] Southwell's subsequent request to Cecil that he proceed to trial, after years in the Tower, also offered a challenge, as he wrote that "I have sent you a sharp sword.... If it please you to draw and to use it, that hand that sent it hath a heart to endure it."[71]

The trial that ensued placed Southwell within a particular tradition that extended back to the early Christian world, in which the martyr was to display himself before a tribunal that illuminated his ordeal as much as the death itself would. After initially refusing to lodge a plea of guilt or innocence—to do so would have acknowledged the legitimacy of the proceedings—Southwell then proclaimed himself not guilty of treason. But his next answer, that he was to be tried "by God and you," only served to emphasize how different the laws were between the divine decree of God and the worldly, persecutory "you." As in the martyrology of John Foxe, authorities—in Southwell's case, no less an authority than attorney-general Edward Coke—were reduced to hurling insults and threats as a result of Southwell's implicit defiance, thus exposing the hollowness and violence of the law that they so insistently professed. In the end, even the prospect of death no longer carried any threat or potency, when Southwell could state, as he did in *An Epistle of Comfort*, that "one death is no more death than another." Indeed, if the end was to be accompanied by a "body quartered" and "quarters boiled," then all the more glorious would be the witness, if it were to be given in the cause of God.[72]

Southwell had once stated that "about Parliament I say nothing, as I desire my letters, like my soul, to have absolutely nothing to do with matters of State."[73] Yet at trial he was forced into a naked confrontational display with power, even if it was a power he exposed, by his actions at trial, as fraudulent. In this, he did not diverge from other martyrs, including Campion or from the other side, Foxe's godly heroes; nor was his confrontational stance before the judges original either, preceded as it was by his *Supplication to Her Majesty*, a treatise written in 1591 which attacked a recent proclamation that had targeted seminarians and Jesuits "of ill character" who had come into the realm by "secret creeks," dreaming of Spanish invasions.[74] The trouble, he wrote, resided not in the queen but in her counselors; but even so, England had become separated from itself, and the queen from herself, in overseeing such iniquities—not least religious iniquities—against its (and her) own people. Southwell, like Greville, nevertheless professed his loyalty; elsewhere, in answer to the famous "bloody question" regarding allegiance, he replied that he would rather be killed than join in with a Catholic invader, revealing (if one takes him at his word here) the line that he drew between religious and civil power. Needless to say, other Jesuits often maintained a different stance in these matters.[75]

It is therefore ironic and somewhat unique, as many have pointed out, that Southwell's poems gained so much acceptance from a Protestant audience, even though a great part of his intent had been to write for conversionary purposes. As Brian Cummings has pointed out, without a strong tradition of Protestant devotional verse, Southwell's poems "answered a need," and with some deletions of overtly Catholic elements, were made "acceptable to Protestant taste."[76] Southwell was not alone in this either, with the Calvinist Edmund Bunny also adapting (if not stealing) a Catholic text, in this case Robert Persons' *First Book of the Christian Exercises*, for a Protestant readership.[77] Though widely printed or disseminated in his own lifetime, Southwell's works would undergo twenty editions in England from the years 1591 to 1636; *St Peter's Complaint* and *Mary Magdalens funeral teares* were especially popular, with Thomas Nashe imitating (or plagiarizing) the latter.[78] With this kind of circulation, in addition to Southwell's subjective and psychologized approach to such scenes as Jesus in Gethsemane, his work could not help but influence the meditative and lyrical Protestant poetry of the following century. More important is that he crossed barriers in accordance with the religious landscape of the time, and in doing so, offered himself in spiritual outreach, despite the extremity— and perhaps the inevitability—of his own death and sacrifice.[79]

Greville and Southwell were thus inseparable from the literary, political, and religious contexts that determined their lives and work, but each pushed against the edges of those contexts in ways that distinguished them from others of their era. Politically they both chafed against Elizabeth, and especially so in the 1590s when she appeared, in their eyes, to be overtaken by the darker forces around her. From the Catholic side, Southwell could hardly have expected that Elizabeth would tolerate such an aggressive missionizing force as the Jesuits, or accept his professed allegiance to two powers; and he never did compromise his own position as a missionary, despite the conciliatory tendencies of his poetry. Greville himself, of course, would not have been so brazen as to write a tract such as the *Humble Supplication*—he was never pushed so far to do so—but his own disillusionments at the queen's court, especially after Essex's death, also led him to put into his characters' mouths incendiary lines, even if he himself always retreated in the end.

Neither Greville nor Southwell would succeed in their respective goals of effecting a united international Protestantism that transcended national lines, or bringing the true Catholic faith back to England. And their afterlives, too, would take on unintended consequences. Southwell's works, as mentioned, went through a number of editions and enjoyed popularity in the next century; but his goal of converting heretics through his poetry would give way instead to that poetry playing a significant role in the flourishing seventeenth-century meditative tradition of the Protestant devotional lyric. Meanwhile, Greville's own *Dedication* was certainly successful in mythologizing his friend Sidney. But the *Dedication* has also been called a "proto-Whig manifesto" by Patrick Collinson,[80] and Greville's thinking contributive to a republican sentiment that would feed into the civil wars to come: none of which Greville the monarchist would have intended.[81] Even Greville's own adopted son Robert, the second Lord Brooke, became a Roundhead in the wars, which Greville in his most "republican" mood would have abhorred.[82]

Where Greville the courtier revised or withheld his writings, Southwell the fugitive actively brought about the publication of his own works; the result was suspicion, if at a financially comfortable remove, for the former and death for the latter. But both were victims in their own way of the Elizabethan (and, with Greville, Elizabethan and Jacobean) regimes. Southwell was ultimately forced to take a stand and died for it, but where he was assured a martyr's crown, Greville went on to live a life of compromise and increasing disillusionment, finding himself, in Kenneth Graham's words, torn between "the temporal claims of his long service and the eternal claims of his protestant belief."[83] The temporal and the eternal would turn even grimmer as the years passed, and in this sense, Greville perhaps suffered more in the end, if one is to go by Southwell's statement that "Better it is to die to life than to live to death."[84] "Reflect upon my soul dark desolation/ And ugly prospects o're the sprites infernall," Greville wrote in his last years: hardly the certitude with which Southwell met his own end. In this way, and for all their similarities in life—their poetic innovations, shared literary influences, and relations toward the kingdom—it was their hour before death that would above all, and finally, divide them the most."[85]

Notes

1 Greville in a letter to Sir John Coke dated 1 February 1613, cited in Joan Rees, *Fulke Greville, Lord Brooke, 1554–1628* (Berkeley: University of California Press, 1971), 6. See also Ronald A. Rebholz, *The Life of Fulke Greville, First Lord Brooke* (Oxford: The Clarendon Press, 1971), 216, 231–232; Richard Waswo, *The Fatal Mirror: Themes and Techniques in the Poetry of Fulke Greville* (Charlottesville: University of Virginia Press, 1972); Geoffrey Bullough, "Fulke Greville, First Lord Brooke," *Modern Language Review* 28 (1933): 1–20; Charles Larson, *Fulke Greville* (New York: Twayne Publishers, 1980); Matthew Steggle, "Fulke Greville: Life and Works," *Sidney Journal* 19 (2001): 1–10. For Robert Southwell see Pierre Janelle, *Robert Southwell the Writer: A Study in Religious Inspiration* (Mamaroneck: Paul O. Appel, 1971); Christopher Devlin, *The Life of Robert Southwell: Poet and Martyr* (New York: Greenwood Press, 1969); Scott R. Pilarz, S. J., *Robert Southwell, and the Mission of Literature, 1561–1595* (Aldershot and Burlington: Ashgate, 2004); Anne R. Sweeney, *Robert Southwell: Snow in Arcadia* (Oxford: Oxford UP, 2013); Frank W. Brownlow, *Robert Southwell* (New York: Twayne Publishers, 1996).
2 Brian Cummings, *The Literary Culture of the Reformation: Grammar and Grace* (Oxford: Oxford UP, 2002), 333.
3 Ibid., 332; Alison Shell, *Catholicism and the English Literary Imagination, 1558–1660* (Cambridge: Cambridge UP, 1999), 80.

4 See for example Peter Lake and Michael Questier (eds.) *Conformity and Orthodoxy in the English Church* (Woodbridge, Suffolk: The Boydell Press, 2000), xii–xiv.

5 Rebholz, *The Life of Fulke* Greville, 8.

6 Ibid., 29.

7 Leonard J. Trinterud, "The Origins of Puritanism," *Church History* 20, no. 1 (1951): 37–57; See also Andrew Pettegree, *Marian Protestantism: Six Studies* (Aldershot: Scolar Press, 1996); C. H. Garrett, *The Marian Exiles: A Study in the Origins of Elizabethan Puritanism* (Cambridge: Cambridge UP, 1996).

8 John Knox, *The Works of John Knox*, ed. David Laing, 6 vols. (Edinburgh: Bannatyne Society, 1846–1864), 5, 171–172. Dewey D. Wallace, *Puritans and Predestination: Grace in English Protestant Theology, 1525–1695* (Eugene: Wipf & Stock, 2004), 20–28; O. T. Hargrave, "The Predestinarian Offensive of the Marian Exiles at Geneva," *Historical Magazine of the Protestant Episcopal Church* 42, no. 2 (1973): 111–123.

9 Patrick Collinson, "The Elizabethan Church and the New Religion," in Christopher Haigh (ed.), *The Reign of Elizabeth I* (Athens: University of Georgia Press, 1985), 169–194.

10 Katherine Duncan-Jones, *Sir Philip Sidney: Courtier Poet* (New Haven: Yale UP, 1991), 26.

11 Freya Sierhuis, "Friendship and Freedom of Speech in the Work of Fulke Greville," in *Passions and Subjectivity in Early Modern Culture*, eds. Brian Cummings and Freya Sierhuis (Routledge, 2016): 131–147.

12 Burnham Carter, Jr., "The Intellectual Background of Fulke Greville," PhD diss., Stanford University (1955), 51.

13 Patrick Collinson, *Godly People* (London: Hambledon Press, 1983), 340; A. F. Scott Pearson, *Thomas Cartwright and Elizabethan Puritanism* (Cambridge: Cambridge UP, 1925), 35–45.

14 Patrick Collinson, *The Elizabethan Puritan Movement* (Cambridge: Cambridge UP, 1967), 27; Patrick Collinson, *Birthpangs of English Protestantism* (London: Palgrave Macmillan, 1988); Peter Lake, *Moderate Puritans and the Elizabethan Church* (Cambridge: Cambridge UP, 1982); Christopher Durston and Jacqueline Eales, *The Culture of English Puritanism, 1560–1700* (Basingstoke: Palgrave Macmillan, 1996).

15 Kelly A. Quinn, "Fulke Greville's Friendly Patronage," *Studies in Philology* 103 (2006): 417–435.

16 Rebholz, *The Life of Fulke Greville*, 30–31; Rees, *Fulke Greville, Lord Brooke*, 42; Cummings, *Literary Culture of the Reformation*, 300; Stephen Clucas, "Giordano Bruno's 'Degli Eroici Furori' and Fulke Greville's 'Caelica,'" *Renaissance Studies* 4 (1990): 201–227.

17 Blair Worden, *The Sound of Virtue: Philip Sidney's Arcadia and Elizabethan Politics* (New Haven: Yale UP, 1996), 50. Sidney's religion has been questioned however; for his "crypto-Catholicism," see Katherine Duncan-Jones, "Sir Philip Sidney's Debt to Campion," in *The Reckoned Expense: Edmund Campion and the Early English Jesuits*, ed. Thomas M. McCoog S. J. (Woodbridge: The Boydell Press, 1996), 85–102; for Sidney as a Philippist, or follower of Philip Melancthon, see Robert E. Stillman, "Philip Sidney and the Catholics: The Turn from Confessionalism in Early Modern Studies," *Modern Philology* 112 (2014): 97–129.

18 Simon Lester Adams, "The Protestant Cause: Religious Alliance with the West European Calvinist Communities as a Political Issue in England, 1585–1630," PhD diss., Oxford University, 1973.

19 Rebholz, *The Life of Fulke Greville*, 30.

20 Worden, *Sound of Virtue*, 89–114; Duncan-Jones, *Sir Philip Sidney*, 161–163.
21 Fulke Greville, "A Dedication to Sir Philip Sidney," in *The Prose Works of Fulke Greville, Lord Brooke*, ed. John Gouws (Oxford: Oxford UP, 1986), 22.
22 Paul E. J. Hammer, *The Polarisation of Elizabethan Politics: The Political Career of Robert Devereux, 2nd Earl of Essex, 1585–1597* (Cambridge: Cambridge UP, 1999); Alexandra Gadja, *The Earl of Essex and Late Elizabethan Political Culture* (Oxford: Oxford UP, 2012); see also Paul Hammer, "The Earl of Essex, Fulke Greville, and the Employment of Scholars," *Studies in Philology* 91 (1994): 167–180; Bradley J. Irish, "The Literary Afterlife of the Essex Circle: Fulke Greville, Tacitus, and BL Additional MS 18638," *Modern Philology* 112 (2014): 271–285.
23 Richard Tuck, *Philosophy and Government, 1572–1651* (Cambridge: Cambridge UP, 1993), 105ff.; J. H. M. Salmon, "Seneca and Tacitus in Jacobean England," in *The Mental World of the Jacobean Court*, ed. Linda Levy Peck (Cambridge, 1991), 169–188; Alexandra Gadja, "Tacitus and Political Thought in Early Modern Europe, c.1530–1640," in *Cambridge Companion to Tacitus*, ed. A. J. Woodman (Cambridge: Cambridge UP, 2010), 253–268; David Womersley, "Sir John Henry Savile's Translation of Tacitus and the Political Interpretation of Elizabethan Texts," *Review of English Studies* new series, 42 (1991): 313–342; Paulina Kewes, "Henry Savile's Tacitus and the Politics of Roman History in Late Elizabethan England," *Huntington Library Quarterly* 74 (2011): 515–551; Edwin B. Benjamin, "Sir John Hayward and Tacitus," *Review of English Studies* 8 (1957): 27; Womersley, "Sir John Hayward's Tacitism," 46–59; David Norbrook, *Poetry and Politics in the English Renaissance* (Oxford: Oxford UP, 2002), 152–153.
24 R. Malcolm Smuts, "Court-Centred Politics and the Uses of Roman Historians, c.1590–1630," in *Culture and Politics in Early Stuart England*, ed. Kevin Sharpe and Peter Lake (Basingstoke: Palgrave Macmillan, 1994), 24–40.
25 Fulke Greville, "A Dedication to Sir Philip Sidney," in *Fulke Greville, The Prose Works* (ed. John Gouws), 23; Norbrook, *Poetry and Politics*, 141.
26 For re-issuings, see Curtis Perry, "Seneca and English Political Culture," in *The Oxford Handbook of the Age of Shakespeare*, ed. R. Malcolm Smuts (Oxford: Oxford UP, 2016), 317–318. For Seneca, see Gregory Staley, *Seneca and the Idea of Tragedy* (Oxford: Oxford UP, 2009), 9–10, 131, 134.
27 Greville, "Dedication," in Gouws (ed.), *Prose Works*, 24.24.
28 Kewes, "Henry Savile's Tacitus," 520.
29 Matthew C. Hansen, "Gender, Power and Play: Fulke Greville's *Mustapha* and *Alaham*," *Sidney Journal* 19 (2001): 125–141.
30 Karen Raber, *Dramatic Difference: Gender, Class and Genre in the Early Modern Closet Drama* (Newark: University of Delaware Press, 2001), 112.
31 Rebholz, *The Life of Fulke Greville*, 131; Rees, *Fulke Greville, Lord Brooke*, 140.
32 Rees, *Fulke Greville, Lord Brooke*, 140–141; Sierhuis, "Friendship and Freedom of Speech," 182.
33 See Rees, *Fulke Greville, Lord Brooke*, 149.
34 See Fritz Levy, "The Theatre and the Court in the 1590s," in *The Reign of Elizabeth I: Court and Culture in the Last Decade*, ed. John Guy (Cambridge: Cambridge UP, 1995), 274–300.
35 See Rebholz, *The Life of Fulke Greville*, 148.
36 Ibid., 154.
37 Rebholz, *The Life of Fulke Greville*, 101–107; see also Gavin Alexander, *After Sidney: The Literary Response to Sir Philip Sidney 1586–1640* (Oxford: Oxford UP, 2006).
38 Mervyn James, *Society, Politics and Culture: Studies in Early Modern England* (Cambridge: Cambridge UP, 1988), 397.

39 Gouws (ed.), *Prose Works*, 103, 128; Worden, *Sound of Virtue*, 356.

40 Norbrook, *Poetry and Politics*, 141–142; John Gouws, "Introduction," in Gouws (ed.), *Prose Works*, xvi–xxi.

41 Greville, "Dedication,"in Gouws (ed.), *Prose Works*, 32.

42 Margo Todd, "Anti-Calvinists and the Republican Threat in Early Stuart Cambridge," in *Puritanism and its Discontents*, ed. Laura Lunger Knoppers (Newark: University of Delaware Press, 2003), 91–93.

43 For Dorislaus, see Norbrook, *Poetry and* Politics, 48; Thomas Dandelet, *The Renaissance of Empire in Early Modern Europe* (Cambridge: Cambridge UP, 2014), 273; Alessandra Maccioni and Marco Mostert, "Isaac Dorislaus (1595–1649): The Career of a Dutch Scholar in England," *Transactions of the Cambridge Bibliographical Society* 8 (1981–1984): 419–470.

44 Quentin Skinner, *Foundations of Modern Political Thought* (Cambridge: Cambridge UP, 1978), 2: 323; Margo Todd, *Christian Humanism and the Puritan Social Order* (Cambridge: Cambridge UP, 1987), 94–95.

45 Richard Cust, "Reading for Magistracy: The Mental World of Sir John Newdigate," in *The Monarchical Republic of Early Modern England: Essays in Response to Patrick Collinson*, ed. John F. McDiarmid (London: Routledge, 2007), 182.

46 Norbrook, *Poetry and* Politics, 152.

47 For the succession question see Kewes, "The Puritan, the Jesuit," 47–70.

48 Victor Houliston, *Catholic Resistance in Elizabethan England: Robert Persons's Jesuit Polemic* (Aldershot and Burlington: Ashgate, 2013), 71. See also Leo Hicks, "Father Robert Persons S. J. and The Book of the Succession," *Recusant History* 4 (1957): 126–127; Peter Holmes, "The Authorship and Early Reception of *A Conference about the Next Succession to the Crown of England*," *Historical Journal* 23 (1980): 415–429; Stefania Tutino, "The Political Thought of Robert Persons in Continental Context," *Historical Journal* 52 (2009): 32–62; Christopher Highley, *Catholics Writing the Nation in Early Modern Britain and Ireland* (Oxford: Oxford UP, 2008), 98–99; John Bossy, "The Heart of Robert Persons," in McCoog (ed.) *The Reckoned Expense*, 141–158.

49 Alexandra Walsham, *Church Papists: Catholicism, Conformity, and Confessional Polemic in Early Modern England* (Woodbridge, Suffolk: The Boydell Press, 1993), 14; Christopher Haigh, *English Reformations: Religion, Politics and Society under the Tudors* (Oxford: Clarendon, Press, 1993), 8.

50 Cummings, *Literary Culture of the Reformation*, 330–332; Shell, *Catholicism and the English Literary Imagination*, 63.

51 John Foxe, *Actes and Monuments* (London: John Day, 1583), 1510, 1517, 1683.

52 Devlin, *Life of Robert Southwell*, 11.

53 Pilarz, *Robert Southwell and the Mission of Literature: Writing Reconciliation*, 13–14, 25.

54 A. C. F. Beales, *Education under Penalty: English Catholic Education from the Reformation to the Fall of James II* (London: Athlone Press, 1963), 39ff.

55 See Janelle, *Robert Southwell the Writer*, 11.

56 Pilarz, *Robert Southwell and the Mission of Literature*, 83–84; Devlin, *Life of Robert Southwell*, 25.

57 Devlin, *Life of Robert Southwell*, 28.

58 Worden, *Sound of Virtue*, 283, 52, 83.

59 Robert Southwell, "The Author to his Loving Cousin," in *The Poetical Works of the Rev. Robert Southwell*, ed. William B. Turnbull (London: John Russell Smith, 1856), 1.

60 Pilarz, *Robert Southwell and the Mission of* Literature, 90–91; see also John Milsom, "Byrd, Sidney, and the Art of Melting," *Early Music* 31 (2003): 437–449.

61 Shell, *Catholicism and the English Literary Imagination*, 62; Louis Martz, *The Poetry of Meditation* (New Haven: Yale University Press, 1954, rev. edn. 1962), 184–210; Janelle, *Robert Southwell the Writer*, 189ff; for a comparative study, see Warren R. Maurer, "Spee, Southwell, and the Poetry of Meditation," *Comparative Literature* 15 (1963): 15–22; Anthony Raspa, *The Emotive Image: Jesuit Poetics in the English Renaissance* (Fort Worth: Texas Christian UP, 1983). Southwell was not entirely original in developing the literature of tears; see Cummings, *Literary Culture of the* Reformation, 333.

62 Humphrey Ely, *Certaine briefe notes upon a briefe apologie* (Paris, n.p., 1602), 29.

63 Thomas M. McCoog, *The Society of Jesus in Ireland, Scotland, and England 1541–1588: "Our Way of Proceeding?"* (Leiden: Brill, 1996), 173ff.

64 Quoted in Janelle, *Robert Southwell the* Writer, 35.

65 For an account of the manuscript and print history of Southwell's publications during his time in England see Nancy Pollard Brown, "Robert Southwell: The Mission and the Written Word," in *The Reckoned Expense*, 251–275 (Woodbridge: Boydell Press, 1996). For Southwell's relations with his family, see Sweeney, 195; Robert Southwell, *The Triumphs over Death*, ed. J. W. Trotman (London: Manresa Press, 1914), 36–64.

66 J. H. Pollen, ed., *Unpublished Documents relating to the English Martyrs* (London: Catholic Record Society, 1908), 5: 361.

67 Philip Caraman, *Henry Garnet, 1555–1606, and the Gunpowder Plot* (London: Longmans, 1964), 78; Sweeney, *Robert Southwell: Snow in* Arcadia, 258.

68 Pilarz, *Robert Southwell and the Mission of* Literature, 276.

69 Anthony Milton, *Catholic and Reformed: The Roman and Protestant Churches in English Protestant Thought, 1600–1640* (Cambridge: Cambridge UP, 2002), 537.

70 Brownlow, *Robert Southwell*, 16.

71 Robert Southwell, *Two Letters and Short Rules of a Good Life*, ed. Nancy Pollard Brown (Charlottesvile: UP of Virginia, 1973), 83–84.

72 Robert Southwell, *An Epistle of Comfort to the Reverend Priests and to the Honourable, Worshipful,* and *Other* of the *Lay Sort, Restrained* in *Durance for the Catholic Faith*, ed. Margaret Waugh (Chicago: Loyola UP, 1966), 146.

73 Quoted from Janelle, *Robert Southwell the* Writer, 51.

74 See Houliston, *Catholic Resistance in Elizabethan England*, 51–52.

75 Brownlow, *Robert Southwell*, 64–72.

76 Cummings, *Literary Culture of the Reformation*, 332.

77 Victor Houliston, "Why Robert Persons Would not be Pacified: Edmund Bunny's Theft of The Book of Resolution," in *The Reckoned Expense*, 159–177.

78 Sweeney, *Robert Southwell: Snow in Arcadia*, 146–150; Devlin, *Life of Robert Southwell*, 267.

79 Shell, *Catholicism and the English Literary* Imagination, 58–62; Barbara Lewalski, *Protestant Poetics and the Seventeenth Century Religious Lyric* (Princeton: Princeton UP, 1979), 104, 427; Brownlow, *Robert Southwell*, 127–128; Cummings, *Literary Culture of the Reformation*, 335.

80 Patrick Collinson, "The Elizabethan Exclusion Crisis and the Elizabethan Polity," *Proceedings of the British Academy* 84 (1995): 61. See also J. G. A. Pocock, *The Machiavellian Moment: Florentine Political Thought and the and the Atlantic Republican Tradition* (Princeton: Princeton UP, 1975), 353.

81 Markku Peltonen, *Classical Humanism and Republicanism in English Political Thought, 1570–1640* (Cambridge: Cambridge UP, 1995), 127, 145.

82 Ann Hughes, *Politics, Society and Civil War in Warwickshire, 1620–1660* (Cambridge: Cambridge UP, 2002), 24–25; Robert Strider, *Robert Greville, Lord Brooke* (Cambridge, MA: Harvard UP, 1958).

83 Kenneth J. E. Graham, *The Performance of Conviction: Plainness and Rhetoric in the Early English Renaissance* (Ithaca: Cornell UP, 1994), 97.
84 Quoted in Brownlow, *Robert Southwell*, 131.
85 Fulke Greville, "*Caelica* XCVIII," 3–6, in *Selected Writings of Fulke Greville*, ed. Joan Rees (London: Bloomsbury, 2013), 43.

Bibliography

Adams, Simon Lester. "The Protestant Cause: Religious Alliance with the West European Calvinist Communities as a Political Issue in England, 1585–1630," PhD diss., Oxford University, 1973.

Alexander, Gavin. *After Sidney: The Literary Response to Sir Philip Sidney 1586–1640*. Oxford: Oxford University Press, 2006.

Beales, A. C. F. *Education under Penalty: English Catholic Education from the Reformation to the Fall of James II*. London: Athlone Press, 1963.

Benjamin, Edwin B. "Sir John Hayward and Tacitus," *Review of English Studies* 8 (1957).

Bossy, John. "The Heart of Robert Persons," in *The Reckoned Expense: Edmund Campion and the Early English Jesuits*. Edited by Thomas M. McCoog, S. J., 251–275. Woodbridge: Boydell Press, 1996, 141–158.

Brown, Nancy Pollard. "Robert Southwell: The Mission and the Written Word." In *The Reckoned Expense: Edmund Campion and the Early English Jesuits*. Edited by Thomas M. McCoog, S. J., 251–275. Woodbridge: Boydell Press, 1996.

Brownlow, Frank W. *Robert Southwell*. New York: Twayne Publishers, 1996.

Bullough, Geoffrey. "Fulke Greville, First Lord Brooke." *Modern Language Review* 28 (1933): 1–20.

Burnham Carter, Jr. "The Intellectual Background of Fulke Greville." PhD diss., Stanford University, 1955.

Caraman, Philip. *Henry Garnet, 1555–1606, and the Gunpowder Plot*. London: Longmans, 1964.

Clucas, Stephen. "Giordano Bruno's 'Degli Eroici Furori' and Fulke Greville's 'Caelica.'" *Renaissance Studies* 4 (1990): 201–227.

Collinson, Patrick. *Birthpangs of English Protestantism*. London: Palgrave Macmillan, 1988.

Collinson, Patrick. *Godly People*. London: Hambledon Press, 1983.

Collinson, Patrick. "The Elizabethan Exclusion Crisis and the Elizabethan Polity." *Proceedings of the British Academy* 84 (1995), 61

Collinson, Patrick. *The Elizabethan Puritan Movement*. Cambridge: Cambridge University Press, 1967.

Cummings, Brian. *The Literary Culture of the Reformation: Grammar and Grace*. Oxford: Oxford University Press, 2002.

Cust, Richard. "Reading for Magistracy: The Mental World of Sir John Newdigate." In *The Monarchical Republic of Early Modern England: Essays in Response to Patrick Collinson*. Edited by John F. McDiarmid, 182. London: Routledge, 2007.

Dandelet, Thomas. *The Renaissance of Empire in Early Modern Europe*. Cambridge: Cambridge University Press, 2014.

Devlin, Christopher. *The Life of Robert Southwell: Poet and Martyr*. New York: Greenwood Press, 1969.

Duncan-Jones, Katherine. *Sir Philip Sidney: Courtier Poet*. New Haven: Yale University Press, 1991.

Duncan-Jones, Katherine. "Sir Philip Sidney's Debt to Campion." In *The Reckoned Expense: Edmund Campion and the Early English Jesuits*. Edited by Thomas M. McCoog, S. J., 85–102. Woodbridge: The Boydell Press, 1996.

Durston, Christopher and Jacqueline Eales, *The Culture of English Puritanism, 1560–1700*. Basingstoke: Palgrave Macmillan, 1996.

Ely, Humphrey. *Certaine briefe notes upon a briefe apologie*. Paris, n.p., 1602.

Foxe, John. *Actes and Monuments*. London: John Day, 1583.

Gadja, Alexandra. "Tacitus and Political Thought in Early Modern Europe, c.1530–1640." In *Cambridge Companion to Tacitus*. Edited by A. J. Woodman, 253–268. Cambridge: Cambridge University Press, 2010.

Gadja, Alexandra. *The Earl of Essex and Late Elizabethan Political Culture*. Oxford: Oxford University Press, 2012.

Garrett, C. H. *The Marian Exiles: A Study in the Origins of Elizabethan Puritanism*. Cambridge: Cambridge University Press, 1996.

Graham, Kenneth J. E. *The Performance of Conviction: Plainness and Rhetoric in the Early English Renaissance*. Ithaca: Cornell University Press, 1994.

Greville, Fulke. "A Dedication to Sir Philip Sidney." In *The Prose Works of Fulke Greville, Lord Brooke*. Edited by John Gouws, 3–136. Oxford: Oxford University Press, 1986.

Greville, Fulke. "*Caelica XCVIII*," 3–6. In *Selected Writings of Fulke Greville*. Edited by Joan Rees, 43. London: Bloomsbury, 2013.

Haigh, Christopher. *English Reformations: Religion, Politics and Society under the Tudors*. Oxford: Clarendon, Press, 1993.

Hammer, Paul. "The Earl of Essex, Fulke Greville, and the Employment of Scholars." *Studies in Philology* 91 (1994): 167–180.

Hammer, Paul E. J. *The Polarisation of Elizabethan Politics: The Political Career of Robert Devereux, 2nd Earl of Essex, 1585–1597*. Cambridge: Cambridge University Press, 1999.

Hansen, Matthew C. "Gender, Power and Play: Fulke Greville's *Mustapha* and *Alaham*." *Sidney Journal* 19 (2001): 125–141.

Hargrave, O. T. "The Predestinarian Offensive of the Marian Exiles at Geneva." *Historical Magazine of the Protestant Episcopal Church* 42, no. 2 (1973): 111–123.

Hicks, Leo. "Father Robert Persons S. J. and The Book of the Succession." *Recusant History* 4 (1957): 104–137.

Highley, Chistopher. *Catholics Writing the Nation in Early Modern Britain and Ireland*. Oxford: Oxford University Press, 2008.

Holmes, Peter. "The Authorship and Early Reception of *A Conference about the Next Succession to the Crown of England*." *Historical Journal* 23 (1980): 415–429.

Houliston, Victor. *Catholic Resistance in Elizabethan England: Robert Persons's Jesuit Polemic*. Aldershot and Burlington: Ashgate, 2013.

Houliston, Victor. "Why Robert Persons would not be Pacified: Edmund Bunny's Theft of The Book of Resolution." In *The Reckoned Expense: Edmund Campion and the Early English Jesuits*, Edited by Thomas M. McCoog, S. J., 159–177. Woodbridge: Boydell Press, 1996.

Hughes, Ann. *Politics, Society and Civil War in Warwickshire, 1620–1660*. Cambridge: Cambridge University Press, 2002.

Irish, Bradley J. "The Literary Afterlife of the Essex Circle: Fulke Greville, Tacitus, and BL Additional MS 18638." *Modern Philology* 112 (2014): 271–285.

James, Mervyn. *Society, Politics and Culture: Studies in Early Modern England.* Cambridge: Cambridge University Press, 1988.

Janelle, Pierre. *Robert Southwell the Writer: A Study in Religious Inspiration.* Mamaroneck: Paul O. Appel, 1971.

Kewes, Paulina. "Henry Savile's Tacitus and the Politics of Roman History in Late Elizabethan England," *Huntington Library Quarterly* 74 (2011): 515–551.

Kewes, Paulina. "The Puritan, the Jesuit and the Jacobean Succession." In *Doubtful and Dangerous: The Question of Succession in Late Elizabethan England.* Edited by Susan Doran and Paulina Kewes, 47–70. Manchester: Manchester University Press, 2014.

Knox, John. *The Works of John Knox*, ed. David Laing, 6 vols. Edinburgh: Bannatyne Society, 1846–1864.

Lake, Peter. *Moderate Puritans and the Elizabethan Church.* Cambridge: Cambridge University Press, 1982.

Lake, Peter and Michael Questier, eds. *Conformity and Orthodoxy in the English Church.* Woodbridge, Suffolk: The Boydell Press, 2000.

Larson, Charles. *Fulke Greville.* New York: Twayne Publishers, 1980.

Levy, Fritz. "The Theatre and the Court in the 1590s." In *The Reign of Elizabeth I: Court and Culture in the Last Decade.* Edited by John Guy, 274–300. Cambridge: Cambridge University Press, 1995.

Lewalski, Barbara. *Protestant Poetics and the Seventeenth Century Religious Lyric.* Princeton, NJ: Princeton University Press, 1979.

Maccioni, Alessandra and Marco Mostert. "Isaac Dorislaus (1595–1649): The Career of a Dutch Scholar in England," *Transactions of the Cambridge Bibliographical Society* 8 (1981–1984): 419–470.

Martz, Louis. *The Poetry of Meditation.* New Haven: Yale University Press, 1954, rev. edn. 1962.

Maurer, Warren R. "Spee, Southwell, and the Poetry of Meditation." *Comparative Literature* 15 (1963): 15–22.

McCoog, Thomas M. *The Society of Jesus in Ireland, Scotland, and England 1541–1588: "Our Way of Proceeding?"* Leiden: Brill, 1996.

Milsom, John. "Byrd, Sidney, and the Art of Melting," *Early Music* 31 (2003): 437–449.

Milton, Anthony. *Catholic and Reformed: The Roman and Protestant Churches in English Protestant Thought, 1600–1640.* Cambridge: Cambridge University Press, 2002.

Norbrook, David. *Poetry and Politics in the English Renaissance.* Oxford: Oxford University Press, 2002.

Peltonen, Markku. *Classical Humanism and Republicanism in English Political Thought, 1570–1640.* Cambridge: Cambridge University Press, 1995.

Perry, Curtis. "Seneca and English Political Culture." In *The Oxford Handbook of the Age of Shakespeare.* Edited by R. Malcolm Smuts, 317–318. Oxford: Oxford University Press, 2016.

Pettegree, Andrew. *Marian Protestantism: Six Studies.* Aldershot: Scolar Press, 1996.

Pilarz, Scott R. *Robert Southwell and the Mission of Literature: Writing Reconciliation.* Aldershot and Burlington: Ashgate, 2004.

Pocock, J. G. A. *The Machiavellian Moment: Florentine Political Thought and the and the Atlantic Republican Tradition.* Princeton: Princeton University Press, 1975.

Pollen, J. H. ed. *Unpublished Documents Relating to the English Martyrs.* London: Catholic Record Society, 1908.

Quinn, Kelly A. "Fulke Greville's Friendly Patronage." *Studies in Philology* 103 (2006): 417–435.

Raber, Karen. *Dramatic Difference: Gender, Class and Genre in the Early Modern Closet Drama.* Newark: University of Delaware Press, 2001.

Raspa, Anthony. *The Emotive Image: Jesuit Poetics in the English Renaissance.* Fort Worth: Texas Christian University Press, 1983.

Rebholz, Ronald A. *The Life of Fulke Greville, First Lord Brooke.* Oxford: The Clarendon Press, 1971.

Rees, Joan. *Fulke Greville, Lord Brooke, 1554–1628.* Berkeley: University of California Press, 1971.

Salmon, J. H. M. "Seneca and Tacitus in Jacobean England." In *The Mental World of the Jacobean Court.* Edited by Linda Levy Peck, 169–188. Cambridge: Cambridge University Press, 1991.

Scott Pearson, A. F. *Thomas Cartwright and Elizabethan Puritanism.* Cambridge: Cambridge University Press, 1925.

Shell, Alison. *Catholicism and the English Literary Imagination, 1558–1660.* Cambridge: Cambridge University Press, 1999.

Sierhuis, Freya. "Friendship and Freedom of Speech in the Work of Fulke Greville." In *Passions and Subjectivity in Early Modern Culture.* Edited by Brian Cummings and Freya Sierhuis, 131–147. London and New York: Routledge, 2016.

Skinner, Quentin. *Foundations of Modern Political Thought.* Cambridge: Cambridge University Press, 1978.

Smuts, R. Malcolm. "Court-Centred Politics and the Uses of Roman Historians, c.1590–1630." In *Culture and Politics in Early Stuart England.* Edited by Kevin Sharpe and Peter Lake, 24–40. Basingstoke: Palgrave Macmillan, 1994.

Southwell, Robert. *An Epistle of Comfort to the Reverend Priests and to the Honourable, Worshipful,* and *Other* of the *Lay Sort, Restrained* in *Durance for the Catholic Faith,* edited by Margaret Waugh, 146. Chicago: Loyola University Press, 1966.

Southwell, Robert. "The Author to his Loving Cousin." In *The Poetical Works of the Rev. Robert Southwell.* Edited by William B. Turnbull, 1. London: John Russell Smith, 1856.

Southwell, Robert. *The Triumphs over Death.* Edited by J. W. Trotman, 36–64. London: Manresa Press, 1914.

Southwell, Robert. *Two Letters and Short Rules of a Good Life.* Edited by Nancy Pollard Brown, 83–84. Charlottesville: University Press of Virginia, 1973.

Staley, Gregory. *Seneca and the Idea of Tragedy.* Oxford: Oxford University Press, 2009.

Steggle, Matthew. "Fulke Greville: Life and Works." *Sidney Journal* 19 (2001). 1–10.

Stillman, Robert E. "Philip Sidney and the Catholics: The Turn from Confessionalism in Early Modern Studies." *Modern Philology* 112 (2014): 97–129.

Strider, Robert. *Robert Greville, Lord Brooke.* Cambridge, MA: Harvard University Press, 1958.

Sweeney, Anne R. *Robert Southwell: Snow in Arcadia.* Oxford: Oxford University Press, 2013.

Todd, Margo. "Anti-Calvinists and the Republican Threat in Early Stuart Cambridge." In *Puritanism and its Discontents*. Edited by Laura Lunger Knoppers, 85–105. Newark: University of Delaware Press, 2003.

Todd, Margo. *Christian Humanism and the Puritan Social Order*. Cambridge: Cambridge University Press, 1987.

Trinterud, Leonard J. "The Origins of Puritanism," *Church History* 20, no. 1 (1951): 37–57.

Tuck, Richard. *Philosophy and Government, 1572–1651*. Cambridge: Cambridge University Press, 1993.

Tutino, Stefania. "The Political Thought of Robert Persons in Continental Context." *Historical Journal* 52 (2009): 32–62.

Wallace, Dewey D. *Puritans and Predestination: Grace in English Protestant Theology, 1525–1695*. Chapel Hill: University of North Carolina Press, 2004.

Walsham, Alexandra. *Church Papists: Catholicism, Conformity, and Confessional Polemic in Early Modern England*. Woodbridge, Suffolk: The Boydell Press, 1993.

Waswo, Richard. *The Fatal Mirror: Themes and Techniques in the Poetry of Fulke Greville*. Charlottesville: University of Virginia Press, 1972.

Womersley, David. "Sir John Henry Savile's Translation of Tacitus and the Political Interpretation of Elizabethan Texts." *Review of English Studies* new series, 42 (1991): 313–342.

Worden, Blair. *The Sound of Virtue: Philip Sidney's Arcadia and Elizabethan Politics*. New Haven: Yale University Press, 1996.

Part I
Fulke Greville (1554–1628)

1 "Freedom Among the Dead"

Greville's *Dedication to Sir Philip Sidney*

Alison Findlay

Fulke Greville's curiously hybrid text, combining a biography of Sir Philip Sidney with a panegyric on Queen Elizabeth, a history of the Elizabethan age and more general observations on poetics, politics, and government, was published as "The Life of the Renowned Philip Sidney" in *The Works of Fulke Greville, Lord Brooke* (1652). As John Gouws notes, this title is "misleading as to both the content and the nature of the work."[1] Only one of the earlier manuscripts in the library of Trinity College, Cambridge, has a title: "A Dedication to Sir Philip Sidney" which refers to Greville's intention to dedicate his own writings: "tragedies, with some treatises annexed" to the memory of his friend, as a means to "imitate or tread in the steps of so great a leader."[2] The tragedies *Alaham* and *Mustapha* are discussed in this volume by Vassiliki Markidou and Brian Cummings respectively, while Robert Appelbaum considers Greville's political writings and Rachel White's essay analyses his *Treatie on Humane Learning* and *Treatise on Religion*.

In the manuscript and printed copies of the *Dedication* which have come down to us, the biography of Philip Sidney has been supplemented by the memoir of Queen Elizabeth and commentary by Greville on his own life and his writings in Chapters XIV–XVI.[3] The *Dedication* went through several rewritings from its first composition *c.*1604 through to 1614, with the majority of the text we have now probably completed by 1612.[4] The *Dedication* can therefore be seen as a lengthy critical introduction to Greville's own works, placed in the contexts of Elizabethan history, political theory, and a literary tradition with classical origins. The life of Philip Sidney provides an anchor in the *Dedication*. It functions as "a seamark" – a landmark to navigation – which holds all the diverse elements together.[5] Joan Rees writes that Greville's friendship with Sidney is at the centre of the most powerful "acretive activity" – emotionally and intellectually charged revision and amendment – that characterises Greville's writing. "What has its origins in a sequence of biographical facts," she argues, "acquires, especially after Sidney's death, an area of associations and significances which reaches far into Greville's political and also his religious experience."[6] Gary Waller has argued that Greville was "deeply scarred by the Protestant dynamic" and Sidney's death in particular, which caused Greville to question the "secret judgements" of an inscrutable God. "He is uneasily aware that the God Sidney served chose to permit his death."[7]

Greville explicitly states that his long-deceased friend gives him "a kind of freedom even among the dead."[8] This refers not just to the text's nostalgic reconstruction of English history, but to Greville's rewriting of himself. The title *A Dedication to Philip Sidney* can be taken literally. As well as being a history, a biography, and a commentary, it is an autobiographical text in which Greville dedicates *himself* to the memory of his "long since-departed friend" and to mortality.[9] The opening of the text points out Greville's reversal of the usual form of dedication to a powerful patron whose support will promote the work and the writer in the future. Instead, Greville self-consciously retires, seeking "employment in the safe memory of dead men" rather than "patronage out of hope or fear in the future." He compares himself to Nestor, "delighted in repeating old news of the ages past," and imagines that, if his own treatises are published and believed by future readers, they shall "rise upon the stage when I am not." He will be dead.[10] Greville's "self-respect of dedication" or self-fashioning is therefore not to the living but to the dead. His *Dedication to Philip Sidney* is a work of mourning in which the process of writing and of rewriting to "imitate or tread in the steps" of Sidney redefines the limits of Greville's own sense of self.[11] As Jacques Derrida points out, "funerary speech and writing do not follow upon death; they work upon life in what we call autobiography."[12]

This essay will argue that the writing process enacts Greville's own precarious identity in characteristically Protestant terms. In *Precarious Life*, Judith Butler claims that mourning "has to do with agreeing to undergo a transformation (perhaps one should say *submitting* to a transformation) the full result of which one cannot know in advance," an uncertainty which makes it futile to "invoke the Protestant ethic" in the face of loss.[13] The passivity and uncertainty which characterises the process of mourning is unsettling because it contradicts the Protestant ethic of both individual effort, hard work and discipline, and faith in a destiny predetermined by God's grace. Early modern identities were undoubtedly transformed by the precarious religio-political environment of post-Reformation Europe, and the Calvinist doctrine of predestination was troubled, for Greville at least, by a deep sense of uncertainty. I argue that the *Dedication to Sir Philip Sidney* materialises the transformative process of mourning outlined by Butler, in which identity is deconstructed and reconstructed through loss:

> [S]omething about who we are is revealed, something which delineates the ties we have to others, that shows us that these ties constitute what we are, ties or bonds compose us. It is not as if an "I" exists independently over here and then simply loses a "you" over there, especially if

the attachment to "you" is part of what composes who "I" am. If I lose you, under these conditions, then I not only mourn the loss, but I become inscrutable to myself. Who am "I" without "you"? When we lose some of those ties by which we are constituted, we do not know who we are or what to do.[14]

Butler goes on to argue that it is "the tie," the relationality between self and other which constitutes identity, a familiar concept for early modern perceptions of self which we label pre-Cartesian. The relationality put into crisis by loss is carefully rebuilt by Greville's writing, especially his depictions of friendship and his technique of *prosopopoeia*, as the essay will go on to discuss. Butler's model is also useful for reading Greville's multi-faceted text because she reorients mourning from a private and depoliticising experience to one which "furnishes a sense of political community" by bringing to the fore "relational ties that have implications for theorising fundamental dependency and ethical responsibility."[15] Political community and the relative responsibility and dependency of those within it are intimately bound up with Greville's memorial for the friend he "observed, honoured and loved ... so much."[16]

The passion which binds the mourning Greville to Sidney beyond death creates an intersubjective relationship as described by Butler. Verses that Greville composed as an engraving for Sir Philip Sidney's tomb celebrated "the sympathies of pure sparcks" which "remaineth between the spirits of the living and the dead." As Sir John Coke remarked to Greville, however, the meaning of these words is "darck and hard to be construed to a literall planie sence."[17] The same is true of the *Dedication*: although Greville's love for Sidney is obvious, at the same time the intersubjective relationship between them which the text seeks to describe and to perpetuate through the act of writing remains mysterious. Reading the dissolution of boundaries between self and other in terms of both personal friendship and religious sympathy helps to illuminate what is at stake. The idea of the friend as another self, "*Amicus alter ipse*" as Erasmus's adage put it, was part of a Renaissance humanist model of idealised friendship, going back to Pythagoras and to Cicero's *De Amiticia*.[18] Greville draws on this classical legacy as a metaphor for his bond to Sidney. He describes the "honour of being bred with him from his youth" and of being chosen by the Aeneas-like Sidney "to be his beloved Achates" in the proposed quest to America with Sir Francis Drake.[19] Although Greville always puts himself in second place, finally entreating the reader to "judge honourably of my friend and moderately of me," the *Dedication* melds their voices, opinions and identities, Greville taking on the authority of Sidney's voice as his spokesman just as Sidney had reciprocated him in the "freedom of our friendship."[20]

The classically derived image of equality in friendship invariably had an unsettling political effect when it was used in writings from the hierarchical societies of the sixteenth and seventeenth centuries, as Laurie Shannon's study *Sovereign Amity* notes.[21] Freya Sierhuis has sensitively argued that Greville's *Dedication* follows this radical tradition and "employs the language of friendship," strategically, "enlarging its boundaries [and] allowing the reader a glimpse of a more stable, more equal political world."[22] In the *Dedication*, intersubjective friendship is characterised as Protestant in nature, underpinned by a perceptible ethos of spiritual and intellectual equality and based in a politically republican ethic of mutual support. Invoking the testimonies of key Protestant figures, Greville pointedly promotes a different kind of sovereignty. He will bring "regnant evidence from the dead" who value "the honour of true worth" much better than those living, who are more likely to profit from discrediting "old friends" in order to promote their own interests in the "markets of selfness," the competitive culture of the present.[23]

The opposite of "selfness" is magnanimous intersubjectivity, a surrendering of self to promote the other which is detailed in Sidney's encounters with these Protestant brothers. Greville reports that Sidney is like the wind Zephyrus "giving life where he blew."[24] He is taught by the Huguenot scholar Hubert Languet, author of the radical *Vindiciae contra tyrannos: A Defence of Liberty against Tyrants. Or, of the Lawfull Power of the Prince over the People, and of the People over the Prince* (1648). Greville depicts a "harmony" of mutual fascination and cultivation between teacher and pupil: "the elder grew taken with a net of his own thread, and the younger taught to lift up himself by a threat of the same spinning."[25] William Nassau, the Protestant Prince of Orange, offers a fuller example of magnanimous and politicised interaction with Sidney and Greville. Michael Gadaleto perceptively argues that Greville's portrait of Orange in the *Dedication* offers a trenchant political critique of the English monarchy and a celebration of the Dutch Republic. Orange, who champions Sidney, is Greville's "ideal hybrid of an older chivalric order centred round action and worth, fused with the republican citizen of the future."[26] The nostalgia and idealism of the text must have been especially poignant when it was published in 1652. Viktor Skretkowicz traces how the subtitle of the published text "WITH the *true Interest of England as it then stood in relation to all Forrain powers*" foregrounds the "immediate relevance" of its political analysis of national and international matters to mid-seventeenth century readers.[27]

Greville deliberately draws on the double meaning of the now obsolete word "assumpsit" to advertise his technique of *prosopopeia*, assuming the voice of another, and his complex relationship with his subjects as narrator of the *Dedication*. The OED defines "assumpsit" as an undertaking, a contract to another undertaken orally or in writing, not sealed but founded upon a consideration in legal terms. It also meant an assumption, or a taking for granted. Both terms are appropriate for Greville's project in the *Dedication*: his commitment to promoting Sidney's forward-looking Protestant politics, alongside a simultaneous recognition that he, Greville, has assumed (silently taken for granted) the voices of others to promote his own political beliefs in Jacobean England. In Chapter II, for example, he ventriloquises both the Prince of Orange and Philip Sidney, recounting, first, the former's fears for the "dangerous fate which the crown of England, states of Germany and the Low Countries" as Protestant territories, faced from "this active King of Spain."[28] A critique of Queen Elizabeth's failure to adequately support the French Protestants "a party raised by God" is neatly reassigned to the Prince of Orange.[29] The unfortunate consequences of Elizabeth's pre-occupation with the Ottomans, which has distracted her from "popish and Spanish invisible arts and counsels" in Europe (especially Austria), is also recorded at length as one of William of Orange's concerns.[30]

Finally, Orange's "free expressing of himself in the honour of Sir Philip Sidney" allows Greville to rehearse the shared feeling among forward-looking Protestants, that Sidney was "underemployed under her" and recommend, via Orange, a more active role for "one of the ripest and greatest counsellors of state, in Sir Philip Sidney."[31] Sidney's refusal to allow Greville to convey this viewpoint to Queen Elizabeth, also ventrilo-quised and narrated by Greville, must have had immediate political bite if this section was written in early Jacobean London, when Prince Henry personified the revival of those hopes, and a match was contracted between his sister, Princess Elizabeth and Frederick the Elector Palatine. The loss of Protestant hopes in Sidney's early death were tragically repeated when Prince Henry died (after contracting what was probably typhoid fever) on 6 November 1612. Perhaps Greville was keenly aware of the fragility of Protestant aspirations when he recited Sidney's determi-nation to leave "the success to His will that governs the blind prosperities and unprosperities of chance and so works out His own ends by the erring frailties of human reason and affection."[32]

Greville goes on to "challenge a kind of freedom, even among the dead" by assuming Sidney's voice and perspective to comment on European affairs.[33] The biographical detail of Sidney's objections to the match pro-posed between Queen Elizabeth and the Duke of Anjou becomes a plat-form for an itemised list of eleven points of anxieties about a Catholic conspiracy to "steal change of religion" into the kingdom.[34] The Duke would use his authority, as a husband over his wife, to metamorphose "our moderate form of monarchy into a precipitate absoluteness," effect-ively a "tyranny" under which the English people would be reduced "to the poverty of the French peasants" by taxation.[35] The "authors and Fathers" of the Reformed English church would be challenged, and her ministers replaced by "indifferent spirits whose God is this world and the Court their heaven."[36] The "crafty" Duke is imagined taking advantage of what Greville sees as "earth-eyed Common Law" on religious conformity in England, to raise up "superstitious idolatry" nationwide.[37] Foreign policy would be affected too in the breaking of alliances with the Protes-tant rulers in Denmark, Sweden, Germany, and the Hanseatic League in the Netherlands. Greville's interpolations "he discerned," "(as he said,)" "he did confess," "he foresaw," "as he conceived" and "he foresaw and prophesied," alluding to Sidney, barely cover the vehemence of Greville's rant against the Catholic threats to the Jacobean court and to the future of the nation.[38]

As a mourning narrator, Greville is ec-static, meaning outside oneself, in Judith Butler's understanding of the term: "to be transported beyond oneself by a passion, but also to be *beside oneself* with rage or grief." Greville's radical Protestant politics are not the same as Butler's but the communal "we" of readers and political activists that his text invokes are perhaps not so distant from the community she addresses "those of us who are living in certain ways *beside ourselves*, whether in sexual passion, or emotional grief, or political rage" or all three.[39]

Greville and Sidney's political passions and misfortunes are deliberately mirrored in the text. Sidney's attempt to join Sir Francis Drake's expedition to America is "imprisoned within the plights of the fortunes" by the Queen's command, just as Greville was later obliged to retire from the Jacobean court.[40] Greville's narrative fantastically supervenes their sense of confinement and elevates them to a "high pinnacle" of transcendent contemplation to overlook "the present map of the Christian world" beneath them.[41] In Chapter VIII Sidney (and Greville) have a panoptic view of "the vast body of this empire resting (as in a dream) upon an immovable centre of self-greatness," and, "under this false assumpsit," failing to take the precautionary measures to counter "the creeping monarchy of Rome (by her arch-instruments the Jesuits)."[42] As well as self-consciously acknowledging the audacity of assuming this panoptic critical overview, Greville draws attention to the dangers of complacency on the part of the English Protestant governors who "sit at home in their soft chairs playing fast and loose with them that ventured their lives abroad."[43] He goes on to itemise, nation by nation, the problems facing the Protestant community. Sidney, via Greville, forecasts that Spanish ambitions in Austria "would soon multiply unavoidable danger, both to themselves [the Austrian cities] and to us."[44] He notes problems in Poland, Denmark, Sweden; observes that the mercenary army of Switzers are "a dangerous body for the soul of Spain to infuse designs into," and, on the bases of these more informed "assumpsits," Sidney "resolves" that an attack on Spain's source of gold in the New World, or an attack at home in Europe should be mounted.[45]

What justification can Greville claim for assuming to speak for others and for assuming such an authoritative, didactic style? At the most obvious level, he situates his duty to write as a necessary supplement and complement to Sidney's actions. "[T]he truth is, his end was not writing even while he wrote, nor his knowledge moulded for tables or schools, but both his wit and understanding bent upon his heart to make himself and others, not in words or opinion, but in life and action, good and great."[46] *The Dedication* laments that Sidney's "short life and private fortunes" afforded him little opportunity to fully display the "ingenuity of his nature" and "public affection" in service to his country.[47] On the shortness of Sidney's life, Greville has no answer to his own implicit question as to why it should have "pleased God, in this decript age of the world, not to restore the image of her ancient vigour in him otherwise than in a lightning before death."[48] Waller suggests that "Greville's Calvinism reads Sidney's death as God's harsh but just judgment on England"[49] and the *Dedication* offers some trenchant criticisms of those governing England for neglecting Sidney's advice and potential in service. Recording that Sidney "never was magistrate, not possessed of any fit stage for eminence to act upon," the *Dedication* observes that the "sparks of extraordinary greatness" in Sidney "lay concealed and in a manner smothered up" because they were given no "clear vent" or expression through great office.[50] The complaints on behalf of Sidney also advertise Greville's own grievance that his talents have been passed over in the Jacobean court. While Sidney is dead, Greville is left on the stage of the world without opportunities for service in "life and action," and must therefore turn to words to proclaim Sidney's virtues to English readers so that "by a right meridian line of their own" they may "learn to sail through the straits of true virtue, into a calm and spacious ocean of human honour."[51]

A Protestant commitment to the word underlies Greville's confident tone as a prophet for the nation. His and Sidney's teacher Hubert Languet endorsed the power of Christian subjects, living by "the sword of the spirit only, to wit, the word of God, wherewith St. *Paul* armes all Christians," to counterbalance the material swords and authority of princes.[52] Greville's own prophetic tone in the *Dedication*, sometimes disguised by *prosopopoeia*, translates the situation of Elizabethan England to the Jacobean present from which Greville is writing. He calls Sidney "our unbelieved Cassandra" for his warnings about "this limitless ambition of the Spaniard" and offers an apocalyptic vision of the growing power of the Inquisition "rising out of the old age of superstitious phantasms, utterly to root out all seeds of human freedom," The "true glass" of insight would prove, according to Sidney (and Greville), "that tyrants be not nursing fathers," and "no anointed deputies of God, but rather lively images of the Dark Prince."[53] Peter Herman has argued that the primary political concern in Greville's *Dedication* is to defend the Ancient Constitution, the English common law balancing power between the monarch and the people, a constitution that was threatened by James I's absolutism. Greville's dedication to the Ancient Constitution, which was embedded in his *Dedication to Philip Sidney*, was highly pertinent when it was published in 1652, after the climactic political clash of royal prerogative and commonwealth.[54]

As well as being a memorial, then, Greville's *Dedication* looks prophetically to the future. Its presentation of Sidney's biography and celebration of Elizabethan history encourages the patriotic Protestant reader to "look upon the stage whereon he is an actor, even the state he lives in," and to turn words into action, following Philip Sidney's model.[55] Greville's idealisation of Sidney and of the Elizabethan age whose best virtues he embodies, is assuredly part of a wider nostalgia for what has been lost, as critics have pointed out.[56] Patrick Crutwell astutely observes that the knights Sidney and the Earl of Essex both appealed, in their own age, to an Elizabethan "Gothick" or nostalgic cult of chivalry which idealised them as figures from a purer, simpler past. Even in the fifteen years between their deaths, perceptions had changed. By 1601, Essex "stood for the 'good old days': hateful modernity had killed him. He died because he was out-of-date. His fate, and Sidney's, are in significant contrast: Sidney dying, in 1586, universally honoured; Essex in 1601, on the scaffold."[57] Greville's Jacobean perspective intensifies the contrast between the idealised past embodied by these Protestant knights, and the wrongness of the present. He attributes the fall of Essex to those "sect-animals" whose malice makes them manufacture and libellously publish texts "against the state" under Essex's name. Unsurprisingly, Greville defines their motives as religious: "[H]is power, by the Jesuitical craft of rumour, they made infinite, and his ambition more equal to it; his letters to private men were read openly by the piercing eyes of an attorney's office, which warrants the construction of every line in the worst sense against the writer."[58]

Justice is perverted and Greville himself is rendered powerless to help because he is "abruptly sent away" to Rochester to guard against "a figurative fleet of danger of nothing by these prosopopeias of invisible rancour."[59] As is clear from these lines, Greville's passion as a historian is driven by religious zeal. Sir John Coke's letter reminded Greville "it is now as necessarie to have diligent historians as learned divines" and equally necessary "that your historian bee also a divine able to ioyne church & comonwealth together wch to seperate is to betray."[60] He also told Greville "(your honor knoweth best) theis tymes neither live, nor govern by honor nor patterns of tymes past," giving voice to a Jacobean nostalgia that was accompanied by a spur to present action: "the chief use of this profession is now the defence of one church and therein of one state."[61] Greville's account of Elizabethan history in the *Dedication* seems to follow Sir John Coke's advice that, in the face of crumbling Catholic authority, Protestant writers should "purse [puruse] them hard" and "so discover their ambition, coteousnes, impostures [,] tyrannies [,] treacheries & al the depths of hel in that Roman gulph" and thus "shew there religion as now it standeth to be incompatible wth al free minds and estates."[62] Greville undertakes this task with fervent energy in his account of Elizabethan history in the *Dedication*. He confesses that he wrote the "short memorial" of Queen Elizabeth in Chapters XV, XVI, and XVII in a state of mental distress. It was not just "false spirits and apparitions of idle grief" that haunted him after the Queen's death but a sense of alienation from the Jacobean present where "the more discomfortable I found those new revolutions of time to my decayed and disproportioned disabilities."[63] He senses that, like Essex, he is out of date. He acknowledges that he has "ever since been dying to all those glories of life" he enjoyed under "the blessed and blessing presence of this unmatchable queen and woman."[64] His sense of loss seems to increase his vehemence in praising Elizabeth as a tolerant, wise, but zealous ruler. Queen Elizabeth is a "she-David" determined to repair "the precipitate ruins of our Saviour's militant church through all her dominions" like the Old Testament king. Not only this, Elizabeth, like David, "ventured to undertake the great Goliath among the Philistines abroad (I mean Spain and the Pope)."[65]

Greville saw writing, both fictional and historical, as a powerful didactic tool. He argued that the "dead images" of Sidney's *Arcadia* served as a caution against neglect of state matters, through which "the conspiracies of ambitious subalterns" can cause "the ruin of states and princes."[66] His own eulogy for Queen Elizabeth I's Protestant rule is a means "to revive myself in her memory," to retain a political voice.[67] This voice is undoubtedly biased; Greville's strict Calvinism which produces polemic. Nevertheless, by using *prosopopeia* to merge his voice with others, the mourning narrator combines his wish for ethical responsibility and political autonomy with a tangible sense of the interdependence of vulnerable human subjects in the collective political sphere. Judith Butler points out that "this way of imagining community affirms relationality not only as a descriptive or historical fact of our formation, but also as an ongoing normative dimension of our political lives, one in which we are compelled to take stock of our interdependence."[68] Discursive interdependence becomes a source of strength in the *Dedication*. When Greville acts as substitute for the voices of Sidney and Orange in Chapter II, for example, he appears to efface himself but in fact cleverly creates the illusion of a collective political voice. Having ventriloquised Orange, Greville ventriloquises Sidney arguing that the Queen would not welcome advice on governing her courtiers from a foreign prince such as Orange. Moreover, if the Queen could not see good enough reasons for promoting Sidney in his actions "daily attending on her," then Orange's report would be of little use.[69] As Gadaleto argues, Greville's account draws attention to Elizabeth's damaging lack of the noble skill of "ingenuous recognition," the ability to perceive Sidney's worth, which Orange displays so magnanimously. Greville's exposure of the Queen's shortcoming is surely part of his wider criticism of absolute sovereignty advocated by James I: "a political system based more upon bonds of idolatrous worship" than upon spiritual and intellectual brotherhood.[70] Elizabeth's neglect of Sidney is repeated in the way Greville himself has been passed over. I would argue that a more important point about testimony is also being argued by the Protestant Greville. While Sidney, the man of action, believes wholly in the power of present deeds, Greville shows a subtle and more modern ingenuity, in implicitly suggesting that the pen is mightier than the sword, that the written words "of dead men," including the *Dedication* and its writer, have greater lasting power as testimonies of worth. As a dedicated Protestant, Greville believes in the power of the word: in the virtue and worth incarnated in Sidney, as witnessed and told as a parable for future ages by Greville himself.

The thunderous warnings about England's future, based on a historical account of religious divisions from the past, undoubtedly give an Old Testament feel to the narrative of the *Dedication*. However, as Victor Skretkowicz argues, "to a strong Calvinist like Greville, the gospels offer an obviously superior model to the biographer of a Christian hero." For Greville, Sidney is "a parable through which to illuminate his own times."[71] The biographical strand of the *Dedication* is gospel-like in its loving celebration of Philip Sidney's life, in contrast with the broader anti-Catholic bombast elsewhere in the text. The testimony of Sir Henry Sidney, Philip's father, opens the account by proclaiming him "*Lumen familiae suae*" [the light of our family] and England soon comes to take him as "a light, or leading star, to every degree within her."[72] Sidney's uncle, Robert Dudley, Earl of Leicester functions as a John the Baptist figure who, having led the expedition to the Netherlands, "saw" in Sidney "the sun so risen above his horizon that both he and all his stars were glad to fetch light from him." Dudley finally acknowledges to Greville that it was by Sidney's natural authority "that he held up the honour of his casual authority" in the campaign.[73] Greville as biographer thus functions as an apostle whose words guide the pilgrim readers. The opening pages of the *Dedication* suggest that he is fully aware of the dangers of slipping into a Catholic pattern of hagiography by praising Sidney's exceptional virtues. He tells readers that in Sidney "the life itself of true worth did (by way of example) far exceed the pictures of it in any moral precepts" written in fiction, that "he himself hath left such an instance in the too short scene of his life as I fear many ages will not draw a line out of any other man's sphere to parallel it."[74] According to Greville, Sidney's life ironically confounds his own thesis in *The Defence of Poesy* that transcendent virtue belongs in the golden world of fiction rather than the brazen world of real life. Greville deftly differentiates the narrative voice of the *Dedication* from such fictional "characteristical kind of poesy" and presents his praise of Sidney as the truth. His record of Sidney's active life in the form of "passing fair and well-drawn lines" is a testimony by which "all pilgrims of this life may conduct themselves humbly into the haven of everlasting rest."[75]

If Greville's text does have beneficial consequences, these would go some way to resolving what Waller calls the "grim Calvinist paradox" between a belief in predestination and the necessity for "continual activity" within the corrupt world as a test of one's election. Waller says Greville "could not escape the responsibility of public duty, even in an unredeemable world."[76] Writing the parable of Sidney's life, even from retirement, was a "continual activity" and public duty of sorts. In Chapter III, Greville makes an explicit intervention in the narrative to say

For the sincere affection which I bear to my prince and country, my prayer to God is that his [Sidney's] worth and way may not fatally be buried with him, in respect that both before his time, and since, experience hath published the usual discipline of greatness to have been tender of itself only, making honour a triumph, or rather trophy, of desire set up in the eyes of mankind either to be worshipped as idols or else, as rebels, to perish under her glorious oppressions.[77]

Far from being a fashionable celebration of Sidney's greatness due to his birth or riches (or, indeed, an idolatrous piece of Catholic hagiography), Greville's *Dedication* will celebrate "true worth" and "noble actions."[78] Ultimately, however, Greville is acutely aware that his written monuments to Sidney or to Queen Elizabeth are not immortal or finally of value in the religious context of divine judgement and eternity. In Chapter XII he self-consciously announces the abrupt ending of his account of Sidney's life: "to suit with the more equally with his fortunes, I will cut off his actions – as God did his life – in the midst, and so conclude with his death."[79] Greville's bleak recognition that he cannot understand why "it pleased God" to determine Sidney's early death is registered candidly in Chapter III.[80] Greville cannot "complain of God" for taking away a person of such "exorbitant worthiness," but, left behind in the world of "our corruptions," he does not stop mourning.[81] He displaces his own anger and bewilderment into the mouth of the Catholic Bishop of Mendoza who expresses sympathy for "the poor widow" England who has been bereaved of the "eminent spirit" that was Sidney "by the hands of a villain."[82] Greville cannot call God a villain but, in the unlikely ally of the Bishop, *prosopopeia* gives him another ecstatic voice in which to confess (and simultaneously condemn) his heretical view and the sexual passion he felt for Sidney. Greville's grief makes him "the poor widow," beside himself in a mixture of yearning, political rage, and despair. Pessimism rather than hope is the dominant tone in the *Dedication*. Greville's text, perhaps as a symptom of his religious uncertainty, deconstructs itself: confident in its purpose to witness Sidney's worth for ages to come, it simultaneously acknowledges the insufficiency of words to create immortality. As Derrida noted in his *Memoirs for Paul de Man*, "We cannot write what we do not wish to erase. We can only promise it in terms of what will always be erased."[83] Writing, in the form of a memoir, cannot be written in certainty; it exists in the moment of composition in the knowledge that it is always under erasure (its testimony being vulnerable to the fate of being forgotten or "mis"read by others). Thus, Greville asks "no exemption" from the "common fortunes of books" whose life depends not on their authors but on the "grace and capacity" of future readers.[84]

In the knowledge that his writing cannot provide certainty for the future, in this world or the next, all that remains for Greville is the truth of his enduring love for Sidney. This passion and dedication annihilates his sovereign subjectivity, reconstituting it across temporal, spatial and mortal boundaries. As I have discussed, Greville's skilful use of *prosopopoeia* merges his own voice with that of Sidney to perpetuate the values he believes Sidney held and he, Greville, continues to hold in the corrupted world of the seventeenth century. It is a playful and liberating form of intersubjectivity through which Greville counters "these prosopopoeias of invisible rancour" made by the "Jesuitical craft of rumour" against the Protestant ideals personified by Sidney.[85] Although Greville does not claim to speak with Sidney in the Catholic sense of talking with the dead as spirits or ghosts, the *Dedication* is a textual version of haunting where Sidney's presence is self-consciously invoked through words. The figure of Sidney allows Greville to cross temporal boundaries. As Gavin Alexander's account of the text brilliantly elucidates: "Sidney never dies for Greville but lives on his mind, evolving and mutating as Greville's life and intellect move on and develop. The events of Sidney's life are always present for Greville, overlaid on to his own present." Thus the Sidney resurrected by the text is strangely omnipresent "he has always been there and is always the same."[86] Paradoxically, Sidney is always the same because he can be read again and again in the light of Greville's own changing experiences, as part of himself that is both past and present.

Skretkowicz refers to the text as a "confession,"[87] and perhaps its most touching words are when Greville tells the reader "I ingenuously confess that it delights me to keep company with him even after death esteeming his actions, words and conversation the daintiest treasure my mind could lay up."[88] It is finally a personal rather than a theological truth that sustains Greville's faith. His writings are "monuments of true affection between us, whereof, you see, death hath no power."[89] Greville's dedication and *Dedication* to Philip Sidney, his love and his writing, is the lifeline of faith that takes him beyond uncertainty and affords him "freedom among the dead."[90]

Notes

1 John Gouws, ed., *The Prose Works of Fulke Greville, Lord Brooke* (Oxford: Clarendon Press, 1986), xiii.
2 *A Dedication to Sir Philip Sidney*, in *The Prose Works of Fulke Greville, Lord Brooke*, ed. John Gouws (Oxford: Clarendon Press, 1986), 89–90. References are to page numbers in this edition.
3 For detailed discussion of the manuscripts and dating see Gouws, *Prose Works*, xv–xxiii.
4 Gouws, xxiii.
5 Greville, *Dedication*, 4.
6 Joan Rees, *Fulke Greville, Lord Brooke, 1554–1628: A Critical Biography* (London: Routledge, 1971), 45.
7 Gary Waller, *English Poetry of the Sixteenth Century*, second edition (London: Routledge, 2013), 126, 131.
8 Greville, *Dedication*, 4.
9 Ibid., 3.

10 Greville, *Dedication*, 3–4, 132.

11 Ibid., 3, 89.

12 Jacques Derrida, *Memoires for Paul De Man*, revised edition, trans. Cecile Lindsay, Jonathan Culler, Eduardo Cadava, and Peggy Kamuf (New York: Columbia UP, 1989), 22.

13 Judith Butler, *Precarious Life: The Powers of Mourning and Violence* (London: Verso, 2004), 21, cf. Derrida *Memoires*, 28.

14 Ibid. 22.

15 Ibid.

16 Greville, *Dedication*, 4.

17 These comments were included in a letter from Sir John Coke to Greville written *c.*1615 as Norman Farmer Jr argued in "Fulke Greville and Sir John Coke: An Exchange of Letters on a History Lecture and Certain Latin Verses on Sir Philip Sidney," *Huntington Library Quarterly*, 33 (1970), 217–236.

18 Desiderus Erasmus, *Proverbes or Adagies with newe addications of thie Chiliardes of Erasmus*, trans. Richard Taverner (London, 1539), notes "Frendshyp (sayth pythagors) is equality & al one mynde or wyll, and my frende is as who shuld say an other I." sigs. C5–C5v. See also Marcus Tullius Cicero, *Laelius De Amiticia* (44 BC), trans. John Harrington, *The Book of freendeship of Marcus Tullie Cicero* (London, 1550).

19 Greville, *Dedication*, 44.

20 Ibid., 155, 44.

21 Laurie Shannon, *Sovereign Amity: Figures of Friendship in Shakespearean Contexts* (Chicago: University of Chicago Press, 2000).

22 Freya Sierhuis, "Friendship and Freedom of Speech in the Work of Fulke Greville," in *Passions and Subjectivity in Early Modern Culture*, ed. Brian Cummings and Freya Sierhuis (Aldershot: Ashgate, 2013), 139.

23 Greville, *Dedication*, 13.

24 Ibid., 21.

25 Ibid., 6.

26 Michael Gadaleto, " 'Prince and No-Prince': William of Orange and the Politics of Friendship in Greville's *Dedication to Sir Philip Sidney*," *Sidney Journal* 35: (2017) Special Issue: Fulke Greville and the Arts, ed. Freya Siurhuis and Brian Cummings, 95–118, 115.

27 Viktor Skretkowicz, "Greville, Politics and the Rhetorics of *A Dedication to Sir Philip Sidney*," *Sidney Journal*, 19:1 (2001): Fulke Greville: A Special Double Issue, ed. Matthew C. Hansen and Matthew Woodcock, 97–124, 103. Gadaleto notes one such reader in Marchamont Needham who cites Greville's portrait of the Prince of Orange in the *Dedication* as a model of republican liberty (117–118).

28 Greville, *Dedication*, 14.

29 Ibid., 15.

30 Ibid., 16.

31 Ibid., 17.

32 Ibid., 18.

33 Ibid., 4.

34 Ibid., 31.

35 Ibid., 32.

36 Ibid., 31.

37 Ibid.

38 Ibid., 29, 30, 33.

39 Judith Butler, *Precarious Life*, 24.

40 Ibid., 46.

41 Ibid.

42 Ibid., 48.

43 Ibid., 52.

44 Ibid., 43.

45 Ibid., 50, 53.

46 Ibid., 12.

47 Ibid., 24–5.

48 Ibid., 23. "her" refers to the world. i.e. Sidney was a short-lived image of the world's "ancient vigour."

49 Waller, *English Poetry*, 131.

50 Greville, *Dedication*, 24, 7–8.

51 Ibid., 12, 4.

52 Hubert Languet, *Vindiciae contra tyrannos: A Defence of Liberty against Tyrants. Or, of the Lawfull Power of the Prince over the People, and of the People over the Prince* (London: Matthew Simmons and Robert Ibbotson, 1648).

53 Greville, *Dedication*, 68.

54 Peter C. Herman, " 'Bastard Children of Tyranny': The Ancient Constitution and Fulke Greville's *A Dedication to Philip Sidney*," *Renaissance Quarterly*, 55:3 (2002), 969–1004.

55 Greville, *Dedication*, 135.

56 Joan Rees summarises these views, noting "It is often observed that the views on politics attributed to Sidney are infected by hindsight, and that the account of Elizabeth's rule is shaped to offer parallels to that of James." Joan Rees, "Past and Present in the Sixteenth Century: Elizabethan Double Vision," *Trivium*, 20 (1985), 112.

57 Patrick Crutwell, *The Shakespearean Moment and its Place in the Poetry of the C17th Century* (London: Chatto and Windus, 1970), 35.

58 Greville, *Dedication*, 93.

59 Ibid, 94.

60 Farmer, "Fulke Greville and Sir John Coke," 221.

61 Ibid., 220.

62 Ibid., 221.

63 Greville, *Dedication*, 130.

64 Ibid., 129.

65 Ibid., 98–99.

66 Ibid., 8.

67 Ibid., 131.

68 Judith Butler, *Precarious Life*, 27.

69 Greville, *Dedication*, 17.

70 Gadaleto, "Prince and No-Prince," 113–115.

71 Skretcowicz, "Greville, Politics and Rhetorics," 120–121.

72 Greville, *Dedication*, 5.

73 Ibid., 18.

74 Ibid., 3.

75 Ibid., 76, 3.

76 Waller, *English Poetry*, 126.

77 Greville, *Dedication*, 23.

78 Ibid., 25.

79 Ibid., 76.

80 Ibid., 23.

81 Ibid.

82 Ibid., 21.

83 Derrida, *Memoires*, 123.

84 Greville, *Dedication*, 135.
85 Ibid., 94.
86 Gavin Alexander, *Writing After Sidney: The Literary Response to Sir Philip Sidney 1586–1640* (Oxford: Oxford UP, 2006), 243.
87 Skretkowicz, "Greville, Politics and Rhetorics," 107.
88 Greville, *Dedication*, 71.
89 Ibid., 86.
90 Ibid., 4.

Bibliography

Alexander, Gavin. *Writing After Sidney: The Literary Response to Sir Philip Sidney 1586–1640*. Oxford: Oxford University Press, 2006.

Butler, Judith. *Precarious Life: The Powers of Mourning and Violence*. London: Verso, 2004.

Cicero, Marcus Tullius. *Laelius De Amiticia* (44 BC). Translated by John Harrington, *The Book of freendeship of Marcus Tullie Cicero*. London: Thomas Berthelette, 1550.

Crutwell, Patrick. *The Shakespearean Moment and its Place in the Poetry of the 17th Century*. London: Chatto and Windus, 1970.

Derrida, Jacques. *Memoires for Paul De Man*, revised edition. Translated by Cecile Lindsay, Jonathan Culler, Eduardo Cadava and Peggy Kamuf. New York: Columbia University Press, 1989.

Erasmus, Desiderius. *Proverbes or Adagies with newe addications of thie Chiliardes of Erasmus*. Translated by Richard Taverner. London, 1539.

Farmer Jr., Norman. "Fulke Greville and Sir John Coke: An Exchange of Letters on a History Lecture and Certain Latin Verses on Sir Philip Sidney," *Huntington Library Quarterly*, 33 (1970): 217–236.

Gadaleto, Michael. " 'Prince and No-Prince': William of Orange and the Politics of Friendship in Greville's *Dedication to Sir Philip Sidney*," *Sidney Journal* 35: (2017) Special Issue: Fulke Greville and the Arts. Edited by Freya Siurhuis and Brian Cummings, 95–118.

Gouws, John, ed. *The Prose Works of Fulke Greville, Lord Brooke*. Oxford: Clarendon Press, 1986.

Greville, Fulke. *A Dedication to Sir Philip Sidney*, in *The Prose Works of Fulke Greville, Lord Brooke*. Edited by John Gouws. Oxford: Clarendon Press, 1986.

Herman, Peter C. " 'Bastard Children of Tyranny': The Ancient Constitution and Fulke Greville's *A Dedication to Philip Sidney*," *Renaissance Quarterly*, 55:3 (2002), 969–1004.

Languet, Hubert. *Vindiciae contra tyrannos: A Defence of Liberty against Tyrants. Or, of the Lawfull Power of the Prince over the People, and of the People over the Prince*. London, 1648.

Rees, Joan. *Fulke Greville, Lord Brooke, 1554–1628: A Critical Biography*. London: Routledge, 1971.

Rees, Joan. "Past and Present in the Sixteenth Century: Elizabethan Double Vision," *Trivium*, 20 (1985): 97–211.

Shannon, Laurie. *Sovereign Amity: Figures of Friendship in Shakespearean Contexts*. Chicago, IL: University of Chicago Press, 2000.

Sierhuis, Freya. "Friendship and Freedom of Speech in the Work of Fulke Greville." In *Passions and Subjectivity in Early Modern Culture*. Edited by Brian Cummings and Freya Sierhuis. Aldershot: Ashgate, 2013.

Skretkowicz, Viktor. "Greville, Politics and the Rhetorics of *A Dedication to Sir Philip Sidney*," *Sidney Journal*, 19:1 (2001): 97–123.

Waller, Gary. *English Poetry of the Sixteenth Century*, second edition. London: Routledge, 2013.

2 Reading might make us know

Vulcan's brothers and Myra's posies in Greville's *Cælica*

Elizabeth Mazzola

> I, that did weare the ring her mother left,
> I, for whose loue she gloried to be blamed,
> I, with whose eyes her eyes committed theft,
> I, who did make her blush when I was named;
> Must I lose ring, flowers, blush, theft and go naked,
> Watching with sighs, till dead loue be awakèd?
>
> (*Cælica* 22.13–18)[1]

Many readers of Fulke Greville's *Cælica* (published after his death in 1633) line up on one side, finding in this collection of poems an almost unrelieved cynicism and despair, especially in the earlier section (which Ronald Rebholz dates to the period between 1577–1587),[2] where the beloved is described by a speaker by turns devoted and frustrated, envious, contemptuous and servile, a double for the infantile cupid in some places, a mirror for the cuckolded Vulcan in others.[3]

But the self-division Greville carefully records is coupled with an unusually detailed picture of the beloved's charms and agency, her capacity for desire aligned with an affinity for language and wish for clarity and freedom. To be sure, this lady has many names—Cala, Myra, Cælica, Cynthia—sometimes even in the same poem; she also has several lovers, sometimes in the same poem, too. But throughout the seventy or so poems which investigate her destabilizing effect on Greville's speaker, her own powers of will or determination to employ her energies, usually marked by her ability to speak and write and think, remain undiminished. *Cælica* describes a beloved who is unfaithful but also intelligible, lustful but not sneaky, nearly divine in her power to wound and to transport, to dare misdeeds and to punish them. So as important as Greville's striking ability to wed delicate form to hard meaning is his abiding interest in a woman interested in many other things, Greville's speaker only occasionally one of them.

If Greville's speaker repeatedly represents himself as alone and embittered and even embarrassed by his efforts, this is not because he has been forced to lie or "perjure himself" the way Shakespeare's sonneteer does, or endure the lady's continued absence as Sidney's Astrophil is forced to do.[4] In fact, it is Greville's estrangement from the Petrarchan project that he wants his beloved to see. Not all readers share this view of Cælica's importance. One scholarly view of Greville as spurned lover associates his dejection with ongoing mourning for a dead master, his friend Sir Philip Sidney. Matthew Steggle, for instance, claims that "Greville's literary activities relating to Sidney—his publication of the *Arcadia*, his biographical account of Sidney, even *Cælica* itself—invite interpretation in terms of a battle over Sidney's legacy."[5] But the Cælica who provides a counterpart to Sidney's Stella takes poetry in a direction very different from *Astrophil and Stella*, suggesting that Sidney's ideas about an inaccessible lady—like his complicated strategy to win her—had proved something of a dead-end for Greville, anyway.[6]

Sidney's experiments with the Petrarchan project start at the outset of *Astrophil and Stella*, where Astrophil's muse immediately faults his thinking about love and courtship and supplies the fledgling poet with new instructions. "Loving in trueth" but "fayne [his] love in verse to show," his muse calls him "Foole" and tells him to "looke in thy heart and write," (1.1, 1.14), thereby coupling secrecy with sincerity and making the lady his collaborator, the ideal lover also an ideal audience whose reading "might make her know."[7] But although Greville's poet–lover does not see his lady as particularly ideal or her literary abilities as useful to him, he rarely doubts his ability to express what he thinks. Instead, he raises questions—sometimes in the course of a single poem—about what his work will mean to readers with their own powers to name and to rhyme. Greville's beloved is a rival maker of meaning and source of authority. In her company, the speaker sees himself as a figure of contradiction and loathing, a failed lover who is not, however, a failed poet.

And although Greville is nearly alone among his contemporaries in not publishing or even circulating his poetry, the suggestion that he guards his writings rather than shares them minimizes the way *Cælica* depicts Greville's poetry as written within a larger circle of poets and lovers inspecting what he says. One cannot "print a kisse," Greville's speaker says at one point, but he then indicates how foolish it would be to print a poem when a poet remains so uncertain of what his readers will think: "lines may deceiue," he concludes (*Cælica* 22. 29–30).[8] My chapter is concerned with the maturity and honesty Greville brings to Petrarchan poetry by describing female readers as suitable readers and partners in love. Maybe Greville puts an end, as Arthur Marotti argues, to amorous sonneteering (418) but in its place Greville pursues reasons for understanding men and women as similar in their experiences, and for seeing poetry as an especially apt tool to register these similarities. Such thinking also underlies Greville's 1589 *Letter to an Honorable Lady*,[9] and I refer to the *Letter* here for evidence of the way Greville imagines a woman's heart in terms of her capacity to know, her sense of herself derived from the way she imagines who she is in time, with words, and all alone.

Paying more attention to Cælica's perspective can change our view of Greville's collection as well as our responses to earlier readings of this work. Elaine Y. L. Ho (1992), for instance, argues that "*Caelica* is a Calvinistic narrative of the self that takes the form and rhetoric of an earlier and ideologically alien, Petrarchan, discourse[,]" its "alternative literary aesthetic" "questioning … the lady's superior virtues" and concluding with an assertion of heaven's better claims. According to Ho, *Cælica* is a story of failure and redemption (35). But I think the collection of poems gathered in *Cælica* reflects Greville's twinned interest in redeeming poetry and in redeeming himself by training his speaker to see what his beloved sees. These goals also inspire Greville's *Letter*. Outlining a love triangle where a husband abandons his wife for another woman, Greville transforms this dreary picture by inventing a fourth figure in the shape of a male writer who sympathizes with the lady and tells her that unrequited love can be explained by "tyme, and mischance" rather than blamed on human failing. Early modern discourses of love come up short, Greville shows the *Letter*'s reader, because their languages of want and betrayal fail to apprehend the ways women and men can also identify with each other.

Such empathy and respect are clear from the outset of the *Letter*, where Greville introduces his subject by first characterizing his relationship with his reader: "Yov are desirous, in regard of the trust you put in me, to vnderstand mine opinion, how you should carry your self through that labyrinth, wherein it seemes time and mischance have imprison'd you" (Grosart, ed. 233). These opening lines describe the relationship between female reader and male author as mutually inflected, so that her "desire" to "understand" his opinion about "how" she "should carry [her] self" as a result of her husband's infidelity is unfolded in a way that absolves her of any taint. Her powers to know give her moral leverage, and showing herself to someone else does not threaten the lady's virtue. Although no fault is assigned to the unfaithful husband at the root of these difficulties, more remarkable still is the way the female reader's needs and wishes—construed as both erotic and philosophical, her desires clearly connected with ethical concerns—can be addressed by her tie to Greville's speaker, one founded on "trust," his sense of how she thinks about how he thinks:[10] if she is "imprison'd" in a "labyrinth," the speaker inserts himself inside with her.

Their close connection and shared perspective about how to view feelings of bitterness, anger, and loss enable the speaker to argue that love has nothing to do with what she owes her husband as his wife, and that what the rest of the world sees has nothing to do with what she thinks. The wife's freedom is reflected in Cælica's movements, too, as I explore more fully below. Here, Greville proposes that if the wife is constrained by the duties prescribed by marriage, she can still train her mind to live nobly, counsel resembling the training Edmund Spenser describes in his "Letter to Ralegh" accompanying *The Faerie Queene*. Spenser's poem aims "to fashion a gentleman or noble person in virtuous and gentle discipline" by transforming submission into a heroic labor men and women alike can perform, knights like Britomart and Artegall enabled to find each other by transforming themselves.[11] Maybe Greville's practical advice to remake oneself rather than renew efforts to win back a lover is also explained by the way Queen Elizabeth forced him and Sidney to curb their ambitions; in Sidney, Marotti argues, Greville found "a symbol of his own victimization" (405). But Greville never really represents himself or the lady as victims or losers in *The Letter* or in *Cælica* because the battles he describes are always personal, men and women more alike than unalike in the solitary contests they undergo.

Many other English poets revised Petrarchan ambitions, and in this section of my chapter I investigate the varied roles women occupied in their poetry, possibly as a result of Elizabeth Tudor's sovereign example. According to Marotti, in Shakespeare's sonnets the role of the beloved is curtailed and her beauty irrelevant because Shakespeare is more occupied by the fierce competition for her favors: rather than consummation of the romance, "friendship as patronage ... is at stake" (406). As other critics have noted, however, Shakespeare's beloved is far from a silent witness because she has considerable fictive talents of her own, her ability to lie aligned with her seductive power. If the sonneteer sees her breasts as "dun" or her hair as "wires" (in sonnet 130), she nevertheless continues to breathe and speak and withstand the collapse of a Petrarchan poetics erected by "false compares."[12] Likewise, in sonnet 138, this Dark Lady's fictive powers are represented as deceptive and corrupting but still a source of pleasures she can share with the speaker:

> When my love swears that she is made of truth
> I do believe her, though I know she lies,
> That she might think me some untutor'd youth,
> Unlearned in the world's false subtleties.
> Thus vainly thinking that she thinks me young,
> Although she knows my days are past the best,
> Simply I credit her false speaking tongue:
> On both sides thus is simple truth suppress'd
>
> (1–8)[13]

Patched together by lies and "seeming trust," the union between self-conscious lover and Dark Lady seems only tentative and uncertain, however. Their "loves" uneasily positioned next to "loves not" in line 12, their faults are not finally forgiven:

> O, love's best habit is in seeming trust,
> And age in love loves not to have years told:

Therefore I lie with her and she with me,
And in our faults by lies we flatter'd be.

(11–14)

Loving Shakespeare's Dark Lady, as Joel Fineman argues, means learning to use language as a tool to falsify or to compromise. Ennobling admiration for a distant beloved has been replaced by nearness and infidelity, such that the speaker and beloved see each other clearly only when they see each other sin. But Queen Elizabeth finds a way to handle loss and compromise without letting her language or station be violated in "On Monsieur's Departure," a poem allegedly written in the wake of the 1580 courtship with Alencon. This poem offers a picture of humbled mastery similar to Shakespeare's sonnet 138, where the lady this time bewails how she must lie to her lover and to herself. Yet Elizabeth's poem also provides a way to represent and guarantee the truthfulness she wants to uphold, balancing her contradictory actions by letting her lover go:

I grieve and dare not show my discontent;
I love, and yet am forced to seem to hate;
I do, yet dare not say I ever meant;
I seem stark mute, but inwardly do prate.
I am, and not; I freeze and yet am burned,
Since from myself another self I turned.[14]

Shakespeare's speaker can only attain such balance or control with the beloved's dangerous help; as the dactyls in the fourth and eighth lines tell us, his "unlearned" state is explained and created by her "subtleties," both truths about the lovers cancelled by the word "suppres'd." In contrast, the dactyls "discontent" and "inwardly" employed in Elizabeth's poem deliberately direct us away from the lover, emphasizing instead what she learns or feels when he disappears because he is irrelevant to the speaker's larger project to shape meaning or position herself. Ilona Bell comments that Elizabeth's poetry helped "transform the monologic male voice of Petrarchan poetry into a characteristically Elizabethan lyric dialogue of courtship."[15] Certainly that is one ironic aim of this poem about rejection, where the Queen carefully explains the cold lady's remove, but the female beloved also seems to crave the same distance the male poet typically does: turning away from "another" allows her to establish her own powers of feeling and thought. If Elizabeth's poem becomes a place to record feelings, the self is the result of adding them up; if she identifies heroic labors with the sublimations Spenser describes in his "Letter," the male lover in "On Monsieur's Departure" is transformed into a set of abstractions Elizabeth can push aside or file away:

My care is like my shadow in the sun –
Follows me flying, flies when I pursue it,

>Stands, and lies by me, doth what I have done;
>His too familiar care doth make me rue it.
>No means I find to rid him from my breast,
>Till by the end of things it be suppressed.

That Elizabeth's "suppressed" requires two rather than the three syllables Shakespeare needs in sonnet 138 suggests how clean and final and brutal the break is. But if the Queen plays the part of the cruel mistress in this scenario, the suffering he inflicts is self-directed, because the lover is elsewhere. And although she craves relief, the release is mental, not physical; she seeks a "gentler passion" to replace her grief—not another opportunity to be with her lover, but another way to experience her thoughts:

>Some gentler passion slide into my mind,
>For I am soft and made of melting snow;
>Or be more cruel, Love, and so be kind.
>Let me float or sink, be high or low;
>Or let me live with some more sweet content,
>Or die, and so forget what love e'er meant.

Elizabeth's "On Monsieur's Departure" is a poem about training her mind, and the subject matter probably explains her decision (like Greville's) not to publish, since Elizabeth is not aiming for love but for a more useful language that can be shared with her readers. This effort characterizes many of Elizabeth's speeches, too, where she positions herself at once as Loving Mother, Henry Daughter, Queen, and King. The poetic style Bell describes in terms of Elizabeth's "moral discrimination, incisive verbal wit, enigmatic multiplicity of meaning, and self-reflexive form" (7) is similarly displayed in the Queen's letters and speeches. But the poetry of Sidney and Shakespeare participates in this "self-reflexive" activity, too, where moral awareness can bridge the gap between speaker and beloved. As Marotti puts it, Sidney "invited his sophisticated readers to exercise their critical faculties to such a degree that the whole work must have begun to take the shape of a metapoem … whose metacommunicative character made the relationship of poet and audience more important than either the ostensible amorous subject-matter or its sociopolitical coordinates" (406). Despite Ho's account of "the spiritual and moral bankruptcy of the Petrarchan self" resulting in the "shutting down [of] the Petrarchan system" (41), the female figures Greville describes in *Cælica* are similarly invested in the moral and linguistic effort to correct what others think. They frequently represent themselves as searching for what Queen Elizabeth calls "some more sweet content" (line 17), a sense of self grounded in what they clearly see, their vision defined by limits that do not, however, reduce them.

The first poem in *Cælica* reverses the dynamic established in *Astrophil and Stella's* opening sonnet, linking a woman's virtue with her active agency rather than with the poet's, outlining how "From her true heart, cleare springs of wisdome flow,/ Which imag'd in her words and deeds, men know." The beloved's virtue instructs those men around her, such that manhood is linked with appreciation of her "wisdome," as if her "words and deeds" will make men "know" (*Cælica* 1.11–12). At the same time, we are told that Greville's speaker is someone whose "innocence" has been "rased" (2.7) and "minde" "darkened" (10.8). "Looking on me, let him know, loue's delights/Are treasures hid in caues, but kept with sp'rits" (5.11–12), the speaker tells us, his defects associated with our difficulties in seeing him, his moral failures typographical ones. Seeing clearly is worth more than "loving in truth" in Greville's poetry. The next few poems describe the speaker's wretchedness and cupid's cruelty as well as time's harsh passage, something which threatens the lady's appearance: "Beauty whose scorching beames make wrinkles florish;/ Time hath made free of teares, sighs, and despaire,/Writing in furrowes deep 'she once was faire'" (8 ll. 10–12). But because Cælica's figure is an amalgam of Shakespeare's ideal young man and Dark Lady, seductive and instructive, culpable and responsible, her now wrinkled figure remains unstained and unblemished, and though older, she is free of corruption. Greville's language has not become debased through contact with her, and her imperfections (unlike breasts that be "dun," or hair like "wires") can be firmly asserted rather than floated as theorems. Greville's poetry continues to operate despite the way the ideal can be ravaged, challenged but never broken apart by lies.

Cælica 9 more clearly suggests how the balance achieved between Cælica's agency and the poet's limits is a way to protect poetry, not indict it. "Loue therefore speake to Cælica for me, /Shew her thy selfe in every thing I doe;/Safely thy powers she may in others see,/ And in thy power see her glories, too;/ Moue her to pitty, stay her from disdaine,/ Let never man loue worthinesse in vaine" (9. 19–24). *Cælica* 11 offers similar evidence of how redemptive (or therapeutic?) the bond with the lady is. Here, the odd identification between Greville's speaker and the mythological Juno resembles the relationship between knowing author and Lady that we find in the *Letter*, both works reconciling love and poetry with a fallen world. In this poem, Greville's speaker links his despair with the suffering of "that poore goddessse" (l. 9) who in turn provides a sign that women know pain as well, and as foolishly, as men do:

> Jvno, that on her head Loues liuerie carried,
> Scorning to weare the markes of Io's pleasure,
> Knew while the Boy in æquinoctiall tarried,
> His heats would rob the heauen of heauenly treasure;
> Beyond the Tropicks she the Boy doth banish,
> Where smokes must warme, before his fire do blaze,

> And children's thoughts not instantly grow Mannish,
> Feare keeping lust there very long at gaze

(1–8)

Greville's image of Juno as someone who feels but also thinks, who "knew" and "scorn[s]," suggests this is a poem about the restitution of reason or recovery of the mind, the goddess as eager to find her husband as she is to banish juvenile behavior. In fact, much of Greville's *Cælica* takes the female point of view, but the women the poet so closely observes are not always watching him. Here Greville represents Juno in terms of her separate responsibilities and authority, as a dignified figure humbled but not ridiculed by betrayal.

More important for Greville's Juno than finding her husband is keeping her head, something we don't see in Lady Mary Wroth's representation of the goddess in one of her sonnets from *Pamphilia to Amphilanthus*: "*Juno* still jealous of her husband *Jove*, / Descended from above, on earth to try,/ Whether she there could find his chosen Love,/ Which made him from the Heav'ns so often flye."[16] Wroth's Juno discovers the poet while looking for her husband, and the two females are depicted as similarly desolate figures who seek rather than create order and thus almost as wayward in their travels as the nymph Jove is chasing. Unlike Greville's Juno, who seeks "some more sweet content" when she banishes cupid, Wroth's goddess discovers the disordered world to be a reflection of her own divisions:

> Close by the place where I for shade did lye,
> She chasing came, but when she saw me move,
> Have you not seene this way (said she) to hye
> One, in whom vertue never grownde did prove?
> Hee, in whom Love doth breed, to stirre more hate,
> Courting a wanton Nimph for his delight;
> His name is *Jupiter*, my Lord, by Fate,
> Who for her, leaves Me, Heaven, his throne, and light.
> I saw him not (said I) although heere are
> Many, in whose hearts, Love hath made like warre.[17]

This Jupiter and Juno seem well matched, both of them childishly unable to use their powers except to hide or hunt, and both of them resembling Wroth's speaker, who links virtue or strength with loss and pain.

In contrast is the balance between female virtue and thinking which not only structures *Cælica* 11 but organizes many other poems. Particularly in the first part of Greville's collection, the speaker routinely contrasts innocent but ineffectual "boy's" "play" (see *Cælica* 13.1, 13.8, 15.11) with images of mature or divine love. To be sure, pictures of female deception are displayed, too, as we see in 38, where the speaker and his mistress making love approach paradise, only for the speaker to discover his lover's betrayal in "that fine soyle" "By broken fence" now "prou'd a common field" (ll. 13–14). In the very next poem, Greville's description of betrayal and infection is given shape in the image of the tower of Babel, but such a picture of corruption or confusion is complicated by the revelation that Cælica "vnderstands all men but me" (l. 14). Coupled with ideas about the speaker's abandonment and the beloved's promiscuity are references to the lady's intelligence, her craft or wisdom, his wit put at the service of hers. She is faulted for loving others, not for making him lie or debase himself.

As a result, it is the speaker who often takes the heat for the failure of this poetry to bring lovers together, more successful poetry defined by the ability to keep the lady's powers separate from the poet's. We see this in the praise of the lady in *Cælica* 17, where the poet says "[e]xcellence can neuer be exprest in measure" (l. 8). His reference to limits does not register defeat, though, for he describes her power as nearly invulnerable but not always wounding:

> Are you afraid, because my heart adores you?/ The world will thinke I hold Endymion's place?/ Hippolytus, sweet Cynthia, kneel'd before you,/ Yet did you not come downe to kisse his face./ Angels enjoy the heauens' inward quires:/ Starre-gazers only multiply desires (17.9–14).

Here is an encounter without corruption, and the empathy between the lovers seems duplicated in the newfound links with other men, the opening to the beloved's mind providing a conduit to the hearts of fellow stargazers. Such a perspective undoes mythological couplings, instead reconciling moral women with mortal men: "Must Danae's lap be wet with golden showers?" Greville's speaker wonders. "Or through the seas must buls Europa beare?/ Must Leda onely serue the higher powers?" (33.9–11). These poetics make room for human anguish but also for human deserving.

This perspective, which divides self-interested loving from selfless reading, underwrites the reworkings of Petrarchan ambition and reward in *Cælica* 22. The speaker's lament over Myra's interest in other men reflects awareness that she was also advancing her own ambitions and desires in loving him:

> I with whose colours Myra drest her head,
> I, that ware posies of her owne hand-making,
> I, that mine owne name in the chimnies read
> By Myra finely wrought ere I was waking:
> Must I looke on, in hope time comming may
> With change bring backe my turne again to play?
>
> (1–6)

Once more Greville aligns female agency with female desire, the "common field" again crowded with other aspirants, supplying a space for males to sadly identify each other as "Vulcan's brothers." Greville's figure of the dejected lover is not only mirrored by the cuckolded husband, but by all of the men he competes against, men who share his aims and history. But the speaker also shares his faults with the lady who writes and steals, her crimes linked with her denial of his identity, her lack of integrity matched by his. If the speaker is reduced to a collection of synecdoches—pieces of who she is, including her eyes and blushes and mother's ring—her love is reduced to a catalog of effects and signs, marked by her attachment to other things. Her linguistic gifts rob him of his virtue, name, and talents—something we see in the third stanza, with the result that the Dark Man, a counterpart to Shakespeare's Dark Lady, is rendered speechless by loving:

> I, that did weare the ring her mother left,
> I, for whose loue she gloried to be blamed,
> I, with whose eyes her eyes committed theft,
> I, who did make her blush when I was named:
> Must I lose ring, flowers, blush, theft, and go naked,
> Watching with sighs till dead loue be awakèd?
>
> (13–18)

In possession of such signs the lady can flee, but Greville's speaker in contrast is empty without love, invisible and silent, even unable to express his pain. He has stopped being a poet; but more than that, Myra has murdered him by looking away. We are thus made to wonder whether it is her language or his that is so dangerous, his love or hers which finally evaporates, his poetry or hers which ultimately betrays:

> I, that when drowsie Argus fell asleep,
> Like Iealousie o'rewatchèd with Desire,
> Was euen warnèd modestie to keepe,
> While her breath speaking, kindled Nature's fire:
> Must I looke on a-cold, while others warme them?
> Do Vulcan's brothers in such fine nets arme them.
> Was it for this that I might Myra see
> Washing the water with her beauties, white?
> Yet would she neuer write her loue to me;
> Thinks wit of change, while thoughts are in delight?
> Mad girles must safely loue, as they may leave;
> No man can printe a kisse; lines may deceiue.
>
> (19–30)

Gary Waller reads this poem as stark evidence of Greville's misogyny, but I think we might instead understand *Cælica* 22 as exploring what happens when a poet looks in his heart instead of looking in the lady's, or insists on writing but gives the beloved all literary authority.

Betrayal is similarly represented in terms of failed communication—rather than sexual corruption—in two later poems. *Cælica* 38 (mentioned briefly above) first registers the complaint that rumor has tainted *Cælica*'s "glassy Honour," making their love something impersonal and impure:

> Cælica, I ouernight was finely vsed,
> Lodg'd in the midst of paradise, your heart:
> Kind thoughts had charge I might not be refused,
> Of every fruit and flower I had part.
> But curious Knowledge, blowne with busie flame,
> The sweetest fruits had in downe shadowes hidden,
> And for it found mine eyes had seene the same,
> I from my paradise was straight forbidden.
> Where that curre, Rumor, runnes in euery place,
> Barking with Care, begotten out of Feare;
> And glassy Honour, tender of Disgrace,
> Stand Ceraphin to see I come not there;
> While that fine soyle, which all these ioyes did yeeld,
> By broken fence is prou'd a common field.

The rhyming pairs of "curre" with "care" and "Rumor" with "Honour" complicate things, however, rendering it unclear whether her virtue or his is at stake, her body polluted, or his imagination. Even before the exposure of her infidelity, the speaker has found her body soiled, after all. If we connect this poem with the next one the way Greville does, then Rumor leads to Babel's Tower, and the sin becomes one of ambition (not lust) or pride (not betrayal). This is why Cælica's ability to love and think in the poem remains ultimately unaffected by the confusion which corrupts men's tongues:

> The pride of flesh by reach of humane wit,
> Did purpose once to ouer-reach the skye;
> And where before God drown'd the world for it,
> Yet Babylon it built vp, not to dye.
> God knew these fooles how foolishly they wrought,
> That Destiny with Policie would breake,
> Straight none could tell his fellow what he thought,
> Their tongues were chang'd, and men not taught to speake;
> So I that heauenly peace would comprehend,
> In mortall seat of Cælica's faire heart,
> To Babylon my selfe there, did intend,
> With naturall kindnesse, and with Passion's art:
> But when I though[t] myselfe of her selfe free,
> All's chang'd: she vnderstands all men but me.

A similar effort to understand how his thinking can be both a route to his beloved and distraction from it is explicitly explored in 42, a rewriting of Spenser's 1596 *Epithalamion*. In Spenser's wedding poem the beloved's "heavenly guifts" are likened to "Medusaes mazeful hed" (11. 187–190), prizes better appreciated when cloaked in night's "sable mantle" (321) and better enjoyed when both husband and wife are "conceald" in darkness (363). But in Greville's speaker's hands, Medusa becomes elusive, not astonishing, an image of mutability rather than of paralysis. Spenser can have his bride because he cannot see her, Greville's speaker betrayed exactly because he so strenuously seeks to control the powers that make her his equal:

> Pelius, that loth was Thetis to forsake,
> Had counsell from the gods to hold her fast,
> Fore-warn'd what lothsome likenesse she would take,
> Yet, if he held, come to her selfe at last.
> He held; the snakes, the serpents and the fire,
> No monsters prou'd, but trauells of desire.
> When I beheld how Cælica's faire eyes,
> Did shew her heart to some, her wit to me;
> Change,that doth proue the error is not wise,
> In her mishap made me strange visions see;
> Desire held fast, till Loues' vnconstant zone,
> Like Gorgon's head transform'd her heart to stone.
>
> (42. 1–12)

Cælica's powers seem to grow as his diminish, and her form hardens as his gives way, the image of "Loue's vnconstant zone" both in his head and on the page. Her shape-shifting is represented as the result of his faulty embrace or imperfect knowing, and the poet is like Juno here, precisely and ironically because Cælica flees his grasp. But maybe Cælica is like the dead Sidney, her disappearance linked with the Petrarchan poet's fading powers.

> From stone she turnes againe into a cloud,
> Where water still had more power than the fire,
> And I poore Ixion to Iuno vowed,
> With thoughts to clip her, clipt my owne desire:
> For she was vanisht, I held nothing fast,
> But woes to come and ioyes already past.
>
> (13–18)

Speaker and beloved do come together, but only in a final moment of loss:

> Thus our delights, like fair shapes in a glasse,
> Though pleasing to our senses, cannot last;

The metall breaks, or else the visions passe,
Onely our griefes in constant moulds are cast:
I'le hold no more: false Cælica, liue free;
Seeme faire to all the world, and foule to me.

In some ways, "On Monsieur's Departure" offers an analogue to this story of capture and release, where the Queen does not punish the beloved for escaping but gives him the means to do so, likening him to shadow and ice, something that can fly or float away. But Greville concludes that his vision is damaged and it is this—rather than Cælica's falsity—which explains why she is set free and left untouched.

The desire of the *speaker* to be seen animates *Cælica 56*, the story of a nighttime assignation. Here Cælica refuses to carry the burden of his vision and evades the poet's efforts, her faithlessness another version of his own. Robert Pinsky nicely comments on the unstable or unequal pairs of nouns in the poem which reflect a "complicated symmetry" at work in the speaker's imagination,[18] but under such pressure it is the poet's form which undergoes metamorphosis and is punished for its instability:

All my senses, like beacon's flame,
Gaue alarum to desire
To take armes in Cynthia's name
And set all my thoughts on fire:
Furie's wit perswaded me,
Happy loue was Hazard's hire,
Cupid did best shoot and see
In the night where smooth is faire;

(56. 1–8)

The speaker's poetry is exposed as a machine designed by fancy, and unrelated to the beloved, who is neither heard nor seen but only thought:

I a God by Cupid dreames;
Cynthia who did naked lye,
Runnes away like siluer streames,
Leauing hollow banks behind
Who can neither forward moue,
Nor if riuers be vnkind,
Turne awaye or leaue to loue.
There stand I, like Articke pole,
Where Sol passeth o're the line,
Mourning my benighted soule,
Which so loseth light diuine.

(56. 30–40)

The reference to the Roman sun god Sol seems curious, but Sol's daughter was Circe, a witch in possession of her own powers to punish and transform. Perhaps allowing Cælica to go, given the speaker's failing powers (the way Elizabeth surrenders her lover) is the only way he can remain a poet in command of what he sees:

> Let no loue-desiring heart
> In the starres goe seeke his fate;
> Loue is onely Nature's art.
> Wonder hinders loue and hate.
> None can well behold with eyes,
> But what vnderneath him lies.[19] (49–54)

Although many readers see these final lines as evidence of the lady's falsity and Greville's contempt for the physical, I think the blame falls squarely on the speaker's eyes, not on Cynthia's form: it is her fate (as moon goddess) to flee and change and hide, and forgetting this is what makes the self-deceiving poet vulnerable to despair. Only when she leaves is he left with lies; in her presence he can dream himself a god.

We should look at *Cælica* for evidence that Greville's ideas about women's sexuality are informed by his ideas about their minds, and that his images of them thinking often dissociate them from their bodies. This is the case in 56, but also in *Cælica* 58, where we hear that *Cælica* had worn a wig when young only to remove it when she gets older, making herself old as a way to register and repair the sufferings of failed lovers by showing herself to be "shadowed in [her] glorie," too:[20]

> The tree in youth proud of his leaues, and springs,
> His body shadowed in his glorie layes;
> For none do flie with art, or others' wings,
> But they in whom all, saue Desire, decayes;
> Againe in age, when no leaues on them grow,
> Then borrow they their greene of misseltoe.
> Where Cælica, when she was young and sweet,
> Adorn'd her head with golden borrowed haire,
> To hide her owne for cold, she thinkes it meet
> The head should mourn, that all the rest was faire;
> And now in age when outward things decay,
> In spite of age, she throwes that haire away.
> Those golden haires she then vs'd but to tye
> Poore captiu'd souls with, she in triumph led,
> Who not content the sunne's faire light to eye,
> Within his glorie their sense dazeled:
> And now againe, her owne blacke haire puts on,
> To mourne for thoughts by her worths ouerthrowne.

This is another poem about how Cælica's moral awareness is linked with her erotic power and ability to pity others—the opposite of Sidney's Stella, because Cælica grows and shares her knowledge. Her youthful falseness is thus set against her thought and conscience; and even earlier artifice is clearly attached to innocence. She is like Shakespeare's Dark Lady, except that Cælica actually *was like* the sun at one point, before Greville began writing, before *Cælica* chronicles *his* fall. But Cælica's difference from the ideal is what is chronicled here, as is her grace arising out of it. That the poem registers this difference without collapsing marks an important step out of Sidney's shadow, and beyond Petrarchan despair.

Ultimately Cælica occupies the very same unstable moral and linguistic grounds the speaker does, and a similar relationship between equals who are unable to love shapes the 1589 *Letter to an Honorable Lady*. Although Greville is advising a betrayed wife, we might also see the *Letter* as written from one mourner to another, both of them bereft at the loss of some remote male figure—maybe even afflicted by the loss of Philip Sidney—and forced to recover the ability to see as well as rework their tie to each other.[21] Greville instructs his reader in the *Letter*: "let it be enough for you henceforwards not to worship idols, 'who have eyes, that see not and eares that heare not' " (Grosart, ed. 270), having already begun with the positing of their moral and intellectual equivalence, his "little wisdom" coupled with her "reverent good will." "[T]hough it be rather a counsel of remorse, then help, to lay before you your errors past" (267), he continues, "they teach you to know," he says, echoing Sidney's Astrophil. His advice is to suffer and yield and accept the fact that "the best is sure to be worst vsed" and "the more goodness, the less return" (270), his assessment of her painful situation making it anything but private: "you poore wiues," he says in Chapter 2 (241), the state of marriage itself ruined. Despite this, however, women can retain their honor. We can see this when the speaker urges the lady to master herself or risk damaging her good name. She is capable of "Genius" (218), and for this reason she "neuer [should] study to be wiser then the truth; and so neither strive to master, mend or please" her unworthy husband (253).

Even more striking than this unusual picture of the betrayed wife is the blurring of conventional gender roles which occurs throughout the *Letter*. One of the earliest, in Chapter 3, occurs when the "Noble Lady" is invited to "pass" through "this false Paradise," as "Vlysses did by the enchanted desarts of Circe; stopping our eares, and closing our eyes, lest our rebellious senses ... lead our misty vnderstandings captiue to perdition" (Grosart, ed. 258). The author and lady occupy the same position as the epic hero; and avoiding snares typically attached to female wiles is now the joint responsibility of men and women, united together against such temptations. In the same chapter, he tells her to "enrich your selfe vpon your owne stocke; not looking out-wardly, but inwardly for the fruit of true peace, whose rootes are there" (Grosart, ed. 260). He then provides another gender reversal, "lay[ing] before [her] the opinions of worthy men, borne vnder tyrants, and bound to obey, though they could not please: the comparison holding in some affinity between a wife's subiection to her husband, and a subject's obedience to his soueraigne" (Grosart, ed. 261). He links her pain as abandoned wife to that of a male noble frustrated by his (female) sovereign, both of them elevated by their suffering, the lady as much a defeated courtier as the courtier a loyal partner. In both relationships, one can love or serve without being ruined. More remarkable still is the sharing of roles and powers in Chapter 5, where the Noble Ladie is encouraged to

> proceed constantly to your end; beare and deale with these weake-
> nesses of your husband's; not with hate of your selfe or of him; but as
> mothers doe with the wantonnesse of children: who cry not to still
> them, nor threaten imperfection and malice with one rod, but first
> take away the offence, then suffer them to enjoy those toyes they
> delight in. For looke what a mother's loue is towards her children, the
> like is an husband's power over a wife: they will not punish; you
> cannot.
>
> (Grosart, ed. 284)

Describing marriage in terms of a necessarily unequal relationship between parents and children explains why these relationships can falter but must continue.

Yet the differences in seeing which Greville describes also supply the reasons the lovers must part in *Cælica* 66, where Cælica advises him "to delight [his] minde with books" (66. 2), and he defies her instructions with the rejoinder that books are "dead," "Which at the second-hand deliuer forth" (66. 22–23):

> I haue for books, aboue my head the skyes,
> Vnder me, Earth; about me ayre and sea;
> The Truth for light, and Reason for mine eyes,
> Honour for guide, and Nature for my way
>
> (66. 13–16)

Echoing the collapse of the relationship outlined in *Cælica* 56, the poet once again questions what a writer can achieve or imagination can do, given Nature's great powers to create and to change. Such a vision can only divide lover from beloved, and again the female figure disappears from the poem the poet finally fashions.

According to Marotti, the love poems end midway in *Cælica* because of the death of Queen Elizabeth (420), and he claims that "when poetry no longer served as a major literary means of expressing social, economic, and political ambitions," sonneteering became a less useful exercise. But maybe more liberating was being able to consign the dead Sidney's memory as lover and poet to the past, for *Cælica* repeatedly details the speaker's efforts to distance himself from the image of the embittered, embattled poet–lover, the unhappy saint, defeated visionary, or confused moralist. This was something Greville could never really do, however, ultimately dedicating his efforts to overseeing his friend's legacy rather than projecting his flaws on the Dark Man, as he does in the *Letter to an Honorable Lady*.[22] Although Greville tells the Noble Lady in the *Letter*, "euen by the prouidence of mischance, you are driuen from these narrow sanctuaries of selfe-affections, which imprisoned you; to take into your heart new idea's, larger ends, and nobler wayes" (Grosart, ed. 290), the remaining portion of *Cælica*, probably completed after 1587, returns to these "narrow sanctuaries," forsaking love and desire for the remoter consolations of God and Protestant sainthood. But perhaps the lady has been charged with the task of keeping love poetry safe for other lovers as Greville seems to suggest in *Cælica* 60. Here the speaker says: "I scorne the world, the world scornes me, 'tis true;/ What can a heart doe more to honour you?" and then concludes: "The world in two I haue diuided fit;/ My selfe to you, and all the rest to it" (11–12, 17–18). If loving her means turning inward, looking through Cælica's eyes can provide a way to see the world outside the two of them. The Noble Lady's perspective is a means for Greville to grasp its "new idea's, larger ends, and nobler ways" because her vision is stronger and her moral authority—like Juno's, or Queen Elizabeth's—still intact.

Acknowledgments

Thanks to Erica Bossier at Louisiana State University Press for her kind help in reprinting excerpts from Mary Wroth's *Pamphilia to Amphilanthus*.

Notes

1 *The Works in Verse and Prose Complete of the Right Honourable Fulke Greville, Lord Brooke.* ed. Alexander B. Grosart. Volumes 3 and 4. Lancashire, 1870. All references to *Cælica* and "A Letter to an Honourable Lady" will be taken from this edition. I have retained Grosart's spelling.

2 See Ronald Rebholz, *The Life of Fulke Greville, First Lord Brooke* (Oxford: Clarendon P, 1971): "Appendix I: The Dating of Greville's Works." 325–240 (327).

3 In *Fulke Greville, Lord Brooke, 1554–1628: A Critical Biography* (London: Routledge & Kegan Paul, 1971) Joan Rees maintains that Greville continued to rework the poems in *Cælica*, such that dating of individual works is impossible: "each [poem] presents a fully integrated statement of its author's mature attitudes and belief" (xi). Gary Waller supplies a less confident picture of the poet's maturity, however, suggesting that Greville's *Cælica* singlemindedly sets itself against "[t]he idolization of the beloved." See "Good Boys, Mad Girls: Greville, Sidney, Wroth and the (Re)construction of Gender Early Modern England" *Sidney Journal* 19, nos. 1–2 (2001): 41–61(49); elsewhere, Waller refers to the

poet's "residual, even archaic, perspective" (60). Arthur F. Marotti more cautiously states that "Greville was obviously uncomfortable with love poetry" (420). " 'Love is not Love': Elizabethan Sonnet Sequences and the Social Order," *English Literary History*, 9, 2: 396–428.

4 See Joel Fineman's account of the moral boundaries crossed by Shakespeare's sonneteer in "Shakespeare's Perjured Eye," *Representations*, 7 (1984): 59–86.

5 See Matthew Steggle, "Fulke Greville: Life and Works." *The Sidney Journal* 9, 1–2 (2001): 1–9 (4).

6 Elaine Y. L. Ho describes a "major critical tendency to trace in *Caelica* development from youthful self-definitions as Petrarchan lover to a more mature and austere Calvinistic inwardness. See "Fulke Greville's *Caelica* and the Calvinist Self," *Studies in English Literature*, 32, 1 (1992): 35–58 (35–36). In *Forms of Discovery* (Chicago: Allan Swallow, 1967), Yvor Winters similarly describes Greville's plain style as belonging to a school "in every respect antithetical to the Petrarchist school" (3), a style in which—as in the case of Sir Thomas Wyatt—"poetry and morality are one" (8–9).

7 All references to Sidney's *Astrophil and Stella* are to the 1591 edition published by Thomas Newman and reprinted by Project Gutenberg. www.gutenberg.org/files/56375/56375-0.txt. Downloaded July 18, 2019. Although Rees analyzes *Cælica* next to *Astrophil and Stella* (94–96), F. J. Levy claims that Greville's work is better understood next to the work of other contemporaries, because Sidney died before Greville began his career as poet in earnest. See "Fulke Greville: The Courtier as Philosophic Poet," *Modern Language Quarterly*, (1972) 33, 4: 33–48.

8 Helen Vincent claims that "writing, rather than reading these poems, was the key activity for the author" (65). "Syon Lays Waste: Secularity, Skepticism, and Religion in *Caelica*," *The Sidney Journal*, 19, nos. 1–2 (2001): 63–84.

9 Joel B. Davis also connects the poems to the *Letter*, but with very different results, arguing that the work "is a symptom of the feminized position of the courtier in an increasingly absolutist regime": "The *Letter* in fact articulates a kind of moral and political agency that appeals to, and modifies, the well-known injunctions that early modern women should be chaste, silent, and obedient." See "Presidents to Themselves: *A Letter to an Honourable Lady*, Merciful Commentary, and Ethical Discourse," *Sidney Journal*, 19, nos. 1–2 (2001): 161–182 (168).

10 In the same way, Mary Ellen Lamb argues, Sidney's dedication of the *Arcadia* to his sister "grants to her reading a determinative role in the very production of that work." See *Gender and Authorship in the Sidney Circle*. Madison, WI: U Wisconsin Press, 1990 (22).

11 See also Marotti, "Love is not love," 418.

12 See Suzanne M. Tartamella, "Reinventing the Poet and Dark Lady: Theatricality and Artistic Control in Shakespeare's *The Taming of the Shrew*," *English Literary Renaissance*, 3, no. 3 (2013): 446–477; Nona Fienberg, "Wroth and the Invention of Female Poetic Subjectivity," in *Reading Mary Wroth: "Representing Alternatives in Early Modern England*, eds. Naomi J. Miller and Gary Waller, 175–190. Knoxville, TN: U Tennessee Press, 1991.

13 All references to Shakespeare's sonnets are taken from *Shakespeare's Sonnets*, ed. Stephen Booth (New Haven: Yale UP: 1980).

14 *Elizabeth I, Collected Works*, eds. Leah S. Marcus, Janel Mueller, and Mary Beth Rose (Chicago, IL: U Chicago P, 2002).

15 Ilona Bell, "Elizabeth Tudor: Poet," *Explorations in Renaissance Culture*, 31, no. 1 (2004): 1–22 (2).

16 Fienberg argues that "Pamphilia's turn inward … is validated by a woman writer whose plots of women's self-discovery turn not on admonitions from male authorities but on the women reading, speaking, and writing stories of

themselves" (179). Naomi J. Miller suggests that "Wroth transforms the role of the lady ... from a breaker into a maker of songs" (298); elsewhere, she explores Wroth's "focus on how love directs the lover's talents outward, toward the beloved, rather than inward, upon the lover's own plight" (302). See "Rewriting Lyric Fictions: The Role of the Lady in Lady Mary Wroth's *Pamphilia to Amphilanthus*," in *The Renaissance Englishwoman in Print: Counterbalancing the Canon*, eds. Anne M. Haselkorn and Betty St. Travitsky, 295–310. Amherst: U Massachusetts Press, 1990.

17 *The Poems of Lady Mary Wroth*. ed. Josephine A. Roberts (Baton Rouge: LSU Press), 140. I use Roberts' edition of Wroth's poetry with kind permission from LSU Press.

18 Robert Pinsky analyzes this poem in a March 2009 issue of *Slate*. See "'All My Senses, Like Beacon's Flame': Fulke Greville's eloquent path to confused arousal." www.slate.com/articles/arts/poem/2009/03/all_my_senses_like_beacons_flame.htm. The imbalance Pinsky describes as slowly unfolding in the poem is actually exhibited from the start, divine power trumping imagination as the poet's powers are immediately crushed by gods at play who fill up the room.

19 The additional lines inserted between lines 24 and 25 in some manuscripts of *Cælica 56* intensify the way Greville's speaker makes himself vanish, just when he should be with his beloved. These lines are also explored in Pinsky's *Slate* posting and Gunn 84 n2.

20 G. A. Wilkes, "A Crux in *Caelica's* LXI," *Notes and Queries*, 45, no. 4 (1998): 434–435; see also Rees, *Critical Biography*, 80–82.

21 The intended audience is unclear, although David offer some speculations, and Margaret Clifford appears to be one possibility.

22 Relying on Rebholz's chronology, Levy argues that the 1589 *Letter* marks a turning point in Greville's thinking (438).

Bibliography

Bell, Ilona. "Elizabeth Tudor: Poet." *Explorations in Renaissance Culture* 31, no. 1 (2004): 1–22.

Davis, Joel B. "'Presidents to Themselves': *A Letter to an Honourable Lady*, Merciful Commentary, and Ethical Discourse." *The Sidney Journal* 19, 1–2 (2001): 161–182.

Elizabeth I, Queen of England. *Elizabeth I: Collected Works*. Edited by Leah S. Marcus, Janel Mueller, and Mary Beth Rose. Chicago: U Chicago Press, 2002.

Fienberg, Nona. "Wroth and the Invention of Female Poetic Subjectivity." In *Reading Mary Wroth: Representing Alternatives in Early Modern England*. Edited by Naomi J. Miller and Gary Waller, 175–190. Knoxville: U Tennessee Press, 1991.

Fineman, Joel. "Shakespeare's Perjured Eye." *Representations* 7 (1984): 59–86.

Greville, Fulke. *Selected Poems of Fulke Greville*. Edited by Thom Gunn. London: Faber and Faber, 1968.

Greville, Fulke. *The Prose Works of Fulke Greville, Lord Brooke*. Edited by John Gouws. Oxford: Clarendon Press, 1986.

Greville, Fulke. *The Works in Verse and Prose Complete of the Right Honourable Fulke Greville, Lord Brooke*. Edited by Alexander B. Grosart. Volumes 3 and 4. Lancashire, 1870.

Ho, Elaine Y. L. "Fulke Greville's *Caelica* and the Calvinist Self." *Studies in English Literature* 32, no. 1 (1992): 35–58.

Lamb, Mary Ellen. *Gender and Authorship in the Sidney Circle*. Madison, WI: U Wisconsin Press, 1990.

Levy, F. J. "Fulke Greville: The Courtier as Philosophic Poet." *Modern Language Quarterly* 33, no. 4 (1972): 33–48.

Marotti, Arthur F. " 'Love is Not Love': Elizabethan Sonnet Sequences and the Social Order." *English Literary History* 49, no. 2 (1982): 396–428.

Miller, Naomi J. "Rewriting Lyric Fictions: The Role of the Lady in Lady Mary Wroth's *Pamphilia to Amphilanthus*." In *The Renaissance Englishwoman in Print: Counterbalancing the Canon*. Edited by Anne M. Haselkorn and Betty S. Travitksy, 295–310. Amherst: U Massachusetts Press, 1990.

Pinsky, Robert. "All My Senses, Like Beacon's Flame: Fulke Greville's eloquent path to confident arousal." www.slate.com/articles/arts/poem/2009/03/all_my_senses_like_beacons_flame.html. Downloaded January 22, 2018.

Rebholz, Ronald. *The Life of Fulke Greville, First Lord Brooke*. Oxford: Clarendon Press, 1971.

Rees, Joan. *Fulke Greville, Lord Brooke, 1554–1628: A Critical Biography*. London: Routledge & Kegan Paul, 1971.

Shakespeare, William. *Shakespeare's Sonnets*. Edited by Stephen Booth. New Haven: Yale University Press, 1980.

Sidney, Philip. *Astrophil and Stella*. London: Thomas Newman, 1591. Reprinted by Project Gutenberg. www.gutenberg.org/files/56375/56375-0.txt. Downloaded July 18, 2019.

Steggle, Matthew. "Fulke Greville: Life and Works." *The Sidney Journal* 19, 1–2 (2001): 1–9.

Tartamella, Suzanne M. "Reinventing the Poet and Dark Lady: Theatricality and Artistic Control in Shakespeare's *The Taming of the Shrew*." *English Literary Renaissance* 43, 3 (2013): 446–477.

Vincent, Helen. "Syon Lays Waste: Secularity, Skepticism, and Religion in *Caelica*." *The Sidney Journal* 19, 1–2 (2001): 63–84.

Waller, Gary. "Good Boys, Mad Girls: Greville, Sidney, Wroth and the (Re)construction of Gender in Early Modern England." *The Sidney Journal* 19, 1–2 (2001): 41–61.

Wilkes, G. A. "A Crux in *Caelica*'s LXI." *Notes and Queries* 45, no. 4 (1998): 434–435.

Winters, Ivor. *Forms of Discovery*. Chicago: Allan Swallow, 1967.

Wroth, Lady Mary. *The Poems of Lady Mary Wroth*. Edited by Josephine A. Roberts, Baton Rouge: Louisiana State University Press, 1992.

3 "The Mind of Man is this worlds true dimension"

Space, knowledge, and the divine in Fulke Greville's *A Treatie of Humane Learning* and *A Treatise of Religion*

Rachel White

During the sixteenth and seventeenth centuries intellectual culture and learning was not only changing but having to justify the legitimate pursuit of knowledge within the prevalent religious and social culture. Fields such as natural philosophy, science, alchemy, magic, geometry, and mathematics were emerging from the same quagmire of potential knowledge, and all were viewed with varying degrees of suspicion as their parameters and methodologies were established. Practitioners sought to legitimise their studies, couching their defences in religious rhetoric and theological reasoning and gradually practices and ideas were dismissed or integrated into intellectual culture. Under Elizabeth I, for example, the philosophic endeavours of John Dee were not only tolerated but patronised, and the excommunicated Dominican friar Giordano Bruno was able to expound cosmological theories about the nature of the universe and publish them during his time in England between 1583 and 1585. The situation under James VI/I was starkly different. With the monarch also the writer of *Daemonologie* (1597), a treatise in the form of a dialogue which justifies witch-hunting within Christian society and differentiates between magical and non-magical practices, the tolerance for intellectual endeavours that pushed perceived boundaries of magic or illegitimate knowledge disappeared. Indeed, in 1604 Dee famously asked to be put on trial to prove that he was not a sorcerer.[1] Furthermore, long-held beliefs about perceived ancient wisdom were also subject to scrutiny and proven to be false, such as the dating of the Hermetic texts, while progress towards science in the modern-day understanding of the word can be seen in texts such as Francis Bacon's *The Great Instauration* (1620) and *The New Atlantis* (1627) which begin to demonstrate the order and methodologies of scientific endeavours.[2]

Having witnessed changes in intellectual culture during his time serving both the Tudor and Stuart dynasties, the poet and courtier Fulke Greville sought to address the nature of knowledge and the appropriate approaches to learning in two poetic treatises written towards the end of his life: *A*

Treatie of Humane Learning (pub. 1633) and *A Treatise of Religion* (pub. 1670).[3] In both treatises, Greville is particularly concerned with the ways in which the human capacity for intellectual enquiry conflicted with divinely ordained boundaries. While critics such as Richard Waswo and Elaine Y. Ho situate Greville's exploration of the continuing effects of the original sin within his Calvinism,[4] I avoid overtly associating Greville's poetic practice with his religious affiliation as "by the end of the sixteenth century the Church of England was largely Calvinist in doctrine."[5] I thus take the view that while Calvinism is an important aspect of Greville's life, its prevalence in doctrine and university learning means that isolating it as an influential part of his poetics is to distort its importance to him as an individual: he "is an unusual writer who does not fit easily into established and accepted categories."[6] Sarah Knight notes that his education at the Shrewsbury School and Cambridge means that "Greville would clearly have been exposed to mid-century reformed ideas that he went on to consider further throughout his life."[7] Greville appears to be a conservative thinker throughout his life, but he does engage with new ideas and considers them in depth in his works. In this chapter, I examine Greville's approach to knowledge in *A Treatie of Human Learning* and *A Treatise of Religion*, and consider how they relate to the overarching questions surrounding the pursuit of legitimate knowledge that are at the core of Greville's concern in both treatises and represent a life-long thought process. I begin by considering the way in which advancements in Elizabethan cosmology influenced Greville and are translated into ways of thinking about and understanding human potential. The notion of measuring and boundaries becomes an important part of Greville's philosophy: unfettered and without limits, the potential of human knowledge is not only vast and incomprehensible, but dangerous as "Men would be Gods."[8] In writing a treaty on human learning, Greville seeks to demarcate boundaries and advise those who pursue knowledge as to the correct modes of study and how to recognise when to stop seeking knowledge. I discuss Francis Bacon's advice to him for gathering knowledge and Greville's understanding of what constitutes knowledge in *Humane Learning* and *Religion*. Finally, I resituate Greville's ideas within a religious framework and discuss Greville's conclusions as to the coexistence of the limitless potential of the human mind within divinely prescribed boundaries.

Even in his earlier writings, Greville is concerned with the position of humankind in relation to the divine which is complicated by the changing understanding of the physical nature of the universe and the world's place within it. In his closet drama *Alaham* (*c.*1600), Greville describes humankind as "a crazed soule, unfix'd;/ Made good, yet fall'n, not to extremes, but to a meane betwixt."[9] Critics have focused on Greville's preoccupation with the corrupt state of humankind since the Fall: Geoffrey Bullough notes his "determination to relate all earthly errors to flaws in human nature which must themselves be placed against a background of eternity";[10] Joan Rees argues that Greville "believed that all human nature and activity are deeply tainted with sin";[11] and Waswo suggests "Greville's main vision of life is fundamentally conditioned by a view of human nature that sees all that takes place within it as a consequence of original sin."[12] However, while Greville is concerned with the effects of the Fall, he recognises the conflicting state of humankind, "Made good, yet fall'n," that complicates its position in creation due to its "unfix'd" nature. It is not simply fallen without hope but has the potential to regain its prelapsarian position. In *A Treatise of Religion*, Greville starts from the premise that humankind is fallen by describing it as "fetter'd [...] and bound" (*TR*, 1), and asks "What is the Chain which draws us back again,/ And lifts Man up unto his first Creation?" (*TR*, 2). In this question, there is an implicit hope of redemption, of being able to reascend to a position lost. However, Greville is quick to note the difficulties facing humankind that reside within its very nature:

> Nothing in him his own heart can restrain,
> His reason lives a Captive to Temptation,
> Example is corrupt, precepts are mixt,
>
> (*TR*, 2)

Greville describes a difficult path back to humankind's former state. Humankind is prone to temptation as even the faculty of reason, which should provide sound logic, is captive to it. Everything in humankind's realm of experience is corrupt and prone to change, and what is known is weak based as it is on "fleshly knowledge" which is innately flawed. From this near hopeless and depraved state, Greville's tone changes with unexpected alacrity in the third stanza:

> It is a Light, a Gift, a Grace inspir'd,
> A spark of Pow'r, a goodness of the Good;
> Desire in him, that never is desir'd;
> An Unity, where desolation stood;
> In us not of us, a Spirit not of earth,
> Fashioning the mortal to immortal birth.
>
> (*TR*, 3)

The object of these attributes is the chain of the previous stanza that "lifts Man up unto his first Creation." It is not a chain of restraint and entrapment, but a direct link to the divine that merely needs to be climbed. Greville's position illustrates Stephen Clucas's point that "Calvinist theology construed salvation as practical, active and operative," while the imagery surrounding the chain invokes the Neoplatonic Great Chain of Being.[13] This indicates the hierarchy of the universe with God at the top and humankind inhabiting a "meane betwixt" being of the physical world but also spiritual by nature. Pseudo-Dionysius argues that the light of God the Father "spreads itself generously toward us, and, in its power to unify, it stirs us by lifting us up."[14] This is to be construed as a divine gift which "cometh down from the Father of Lights, with whom is no variableness, neither shadow of turning."[15] Greville's invocation of light and the goodness of God further accentuates the precarious position of humankind whose knowledge is "never fixt," which contrasts with the divine lack of "variableness."

This state of being between two extremes is further complicated by new cosmological theories that remove the world and humankind from the "cosy, man-centred world of Ptolemy" to the heliocentric model, where the position of the world and humankind is no longer central but "unfix'd," and which is further developed to a potentially limitless and infinite universe.[16] One of the main proponents of this theory is Giordano Bruno, whose "brief stay in London during the 1580s demonstrated the conflict of traditional cosmological teachings in opposition to the epistemological and metaphysical innovations of higher learning at the time."[17] With a meeting at his house to discuss the new cosmology as the setting of Bruno's *La Cena de la Ceneri* [*The Ash Wednesday Supper*] (1584) and a reference to an offence committed towards Greville in *The Expulsion of the Triumphant Beast*,[18] Greville's tacit engagement with Brunian cosmology translates from the physical nature of the universe itself to the implications this has for humankind in his later writings. While the position of the ghost in the opening of *Alaham* negotiates both the lack of a purgatorial space in the Protestant cosmos but also that this lack of defined space is now infinite, Greville continues to question the implications of infinitude in his later work. Steven Shapin notes that the sixteenth and seventeenth centuries were "the first periods in European culture when cosmic infinity challenged the more comfortable dimensions of common experience."[19] The implications of the new cosmology are manifest even in the nature and potential of human knowledge. *A Treatie of Humane Learning* opens with clear Brunian resonances as the mind is compared to an infinite universe containing multiple worlds:

> The Mind of Man is this worlds true dimension
> And *Knowledge* is the measure of the minde:
> And as the minde, in her vast comprehension
> Containes more worlds than all the world can finde:
> So Knowledge doth it selfe farre more extend,
> Than all the minds of Men can comprehend.
>
> (*HL*, 1)

For Greville, the world is measured by human potential: "the Mind of Man is this worlds true dimension." As the stanza develops, the measurability of the mind becomes precluded by its immensity and the limitless potential of knowledge, which circumscribes the mind's limits. Within a few lines, Greville moves from describing the world through the limitations of the mind, to suggesting that those limitations do not exist at all as knowledge extends far beyond what "all the minds of Men can comprehend": knowledge, and therefore the human capacity for it and the measure of the world itself, is infinite. In *The Ash Wednesday Supper*, Bruno argues that:

> The universe is infinite, whence it follows that no body can be simply in the middle of the universe or at its periphery or anywhere between these two limits except through certain relations to other bodies and artificially imposed limits.[20]

Measurement and location, for Bruno, are negated through cosmological infinitude. Without boundaries, spatial dimensions cannot be assigned without artificially imposing limits or through the relation of bodies to one another in space. In another of his Italian dialogues written during his time in England, the characters question the infinitude of space: Elpino asks "Where will you put all that vastness?" to which Filoteo answers "Where will you put the borders?"[21] For Bruno, the notion of a cosmological boundary can never be more than arbitrary and artificial; measurement can only occur through imposing limits. *A Treatie of Humane Learning* begins with the limit of the human mind, but as the stanza continues it becomes clear that this is an artificially imposed limit by Greville which soon breaks its own boundaries. The world's "dimension" is really our comprehension which is subject to restriction, but the "worlds true dimension" is limitless because knowledge, the potential of which constitutes the human mind, has unending potential.

In linking the human mind to the infinite cosmological model, Greville's use of the word "dimension" in describing the world's true spatial extent becomes indicative not only of measurement and spatial extent, but of proportion too.[22] This concept is explored by John Dee in his *Mathematicall Praeface* (1570), in which he describes proportion as a "necessary, wonderfull and Secret doctrine."[23] For Dee, mathematically based relationships of proportion reflect the perfection of the universe, thus the identification of the human mind as the "true dimension" of the world also invokes the notion of mirroring the cosmos through a proportional relationship between the human mind and the terrestrial world. The human mind is not only a conceptual boundary of the world; it is also measurable by knowledge which is "the measure of the minde." Knowledge thus gains the paradoxical status of demarcating both the limit and the potential of the world through its identification of being what the mind is contained by, while also being the essence of the mind itself. The second part of the stanza invokes the infinitude of Brunian cosmology as the mind "contains more worlds than all the world can finde." If the world is measurable by the mind's potential for knowledge, the mind itself contains multiple worlds, each of which is measured by knowledge. Thus Greville's first stanza of *A Treatie of Humane Learning* not only invokes notions of measurement and space, but also of the proportional relationship of the cosmos which is reflected in the human mind.

The opening stanzas of *A Treatie of Humane Learning* continue with Greville describing the limitless extent of knowledge, and therefore of the human mind:

> A climing Height it is without a head,
> Depth without bottome, Way without an end,
> A Circle with no line invironed,
> Not comprehended all it comprehends;
> Worth infinite, yet satisfies no minde,
> Till it that infinite of the God-head finde.
>
> (HL, 2)

Knowledge is described as an entity of continually growing proportions as it is a "climing Height" without a discernible peak, which is reinforced by the oxymoronic phrases "depth without bottom" and "a Circle with no line invironed": knowledge cannot have either depth or shape without the imposition of boundaries or ends. This infinitude of knowledge is not just one of its attributes, but is a condition of the human mind that cannot be satiated until it has found "that infinite of the God-head." Despite the apparent positivity and hope for human learning with which Greville opens his poetic treatise, by the third stanza he curtails this by defining exactly what knowledge is:

> This Knowledge is the same *forbidden tree*,
> Which man lusts after to be made his Maker;
> For Knowledge is of Powers eternity.
> And perfect Glory, the true image-taker;
>
> (HL, 3)

In harking back to Genesis and the Fall Greville reminds his readers that despite the apparently limitless potential of the human capacity for knowledge and learning there remain divinely prescribed boundaries that should not be crossed. The taint that has existed in humankind ever since the Fall becomes Greville's main concern throughout the rest of *A Treatie of Humane Learning*.

What does Greville have in mind when he refers to knowledge or learning? This is an important consideration, as the differentiations between types of study and subject matter were not so clearly defined in the sixteenth and seventeenth centuries. This apparent lack of classification has been the source of consternation among critics, as it is difficult to fathom with a post-Enlightenment sensibility how seemingly incongruous subjects like magic and science could be mutually practised by those with advanced learning and intellectual capabilities: for example Isaac Newton, the father of modern-day physics, was also a practising alchemist. Such incongruity has led critics such as Brian Vickers to claim that seventeenth-century scientists were "able to live mutually incompatible mental categories."[24] The urge to categorise is our own however, and placing such expectations upon seventeenth-century intellectualism creates anachronistic demarcations and leads to inaccurate interpretations of early modern approaches to knowledge. It would be wrong to assume an anachronistic reading of Greville's interpretation of knowledge when he is writing at a time when the real differentiations between types of knowledge are only beginning to emerge. The main question for philosophers and those concerned with learning remained one of legitimacy: how was it possible to know if one's enquiries had crossed the line into illegitimate or forbidden knowledge?

Greville's concern is one of legitimacy: he recognises the limitless potential of the human mind in the opening stanzas of *Humane Learning*, but uses his poetic treatise to advise the reader as to the application and limits of learning. Matthew Woodcock suggests Greville "reaches a climax of almost breathless urgency" in his despair over the status of knowledge in *A Treatie of Humane Learning*. However, there is a turn at the sixty-third stanza where he argues for "careful, conscious reorientation of the human sciences" rather than their complete abandonment.[25] He discusses the skill of judging one's knowledge and exercising care over choosing subject matter, describing learning as "A bunch of grapes sprung up among the thornes,/ Where, but by caution, none the harme can misse" (*HL*, 62). The fruits of knowledge are plentiful but surrounded by the potential for danger and harm without proper discernment on the part of the person seeking to learn. In these stanzas, Greville starts to interrogate the notion of necessity in relation to knowledge, that is to say, he claims that the knowledge gained needs to serve a purpose and not be in any way frivolous or excessive:

> Againe the active, necessarie Arts,
> Ought to be brief in books, in practise long;
> Short precepts may extend to many parts,
> The practise must be large, or not be strong.
> *And* as by artlesse Guides, States ever waine:
> So doe they where these uselesse dreamers reigne.
>
> (*HL*, 68)

Here, Greville gives guidance as to how necessary knowledge is to be communicated and learned, and he suggests that it is understood through lengthy practice and limited book learning. In the final couplet, he plays on the word "art" to move away from connecting it with specific types of learning to a lack of skill and competency through drawing a parallel to the decline of states through the inadequacy of those in power. The "uselesse dreamers" are thus those that pursue unnecessary knowledge and whose contributions of knowledge are without purpose. Such somnolent language also indicates inactivity and laziness: that searching for unnecessary knowledge is not only undisciplined but the prey of indolent and idly curious minds that resist proper structure and training.

Greville goes on to provide a solution to guide learners and to create a sense of cohesion and uniformity within each area of knowledge:

> To which true end, in every *Art* there should
> One, or two *Authors* be selected out,
> To cast the learners in a constant mould;
> Who if not falsely, yet else goe about;
>   And as the Babes by many Nurses doe,
>   Oft change conditions, and complexions too.
>
> (*HL*, 78).

Greville's solution for ensuring that knowledge remains consistent between learners is to select writers that are representative of that subject area for all learners to read and so be cast "in a constant mould," thus removing the possibility of differentiations within the same area of study and providing a source of internal regulation. This would not only help to prevent a subject being explored through idle curiosity and a lack of proper knowledge, the consequences of which could be dangerous, but protects the subject from fashions and changing trends in thought. Constancy within learning is important to Greville; it should not be exposed to the fluctuations in human behaviour and desire. Like babies, learners are prone to change moods and desires quickly, so Greville claims that having one or two selected authors as the foundation of any area of study would help to provide constancy but not adequacy and completeness in learning.

Greville's solution would also help to combat curiosity and the search for unnecessary knowledge. William Eamon points out that to be curious in the early modern period was "neither innocent nor virtuous" and that to pry into the mysteries of the world that God chose not to reveal "was to trespass the boundary of legitimate intellectual inquiry, to challenge God's majesty, and to enter into the territory of forbidden knowledge."[26] Indeed, multiple passages in the Bible warn against looking too deeply into the mysteries of the divine and overstepping proscribed boundaries as God alone is allowed access to secrets that are beyond the reach of humankind: "The secret things belong unto the Lord our God: but those things which are revealed belong unto us and our children forever, that we may do all the words of this law."[27] Peter Harrison also notes that knowledge acquired through curiosity did not serve a purpose: "the curious inquirer aspired to those things that lay beyond the natural powers of the human intellect or to knowledge that was without profit, useless, or – in a word – 'vain'."[28] While curiosity came to be viewed as an essential element for discovery, for Greville and his contemporaries it was to be curtailed and controlled as it would lead to fruitless, unnecessary, or pointless knowledge. Indeed, the word *curiositas* referred to excessive intellectual inquiry, not the pursuit of knowledge itself.[29] Inquiry into nature or creation needed to have a purpose; knowledge for knowledge's sake was not deemed acceptable. Greville addresses this idea towards the end of *A Treatie of Humane Learning*:

> Yet *some seeke knowledge, meerely to be knowne*,
> And idle Curiositie that is;
> Some but to *sell*, not freely to bestow,
> These gaine and spend both time, and wealth amisse;
> Embasing Arts, by basely deeming so,
>   Some to build others, which is Charity,
>   But these to build themselves, who wise men be.
>
> (HL, 144)

Here, Greville identifies the vices associated with unnecessary knowledge which are the desire to beget both fame and fortune. The ambiguous first line "some seeke knowledge, meerely to be knowne" implies both the desire to know for the sake of knowing and to be known for one's knowledge. Greville condemns the former as "idle Curiositie," purposeless and of no benefit to humankind, while the invocation of fame is linked to the following notion of selling knowledge and not "freely" bestowing it. Greville admonishes both of these results of curiosity, arguing that they lower or "embase" all arts and knowledge. This stanza exemplifies Warren Boutcher's view that the treatise is "not a critique of all learning in the arts but of corrupted learning, learning which forgets that reason is an endowment from God for the common good, not for idle contemplation and particular profit."[30] The final couplet of this stanza takes the virtuous extremes of seeking knowledge to provide a counterweight to its aforementioned vices of fame and fortune, arguing that knowledge can be imparted to others to "build" them as a charitable act, and to build the self which leads one to wisdom.

In *A Treatise of Religion*, Greville once again considers curiosity and how it affects humankind's relationship with God. He recognises that to be curious is a natural human state, yet points out that its results are not desirable:

> Questions again, which in our hearts arise
> (Since loving knowledge, not humility)
> Though they be Curious, Godless, and Unwise,
> Yet, prove our nature feels a Deity,
> For if these strifes rose out of other grounds,
> Man were to God, as deafness is to sounds.
>
> (TR, 9)

Greville's description of questions arising within our hearts suggests that there is an active attempt to repress them, but humankind's love of knowledge over humility ultimately releases them. These questions are "Curious, Godless, and Unwise," features that are all facets of unnecessary knowledge. The essential problem that Greville identifies with the nature of these questions and unchecked inquisitiveness is that there is a danger of feeling Godlike – "our nature feels a Deity" – and therefore instead of perceiving our imperfect and fallen state, we start to lose sight of God in the face of human potential. This notion of overreaching echoes Greville's earlier description of humankind's desire "to binde, and never to be bound,/ To governe God, and not bee governed" (*HL*, 59). This inversion of the status quo subjects God to humankind, violating the divinely ordained order as "Men would be Gods" (*TR*, 84). Greville warns against such desires that come out of unrestrained inquisitiveness and curiosity, stating that it is in fact impossible to know God via these means:

> Then by affecting pow'r, we cannot know him.
> By knowing all things else, we know him less,
> Nature contains him not, Art cannot shew him,
> Opinions Idols and not God express.
> Without, in Pow'r, we see him every where,
>
> (*TR*, 7)

Greville's point is that the relationship between knowledge and proximity to God in terms of understanding the divine is one of inversion: the more knowledge one has of the world and nature, particularly knowledge achieved through curiosity, the less one knows of God and the further away one is from understanding Him. The reason for this, according to Greville, lies in where we look for God, within or without. It is our corrupted knowledge that encourages us to seek God in the wrong places as it "Serves to convince our Consciences within,/ [...] To seek God and Religion from without" (*TR*, 14). It is this erroneous guidance from the conscience that leads humankind to seek God externally to ourselves through acquiring knowledge and arts, a fact which ultimately serves to further the distance between God and humankind.

The methodology of learning seems to have concerned Greville beyond his treatise. A short letter by Francis Bacon advises Greville in his studies, apparently addressing questions from the latter possibly in preparation for writing *Humane Learning*.[31] Bacon opens his "Advice to Fulke Greville on his Studies" by stating Greville's intent:

> Cousin Fulke, you tell me you are going to Cambridge, and that the ends of your going are, to get a scholar to your liking to live with you, and some two or three others to remain in the University, and gather for you; and you require my opinion, what instruction you shall give these gatherers.[32]

Greville's intention, it seems, was to return to Cambridge and to lead a group of "gatherers" of knowledge in order to produce "abridgements" and "epitomes." Bacon voices his disapproval of the enterprise as a whole, arguing that those who learn through the notes and abridgements of others may have a wide-ranging knowledge but will never achieve more than a general understanding of a subject: "I do not deny, but he that hath such abridgments of all arts shall have a general notion of all kinds of knowledge. But he shall be like a man of many trades, that thrives less than he that seriously follows one."[33] It seems that even in asking for Bacon's advice Greville was concerned with the vastness of knowledge and was seeking a way to make swathes of it available so that a single person could expand their knowledge-seeking potential. Bacon recognises Greville's aim, but remains steadfastly against such an endeavour:

> It may be objected that knowledge is so infinite, and the writers of every sort of it so tedious, as it is reason to allow a man all helps to go the shortest and nearest way. But they that only study abridgments, like men that would visit all places, pass through every place in such post as they have no time to observe as they go, or make profit of their travel.[34]

Bacon's advice is that abridgments only provide a surface knowledge of a topic, one learning solely through this method can never hope to achieve a profound understanding of it and therefore they will be ill equipped to use that knowledge in any productive way. Greville's suggestion emerges from early modern encyclopaedism, and Neil Kenny argues that "its diverse manifestations all share the goal of selecting a body of learning from the formless mass of the knowable, and relating the constituent parts to each other logically, so that together they form a circle of learning."[35] While abridgements would lend themselves to this "circle of learning," Bacon sees them as shortcuts that do not ultimately provide one with a sound understanding of the topic at hand but merely an overview.

It is perhaps surprising that Greville would suggest an intellectual endeavour that aimed at gathering and epitomising knowledge, given his view that human understanding is already tainted because of the Fall. In *A Treatie of Humane Learning*, he describes Understanding as "the last chiefe oracle of what man knowes" after sense, imagination, and memory. However, this faculty is flawed as it contains:

> Some ruinous notions, which oure Nature shows,
> Of generall truths, yet have they such a staine
> From our corruption, as all light they lose;
>   Save to convince of ignorance, and sinne,
>   Which where they raigne let no perfection in.

(HL, 15)

Greville alludes to the Fall once again, and argues that while humankind has an innate understanding of "generall truths," that very faculty is itself stained with sin and so a state of perfect and pure understanding can never be truly achieved. He continues to explore this in *A Treatise of Religion*:

> But there remains such natural corruption
> In all our Pow'rs, even from our Parents feed,
> As to the good gives native interpretation;
> Sence stains affection; that Will, and Will Deed,
>   So that what's good in us, and others too
>   We praise; but what is evil, that we do.

(TR, 13)

This stain is inescapable and not only draws us to evil, but makes our understanding and senses imperfect. It is the mark of original sin as following Adam and Eve's expulsion from the Garden of Eden "human senses had been defiled, and the possibilities of human knowledge were understood to be severely limited."[36] For Greville, this stain is not a dried mark that might fade with time: his use of it in the present tense "Sence stains affection" suggests that it is something which occurs continually, a staining that persists with the same potency it had at the moment of the original sin. He goes on to suggest that without faith and obedience to Christ, the alternative paths are "Flesh and the Devil" which "stain our knowledge and enlarge our evil" (TR, 105). An active besmirching presence, this stain alters our senses, wills and deeds, leading us down the path of evil instead of good and makes the knowledge we do have impure.

Greville explores the ongoing degeneration of humankind's faculties, or "defects in Nature" (HL, 5), in the opening stanzas of *A Treatie of Humane Learning* and, beginning with Sense, shows how this corruption precipitates through the other faculties of wit, fancy, imagination and finally understanding:

> Which *Sense, Mans first instructor*, while it showes,
> To free him from deceipt, deceives him most;
> And from this false root that mistaking growes,
> Which truth in humane knowledges hath lost:
> So that by judging Sense herein perfection,
> Man must deny his Natures imperfection.

(HL, 6)

Greville identifies the contradictory essence of human Sense as it is the faculty we rely upon the most, our "first instructor," that provides us with sensory and perceptive information about the world, our relation to things in it and our existence within it. The information provided by the Sense is unfiltered and raw; it is through this that we experience Nature and life before processing it cognitively. However, Greville shows that Sense is dissembling and claims to provide truthful knowledge of the world around, when in fact it "deceives him most." Thus, the most primitive knowledge of the world that comes through Sense is flawed, and this falsehood grows like a tree, leading ultimately to the inability of humankind to recognise its own imperfect nature as the information received via the Sense does not correlate to the true human state. In this, Greville suggests that animals have a better understanding of their place in the world as "every Beast in it doth us exceed" (*HL*, 7): that is, the human Sense deceives us into believing we are not imperfect or corrupt and so taints our other cognitive faculties with this basic misconception, whereas animals do not believe themselves to be anything other than what they are: their Sense provides them with a more truthful knowledge of themselves and so they "exceed" humankind.

It is this notion of excess that ultimately increases the separation between humankind and God. In a seemingly paradoxical statement Greville claims that "by knowing all things, we know him lesse" (*TR*, 7). For Greville, knowledge is a way of coming to know God, not in the way of the natural philosopher who "reads" the Book of Nature to slowly reveal the face of its maker, but as a way of knowing the self and finding the good within. Thus, knowledge for the sake of knowledge will be counterproductive in trying to reach the divine. In *A Treatie of Humane Learning* he claims that "the use of knowledge is not strife" (*HL*, 84), it should be productive and enriching for the individual. The most pertinent issue for Greville in terms of seeking knowledge is that it does not supercede the divine. The ultimate end of learning is to know the self and, in so doing, to recognise God and be drawn to him; if one seeks "more light to cleare the mind" (*TR*, 80) then God's written word is the place to look and also contains warnings about the consequences of breaking His laws:

> That *Adams* fall was breach of Law enacted,
> By which in stained womb the chosen seed
> Together with the reprobate did breed.
>
> (*TR*, 80)

For Greville, the story of the Fall illustrates that the uncurbed pursuit of knowledge is unlawful as it breaks the limits which have been set for human-kind. Once again, Greville's notion of being tainted is continual as the entire human race issues from that "stained womb," thus the stain is passed from generation to generation and cannot be removed.

Both treatises conclude by placing productive and useful learning within religious parameters. In *A Treatie of Humane Learning* Greville advises that caution should accompany learning:

> With which faire cautions, Man may well professe
> To studie God, whom he is borne to serve
>
> (*HL*, 148)

For Greville, the study of God is not about the accrual of knowledge of the terrestrial world and trying to understand the secrets of nature, but is an active journey of self-discovery of the inner self that will lead to a reconnection with the divine as there "are true Learnings in the humble heart" (HL, 150). Ultimately for Greville, "knowledge is to obey" (TR, 114). Though he engages with new and radical ideas and appears inclined to advocate an unfettered pursuit of knowledge, for Greville true knowledge is a realisation and acceptance of the place of humankind in the divine order, and an active participation in seeking God from within. The pursuit of the knowledge of God does not allow for abridgements or epitomising, but must be done to the whole of one's capacity. Thus, while Greville acknowledges the potentially limitless mine of knowledge, he advocates knowing and obeying divinely prescribed boundaries so that we may better learn of ourselves and, in so doing, begin to reclaim what was lost at the Fall.

Notes

1 John Dee, "To the Honorable Assemblie of the Commons in the Present Parlament" (London, 1604).
2 Isaac Casaubon identified them as having been written in the second or third centuries AD in 1614.
3 Ronald A. Rebholz suggests that *Humane Learning* was composed between 1620 and 1622, and that *Religion* was composed between 1622 and 1628 though a later date is more likely. With the exception of an unauthorised publication of *Mustapha* (1609), all of Greville's works were published posthumously making it difficult to accurately date them. Rebholz's chronology remains a useful guideline for dating Greville's texts, but remains conjectural. Rebholz, *The Life of Fulke Greville, First Lord Brooke* (Oxford: Clarendon Press, 1971). See also G. A. Wilkes, "The Sequence of the Writings of Fulke Greville, Lord Brooke," *Studies in Philology*, 56, no. 3 (1959), 489–503.
4 See Richard Waswo, *The Fatal Mirror: Themes and Techniques in the Poetry Fulke Greville* (Charlottesville: UP of Virginia, 1972); Elaine Y. L. Ho, "Fulke Greville's *Caelica* and the Calvinist Self," *Studies in English Literature, 1500–1900*, 32, no. 1 (1992), 35–57.
5 Nicholas Tyacke, *Anti-Calvinists: The Rise of English Arminianism c.1590–1640* (Oxford: Clarendon Press, 1987), 3.
6 Andrew Hadfield, "The Political World of Fulke Greville" in *Fulke Greville and the Culture of the English Renaissance*, ed. by Russ Leo, Katrin Röder and Freya Sierhuis (Oxford: Oxford UP, 2018), 260–276, 260.
7 Sarah Knight, "'Not with the Ancient, nor yet with the Modern' Greville, Education, and Tragedy" in *Fulke Greville and the Culture of the English Renaissance*, ed. by Russ Leo, Katrin Röder and Freya Sierhuis (Oxford: Oxford UP, 2018), 195–209, 198.
8 Fulke Greville, *A Treatise of Religion* in *The Remains of Sir Fulk Grevill Lord Brooke: Being Poems of Monarchy and Religion: Never before Printed* (London: 1670), 177–205, stanza 84. Future references to *A Treatise of Religion* will be referred to in parentheses as TR followed by the stanza number. *A Treatie of Humane Learning* is from *Certaine Learned and Elegant Workes of the Right Honorable Fulke Lord Brooke, Written in his Youth, and familiar Exercise with Sir Philip Sidney. The severall Names of which Workes the following page doth*

declare (London: 1633) and will be referred to in parentheses as *HL*, followed by the stanza number.

9 Fulke Greville, *Alaham* in *Certain Learned and Elegant Workes*, sig. F2ʳ.

10 Geoffrey Bullough, Introduction in *Poems and Dramas of Fulke Greville, First Lord Brooke*, ed. by Geoffrey Bullough, 2 vols. (Edinburgh: Oliver & Boyd, 1939), 4.

11 Joan Rees, *Fulke Greville, Lord Brooke, 1554–1628: A Critical Biography* (London: Routledge & Kegan Paul, 1971), 6.

12 Waswo, *The Fatal Mirror*, 6.

13 Stephen Clucas, "'Wondrous Force and Operation': Magic, Science and Religion in the Renaissance" in *Textures of Renaissance Knowledge*, ed. Philippa Berry and Margaret Tudeau-Clayton (Manchester: Manchester UP, 2003), 35–57, 48.

14 Pseudo-Dionysius, *Pseudo-Dionysius: The Complete Works*, trans. Colm Luibheid (Mahwah: Paulist Press, 1987), 145.

15 James 1:17. Quotations from the Bible are from the Authorised Version (King James) (1611).

16 Keith Thomas, *Religion and the Decline of Magic: Studies in Popular Beliefs in Sixteenth and Seventeenth Century England* (London: Weidenfeld and Nicolson, 1973), 349.

17 Ryan Curtis Friesen, *Supernatural Fiction in Early Modern Drama and Culture* (Eastbourne: Sussex Academic Press, 2010), 2.

18 The dedication in this text suggests a falling out between Greville and Bruno. However, Bruno may have been seeking patronage and never come into contact with Greville. See Giordano Bruno, *The Expulsion of the Triumphant Beast*, ed. and trans. Arthur D. Imerti (Lincoln and London: University of Nebraska Press, 2004), 70.

19 Steven Shapin, *The Scientific Revolution* (Chicago: University of Chicago Press, 1996), 26.

20 Giordano Bruno, *The Ash Wednesday Supper*, ed. and trans. Edward A. Gosselin & Lawrence S. Lerner (Toronto: University of Toronto Press, 1995), 142.

21 Giordano Bruno, *On the Infinite, the Universe and the Worlds*, trans. Scott Gosnell (Port Townsend: Huggin, Munnin & Co., 2014), 35. Originally published in Italian in 1584.

22 *OED*, "dimension" n. 2a "Measurable or spatial extent of any kind, as length, breadth, thickness, area, volume; measurement, measure, magnitude, size. (Now commonly in plural: cf. *proportions*.)"

23 John Dee, "Mathematical Praeface" in *The Elements of Geometrie of the Most Auncient Philosopher Euclide of Megara* (London: 1570), sig.*ijʳ.

24 Brian Vickers, "Introduction" in *Occult and Scientific Mentalities in the Renaissance*, ed. Brian Vickers (Cambridge: Cambridge UP, 1984), 1–55, 33.

25 Matthew Woodcock, "'The World is Made For Use': Theme and Form in Greville's Verse Treatises," *Sidney Journal*, 19, nos. 1–2 (2001), 143–160, 154; 155.

26 William Eamon, *Science and the Secrets of Nature: Books of Secrets in Medieval and Early Modern Culture* (Princeton: Princeton UP, 1994), 59–60.

27 Deuteronomy 29:29. See also Proverbs 25:27; 1 Corinthians 8:1; Romans 12:3.

28 Peter Harrison, "Curiosity, Forbidden Knowledge, and the Reformation of Natural Philosophy in Early Modern England," *Isis*, 92, no. 2 (2001), 265–290, 274.

29 Eamon, *Secrets of Nature*, 61.

30 Warren Boutcher, "'Rationall Knowledges' and 'Knowledges … Drenched in Flesh and Blood': Fulke Greville, Francis Bacon and Institutions of Humane Learning in Tudor and Stuart England," *Sidney Journal*, 19, nos. 1–2 (2001), 11–40, 14.

31 Brian Vickers, ed., *Francis Bacon The Major Works* (Oxford: Oxford UP, 2002), 558.

32 Francis Bacon, "Advice to Fulke Greville on His Studies," 102. It is generally
    accepted that this letter is by Francis Bacon since James Spedding's attribution in
    The Works of Francis Bacon (London: Longman, 1858). See also Vernon F.
    Snow, "Francis Bacon's Advice to Fulke Greville on Research Techniques," *Hunt-
    ingdon Library Quarterly*, 23, no. 4 (1960), 369–378; Vickers's note in *Francis
    Bacon The Major Works*, 557–558.
33 Bacon, "Advice," 202.
34 Bacon, "Advice," 202–203.
35 Neil Kenny, *The Palace of Secrets: Béroalde de Verville and Renaissance Con-
    ceptions of Knowledge* (Oxford: Clarendon Press, 1991), 1.
36 Shapin, *Scientific Revolution*, 24.

Bibliography

Bacon, Francis. "Advice to Fulke Greville on His Studies." In *Francis Bacon
    The Major Works*. Edited by Brian Vickers, 102–106. Oxford: Oxford UP,
    2002.
Boutcher, Warren, " 'Rationall Knowledges' and 'Knowledges … Drenched in Flesh
    and Blood': Fulke Greville, Francis Bacon and Institutions of Humane Learning
    in Tudor and Stuart England." *Sidney Journal* 19, nos. 1–2 (2001): 11–40.
Bruno, Giordano. *The Ash Wednesday Supper*. Edited and translated by Edward A.
    Gosselin and Lawrence S. Lerner. Toronto: University of Toronto Press, 1995.
Bruno, Giordano. *The Expulsion of the Triumphant Beast*. Translated by Arthur
    D. Imerti. Lincoln and London: University of Nebraska Press, 2004.
Bruno, Giordano. *On the Infinite, the Universe and the Worlds*. Translated by
    Scott Gosnell. Port Townsend: Huggin, Munnin & Co., 2014.
Bullough, Geoffrey. ed. *Poems and Dramas of Fulke Greville, First Lord Brooke*.
    Edinburgh: Oliver & Boyd, 1939.
Clucas, Stephen. " 'Wondrous Force and Operation': Magic, Science and Religion
    in the Renaissance." In *Textures of Renaissance Knowledge*. Edited by Philippa
    Berry and Margaret Tudeau-Clayton, 35–57. Manchester: Manchester Univer-
    sity Press, 2003.
Dee, John. "Mathematical Praeface." In *The Elements of Geometrie of the Most
    Auncient Philosopher Euclide of Megara*. London: Henry Billingsley, 1570.
Dee, John. "To the Honorable Assemblie of the Commons in the Present Parlament"
    (London, 1604).
Eamon, William, *Science and the Secrets of Nature: Books of Secrets in Medieval
    and Early Modern Culture*. Princeton: Princeton University Press, 1994.
Friesen, Ryan Curtis. *Supernatural Fiction in Early Modern Drama and Culture*.
    Eastbourne: Sussex Academic Press, 2010.
Greville, Fulke, *Alaham in Certaine Learned and Elegant Workes of the Right
    Honorable Fulke Lord Brooke, Written in his Youth, and familiar Exercise with
    Sir Philip Sidney*. London, 1633, sigs D1ᶜ–N4ᵛ.
Greville, Fulke, *A Treatie of Humane Learning in Certaine Learned and Elegant
    Workes of the Right Honorable Fulke Lord Brooke, Written in his Youth, and
    familiar Exercise with Sir Philip Sidney*. London, 1633, sigs. d1ᶜ–g3ᵛ.
Greville, Fulke, *A Treatise of Religion in The Remains of Sir Fulk Grevill Lord
    Brooke: Being Poems of Monarchy and Religion: Never before Printed*. London:
    1670, 177–205.

Hadfield, Andrew. "The Political World of Fulke Greville." In *Fulke Greville and the Culture of the English Renaissance*. Edited by Russ Leo, Katrin Röder and Freya Sierhuis, 260–276, 260. Oxford: Oxford University Press, 2018.

Harrison, Peter, "Curiosity, Forbidden Knowledge, and the Reformation of Natural Philosophy in Early Modern England." *Isis* 92, no. 2 (June 2001): 265–290.

Ho, Elaine Y. L. "Fulke Greville's *Caelica* and the Calvinist Self." *Studies in English Literature, 1500–1900*, 32, no. 1 (Winter 1992): 35–57.

Kenny, Neil. *The Palace of Secrets: Béroalde de Verville and Renaissance Conceptions of Knowledge*. Oxford: Clarendon Press, 1991.

Knight, Sarah. " 'Not with the Ancient, Nor Yet with the Modern' Greville, Education, and Tragedy." In *Fulke Greville and the Culture of the English Renaissance*. Edited by Russ Leo, Katrin Röder and Freya Sierhuis, 195–209, 198. Oxford: Oxford UP, 2018.

Pseudo-Dionysius. *Pseudo-Dionysius: The Complete Works*. Translated by Colm Luibheid. Mahwah: Paulist Press, 1987.

Rebholz, Ronald A. *The Life of Fulke Greville, First Lord Brooke*. Oxford: Clarendon Press, 1971.

Rees, Joan. *Fulke Greville, Lord Brooke, 1554–1628: A Critical Biography*. London: Routledge & Kegan Paul, 1971.

Shapin, Steven. *The Scientific Revolution*. Chicago: University of Chicago Press, 1996.

Snow, Vernon F. "Francis Bacon's Advice to Fulke Greville on Research Techniques." *Huntingdon Library Quarterly* 23, no. 4 (January 1960): 369–378.

Spedding, James. *The Works of Francis Bacon*. London: Longman, 1858.

Thomas, Keith. *Religion and the Decline of Magic: Studies in Popular Beliefs in Sixteenth and Seventeenth Century England*. London: Weidenfield and Nicolson, 1973.

Tyacke, Nicholas. *Anti-Calvinists: The Rise of English Arminianism c.1590–1640*. Oxford: Clarendon Press, 1987.

Vickers, Brian. "Introduction." In *Occult and Scientific Mentalities in the Renaissance*. Edited by Brian Vickers, 1–55. Cambridge: Cambridge University Press, 1984.

Waswo, Richard. *The Fatal Mirror: Themes and Techniques in the Poetry Fulke Greville*. Charlottesville: University Press of Virginia, 1972.

Wilkes, G. A. "The Sequence of the Writings of Fulke Greville, Lord Brooke." *Studies in Philology* 56, no. 3 (January 1959): 489–503.

Woodcock, Matthew. " 'The World is Made For Use': Theme and Form in Greville's Verse Treatises." *Sidney Journal* 19, nos. 1–2 (2001): 143–160.

4 Duality and aporia in Greville's political writings

Robert Appelbaum

> It must be extreme hard to find out the opinions and meanings of those men that are gone from us long ago, and have left us no other signification but their books.
>
> Thomas Hobbes, *The Elements of Law*[1]

As an interpretive science, the history of ideas—along with its corollary in literary studies, the history of ideas in literature—may often find itself trying to explain the inexplicable. In "the opinions and meanings of those men that gone from us long ago," as Thomas Hobbes put it, especially in the case of political writings, we may well find ourselves baffled.[2] Ideas may seem so compromised at the outset by the factional disagreements that have fueled and ignited their expression, but which are no longer extant; by apparent self-contradictions, unexamined assumptions, thoughtlessly or craftily adopted conventions of artifice; by ambiguous word choices, rhetorical ruses, and polemical attacks—not to mention obvious statements that defy our own prejudices and principles, including the biases of class, nation, and ethnicity—that the historian's task is all but inevitably a kind of smoothing. What once (we suppose) seemed salient and reasonable may later seem incoherent, misplaced, mistaken, or irrational. What once may have been a convincing argument may now seem to be riddled with erratic emphases, mistakes, inconsistencies, and aporia—not to mention strong beliefs which to us are by now incredible. How could any rational person, to give an obvious example, believe that monarchs were the "head" of their states and subjects their "body"? And yet a few centuries ago many very rational individuals believed in just that idea—some were even willing to die for it, or at least some version of the idea, given the interests of the individuals as well as their convictions. Thus Quentin Skinner has referred to the "opacity" of texts in the field of the history of political ideas, and J. G. A. Pocock to their "indefinite rationality." By themselves, texts of the past do not seem to mean what they say, or say what they mean. How could they? Brought back into context, however, above all to their linguistic and pragmatic or performative dimensions, the texts as it were learn to speak, clearly, distinctly, and determinatively, if also, sometimes, ambiguously or inconclusively. Neither Skinner nor Pocock would call this "smoothing," and would probably resent the term being applied to what they do, for in their own work paradoxes are allowed to remain paradoxes, and failures are allowed to remain as failures. One of Skinner's first complaints about the history of political thought was that it too often subscribed to a "myth of coherence."[3] But still, the discipline of the history of the literatures of political thought seem to demand that historians find some form of coherence in what they study.

If anyone's political writings seem to demand some smoothing, some overcoming of opacity and indefiniteness, Fulke Greville's would be high among them. In Greville's work, calls for virtue jostle with maxims concerning the impossibility of virtue. Calls for a strong monarchy jostle with resentment over social inequality and a faith in constitutionalism. Objections to tyranny jostle with appeals to patience and the punishments of God, and sometimes to recommendations to tyrants concerning how they should comport themselves in order to keep their tyrannies in place.[4] Meanwhile, the praise of nature and natural law jostle with complaints about natural corruption. Hopelessness jostles with hope. Examples from history serve as models of what not to do, while examples from mythology provide models for what cannot be achieved anymore, but ought to be achieved. Assertions about the fruits of peace jostle with recommendations on the conduct of war. The claims of Christianity jostle with the claims of secular order. And all this comes in fragments, in chapters that seem to contradict one another, and yet in a verse (when verse, as usual, is used) that combines a suppleness with a convincing sententiousness that almost rivals Ben Jonson's.[5]

In order to make sense of all this, it would seem that a recourse to Pocock's and Skinner's methodology of finding the paradigmatic "language" would be appropriate, in keeping with which a political thinker's works are addressed. Find the controlling paradigm; find the language game; find the inherent assumptions, conventions, and points of view that writers adopt in order to write, and you are on the way to explain an otherwise puzzling text. Many of the recent commentators on Greville's political work have followed suit. David Norbrook has associated Greville's work with Etienne de la Boétie and the discourse of voluntary servitude; Peter Herman with the discourse of the ancient constitution; Freya Sierhuis, following many earlier scholars, with the discourse of Calvinism; Ethan John Guagliardo with George Puttenham and a shared "political atheology," Bradly J. Irish, also following many earlier scholars, with Tacitism and its historical pessimism, which many have shown to have been rampant in Greville's lifetime, and highly popular among his circles of associates, including the Earl of Essex.[6] But what is the effect of all this? Sierhuis summarizes the critical history of Greville's political writings by saying that criticism "has for long been locked in a kind of critical aporia, with opinion divided almost equally between those who see him as a defender of absolute monarchy and those who see him as its most trenchant, albeit circumspect, critic"[7] Putting the critical history in this light makes it seem as if critics are looking for what Greville was *for* and what he was *against*. It makes the critical problem seem to be how to establish the one or the other, and how to establish it by unlocking a key—Tacitism, Calvinism, constitutionalism—that opens the door toward a legible coherence, in fact, a coherence that boils down to an unerring if controversial statement of belief, expressed in the context of a coherent and systematic theory. Add to this what is known about the author's life and circumstances, and what the conditions for political writing were like (it was dangerous to speak critically of the great) and one can come very near a smooth appreciation of a very rough literary episode.

But what if the opacities, indeterminacies, inconsistencies, and aporia that have divided the critical community are embedded in Greville's ideas themselves? And what if these qualities, instead of being hindrances to a writer's project, actually enable it?

In this chapter I am going to take a brief look at four related texts by Fulke Greville, *A Treatise of Monarchy* (probably completed by 1610; first published 1670), *A Treatie of Warres* (probably from the early 1620s; first published in the twentieth century), *An Inquisition Upon Fame and Honour* (1612–1614; first published in the twentieth century) and *The Five Years of King James* (after 1613; first published 1643). The latter, in my opinion, is not by Greville. (It is in fact seldom attributed to him today, although his name appears on the title page.) The text lacks the suppleness of thought and style and the sententiousness evident in his other writings, and therefore I will not put much stress on it. But even the King James tale (focused on the plot to poison Thomas Overbury) displays a kind of enabling self-contradiction, which shows consistency with Greville's discourse.

I am not the first to note this. Geoffrey Bullough refers to "the baffling 'dualism'" in Greville. "He deliberately takes up two points of view in assessing human actions. *Sub specie aeternitatis* our errors are vile; seen in the light of expediency and practical use, they may be valuable."[8] I shall modify this position in what follows, but it is a fair indication of what is at stake—a dualism, with or without quotes, that cannot be resolved. The great literary historian Hugh N. Maclean later also observed the dualism inherent in Greville's political thought, and by dualism, somewhat unlike Bullough, he referred to polarities that could not be synthesized, tensions that could not be relaxed, but which Greville addressed for just that reason. On the subject of *a Treatise of Monarchy*, for example, analyzing Greville's concept of sovereignty, Maclean concludes, "factors pulling in opposite directions must be combined to describe at all completely Greville's conception of sovereignty."[9] On the subject of *A Treatie of Warres* he writes, more capaciously, that Greville's dualism places the Christian in something of a dilemma. If men regard the natural world as "real," and if, accordingly, mere "shows divine" (stanza 64) serve them for a so-called "super-natural" world, they are quite right to adopt a Turkish viewpoint, i.e., to equate "Court" with "camp," and govern themselves and others by the "discipline" of natural war. If, however, men claim to "Measure themselves, by Truths eternal doom" (stanza 59), and identify their "end in this World" with "the World to come," they must abstain from all wars whatsoever, including those "built on Piety" (stanza 53).[10]

On the subject of monarchy and sovereignty Greville is unable to resolve the conflict between divine and popular sovereignty, between an impulse toward absolutism and an impulse toward constitutionalism. On the subject of war, Greville is unable to resolve the conflict between peace as an unqualified good and the conduct of war as a virtuous necessity. Similarly, in his work on honor and fame he cannot resolve the conflict between understanding fame and honor as virtues, on the one hand, and as sins on the other. And in the work on James I, whether or not it is by Greville, similar contradictions appear. The court of King James was a court of high ideals; it was also a den of corruption.

To claim that Greville's political writing is animated by fundamental dualisms is perhaps just to find another form of coherence in the work— the coherence of self-opposition, maybe even what Keats called "negative capability." But the claim goes deeper than that. It is to assert that aporia is what makes Greville's political writings possible. It is to assert that the space of aporia, this tugging of thought in mutually incompatible directions, is what enjoins Greville to write.

There is no future, and we have to prepare for it. That is one of the main premises, put in modern terms, that I think is behind Greville's project. There is no future; there is no progress to come, nor even such a notion of an evolutionary process by which the "real world," as Maclean puts it, can develop into the "world to come." Instead, there is an unresolvable duality, where the future is unforeseen, unhoped for, unimaginable, but where it nevertheless weighs on the present and demands our attention. It must be addressed. And so it comes into a kind of suspended existence, as I will show, viewed from a vehement yet detached hortatory perspective, often expressed in the subjunctive mood.

There is no past, and we continue to suffer the effects of it. That is another of the main premises, put in modern terms. Of course, Greville was a student of the past. Tacitus was a historian and Greville once tried to establish a lectureship in history at Cambridge.[11] But in the main, Greville uses the past in either of two rather anti-historicist ways: Either the past is comprised of an exemplary mythology (not again, as a process from which the modern period has evolved, but rather as a model of what we are not anymore and can never become); or else the past is comprised of incidents from mythology, ancient history, or recent history which serve as examples of what not to do. There are perhaps a few passages in the political poems where history is engaged with directly; but they are rare. As for the prose work, *Five Years of King James*, it is incomplete, breaking off with the unfinished tale of the aftermath of Overbury's death.

Originally, when preparing to write this chapter, I thought that I might myself be able to resolve the problem by focusing on Greville's discussions of conflict resolution. Like other political thinkers of his time, including Sir Francis Bacon, as well as many of the contemporary political thinkers, the idea seems to be that there must not be conflict, that political and social conflict is wrong in all sorts of ways; but still, there is conflict, and both the theorist and the historian can show how conflict can be or has been overcome. Bacon's history of the life Henry VII provides a model.[12] Recourses to (defensive or offensive) war, assertions of sovereignty over others, contests for honor, the mustering of a court to rule over a nation, the violent enforcing of laws, the pragmatic, not to say Machiavellian shaping of the loyalties of the state—all these activities respond to ineluctable phenomena in the real world, and from time to time have to be carried out. As Sierhuis puts it,

> Critics who have attempted to make Greville either an apologist for absolute monarchy or a defender of the ancient constitution would do well to remember that Greville regards no existing political arrangement as corresponding to an 'ideal' state. The best that man in his fallen state can aspire to is some modicum of stability—not a harmonious equilibrium but a temporary balance of forces.[13]

That too was my own first impression, that Greville was one among many practical men devoted to finding how to settle the conflicts and imbalances of the day, however temporary and unideal the settlement might be. But Greville the writer is not really a pragmatist, as Bullough began to point out. He is a writer for whom pragmatism is at most only one half of the equation; the other half is a devout fatalism according to which the world is always in a condition of what Greville calls "declination" and cannot measure up to our expectations and our faith. So instead of pragmatism, however much it might be desirable, Greville's offers statements like these, in stanza 106 of *A Treatise of Monarchy*:

> How to prevent, or stay those declinations.
> And desperate diseases of estate,
> As hard is, as to change the inclinations
> Oh humane nature in her love, or hate.
>   Which whosoever can make straight or true,
>   As well is able to create her new.

Greville does not believe that a state could be remade "new," no more than he believes human nature can be changed anew. He knows that we have values and wishes, but they are not really for us, we pitiful humans, in this world without a future or a past. He is by no means alone in this. Among the founding fathers of this kind of dualism was Saint Augustine, struggling so mightily against the disparities between the City of God and the City of Man. Calvin too entertained dualisms of this kind, and a long line of English intellectuals of the Renaissance and Reformed theologians followed suit.[14] "What a piece of work is a man," Hamlet began in his address to Rosencrantz and Guildenstern. "And yet to me, what is this quintessence of dust?"

Maclean explains Greville's dualism in part by showing him to have been caught between a past he liked to idealize, when Sir Phillip Sidney and Queen Elizabeth were alive, and a present which seemed doomed to corruption. Herman rebuts this analysis, claiming that Greville continually upheld if not without nostalgia a monist doctrine of the "ancient constitution," a concept of course that Pocock originally brought to historiographical attention, and that was alive and kicking, as Herman shows, in many of Greville's contemporaries and forebears. I think that Maclean and Herman are both right—but not entirely in the way they claim to be. If *Five Years of King James* is indeed Greville's work, how can the idealization of Elizabeth be squared with an opening passage where the author claims, "No state of government can be said to be permanent, but that oftentimes those are said to good, are little by little converted unto those that be evil, and oftentimes changed from worse to worse, until they come to utter desolation?"[15] Greville makes similar claims in *A Treatise of Monarchy* with reference to ancient and early modern European history. For example, he at one point extolls the balance of the Roman senate, which "kepte uprighte/Her farr extended government and law," only in the next lines to say that the balance was ultimately overturned, because of war and "martiall mutinous election" (stanza 306). In other words, the best of political solutions are fated eventually to fail, so that they must be at once praised and mourned, in the immediate context of a narrative of James's ascension, we find that there were already insuperable problems in the kingdom of England, and that James when coming to power did his best to overcome them. "[James] established a peace, both honourable and profitable, with all neighbour princes, and by relation through all Europe; so that neither out friends, nor our enemies, might be either feared or suspected."[16] Even James could be idealized; Greville did not need a Sidney or an Elizabeth in order to write about a fortunate state of affairs that exists no longer. All he needed to note was that, again, the best political solutions are at once to be praised and mourned. As for the ancient constitution, it is to be noted that even that idea was founded on a contradiction. For although there was assumed to be an ancient constitution, no one had ever seen it. In fact, the idea that the ancient constitution came from "time immemorial," in other words that the constitution had no real past, was considered as one of its saving graces.[17] There was no past, and we are still benefiting from it.

A few more irresolvable dichotomies are worth calling attention to. To begin with, the dualities between the human and the divine and the past and the present are modified by a duality between nature and custom, or between natural law and positive law. Nature is a fundamental, unassailable, undeniable; it is necessity itself. And it is assumed that nature is benign. But custom can override, improve, or corrupt it. Natural law is inherent in every living being, and especially in every living human being, who will know, as Aquinas originally put it, that every human being naturally seeks to do good and avoid doing evil. But natural law is not enough. For human beings are subject to corruption. And positive law may require individuals to do evil to one person in order to do good toward another. It will, as Greville mentions many times, rightly enforce inequality—even though natural law begins by equating all living beings. And even worse: "Nature it self declines unto privation," Greville writes toward the beginning of the *Treatise Of Monarchy*, "As mixed of real ill and seeming good" (stanza 27).[18] Good nature becomes bad nature, in the course of a natural process. And, as the alert reader will have noticed, there is still another duality at play: not only between fullness and privation, or between "ill" and "good," but between reality and appearance. Nature may *seem* to be one thing—benevolent—but it can actually *be* quite another. There is no trusting nature, even though it is the one thing we are required to trust.

The dualism in Greville's work is in part rhetorical and methodological. Greville is enchanted with the antithesis, the paradox, the oxymoron, along with ironic resolution, accentuated by quibbling repetitions, puzzling parallelisms, chiasma, and other aggressive poetic devices that operate to put contrasting ideas in tense relation with one another. In a stanza among others that calls attention to how men become addicted to a desire for fame, we find Greville writing

> Hence they that by their words would Gods become
> With pride of thought deprave the pride of deeds,
> Upon the active cast a heavy doom,
> And mark weak strengths, to multiply strong weeds:
>   While they conclude Fame's trumpets, voice, and pen
>   More fit for crafty States, than worthy Men.
>
> (stanza 27)

The ultimate point, here and through most of the treatise, seems to be that men should seek fame without seeking fame; that the "pride of deeds" is undermined by the "pride of thought" (where "pride" appears to have different meanings in each expression); that the discourse of fame is unworthy of the men who deserve it. Meanwhile, the argument is structured by such verbal juxtapositions as "pride of thought/pride of deeds," "weak strengths/strong weeds," "crafty States/worthy Men." There is an argument and there is a structure of poetic argumentation, and they both are motivated by a dialectical, interrogative, sometimes ironic, sometimes indecisive and sometimes emphatic joining or juxtaposing of contraries. The strategy is as old as Petrarch. And it is what Greville does when he writes poems.[19]

But I am claiming that something even deeper is at work in the political writings, which is not to say that there is not also something deeper at work in the love poems and other works, but that this "something deeper" in the political writings is at least in some ways sui generis. Among the distinctive characteristics of political writing is its relation to time. Political writing, to the extent that it is political, has to address itself to a past, a present, and a future, that is to human life in its ongoing political dimension. For political science is a form of what Aristotle originally called practical wisdom. Pocock and Skinner began their careers by emphasizing this performative and interventionist notion of political discourse.[20] Conversely, political writing may also have to address itself to a timeless set of principles and conditions, to a pre-political and therefore natural past or to a future which is imagined to come after a sharp break from the future at hand, the one seen to be continuous with the present. For political science, practical though it may be, is frequently also a search for first and last principles, for natural unchanging conditions, for laws of evolutionary and de-evolutionary change, and for the ultimate purposes or eschaton of political action. Such is the complex temporality of political discourse. The issue has been much discussed in recent political thought with regard to the work of Walter Benjamin, Giorgio Agamben, and Alain Badiou, all of whom have argued (from a post-Marxist point of view) that political thought needs to address not just a "now" but a "time to come," a time after an unforeseeable Event which shall change political conditions.[21] But not enough has been said on this subject with regard to early modern thought, except on the subjects of apocalypticism and millenarianism.[22] Be that as it may, Greville shows few signs of apocalyptic consciousness and none of millenarianism or of what Agamben calls "messianic time." Nor, as I have suggested, does he express much concern for historical process. Though he will sometimes argue his preferences (whether for ancient constitutions or a strong monarchy) he does not address how particular constitutions have developed, or how particular monarchs and tyrants have come to power, or even how particular constitutions, monarchies, and tyrannies have declined. Nor, by the same token, does he have anything to say about how present constitutions and governments might change or improve in the future. That might not be remarkable except that Greville's interest in Machiavelli and Tacitus and his own tragedies *Mustapha* and *Alaham* shows that Greville was familiar with the drama of historical processes and even with, from the examples of Machiavelli or his associate Francis Bacon, how a political writer might propose historical change.[23]

In Greville's political poems, there is no future, although we have to prepare for it. And by the same token, there is no past, although we have to learn from it. In Greville's hands, the verse treatise becomes a form of meditation which derives from historical precedent and subjects it to a dialectical analysis. This dialectic, in turn, instead of reaching for a synthesis, gestures toward what I would characterise as a corrupt and conditional politics *sub specie aeternitatis*. That is not quite the same thing as Bullough was saying: for Bullough the eternal is expressed simply with maxims of eternal truth. Here I am saying, in effect, that for Greville the eternal is not eternal. It is a limit toward which we can only gesture, and only with a measure of futility. Following Brian Cummings we might associate this form of versification the "ambiguity of Calvinism"[24]—if we also associate it with an ambiguity of Tacitism, of constitutionalism, of Augustinianism, and so forth. All of these trends of thought gesture toward and miss the ideal of eternal perfection. But apart from its intellectual partners, Greville's political verse is precisely an attempt to enter the space of this essential contradiction: and so comes a corrupt and conditional politics of eternity. Although corruption and conditionality would seem to belong to the pragmatic world, Greville speaks from corruptible and the conditional *towards* the eternal without ever really getting there.

The strategy is not unique to Greville. Many of his contemporaries were inclined—or even limited—to a strictly rhetorical use of history, to viewing history as a repository of exempla, whose teaching were timeless and universal, yet also particular to circumstances and contingent and even often futile.[25] But given what appears to be Greville's ambition in his political writings, and his evident understanding of chronology and sequence in history, the strategy must be seen, as Bullough and Maclean agree, to be to some degree deliberate. To the modern reader it can often result in what seems like tendentiousness. For example, in stanzas 235 and 236, in the section of the *Treatise of Monarchy* called "Of Church," Greville alludes to the story of Salamoneus, the mythical king of Elis, who built a bridge of brass and commanded his subjects to worship him as a god, only to be struck down by a thunderbolt sent by Zeus. Greville concludes the story this way:

> Salamoneus, who while he his Caroche drave
> Over the brazen bridge of Elis stream,
> And did with artificial thunder brave
> Jove, till he pierced him with a lightning beam:
>   From which example, who will an idol be,
>   Must rest assured to feel a deity.

(stanza 236)

It is to be noticed, first, that the story is mythical, and Greville must have known that. It is to be noticed, second, that whether or not the story is mythical, a single case is taken to prove a universal truth. Even if we grant Greville the licence of allegorical thinking, and Zeus and the Christian God are lined up with one another, the alacrity with which the particular becomes the universal, and an event from the distant past comes to represent a warning to the future—"who will be"—indicates a hortatory relationship to the material at hand, a cry to the unknown and unknowable future, managed over-confidently. Here and on many occasions it seems that Greville is suggesting that he who imitates the past is doomed to repeat it, so don't imitate it—although of course, Greville uses history selectively, to prove what he is inclined to prove.

What seems to warrant Greville's tendentiousness is the context: a sequence on "The Church" where his main purpose seems to be to reiterate a Calvinist critique of idolatry and the worldliness of the Catholic Church. In the context of a work on monarchy, the tendentiousness is further supported by a project which dismisses the idea that princes are in any way divine and therefore above the exigencies of nature and law. To claim authority by divinity, whether in the church or the state, is fundamentally contrary to both religion and political right. That seems to be the governing idea.

But does the idea warrant the anecdote and the conclusion drawn from it? Is there not a divide even between such principles as can be abstracted from Greville's work and what Greville actually writes? Isn't what Greville writes something in excess of the principles? Or is the governing idea already a problem? One doesn't have to look far elsewhere in the *Treatise*—in fact it is embedded in the anecdote about Salamoneus—that although it is wrong to claim authority by divinity, still all authority comes from God. Or rather, although it *must* come from God, still God has left us to our own resort. There is no direct and audible command from God about how to set up a state and govern it. Nor is God immanent in human government. For that reason,

> Where if this outward work which power pretends
> Were life indeed, not frail hypocrisy,
> Monarchs should need no other friend,
> Conscience being base of their authority.

> (stanza 238)

In other words, though God intervenes now and then to punish tyranny and idolatry, all human government is tainted with tyranny and idolatry. If it were not tainted, conscience would be enough, for through conscience we would recognise what God wants us to do and act accordingly. But government is tainted—separated from the divine order it would perforce emulate—and therefore government must be ruled in keeping with law, prudence, community standards, and so forth, along with the weak help of conscience, and an awareness of the inevitability of decline.

All authority comes from God, but God has nothing to do with it—at first, and not in the meantime either. That is a corollary paradox. That is why there is neither a past nor a future. Whether God will intervene at any point we cannot know, except that we believe God will intervene, and know that He has intervened in the past. And as to whether God has set us on the way to government—that is emphatically denied. Instead, and for this reason, when Greville develops a poetic discourse on a political subject, he repeatedly turns to the device of a phantasmatic allegory depicting a sort of golden past which is all but impossible to believe in, and yet that establishes a foundation for political discourse as a whole.

Most well known are the opening two stanzas of *Monarchy*:

1.
There was a time before the times of Story,
When Nature reined instead of Laws or Arts,
And mortal Gods, with Men made up the Glory
Of one Republic by united Hearts.
     Earth was the common seat, the Conversation
     In saving Love, and ours in Adoration.

2.
For in those Golden days, with Natures Chains
Both King and People seemed conjoined in one,
Both nearest alike, with mutual feeding veins
Transcendency of either side unknown,
     Princes with Men using no other Arts,
     But by good dealing to obtain good hearts.

This Hesiodic–Ovidian myth, referring to the natural and golden state of humankind, opens a treatise which will then deal with the aftermath of the fall from nature, when "by decree of Fate this Corporation/Is altered" (stanza 17).[26] But anyone who knows the original myth can see that Greville corrupts it. Greville imagines a long ago age when gods, monarchs, heroes, and peoples lived out their lives in monarchic harmony—Hercules, Jason, and even Midas make their appearances in the midst of this age, even though this is supposed to be before the "time of Story." In the original myths, above all, though it is true that humanity lives in a natural, blissful state, there are no kings or princes. There is no need for them, no need for rulers of any kind, and no need for anyone to "obtain the hearts" of others. And of course, none of this has anything to do with the Christian story of origins in Genesis.

Why does Greville open his treatise with such a myth, and why does he do so with deliberate inaccuracy? Again, this is not the only time Greville uses such a device (which he himself might associate with the figure of *Ironia*[27]). It is very common, almost mandatory. In order to structure an account of political realities, whether on the subject of monarchy, religion, law, honor, commerce, or war, Greville is inclined to begin a chain of thought with a myth about an age of perfection from which we have since declined. It is part of the structure of his poetic imagination, not to mention his irony. It is as if to argue, we are not what we were; we ought to be what we were; we are not what we ought to be, and there is no disputing the fact, since the age of gold or harmony or nature or godliness is over. It is to argue, moreover, that *we must begin* with that premise. But it is to argue that premise *in myth*. It is to argue that we ought to be our mythical selves, which is the one thing we cannot be. We are detached from the past of what we ought to be. And we continue to suffer for it.

Such an argument, as I have suggested, is based on an unresolvable dualism, a dualism that Greville discloses through the appeal to myth. Precisely because what we ought to be is (a) a myth and (b) something we cannot be, we are faced with an insuperable duality. And what I wish to emphasize above all is that whatever Greville maintains on any particular issue—and lots of beliefs and reasons for them can be culled from his writings—as a political writer Greville invites the experience of a play of ironic unresolvability.

Maxims are made to follow from this condition into which we are plunged. For example, we need to have good, strong, transparent laws, Greville argues directly, fitted as closely to nature and divinity as possible, written in the vernacular. And that is because left to our own devices we are deficient, inadequate, weak, and find it difficult to interpret what statutes require of us. Consider the main metaphor in what follows:

> For as the man that means to write, or draw,
> If he unperfect be in hand, or head,
> Make his straight lines unto himself a law.
> By which his afterworks are governed;
> So be these lines of life in every Realm,
> To weight men's acts, a well contenting beam.

"So be these lines," i.e., laws: this is a characteristic gesture toward an unknown future, placed in an indeterminate subjunctive. So be it. The state is enjoined—so be it—to form good laws the way a man who has trouble writing or drawing finds the few examples from his own hand of that which is straight, and rules himself against that straightness.

It is not bad advice. But it demands that we recognise a basic condition of imperfection. It demands what Greville calls "art" as opposed to "nature." And it is ultimately doomed. People will misbehave, princes will tyrannise, and laws will be compromised by passion and interest. Our straight lines are ephemeral. Things fall apart. Yet we must work to keep them together.

Let me conclude here by the example of *A Treatie of Warres*, which begins by extolling the fruits of peace and ends up remarking on the necessity of war. Greville asks, how can humanity survive its own inclination toward violence? Why do humans keep going to war when it is clear that war doesn't do them any good? One explanation comes from another part Ovidian, part biblical myth, which also links to the *Treatise on Fame and Honour*:

> Yet since the Earth's first age, brought Giants forth,
> Greatness for good hath so past everywhere,
> As even this cloud, of Giant-making worth.
> Proudly the style of Fame, and Honour bears;
>   Kings are here creatures, so is virtue too,
>   And beings take from what the valiant do.
>
> (stanza 13)[28]

In other words, the giants, whatever they were, came into being and made people confuse greatness with moral worth, so that people began making war to make themselves "great." The chief example is Nimrod, who raised a kingdom through warfare, and set an example to bellicose princes everywhere. That is a shame. The "most famous" princes are those who "stain most earth, with human blood in war" (stanza 14).

So here is an unequivocal position. War is vainglorious and cruel. But its vainglory is established through a myth which implies that once upon a time there were no giants, and therefore no vainglory or war. And yet later Greville changes the subject to how *God* brings war upon people. From being a sign of human immorality, war becomes a sign of human "Mortality … Change's proper stage" (stanza 42). From being an expression of human resistance to humility and fraternity, it becomes an irresistible ontological condition. Man is doomed to war because man is doomed. And it is God who has done the dooming. "All great Empires, Cities, Seats of Power/ Must rise and fall" (stanza 38), and war is one of the means through which the fall of civilisations is accomplished. In fact, this is God's plan:

> God then sends *War*, commotion, tumult, strife,
> Like winds and storms, to purge the air and earth;
> Disperse corruption; give the World new life …
>
> (stanza 43)

War, like other signs of mortality and "discord" in the world,

> All prove God meant not Man should here inherit:
> A *time-made* World; which with time should not fade:
>   But as Noah's flood once drowned woods, hills, and plain,
>   So should the fire of Christ waste all again.
>
> (stanza 48)

Finally, apocalypticism rears its head. But it rears its head not as a fulfilment of time, but as an abrupt end to time. There is no future, in precisely this sense: Greville refuses what Agamben calls "messianic time," in favor of a time that leads nowhere until it gets abolished by a divine power. The phenomenon of war, like the phenomena of government, laws, fame, honor, and even established religion exists without reference to the time to come; in fact, all these phenomena show that humanity is incapable of living with eye toward the time to come.[29]

Greville's dualism is not a question of the difference between the mind and the body; it is between this world and the other world; it is between pragmatism and idealistic pessimism, between intentions and results; it is between heaven and earth, eternity and the "time-made world," where it turns out that there is no time, just a succession of rises and falls. The dualism is also a constituent of the space of political poetry, where many axioms and recommendations are compiled which in the end have no *telos*, no final consequences, and no future, only an ironic gesture toward what will be or what we may let be. If there is anything that connects Greville and his contemporaries to us, it may be first of all to this: the aporia of time and intention; of here, yesterday and tomorrow; of pragmatic ambition and futurelessness; a sense in fact that there is neither past nor future, but we still suffer or benefit from the first, and we have to prepare for the latter. But all this is not a doctrine as much, again, as it is a space of articulation, of the poetry of political hope and political despair. The dualism makes the poetry, and the poetry makes the dualism.

Notes

1 Cited in Quentin Skinner, "A Reply to My Critics," in *Meaning and Context: Quentin Skinner and His Critics*, ed. James Tully (Princeton: Princeton UP, 1988), 235.

2 Ibid.

3 Quentin Skinner, "Meaning and Understanding in the History of Ideas," *History and Theory*, 8, no. 1 (1969): 3–53. J. G. A. Pocock, "The History of Political Thought: A Methodological Inquiry" [1962], in *Political Thought and History: Essays on Theory and Method* (Cambridge: Cambridge UP, 2009), 3–19. The literature by and about the work of Skinner and Pocock is voluminous, and this is probably not the place to rehearse it. In this chapter I limit myself to citing, qualifying, and challenging a few salient points of the work of the two historians, with the help of a few other scholars, on the way toward developing a reading strategy of my own. For commentary on the problem of coherence see Michelle T. Clarke, "The Mythologies of Contextualism: Method and Judgment in Skinner's Visions of Politics," *Political Studies*, 61 (2013): 767–783.

4 See for example, *A Treatise of Monarchy*, stanza 191, in Fulke Greville, Lord Brooke, *The Remains. Being Poems of Monarch and Religion*, ed. G. A. Wilkes (Oxford: Oxford UP, 1965):

> But if power will exceed, then let mankind
> Receive oppression, as fruits of their error:
> Let them again live in their duties' shrine,

As their safe haven from the winds of terror.
Till he that raised power, to mow man's sin down.
Please, for power's own sins, to pluck off her crown.

All further citations will be from this edition and noted in the text by stanza. I have modernized spelling of Greville's texts throughout.

5 Such was the opinion at least of Yvor Winters in "Aspects of the Short Poem in the English Renaissance," *Forms of Discovery: Critical And Historical Studies on The Forms of the Short Poem in English* (1967), 1–120, esp. 44–52.

6 David Norbrook, "Fulke Greville and the Arts of Power," in David Norbrook, *Poetry and Politics in the English Renaissance* (Oxford: Oxford UP), 140–154; Peter C. Herman, " 'Bastard Children of Tyranny': The Ancient Constitution and Fulke Greville," *Renaissance Quarterly*, 55, no. 3 (2002), 969–1004; Freya Sierhuis, "The Idol of the Heart: Liberty, Tyranny, and Idolatry in the Work of Fulke Greville," *Modern Language Review*, 106, no. 3 (2011), 625–646; Ethan John Guagliardo, "The Political Atheology of George Puttenham and Fulke Greville," *Modern Philology*, 112, no. 4 (2015): 591–614; Bradley J. Irish, "The Literary Afterlife of the Essex Circle: Fulke Greville, Tacitus, and BL Additional MS 18638," *Modern Philology*, 112, no. 1 (2014), 272–285.

On Tacitism, some of the key texts are as follows: J. H. M. Salmon, "Stoicism and Roman Example: Seneca and Tacitus in Jacobean England," *Journal of the History of Ideas*, 50 (1989): 199–225; David Womersley, "Sir Henry Savile's Translation of Tacitus and the Political Interpretation of Elizabethan Texts," *Review of English Studies*, 42 (1991): 46–59; Peter Burke, "Tacitism, Scepticism, and Reason of State," in *The Cambridge History of Political Thought, 1450–1700*, ed. J. H. Burns (Cambridge UP, 1991), 479–498.

7 Sierhius, "The Idol of the Heart," 634.

8 Hugh N. Maclean, "Fulke Greville: Kingship and Sovereignty," *Huntington Library Quarterly* 16, no. 3 (1953): 237–271, 271.

9 Hugh N. Maclean, "Fulke Greville on War," *Huntington Library Quarterly* 21, no. 2 (1958): 95–109, 106.

10 Geoffrey Bullough, "Introduction," in *Poems and Drama of Fulke Greville, First Lord Brooke*, 2 Volumes, ed. Geoffrey Bullough, 1, 13 (Edinburgh and London: Oliver and Boyd), 1:13.

11 Joan Rees, Fulke Greville, Lord Brooke, 1554–1628: A Critical Biography, 40 (London: Routledge and Kegan Paul, 1971).

12 Sir Francis Bacon, *The Historie of the Raigne of King Henry the Seventh* (London: 1622). For an insightful analysis see Jerry Weinberger, "The Politics of Bacon's History of Henry the Seventh," *Review of Politics*, 52, no. 4 (1990): 553–558. Also see F. Smith Fussner, "Sir Francis Bacon and the Idea of History," in *The Historical Revolution: English Historical Writing and Thought 1580–1640*, ed. F. Smith Fussner (New York: Columbia UP, 1962), 253–274.

13 Sierhuis, "The Idol of the Heart," 634.

14 David Vandrunen, "The Two Kingdoms Doctrine and the Relationship of Church and State in the Early Reformed Tradition," *Journal of Church and State* 49, no. 4 (2007): 743–763.

15 *The Five Yeares of King James, or, The Condition of the State of England and the Relation It had to Other Provinces* (London: 1643), 1.

16 Greville, *Five Yeares*, 2.

17 Glenn Burgess, *Absolute Monarchy and the Stuart Constitution* (New Haven: Yale UP, 1996) offers an astute analysis of this topic, in what a amounts to a gentle revision of J. G. A. Pocock, *The Ancient Constitution and the Feudal Law: A Study of English Historical Thought In The Seventeenth Century*, Second Edition (Cambridge: Cambridge UP, 1987).

18 Sierhuis, "The Idol of the Hear" (633) also discusses this passage.
19 See Kathryn Murphy, "Fulke Greville's Figures of Repetition," *Essays in Criticism*, 65, no. 3 (2015): 250–294.
20 Some of Skinner's main methodological essays are included in James Tully, ed. *Meaning and Context: Quentin Skinner and His Critics* (Princeton: Princeton UP, 1988). For Pocock see J. G. A. Pocock, *Politics, Language and Time Essays On Political Thought and History*, Second Edition (Chicago: University of Chicago Press, 1989).
21 Most relevant in this context is probably Giorgio Agamben, *The Time That Remains: A Commentary on the Letter to the Romans*, trans. Patricia Dailey (Stanford: Stanford UP, 2005).
22 See Matt D. Goldish, Richard H. Popkin, *et al.*, eds. *Millenarianism and Messianism in Early Modern European Culture*, four volumes (London: Springer, 2001–2011).
23 Paul Hyland Harris, "Within Machiavellianism," *Italica*, 25 (1948): 28–41.
24 Brian Cummings, *The Literary Culture of the Reformation: Grammar and Grace* (Oxford: Oxford UP, 2002), 300.
25 See Timothy Hampton, *Writing from History: The Rhetoric of Exemplarity in Renaissance* (Ithaca: Cornell UP, 1990).
26 The critical *locus classicus* of this phenomenon is Harry Levin, *The Myth of the Golden Age in the Renaissance* (New York: Oxford UP, 1969).
27 The passage comes in *A Dedication to Sir Philip Sidney*, and it itself deserves more analysis than I have space to devote to it here: "… a new counsel rose up in me, to take away all opinion of seriousness from these perplexed pedigrees, and to this end carelessly cast them into that hypocritical figure ironia, wherein men (commonly to keep above their works) seem to make toys of the utmost they can do." *The Prose Works of Fulke Greville*, ed. John Gouws (Oxford: Clarendon Press, 1984), 91–92. And see Joan Rees, *Fulke Greville*, 119–122.
28 Fulke Greville, *A Treatie of Warres*, in Bullough, Editor, *Poems and Drama of Fulke Greville*, 1: 214–230.
29 It is to be noted, all the same, that in the section "Of Warr" in the *Treatise of Monarchy* Greville is less pacifistic, less pessimistic, and less indirect. There he cautions princes to be ready for war, just in case, and expansively attacks the Catholic Church's militant ambitions.

Bibliography

Agamben, Giorgio. *The Time That Remains: A Commentary on the Letter to the Romans*, trans. Patricia Dailey. Stanford: Stanford University Press, 2005.
Bacon, Sir Francis. *The Historie of the Raigne of King Henry the Seventh*. London: 1622.
Bullough, Geoffrey. "Introduction." In *Poems and Drama of Fulke Greville, First Lord Brooke*, 2 Volumes. Edited by Geoffrey Bullough, 1, 13. Edinburgh and London: Oliver and Boyd.
Burgess, Glenn. *Absolute Monarchy and the Stuart Constitution*. New Haven: Yale University Press, 1996.
Burke, Pete. "Tacitism, Scepticism, and Reason of State." In *The Cambridge History of Political Thought, 1450–1700*, Edited J. H. Burns, 479–498. Cambridge: Cambridge University Press, 1991.
Clarke, Michelle T. "The Mythologies of Contextualism: Method and Judgment in Skinner's Visions of Politics." *Political Studies* 61 (2013): 767–783.

Cummings, Brian. *The Literary Culture of the Reformation: Grammar and Grace*. Oxford: Oxford University Press, 2002.

Fussner, F. Smith. "Sir Francis Bacon and the Idea of History." In *The Historical Revolution: English Historical Writing and Thought 1580–1640*. Edited by F. Smith Fussner, 253–274. New York: Columbia University Press, 1962.

Goldish, Matt D., Richard H. Popkin, *et al.*, eds. *Millenarianism and Messianism in Early Modern European Culture*. Four volumes. London: Springer, 2001–2011.

Greville, Fulke. *Poems and Dramas of Fulke Greville, First Lord Brooke*, 2 Volumes. Edinburgh and London: Oliver and Boyd, 1939.

Greville, Fulke. *The Five Yeares of King James, or, The Condition of the State of England and the Relation It had to Other Provinces*. London, 1643.

Greville, Fulke. *The Prose Works of Fulke Greville*. Edited by John Gouws. Oxford: Clarendon Press, 1984.

Greville, Fulke Lord Brooke. *The Remains. Being Poems of Monarch and Religion*. Edited by G. A. Wilkes. Oxford: Oxford University Press, 1965.

Guagliardo, Ethan John. "The Political Atheology of George Puttenham and Fulke Greville." *Modern Philology* 112, no. 4 (2015): 591–614.

Hampton, Timothy. *Writing from History: The Rhetoric of Exemplarity in the Renaissance*. Ithaca: Cornell University Press, 1990.

Harris, Paul Hyland. "Within Machiavellianism." *Italica* 25 (1948): 28–41.

Herman, Peter C. "'Bastard Children of Tyranny': The Ancient Constitution and Fulke Greville." *Renaissance Quarterly* 55, no. 3 (2002): 969–1004.

Irish, Bradley J. "The Literary Afterlife of the Essex Circle: Fulke Greville, Tacitus, and BL Additional MS 18638." *Modern Philology* 112, no. 1 (2014): 272–285.

Levin, Harry. *The Myth of the Golden Age in the Renaissance*. New York: Oxford University Press, 1969.

Maclean, Hugh N. "Fulke Greville: Kingship and Sovereignty," *Huntington Library Quarterly* 16, no. 3 (1953): 237–271, 271.

Maclean, Hugh N. "Fulke Greville on War," *Huntington Library Quarterly* 21, no. 2 (1958): 95–109, 106.

Murphy, Kathryn. "Fulke Greville's Figures of Repetition." *Essays in Criticism* 65, no. 3 (2015) 250–294.

Norbrook, David. "Fulke Greville and the Arts of Power." In *Poetry and Politics in the English Renaissance*. Edited by David Norbrook, 140–154. Oxford: Oxford University Press, 1984).

Pocock, J. G. A. *The Ancient Constitution and the Feudal Law: A Study of English Historical Thought In The Seventeenth Century*, Second Edition. Cambridge: Cambridge University Press, 1987.

Pocock, J. G. A. *Politics, Language and Time Essays On Political Thought and History*, Second Edition. Chicago: University of Chicago Press, 1989.

Pocock, J. G. A. "The History of Political Thought: A Methodological Inquiry" [1962]. In *Political Thought and History: Essays on Theory and Method*. Edited by J. G. A. Pocock, 3–19. Cambridge: Cambridge University Press, 2009.

Rees, Joan. *Fulke Greville, Lord Brooke, 1554–1628: A Critical Biography*. London: Routledge and Kegan Paul, 1971.

Salmon, J. H. M. "Stoicism and Roman Example: Seneca and Tacitus in Jacobean England." *Journal of the History of Ideas* 50 (1989): 199–225.

Sierhuis, Freya. "The Idol of the Heart: Liberty, Tyranny, and Idolatry in the Work of Fulke Greville." *Modern Language Review* 106, no. 3 (2011): 625–646.

Skinner, Quentin. "A Reply to My Critics." In *Meaning and Context: Quentin Skinner and His Critics*. Edited by James Tully. Princeton: Princeton University Press, 1988.

Skinner, Quentin. "Meaning and Understanding in the History of Ideas." *History and Theory*, 8, no. 1 (1969): 3–53.

Tully, James, ed. *Meaning and Context: Quentin Skinner and His Critics*. Princeton: Princeton UP, 1988.

Vandrunen, David. "The Two Kingdoms Doctrine and the Relationship of Church and State in the Early Reformed Tradition." *Journal of Church and State* 49, no. 4 (2007): 743–763.

Weinberger, Jerry. "The Politics of Bacon's 'History of Henry the Seventh'." *Review of Politics*, 52, no. 4 (1990): 553–558.

Winters, Yvor. "Aspects of the Short Poem in the English Renaissance," *Forms of Discovery: Critical And Historical Studies on The Forms of the Short Poem in English* (Ohio: Swallow Press, 1967), 1–120.

Womersley, David. "Sir Henry Savile's Translation of Tacitus and the Political Interpretation of Elizabethan Texts." *Review of English Studies* 42 (1991): 46–59.

5 Monarchy and patriarchy in Fulke Greville's *Mustapha*

Brian Cummings

Forty years after his death, Sir Fulke Greville still had the capacity to cause trouble. In 1670, Henry Herringman, the publisher of John Dryden, and of the Fourth Folio of Shakespeare, finally felt able to set forth into the world the last unpublished literary *Remains* of Greville, one of the very few men to have served at the courts of all three of Elizabeth, James I, and Charles I.[1] The so-called *Life of Sir Philip Sidney*, in reality a dedication of his own works to the memory of his late friend, had been kept back from print until 1651, no doubt because of its critique of Jacobean policy.[2] Herringman's edition of the *Remains* contained the still more incendiary verse treatises of Greville on the subjects of *Monarchy* and *Religion*. The second of these works Greville had intended, as shown by its place at the forefront of the author's personal manuscript copy of his work (now known as the Warwick Manuscripts in the British Library), to be printed as the first of his philosophical poems in his complete works.[3] However, in 1633, when *Certaine Learned and Elegant Vvorkes of the Right Honorable Fulke Lord Brooke Written in his Youth, and Familiar Exercise with Sir Philip Sidney* first appeared, *Monarchy* was left out.[4]

The reason is that Greville's writing is so close to the nerve ends of Stuart politics. Greville is a monarchist who nonetheless perpetrates a devastating critique of monarchy; and an orthodox Christian who nonetheless exposes the most disturbing energies of his religion. At the heart of these critiques Greville also retains the sensitive range of the love poet. Not least of his contributions to seventeenth-century political writing is his understanding of how the representation of Jacobean sovereignty is bound up with the sexual politics of gender. King James is a patriarch through and through, and yet the link between power and masculinity is never stable. Greville's poetry brings this to life with thrilling anxiety, and in the process becomes one of the prime analyses of patriarchy in the Stuart period.

Thus it was that only 100 years after his birth, following a revolution and a restoration, that the *opus* of Greville's assimilation of the lessons of Tudor and Stuart power finally emerged in full. His works operated on the boundaries of censorship and self-censorship, emerging only in stages.

Certaine Learned and Elegant Vvorkes did contain a text of the two plays which Greville wrote on the politics of the Muslim world, *Mustapha* and *Alaham*. In fact, *Mustapha* may have been started in the 1590s, and had already appeared in a quarto in 1609. The play published in 1633 is clearly a revised version. These two distinct texts are complicated by the hasty decision by Sir Kenelm Digby, at the last minute, to interpolate Greville's "Chorus Sacerdotum" into *Mustapha* in the printing of *Certaine Learned and Elegant Vvorkes*. Neither of the printed versions is satisfactory, and the text of the Warwick Manuscript is preferable to either.[5] However, the revision of *Mustapha* after the 1609 quarto shows how Greville continued to reflect on the political culture of the Ottoman Empire, and its theological ramifications. By this time, Greville had experience of office in government, as Treasurer of the Navy (1599–1603), and after the death of Sir Robert Cecil, Under-Treasurer and then Chancellor of the Exchequer (1612–1621).[6] *Mustapha* deals with a sensational event of recent history—the murder, in 1553, on the orders of Suleiman the Magnificent (1494–1566), of his eldest son, Şehzade Mustafa Muhlisi (1515–1553). After the death of the prince, the Janissaries and Anatolian soldiers of Mustafa rebelled against Suleiman's decision. The play thus wrestles with classical resistance theory at a point when this was being openly discussed at the court of James I. At the same time, it directly addresses the question in terms of a relation between a father and son – exactly the metaphor in which James himself couched the problem of loyalty and rebellion. And yet Greville's version of the story of Solyman clearly poses contradictory evidence: Mustapha is not a rebel, and his death, far from bringing peace, incites resistance against the monarch.

"Acts upon their true stage": the Ottoman Empire in early modern England

Mustapha and *Alaham* are, as Greville states in the "Dedication," "no plays for the stage."[7] However, they are more politically radical than many that had to pass the censors for the public stage. The dramas gave Greville the rein for a covert exposition of the vicissitudes of English political circumstances. The representation of Islam in Britain was undergoing a transformation in the early modern period.[8] The Ottoman Empire gave the focus for a range of treatises, pamphlets, and in time, plays.[9] In *Mustapha* and *Alaham*, Greville appropriates these contemporary representations of the Ottoman Empire, in order to undertake a complex investigation of their practices of power. *Mustapha*, especially, conceals its political and religious message through its setting in the Islamic court of Suleiman, the longest-reigning Sultan in the history of the Ottoman Empire. The Ottoman Sultan was both exemplar and rival in relation to Tudor royal power.[10] Suleiman appeared often in English plays.[11] The image of the historical Turkish Prince Mustapha became powerfully symbolic in the reign of Elizabeth as a reflection of the problem of succession, with a male heir murdered on the order of his reigning father. For the English nation, transfixed by the problem of producing a male heir at all, such paternal behaviour needed cultural explanation. The story of Mustapha and his father became familiar in sources like William Painter's *Palace of Pleasure*, John Foxe's *Actes and Monuments*, and Richard Hakluyt's *Voyages*, before being standardized in Richard Knolles's *Historie of the Turkes* (1603).[12] In plays like Robert Greene's *The Tragical Reign of Selimus*, and *The Tragedie of Soliman and Perseda*, usually attributed to Thomas Kyd, narratives of the violence of the Turkish court transferred to the stage.[13]

The European fear of Turkey was important in Elizabethan politics and Kyd's play panders to the image of Suleiman as an oriental despot, lusting for power and sexual gratification. Greville's source for his play appears to have been Nicholas de Moffan's history of Suleiman translated by Hugh Goughe in *The Ofspring of the House of Ottomano* (1569). Greville may also have known Gabriel Bounin's French play of 1561, which represents the assassination of Mustafa by his father.[14] However, Greville resists the temptation offered by Goughe to stereotype the Ottoman court in a monolithic way, by carefully delineating different strands of his argument through his dramatic principals. He presents the Turkish prince admiringly, emphasizing his Stoic indifference to his fate at the hands of a tyrant. Greville's Solyman, by contrast, cares only for his crown while sacrificing the blood of his son. His wife Hürrem Sultan (known to Europeans as Roxelana and by Greville as Rossa) is presented as a scheming woman who plots the demise of Mustapha to save the crown for her own son. By an irony of fate, Rossa ends up a victim to her own plot. Though all this, Greville finds the sophistication of the Turkish court alluring, but is apprehensive of the despotism of the Sultanate.

Jonathan Burton has commented on the play's expression of religious and political tolerance but is surely wrong in putting this down to an "accident of the story."[15] The tragedy of *Mustapha* is intricately related to an analysis of the nexus of monarchomach politics and neo-Calvinist religion. At some point between the two versions of *Mustapha*, Greville composed *A Treatise of Monarchy*, perhaps as early as 1610, focusing on the origin and nature of monarchy, and on the practical wisdom required to rule effectively. By 1625, *Monarchy* was excluded from Greville's plans for posthumous publication, presumably because he was aware that a discussion of the fallibility of monarchy might be prone to censorship.[16] Among the difficult subjects raised in *Monarchy* is the relationship of sovereignty to tyranny:

> Thus as we see these guides of humane kinde,
> Changed from Gods, and fathers to oppressors;
> Soe see wee tirannyes excesse of minde
> Against her own estate become transgressor;

> And either by her subjectes craft betray'd,
> Slayne by themselves, or by Gods judgementes sweyd.[17]

Kingship since the golden age has been in decline, a decline evident in the representation of the monarch as a kind of natural father. The theory of monarchy pursued by James I famously structured itself on an analogy with fatherhood, in which the king acts towards his subjects as a father does towards his children. Greville's text therefore intervenes directly in one of the most sensitive aspects of the Stuart ideology of the divine authority of kings.

In *A Treatie of Warrs*, the idea of the political father is given due observance:

> Is not even age due oddes to everie father,
> From whence we children owe them reverence?
> If he that hath have latitude to gather,
> Must he not yeild that cannot make defense?
> Have subjectes lawes to rectifie oppression;
> And Princes wronges no lawe, but intercession?[18]

Yet no sooner has the idea been broached, than it is exposed to a relentless questioning. Nine question marks appear in two stanzas, as political proposition and ideological statement run aground in doubt and uncertainty:

> Are there by nature Lordes, and servantes too?
> Was this world made indifferent to man?
> Doe Power, and honor followe them that doe?
> And yet are Kinges restrain'd from what they can?
> Gave nature other bounds of habitation
> Then strength, or weakenesse unto euery nation?
>
> (*Warrs*, st. 57)

Greville's writing here encounters a resistance to power that proves irresistible. This creates a paradoxical encounter with the metaphorics of sovereignty.

The *Dedication* indicates explicitly that Greville expects his plays to be read in relation to the politics of his own time and state, whatever their origin in the vexed religion and policy of the Ottoman Empire:

> But he that will behold these acts upon their true stage, let him look on that stage whereon himself is an actor, even the state he lives in, and for every part he may perchance find a player, and for every line (it may be) an instance of life beyond the author's intention or application.[19]

In the plays, Greville draws on the resources of humanist neo-Senecan tragedy both in English and in French in order to comment on problems of government and theories of state that are central to late sixteenth-century humanism.[20] Greville's plays share much of the intellectual framework of Marc-Antoine Muret's French *Julius Caesar*, translated into English by the Countess of Pembroke; Thomas Kyd's *Cornelia*; George Gascoigne's *Jocasta*; and Samuel Daniel's *Cleopatra*. In particular, Greville shows an obsession with familial fortunes. The representation of fathers and sons, and of mothers and sons, and indeed every filial relation, is fraught with difficulty.

In *Alaham*, there is a debate on fatherhood in the very first scene of the play:

> Alaham. Father, descendinge kindnesse signifies:
> Our State is there, where our well beinge lies.[21]

The priest, Heli, doubts whether Alaham's glory will be short-lived if he stands against his father. The *Chorus Primus* at the end of this scene once again expresses the conventional view, that a son must never rise against his father:

> Out of which fatall guide *Alaham* nowe vndertakes
> The ruine of his Kinge, and father, for ambitions sake;
> Against the lawes of Nations, power, and natiue blood;
> As if the uttermost of ill a sceptre could make good.
>
> (1.Chorus, 53–6)

The rest of the play in some ways confirms the orthodox position on resistance theory. And yet *Alaham* is also charged with anxiety, as if the dynamics of family relations have contorted the state of political theory. In *Mustapha*, as we shall see, these tensions come to the surface and occupy the whole play. In this respect, *Mustapha* proves to be central to Greville's political concerns. Among other things, the play is a kind of ironic commentary on divine right theory, and particularly on the patriarchalist model. Solyman has a pathological paranoia that his son Mustapha is conspiring to murder him. Despite overwhelming evidence to the contrary, the king will not believe his eyes but instead gives into a filicidal jealousy; ironically, the death of his son gives rise immediately to an attempted rebellion. Some of the most interesting passages in the play therefore concern Soliman's discourses on fatherhood and kingship with his judicious counsellor Achmat.

Greville's analysis of the politics of patriarchy has political, philosophical, and theological sources. Freya Sierhuis demonstrates that Greville's resistance to patriarchalism shares common ground with Étienne de la Boétie's *Discours de la servitude volontaire*.[22] Greville indeed shows a complex neo-Calvinist resistance to the image of fatherhood in the ideological formation of nationhood. But he is also a pronounced monarchist.

His writings ponder political conformity and absolutist ideology, and yet also express a pervasive scepticism. He combines an attachment to Roman Stoic political values (notably Tacitus and Seneca), with an increasingly pessimistic version of Calvinist predestinarianism.[23]

The politics of patriarchy in the seventeenth century

The idea of fatherhood is central to the Stuart debate about kingship. James I himself outlined this theory of monarchy in a speech to parliament in March 1610:

> There be three principal similitudes that illustrate the state of mon-
> archy: one taken out of the word of God; and the two other out of the
> grounds of policy and philosophy. In the Scriptures kings are called
> gods, and so their power after a certain relation compared to the
> divine power. Kings are also compared to fathers of families; for a
> king is truly *parens patriae*, the politic father of his people. And lastly,
> kings are compared to the head of this microcosm of the body of
> man.[24]

James presents the relation in metaphorical terms as a "similitude" to "illustrate" an idea. This helps restrain the implicit blasphemy of comparing himself directly with God. The phrase, "after a certain relation," is therefore circumspect. Yet this contrasts with the certainty with which the idea then becomes reified: "for a king is truly *parens patriae*, the politic father of his people." James may find problems with identifying himself as God, but not as a parent with quasi-divine rule over his family.

The idea was the source of controversy leading up to, during, and after the civil wars, and survived them into the Restoration. Sir William Temple, shortly after his removal as ambassador to the United Netherlands due to his support of a Dutch alliance, produced in 1673 his *Observations Upon the United Provinces of the Netherlands*, which justified the idea of alliance with the Dutch against France and which also endeavoured (stylishly and with sympathetic humour) to explain the idiosyncrasies of Dutch behaviour and customs to their sceptical English brethren and neighbours. At much the same time Temple wrote his *Essay upon the Original and Nature of Government*, where despite explicitly disavowing a Hobbesian model of government as social contract, he revived what by the 1670s appeared to be a decidedly old-fashioned characterization of the nation as a kind of natural family:

> the Governour or King of a Nation, ... is indeed a *Pater patriae*, as the
> best Kings are, and as all should be; and as those which are not, are
> yet content to be called. Thus the peculiar compellation of the Kings
> in France, is by the name of *Sire*, which in their ancient language is

nothing else but Father, and denotes the Prince to be the Father of the Nation. For a Nation properly signifies a great number of Families, derived from the same Blood, born in the same Countrey, and living under the same Government and Civil Constitutions: As *Patria* does the land of our Father; and so the *Dutch* by expressions of deerness, instead of our Countrey, say our *Father-land*. With such Nations we find in Scripture all the Lands of *Judea*, and the adjacent Territories, were planted of old. With such we find the many several Provinces of *Greece* and *Italy*, when they began first to appear upon the Records of Ancient Story or Tradition. And with such was the main Land of *Gaul* inhabited in the time of *Caesar*; and *Germany* in that of Tacitus. Such were the many Branches of the old *British* Nation.[25]

A nation in Temple's terms is a form of extended family. It does not primarily describe a geographical unit or a convenience of political arrangement, although both of these principles are adumbrated within it; it describes a blood-line or common ancestry, and a mutual loyalty based on family ties. This principle Temple identifies as universal to human societies, whether ancient or modern, Christian or Jewish, theocratic or pagan.

J. P. Sommerville has argued that the strength of patriarchalist political theory lies precisely in its basis in a social norm derived from nature.[26] Temple, a dozen years after the restoration of King Charles II, re-establishes the monarch as the head of this family. The ties of blood and filial duty make national identity and political structure a law by nature rather than by theory or election. In this way, Temple's discussion brings to fruition a famous work by Sir Robert Filmer, *Patriarcha: The Naturall Power of Kings defended against the Unnatural Liberty of the People*. Although first published in 1680, it pre-dates Hobbes's *Leviathan*; Sommerville dates one manuscript to before 1631 and the other to 1635–1642.[27] Because of its late printing, it acquired wide currency among supporters of royal authority in the 1680s and 1690s; John Locke spent a large part of his *First Treatise of Government* refuting it. The first chapter, however, Sommerville surmises may have been written in the 1620s. It can therefore be seen as a culmination of Jacobean theory of kingship. Here is an unapologetic statement of absolute monarchy in English, and at the same time an astonishingly frank assertion of patriarchal thinking, making it newly notorious in recent years among feminist historians.[28]

In making his argument, Filmer constantly draws on the writings of the sixteenth-century political theorist, Jean Bodin, from whom every seventeenth-century discussion of sovereignty draws extensively.[29] Filmer himself issued a pamphlet called *The Necessity of the Absolute Power of all Kings* in 1648, virtually an anthology of quotations from Richard Knolles's English translation of Bodin's *The Six Bookes of a Commonwealth* (1606).[30] To Bodin's outline theory, Filmer adds the status of fatherhood as a definition of authority and the nation:

In all Kingdoms or Commonwealths in the World, whether the Prince be the Supreme Father of the People, or but the true Heir of such a Father, or whether he come to the Crown by Usurpation, or by Election of the Nobles, or of the People, or by any other way whatsoever; or whether some Few or a Multitude govern the Commonwealth: yet still the Authority that is in any One, or in Many, or in All these, is the only Right and Natural Authority of a Supreme Father. There is and always shall be continued to the End of the World, a Natural Right of a Supreme Father over every Multitude.[31]

It is an odd assertion, as it asserts a "natural right" while denaturalizing the circumstances of that right. A king rules as a father even when he is not a father or even a single individual. Locke scoffed that of course a natural father has no such absolute power, as he is a mere subject.[32] In time, Filmer's patriarchalist theory came head to head with the theory of contract, and never really recovered.[33] For Filmer virtually contradicts himself by deriving the king's powers from a principle in nature, which transcends nature itself.

This sets up a profound problem of metaphor in the idea of the father of the nation. With a certain wicked genius, Hobbes created his proof that political relationships are conventional and not natural, by stating that "it cannot be known who is the Father, unlesse it be declared by the Mother."[34] Yet Filmer denies the idea that he is being hopelessly literal-minded here. He agrees that "It may seem absurd to maintain that Kings now are the Fathers of their People, since Experience shews the contrary. It is true, all Kings be not the Natural Parents of their Subjects."[35] But fatherly rule, while not to be taken literally, acts with more force than a metaphor. The prince has the same rights in the real world as a natural father has over his children. In such a way a prince is allowed to act against the ordinary rules of the natural world, and has authority over his elders. Indeed, he says, "many a Child, by succeeding a King, hath the Right of a Father over many a Gray-headed Multitude, and hath the Title of *Pater Patriae*."[36]

Pater patriae *and English political theory*

The ancient title of *pater patriae* takes us into the heart of the nexus of sovereignty, nation, and fatherhood. In classical Rome it was an honorific title, first bestowed on Cicero during his consulate in 63 CE, because of his part in the suppression of Catiline's conspiracy. It was conferred on Julius Caesar and then on Augustus, but while thereafter it was often granted to the Roman emperor, it was not part of the office or *imperium* of state. Rather it implied a special status, perhaps after a long reign or as a mark of esteem, as an elder statesman or venerable ruler. It suggested an emotional bond between sovereign and people, which went beyond the logic of the law. As such it then passed into post-classical usage. In Renaissance Italy, it was used by Cosimo de' Medici in Florence.[37] In the Netherlands, it was translated into Dutch as early as 1571 for the benefit of William the Silent as *vader des vaderlands*.[38] It was used on occasion in England by Henry VIII, and later adopted, at times aggressively, by the Stuart kings before and after the Restoration.[39]

The word *patria* does not always make its etymology obvious, but lurks as a buried metaphor. The *patria* is the land of our fathers, or is like a father to us. It bears us, nurtures us, looks after us, but also rules us and punishes us if we do wrong. In Dutch (or German) the phrase *vader des vaderlands* is a tautology. In Latin it works more like a pun: there is a happy coincidence between the role of the ruler as a *pater* and the nation as a *patria*. In English, however, lacking an available natural idiom of "fatherland," the connection either has to be forced or else brought in via a foreign language. Just as Latin inflects a paronomasia between *pater* and *patria*, Filmer tries to retrieve this from Latin via the inkhorn term *patriarchia* or the English "patriarchy." The word "patriarchy," in the sense of a social organization with a father as its head, was still a new word.[40] Within the metaphorics of the vocabulary of nationhood and fatherland lie the parameters of political theory and ideology.

Filmer uses the analogy of fatherhood not only to enforce a principle of natural authority of rule, but also to counter an alternative theory of liberty or of choice in the selection of government. In the first page of his treatise he rebuts the notion that:

> Mankind is naturally endowed and born with Freedom from all Subjection, and at liberty to choose what Form of Government it please: And that the Power which any one Man hath over others, was at first bestowed according to the discretion of the Multitude.
>
> (2)

Naturally, he says, this idea is popular with the common people, and most especially "the meanest of the multitude," because of its "prodigal" distribution of rights and freedoms to all. Filmer's repudiation is based first of all on Holy Scripture: those who regard liberty as "the height of human felicity" have obviously forgotten the example of our common father Adam, for whom "the desire of liberty was the cause of the fall." This argument from Scripture is backed up by a reading of history, which shows that the idea of liberty of choice contradicts the practice of all the ancient monarchies. Yet behind all of Filmer's argument lies a conviction even stronger, that his understanding of political theory is written into the very "law of nature." Parental rights underscore political rights, and guarantee the rule of law and the chain of authority. Giving the people the liberty of choosing their ruler is like giving a child the choice of its own parents, that is, an impossibility. Deriving the power of a ruler from its investment in the will of the people is similarly tantamount to allowing a child the right to choose who will rule him instead, a thing equally ridiculous in nature. This is not only unnatural but also insane. "It is hard to say," Filmer concludes, "whether it be more erroneous in divinity or dangerous in policy."

As if to clinch his case Filmer attributes the erroneous opinion to Catholics and Calvinists. On the basis of the argument from liberty, "both Jesuits and some over zealous favourers of the Geneva discipline," he writes with horror, have argued for the right of the multitude to "punish" their prince or "deprive" him from power, if he transgresses the laws of the kingdom. He cites with equanimity theological opposites: the Jesuit Robert Persons from *A Conference about the Next Succession to the Crown of Ingland* (1594) and the humanist quasi-Protestant George Buchanan from *De Iure regni apud Scotos*. Further evidence of such seditious support of resistance theory is adduced from both Bellarmine and Calvin. These references to the Jesuits and Calvinists, however, as well as shoring up Filmer's orthodoxy in relation to the Stuart kings, also show the vulnerability of his argument to a theological counter-attack from either wing. It is always wise to remember, as Jonathan Scott has argued, how much seventeenth-century English political thought needs to be understood in the context of radical religion, even when expressed by someone religiously conformist.[41] This also shows us some of the reasons why, despite Filmer's assertiveness, the figure of the father was prone to ambiguity and controversy. Indeed, Filmer's assertiveness may itself be a symptom of the difficulty of establishing these notions within an English-speaking idiom.

Mustapha *and the fall of the father*

In his *Trew Lawe of Free Monarchies*, written in 1598 while he was still king of Scotland only, James VI extolled the care of a king for his subjects as identical to "the naturall love" of a father to his children.[42] Monarchical rule is based on the power of his emotional connection with his people, a kind of triumph of empathy. The king feels the same "toile and paine," he foresees "all inconueniences and dangers that may arise towards his children" and, without any consideration of personal safety, like a parent he forestalls every threat or anxiety that his offspring encounters.[43] By the same token, when his people err and stray from the path of virtue, the kingly father adjusts his empathetic emotion accordingly, and feels instead "wrath and correction" (65). His emotions never let him down; like the scriptural God who feels anger or jealousy, his feelings are a direct reflection of the true state of things.

Some explanation is needed here, since the idea of sympathetic emotion is a tenuous one in the early modern period. The emotions or "passions" in general were undergoing a systematic re-evaluation.[44] "Sympathy" in particular has usually been seen as an invention of the eighteenth century, although Seth Lobis's book has gone some way to redressing this balance.[45]

However, the origins of "sympathy" in English lie in physics and magic: a property which connects material things, as metals attract each other by magnetism. Lobis shows the beginnings of a transference of this meaning to the world of emotions. In the early seventeenth century there is a move towards identifying a kind of fellow-feeling, in which one person's feelings can be matched by their presence in another. A writer who is especially interesting in this regard is John Donne. God not only wills man and woman to become one flesh, but also "to become one soule so, as that they might maintaine a simpathy in their affections, and haue a conformity to one another."[46] At such a point, Donne develops what might be called a prototype theory of empathy, in which feeling becomes physically transferable from one human body to another, via a kind of metempsychosis.[47]

Greville's play *Mustapha* uses these developments to turn the theory of *pater patriae*, which acts as a deep-lying metaphor in Jacobean policy, into a living embodiment. The struggles of Mustapha become a trope for political analysis.[48] It is the revised version in the Warwick Manuscript which is the subject of the discussion here. In the opening scene of the play, Solyman gives voice to the empathy of kings in a way that appears to do apt justice to James's *Trew Lawe of Free Monarchies*:

> Solyman. *Rossa!* Th'eternall wisdome doth not covet
> Of man, his strength, or reason; but his love.
> And not in vayne: Since love, of all the pow'res,
> Is it which governs everie thought of ours.[49]

Solyman has a seeming inalienable certainty about his emotions as he begins the play. Yet almost immediately, the affective power of monarchy is exposed to conflict. Solyman develops the concept of kingly "love" into an idea of "kindness," as a natural power beyond any other. However, having declaimed his love as his own governor, "kindnesse" he sees as a weakness. Just as Alaham descends into multiple self-questioning, Greville deploys the interrogative with sensitive power in making Solyman sense his emotional conundrum. "Doth kindnesse lessen Kinges authoritie? (1.1.12)," he asks, rhetorically. Solyman believes he must put kindness to one side:

> Solyman. This frayltie in my selfe I conquer must,
> And stay the false untimely hopes it worckes,
> Threatninge the fathers ruine in the sonne.
> Manye with trust, with doubt fewe are undonne.

(1.1.15–18)

How are we to explain his *volte face*? Here, it is interesting that Solyman perceives "kindnesse" as a form of "frayltie." It is a feminine emotion at odds with the expression of patriarchy.

However, if the reader is tempted to follow Solyman in his self-justification, and accept this conveniently gendered rule of emotion, it is exposed to further insinuation by the intervention of Solyman's wife, Rossa. Rossa is Mustapha's step-mother and eagerly supports Solyman in the interpretation of his dilemma in order to press the advantage for her own son as a rival heir.

> Rossa. [*aside*] This is the glasse which father lookes not in;
> The worckman hides, the instrumentes discover:
> See how it fittes a Kinge to be a louer?
>
> (1.2.116–118)

If Solyman has been tempted to espouse his own virtue as a noble rejection of his feminine side, Greville reveals to the reader how he is only deceiving himself. Rossa plays the part of masculine virtue to perfection in projecting Solyman's assumption of patriarchal values as a convenient fiction.

As a closet drama, Greville's play revels in set-piece debates of a formal kind in which the two interlocutors speak at cross purposes. The scene between husband and wife is followed by one between king and counsellor. In the magnificent Act 2, scene 2, Solyman and Achmat act out a dialogue on kingship in which the arch positions of Jacobean theory go head to head. Solyman by now is in full torment between opposing views of his own identity as pater patriae. If James's theory implies the two principles act in harmony, Solyman is wracked by self-analysis. On the one hand, he recognizes the thought that his emotion and his monarchy must be indivisible. On the other hand, this very indivisibility is the source of his problems. His emotions are making him into a tyrant, and a homicidal monster:

> Solyman. Doth Kinges restraint of wrath appeare like feare?
> Shall our remissenesse suffer more then this?
> Can horror onely, adoration beare?
>
> (2.2.9–11)

James in his speech to parliament invokes the theory of the body politic in order to efface the distinction between the king's two bodies. However, Solyman digresses into this theory only to deconstruct it:

> Must Kinges that change this likenesse loose their owne?
> Two states I beare: his Father, and his Kinge;
> Theise two, being relatives, have mutuall bondes;
> Neglect in either, all in question bringes.
>
> (2.2.14–17)

The division between natural and political monarchy only serves to create a divided state. If the two go together, they also fall together, as the state splits in two.

Solyman is no longer able to maintain the distinction between a masculine "love" and a feminine "kindness," and questions fatherly love altogether:

> And shall love be a chayne, tied to my Crowne,
> Either to helpe him up, or pull me downe?
>
> (2.2.36–37)

There follows an extraordinary disavowal of the central doctrine of Stuart monarchy:

> No: No. This *Father*-Language fittes not *Kinges*,
> Whose publique, universall providence
> Of *Thinges*, not *Persons*, alwayes must haue sense.
> With justice I these mistie doubtes will cleare.
> And he that breakes Divine, and Humane lawe,
> Shall no protection out of either drawe.
>
> (2.2.38–43)

Monarchy requires the rejection of emotion, not its triumph. The moment is so powerful it reads like a kind of sovereign nervous breakdown. David Norbrook has commented brilliantly on how it is characteristic of Greville's writing to raise "radical sentiments" but almost as quickly to repress them.[50] Greville is certainly brazen enough in showing a repudiation of the pieties of Jacobean patriarchy ("This *Father*-language fittes not *Kinges*"), but then immediately checks the moment in an effort of self-censorship. No sooner is Solyman's radical idea uttered than it is exposed to further revolution. Achmat attempts to soften his king's purpose and advises against Solyman's renewed determination to seek the death of his supposedly seditious son. Yet Solyman replies with further self-contradiction.

Having just recanted the emotional solipsism of kingship, he now justifies his course of action by rejecting his recantation. Whatever rational advice is offered by his counsellor Achmat, the king knows better, because he feels it as a king, and a king's feelings are never in the wrong:

> Sol. Thought is with God an act: Kinges cannot see
> Th'intentes of mischeife, but with jealousie.
>
> (2.2.71–72)

Solyman's nervous breakdown is now in full swing. Yet if so, he is now back in accord with the orthodoxy of Jacobean political theory. James had said in *Trew Lawe of Free Monarchies* that "Kings are called Gods" (64), a view discussed at still greater length in his *Basilicon Doron*.[51] So

Solyman now refers to his judgements in terms of divine intuitions. Just as God's speech acts eliminate the gap between saying and doing, so God's emotional instincts eradicate any distinction between feeling and acting. If the king feels jealous, the object of his jealousy must be planning assassination or sedition. Solyman's suspicions of his son are de facto evidence of his son's intentions towards rebellion.

Achmat replies in alarm, perhaps thinking his king has lost his mind. The debate now becomes brittle, as the formal speeches fragment into an abrupt stychomichia:

> Achmat. In what protection then lives innocence?
> Sol. Belowe the dangers of Omnipotence.
> Achmat. Are thoughtes, and deedes confounded anie where?
> Sol. In Princes lives, that may not suffer feare.
>
> (2.2.73–76)

This is, Achmat states, a theory without limits, and further implies that it is a route into inevitable tyranny. His king has become an emotional despot and at the same time a slave to his emotions. But however much Achmat demurs, Solyman only redoubles his certainty. Indeed, the opposition of the subject only proves the monarch must be right.

Achmat replies that Solyman's theory is an invitation to rebellion rather than a bulwark against it:

> Achmat. This is the way to make Accusers prowd,
> And feede up starved spite with guiltlesse bloode.
>
> (2.2.79–80)

He advises a compromise: disinherit Mustapha and let Rossa's sons ruke after him. This way, a mother's jealousy can be assuaged, and order restored. But Solyman replies that Achmat, too, is a victim of emotional cliché in assuming that Rossa is acting only out of jealousy. He knows, by a king's instinct, that Mustapha is plotting "Parricide" (2.2.108). Not to act on this by arresting and condemning Mustapha would be a negligence of kingly duty. At this point, Achmat accuses Solyman outright of "tyranny":

> Achmat. Tyrantes they are that punishe out of feare.
> States wiser than the truth decline, and weare.
>
> (2.2.112–113)

Perhaps it is no surprise that Solyman counters in kind by calling out Achmat as a "Traitor":

> Solym. Traytor! Must I doubt all to creditte thee?
>
> (2.2.119)

Achmat's reply is full of resigned irony:

> Ach. No lesse is truth, where Kinges deceiv'd will be.
>
> (2.2.120)

He appeals to a power even beyond monarchy, in its original form as divine law:

> Ach. God, euen to himselfe, hath made a lawe.
>
> (2.2.128)

This not a challenge of the king's authority, more of a reminder to the king of the basis on which he claims to have authority.

However arbitrary Soyman's rule has now become, and however closely he is made to imitate a Jacobean mental framework, an observer might still be surprised at Solyman's forebearance at this point: would James I have tolerated Achmat's honesty? Solyman instead earnestly seek Achmat's advice. This comes in the form of axiomatic principles of adamantine reasonableness:

> Ach. Sir! where Kinges doubt, wisdome, and lawes provide
> Due triall, and restraint of libertie;
> And unto caution their estate is tied:
> But where Kinges rage becomes superlative,
> There people doe forbeare, but not forgive.
>
> (2.2.141–145)

In the process, some of the cornerstones of Greville's politics emerge in Achmat's voice. Of note first of all, are certain points of principle: the sovereignty of law in an abstract sense rather than in either the person or the institution of monarchy. This puts Greville apparently on the same side as the monarchomachs, and superficially the play at this point reads like a trenchant critique of absolutism. Yet this is allied to a sceptical position on the limits of liberty in relation to sovereignty. The law provides "Due triall, and restraint of libertie": freedom is not his overaching principle, as it is of many opponents of absolutism. Yet just as important as these issues of theory is Achmat's sceptical tone. This is as much literary as it is philosophical. Achmat follows the stoic pattern of Seneca in providing "caution": he desists from Solyman's position because his master has given in to "Kinges rage" and thus transgressed the proper boundaries of the passions. To stoicism, Greville adds a dose of Calvinist theology. The appeal to divine right goes beyond the limits set to power within a Calvinist polity. All of this intellectual turmoil is reflected in the terse, energetic argumentation of Greville's verse.

The further twist here is how Greville takes advantage of the Islamic context to say things that might be unsayable in relation to Christian

Europe. Since Solyman is a Muslim king, anything politically inappropriate to the Stuart sensibility can be attributed to his apostate circumstances. And yet Greville is not negative towards Islam, indeed in many ways he is openly fascinated and even sympathetic. The king's piety and devotion are not in doubt, and his religion endows him with complex values: steadfastness, sensitivity, self-criticism, and a constant yearning for improvement in the ways of virtue. He is caught on the horns of an impossible dilemma, and he falls increasingly into making wrong decisions. Nonetheless, the decisions are sophisticated ones, as his tortuous conflict over fatherhood. He is caught between an image of paternity based on reason and necessity; and another based on passion and chance. Much of this dilemma would be virtually unsayable in relation to a Christian God, or a Calvinist theodicy. Solyman treads on the most sensitive territory of theological politics in the post-Reformation world, and he is free to do so because he is Muslim.

The grand political theatre of Act 2, scene 2 is matched by another set-piece drama of the intellect in Act 4, scene 4. By now Solyman is committed to the murder of Mustapha, who is now placed in a parallel dilemma of action: should he rebel, and hence justify the king's suspicions, or submit and die at his command. The agony of the father in Act 2 is now matched by the agony of the son in Act 4. The symmetry between the scenes is not just one of patriarchal values. It also opens out the nervous energy of the early modern passions, as the principle of active virtue finds its fruition in a decisive moment of passive humiliation. There is one further ideological collision, as Mustapha feels himself drawn towards an existential crisis: to prove himself loyal in reality, he has to admit to his father's fantasy that he is a rebel; and to create for himself the space for stoic freedom, he has to submit to the logic of necessity, in which his own agency is annihilated. Out of the narrative elements of the reign of Solyman the Magnificent, and from the seemingly intractable folly of the central act of his reign, Greville distils his distinctive political philosophy. Sovereignty conceived as personal agency is a dystopian myth which leads to fatalistic violence.

Just as the wise counsellor Achmat is the foil for Solyman, so now the priest performs the same role for Mustapha. By this means the theological stakes are raised. Mustapha now knows the score, but he stands by his father even though his father will kill him. This is dangerous ground for Greville, but once again he conceals his radical argument behind the Islamic context. To submit to the necessitarian dogmatics of Solyman's patriarchal theology, is like a literalization of the Calvinist theory of predestination. *God has made me this way; I am his to do with as he wishes.* If he must murder me, who am I to stand in his way. Greville proposes this with breathtaking theological flair. But like Calvin before him, he does not flinch. In a passage added to the *Institutio* in the final edition of 1559, Calvin declares: *Decretum quidem horribile, fateor*

("The decree is dreadful indeed, I confess").[52] Calvin is made out by his opponents, then and now, to be implacable in his certainty: but the word *horribile*, repeated from an earlier phrase in Book III, *horribilis Dei maiestas* ("God's dread majesty,") shows that his doctrinal stance is complex.[53] He includes the force of the objection (*fateor*, "I confess") rather than deflects it; he understands the emotional gravity of his opponents; he is forced as if against his will to believe the fierce majesty of what he is expressing. This is all the more reason for believing it, and for rejoicing in that belief. Predestination does not come under the heading of the doctrine of God in Book I, but is reserved until Book III as part of the doctrine of salvation. It is presented as the clear result of a correct reading of scripture, whereby God predestinates some to salvation, others to destruction. Otherwise grace would not be grace (Romans 11:5). Yet it is also presented, from the beginning, as an idea which inspires opposition.

Greville borrows from Calvin this rhetoric of the unsayable: the structure of the world is ineluctable, but it is not therefore unliveable.[54] Stoicism meets Calvinism head on in Mustapha's graceful acceptance of the father's demand. Jonathan Dollimore has argued that Greville's play shows the "disintegration of providentialist belief."[55] Yet this suggests that scepticism can only exist outside the Christian framework. Greville's analysis is both more sensitive and more stark: God may be darker than we thought, making demands of us that we cannot answer for. The scene begins calmly, the dialogue resembling a fugue formed out of a lucid realm of ideas which lie outside and beyond the personal:

> Priest. Can'st thou forgive? Rather avoyd the cause,
> Which else makes mercie more severe then lawes.
> Mustapha. From man, to man duties are but respectes,
> The groundes wherof are meere humanitie:
> Can justice other there then mercie be?
>
> (4.4.77–81)

"Thought is an act," the Priest reflects (4.4.82). Is he repeating the mantra of Solyman, "Thought is with God an Act" (2.2.71)? Solyman used the dictum to justify his own arbitrary absolutism, but the Priest utters it in a manner seemingly purified of the personal. Mustapha redescribes patriarchal absolutism as a transcendental law of truth:

> Must. Good world; where it is danger to be good.
> Yet grudge I not power of my selfe to Power:
> This basenesse onely in mankinde I blame,
> That indignation should give lawes to fame.
> Shewe me the truth. To what rules am I bound?
>
> (4.4.105–109)

Up to this point, Mustapha presents his action as one of choice; but from half way through the scene, a different logic, of necessity, takes over:

> Priest. Fatall necessitie is never knowne
> Untill it strike: and till that blowe be come,
> Who falles, is by false visions overthrowne.
>
> (4.4.139–141)

A play about human monarchical command now becomes a tragedy of necessity.

The crucial context here to understand is once again that Greville is able to distinguish between divine and monarchical absolutism because the God in question is the Muslim God:

> Must. Is it in vs to rule a *Sultans* will?
> Priest. We made them first for good, and not for ill.
> Must. Our Gods they are, their God remaines above.
>
> (4.4.148–150)

This enables Greville to give voice to a political trajectory which was almost unthinkable in Jacobean England:

> Priest. Are men no more? Are Kinges annoynted blood
> Prophane to them, and sacred vnto vs?
> Playes Power with lawes of God, and Nature thus?
> Shall sorrowe write this storie of oppression
> Onely in idle teares, and not in blood?
>
> (4.4.182–186)

Scepticism about the divine right of kings has become open, and is allowed to be so because the divine right is not Christian. Yet Greville is artful in this obliquity. He can hold open one line of inquiry by shutting off another. A good example is the way that he suggests a belief in absolutism is a result of human error, or what he calls the "false *Labyrinth* of humane feare" (4.4.188). The result is that while Solyman descends into tyrannical solipsism, Mustapha aspires to a Christ-like equanimity in the face of death, an apotheosis described by Achmat at the tragic dénouement of the play in Act 5, scene 2:

> Achmat. Till *Mustapha*, in haste to be an Angell,
> With heavenlie smiles, and quiet wordes, foreshowes
> The joy, and peace of those soules where he goes.
> His last words were: O *father! Nowe forgive me.*
> *Forgive them too, that wrought my ouerthrowe:*
> *Let my graue never minister offences.*

> For, since my Father coveteth my death,
> Behold, with joy, I offer him my breath.

                                                    (5.2.81–88)

Mustapha finds redemption in an ultimate act of humility.

The play thus represents to the full the dilemma of seventeenth-century political theology. By Solyman's analysis, to be a good king is to relinquish the desire to be a good father. The personal life must be abandoned for the public good. Yet this is a contradiction, because as a good king he is applying the feelings that a good father normally has for his child, only projected now onto the people, his subjects at large. The public good is based on the fatherly instincts of the king. At some level, then, Greville exposes the patriarchal conception of kingship as contradictory. In the process he exposes it as dangerous and violent. If James felt that the dangers of the state could be averted by mirroring family life within the practice of the state, Greville finds this emotional symmetry the greatest danger of all. *Mustapha* the play manifests not so much a triumph of empathy as a tyranny of empathy. A rule of authority based on this principle seems to him not to follow the "law of nature" as Filmer later expressed it, but on the contrary a descent into the realm of the arbitrary whims of desire and the passions.

Greville formulates a suspicion of and reluctance for what he dubs "father-language." Yet he was also a principled monarchist and not an overt defender of resistance theory. His position on kingship and on authority is notably conservative. J. G. A. Pocock therefore regards any radical tendencies in Greville to be submerged in orthodoxy.[56] However, *Mustapha* maintains a classical balance between opposing poles of theory. It allows a radical stance on patriarchalism to exist alongside a pessimistic view of human nature. In this way, neo-Calvinism is still a form of critique, certainly enough for Greville's contemporaries to view him as subversive, even after the civil wars. This is expressed at greater length in Greville's philosophical poems, *Monarchy* and *Of Religion*, which show the same recoil from an idealization of fatherhood as in *Mustapha*, combined with epigrammatic rejection of the optimism of the Stuart claim to socially normative standards of sovereignty:

> And though they serve ambitious Princes use,
> While they protecte them, like a nursinge father;
> And while this common traffique of abuse
> Mutuallie helpeth either side to gather:
> Yet marcke the end of false combined trust;
> It will divide, and smart the people must.[57]

This reads in a way like a prophecy of civil war and political breakdown. Yet if Greville foresaw the catastrophe of Stuart political absolutism, he chose to identify it most vividly, in ironic form, in his Islamic tragedies of state.

Notes

1 *The Remains of Sir Fulk Grevill Lord Brooke Being Poems of Monarchy and Religion: Never Before Printed* (London: Henry Herringman, 1670).
2 *The Life of the Renowned Sr Philip Sidney. With the True Interest of England as it Then Stood in Relation to All Forrain Princes: And Particularly for Suppressing the Power of Spain Stated by Him. Written by Sir Fulke Grevil Knight, Lord Brook, a Servant to Queen Elizabeth, and His Companion & Friend* (London: Henry Seile, 1651).
3 London, British Library [henceforth BL], MS Add. 54567, fo. 1r.
4 *Certaine Learned and Elegant Vvorkes of the Right Honorable Fulke Lord Brooke Written in His Youth, and Familiar Exercise with Sir Philip Sidney* (London: Henry Seyle, 1633).
5 There is also a MS copy of the early text: Cambridge University Library MS Ff. 2. 35. See *The Complete Poems and Plays of Fulke Greville, Lord Brooke (1554–1628)*, ed. G. A. Wilkes, 2 vols (Lewiston: Edwin Mellen Press, 2008), i.9 and i.13–5. Until the appearance of the forthcoming *Clarendon Edition of the Works of Fulke Greville* (5 vols), Wilkes is preferred here to the edition of Geoffrey Bullough (*Poems and Dramas of Fulke Greville*, 2 vols (Edinburgh: Oliver & Boyd, 1939)), since Wilkes bases his text on the MSS rather than *Certaine learned and elegant vvorkes*.
6 Ronald A. Rebholz, *The Life of Fulke Greville: First Lord Brooke* (Oxford: Clarendon Press, 1971), 237–246 and 255–271.
7 "Dedication to Sir Philip Sidney," in *The Prose Works of Fulke Greville, Lord Brooke*, ed. John Gouws (Oxford: Oxford UP, 1986), 134.
8 Nabil Matar, *Islam in Britain 1558–1685* (Cambridge: Cambridge UP, 1998), 1–20.
9 Matthew Dimmock, *New Turkes: Dramatizing Islam and the Ottomans in Early Modern England* (Aldershot: Ashgate, 2005), chs 1–2.
10 Jerry Brotton, *The Sultan and the Queen: The Untold Story of Elizabeth and Islam* (London: Penguin Books, 2017).
11 Dimmock, *New Turkes*, 189–195.
12 Richard Knolles, *The Generall Historie of the Turkes from the First Beginning of That Nation to the Rising of the Othoman Familie* (London: Adam Islip, 1603).
13 Daniel Cadman, *Sovereign and Subjects in Early Modern Neo-Senecan Drama: Republicanism, Stoicism and Authority* (Farnham and Burlington: Ashgate, 2015), 74.
14 Gilian Jondorf, *French Renaissance Tragedy: The Dramatic Word*, rev. ed. (Cambridge: Cambridge UP, 2006), 155.
15 Jonathan Burton, *Traffic and Turning: Islam and English Drama, 1579–1624* (Cranbury: University of Delaware Press, 2005), 193.
16 John Gouws, "Greville, Fulke, first Baron Brooke of Beauchamps Court (1554–1628)," in *Oxford Dictionary of National Biography*, Oxford UP, 2004; online edition, May 2007 www.oxforddnb.com.libproxy.york.ac.uk/view/article/11516.
17 *A Treatise of Monarchy*, stanza 79; in *Poems and Plays*, ed. Wilkes, II, 51.
18 *A Treatie of Warrs*, stanza 56; in *Poems and Plays*, ed. Wilkes, II, 227. Further refs in text citing stanza number.
19 Gouws, ed. "Dedication," 135.
20 Cadman, *Sovereign and Subjects*, 69–91.

21 *Alaham*, 1.1.211–12; ed. Wilkes, op. cit., i.322. Further refs in text, citing act, scene, and line number. Wilkes's text is based on the Warwick MS (BL MS Add. 54568), in scribal hand *d*, with corrections in Greville's hand.

22 "The Idol of the Heart: Liberty, Tyranny, and Idolatry in the Work of Fulke Greville," *The Modern Language Review*, 106 (2011)" 625–646, this ref. 631.

23 Alan T. Bradford, "Stuart Absolutism and the 'Utility' of Tacitus," *Huntington Library Quarterly* 46 (1983): 127–155.

24 Speech by James I to Parliament (21 March 1609/10); the original manuscript version is in the National Archives, TNA SP 14/53/31. King James VI and I, *Political Writings*, ed. Johann P. Sommerville (Cambridge: Cambridge UP, 1994), 179–203.

25 William Temple, *Miscellanea. By a Person of Honour* (London: [A.M.] and [R.R.], 1680), 66.

26 Johann Sommerville, *Politics & Ideology in England 1603–1640* (London: Longman, 1986), 27.

27 Robert Filmer, *Patriarcha and Other Writings*, ed. Johann P. Sommerville (Cambridge: Cambridge UP, 1991), xxxiii. Sommerville draws on the argument of Richard Tuck, "A New Date for Filmer's *Patriarcha*," *Historical Journal*, 29 (1986): 183–186.

28 On the origins of patriarchal thinking in the seventeenth century, see James Daly, *Sir Robert Filmer and English Political Thought* (Toronto: University of Toronto Press, 1979), 59–61.

29 Daly, *Filmer and English Political Thought*, 21.

30 *Patriarcha*, xii.

31 Cited here using capitalization following the printed edition of *Patriarcha, or, The Natural Power of Kings* (London: Walter Davis, 1680), 22–23; see also the MS text in *Patriarcha*, 11.

32 *Selected Political Writings*, ed. Paul E. Sigmund (New York: W.W. Norton, 2005), 11.

33 Victoria Kahn, *Wayward Contracts: The Crisis of Political Obligation in England, 1640–1674* (Princeton: Princeton UP, 2009), 3; Joanna Picciotto, *Labors of Innocence in Early Modern England* (Cambridge, MS: Harvard UP, 2010), 78.

34 *Leviathan* (1651), "Of Dominion Paternall, and Despoticall," chapter 20 in *The Clarendon Edition of the Works of Thomas Hobbes*, vol. 4, *Leviathan: The English and Latin Texts*, ed. Noel Malcolm (Oxford: Oxford UP, 2013), 310. See also Kahn, *Wayward* Contracts, 166.

35 Filmer, *Patriarcha* (1680), 19.

36 Filmer, *Patriarcha* (1680), 20.

37 Alison M. Brown, "The Humanist Portrait of Cosimo de' Medici, *Pater Patriae*," *Journal of the Warburg and Courtauld Institutes*, 24 (1961): 186–221.

38 K. W. Swart, *Willem van Oranje en de Nederlandse opstand 1572–1584* (The Hague: Sdu, 1994), 128.

39 Su Fang Ng, *Literature and the Politics of Family in Seventeenth-Century England* (Cambridge: Cambridge UP, 2007), 12.

40 The *Oxford English Dictionary* gives as its first citation 1626, from a speech by Francis Bacon. "Patriarchy, *noun*." OED Online. June 2017. Oxford UP www. oed.com.libproxy.york.ac.uk/view/Entry/138873?redirectedFrom=patriarchy.

41 Jonathan Scott, *England's Troubles: Seventeenth-Century English Political Instability in European Context* (Cambridge: Cambridge UP, 2000), 229–245.

42 *Political Writings*, ed. Sommerville, 78.

43 *Political Writings*, ed. Sommerville, 65.

44 In a vast field, see especially: Thomas Dixon, *From Passions to Emotions: The Creation of a Secular Psychological Category* (Cambridge: Cambridge UP,

2003); Gail K. Paster, Katharine Rowe, and Mary Floyd-Wilson, eds., *Reading the Early Modern Passions: Essays in the Cultural History of Emotion* (Philadelphia: University of Pennsylvania Press, 2004); Brian Cummings and Freya Sierhuis, eds., *Passions and Subjectivity in Early Modern Culture* (Aldershot: Ashgate, 2013); Richard Meek and Erin Sullivan, eds., *The Renaissance of Emotion: Understanding Affect in Shakespeare and his Contemporaries* (Manchester: Manchester UP, 2015).

45 Seth Lobis, *The Virtue of Sympathy: Magic, Philosophy, and Literature in Seventeenth-Century England* (New Haven and London: Yale UP, 2015).

46 John Donne, *Devotions vpon emergent occasions* (London: Thomas Jones, 1624), sig. 2A2v–2A3r.

47 Brian Cummings, "From Sympathy to Empathy: Donne and Milton," *Sympathy in Transformation: Dynamics between Rhetorics, Poetics, and Ethics*, ed. Roman Alexander Barton, Alexander Klaudies and Thomas Micklich, Transformationen der Antike, 51 (Berlin and Boston: De Gruyter, 2018), 109–124.

48 Katrin Röder, *Macht und Imagination: Fulke Grevilles Konstruktion diskreter Autorschaft* (Heidelberg: Winter, 2006), 221–225.

49 *Mustapha*, 1.1.1–4; ed. Wilkes, op. cit., I, 211. Further refs in text, citing act, scene, and line number. Wilkes's text is based on the Warwick MS (BL MS Add. 54569), in scribal hand *d*, with corrections in Greville's hand.

50 David Norbrook, *Poetry and Politics in the English Renaissance*, rev. ed. (Oxford: Oxford UP, 2002), 142.

51 See also *Basilicon Doron*, in *Political Writings*, ed. Sommerville, 1.

52 *Institutio*, 3, 23, 7; in Jean Calvin, *Opera selecta*, ed. Peter Barth and Wilhelm Niesel, 2nd ed., 5 vols (München: Christian Kaiser, 1926–1962), III, 401, trans. by F. L. Battles in *The Institutes of the Christian Religion*, ed. John T. McNeill, 2 vols (Philadelphia: Westminster Press, 1960), II, 955.

53 *Institutio*, 3, 20, 17; *Opera selecta*, III, 322; *Institutes*, ed. McNeill, II, 874.

54 Brian Cummings, *The Literary Culture of the Reformation: Grammar and Grace* (Oxford: Oxford UP, 2002), 300.

55 Jonathan Dollimore, *Radical Tragedy: Religion, Ideology and Power in the Drama of Shakespeare and his Contemporaries*, 3rd ed. (Durham, NC: Duke UP, 2004), 83–86, 120–133.

56 J. G. A. Pocock, *The Machiavellian Moment: Florentine Political Thought and the Atlantic Republican Tradition*, rev. ed. (Princeton: Princeton UP, 2016), 587.

57 *Of Religion*, stanza 31; in *Poems and Plays*, ed. Wilkes, II, 336–337.

Bibliography

Bradford, Alan T. "Stuart Absolutism and the 'Utility' of Tacitus." *Huntington Library Quarterly* 46 (1983): 127–155.

Brotton, Jerry. *The Sultan and the Queen: The Untold Story of Elizabeth and Islam.* London: Penguin Books, 2017.

Brown, Alison M. "The Humanist Portrait of Cosimo de' Medici, *Pater Patriae*." *Journal of the Warburg and Courtauld Institutes* 24 (1961): 186–221.

Bullough, Geoffrey. *Poems and Dramas of Fulke Greville*, 2 vols. Edinburgh: Oliver & Boyd, 1939.

Burton, Jonathan. *Traffic and Turning: Islam and English Drama, 1579–1624.* Cranbury: University of Delaware Press, 2005.

Cadman, Daniel. *Sovereign and Subjects in Early Modern Neo-Senecan Drama: Republicanism, Stoicism and Authority.* Farnham and Burlington: Ashgate, 2015.

Calvin, Jean. *Opera selecta*. Edited by Peter Barth and Wilheim Niesel, 2nd edition, 5 vols. München: Christian Kaiser, 1926–1962.

Calvin, Jean. *The Institutes of the Christian Religion*. Edited by John T. McNeill, translated by F. L. Battles, 2 vols. Philadelphia: Westminster Press, 1960.

Cummings, Brian. "From Sympathy to Empathy: Donne and Milton," *Sympathy in Transformation: Dynamics between Rhetorics, Poetics, and Ethics*. Edited by Roman Alexander Barton, Alexander Klaudies and Thomas Micklich, Transformationen der Antike, 51, 109–124. Berlin and Boston: De Gruyter, 2018.

Cummings, Brian. *The Literary Culture of the Reformation: Grammar and Grace*. Oxford: Oxford University Press, 2002.

Cummings, Brian and Freya Sierhuis, eds. *Passions and Subjectivity in Early Modern Culture*. Aldershot: Ashgate, 2013.

Daly, James. *Sir Robert Filmer and English Political Thought*. Toronto: University of Toronto Press, 1979.

Dimmock, Matthew. *New Turkes: Dramatizing Islam and the Ottomans in Early Modern England*. Aldershot: Ashgate, 2005.

Dixon, Thomas. *From Passions to Emotions: The Creation of a Secular Psychological Category*. Cambridge: Cambridge UP, 2003.

Donne, John. *Devotions vpon emergent occasions*. London: Thomas Jones, 1624, sig. 2A2v–2A3r.

Dollimore, Jonathan. *Radical Tragedy: Religion, Ideology and Power in the Drama of Shakespeare and his Contemporaries*, 3rd edition. Durham, NC: Duke University Press, 2004.

Filmer, Robert. *Patriarcha and Other Writings*. Edited by Johann P. Sommerville. Cambridge: Cambridge University Press, 1991.

Filmer, Robert. *Patriarcha, or, The Natural Power of Kings*. London: Walter Davis, 1680.

Gouws, John. "Greville, Fulke, first Baron Brooke of Beauchamps Court (1554–1628)." *Oxford Dictionary of National Biography*, Oxford University Press, 2004; online edition, May 2007 [www.oxforddnb.com.libproxy.york.ac.uk/view/article/11516, accessed 20 October 2017].

Greville, Fulke. *Certaine Learned and Elegant Vvorkes of the Right Honorable Fulke Lord Brooke Written in His Youth, and Familiar Exercise with Sir Philip Sidney*. London: Henry Seile, 1633.

Greville, Fulke. *The Complete Poems and Plays of Fulke Greville, Lord Brooke (1554–1628)*. Edited by G. A. Wilkes, 2 vols. Lewiston: Edwin Mellen Press.

Greville, Fulke. *The Life of the Renowned Sr Philip Sidney. With the True Interest of England as it Then Stood in Relation to All Forrain Princes: And Particularly for Suppressing the Power of Spain Stated by Him. Written by Sir Fulke Grevil Knight, Lord Brook, a Servant to Queen Elizabeth, and His Companion & Friend*. London: Henry Seile, 1651.

Greville, Fulke. The *Prose Works of Fulke Greville, Lord Brooke*. Edited by John Gouws. Oxford: Oxford University Press, 1986.

Greville, Fulke. *The Remains of Sir Fulk Grevill Lord Brooke Being Poems of Monarchy and Religion: Never before Printed*. London: Henry Herringman, 1670.

Hobbes, Thomas. *The Clarendon Edition of the Works of Thomas Hobbes*, vol. 4, *Leviathan: The English and Latin Texts*. Edited by Noel Malcolm. Oxford: Oxford University Press, 2013.

James VI and I. *Political Writings*. Edited by Johann P. Sommerville. Cambridge: Cambridge University Press, 1994.

Jondorf, Gilian. *French Renaissance Tragedy: The Dramatic Word*, rev. edition. Cambridge: Cambridge University Press, 2006.

Kahn, Victoria. *Wayward Contracts: The Crisis of Political Obligation in England, 1640–1674*. Princeton: Princeton University Press, 2009.

Knolles, Richard. *The Generall Historie of the Turkes from the First Beginning of That Nation to the Rising of the Othoman Familie*. London: Adam Islip, 1603.

Lobis, Seth. *The Virtue of Sympathy: Magic, Philosophy, and Literature in Seventeenth-Century England*. New Haven and London: Yale UP, 2015.

Locke, John. *Selected Political Writings*. Edited by Paul E. Sigmund. New York: W.W. Norton, 2005.

Matar, Nabil. *Islam in Britain 1558–1685*. Cambridge: Cambridge University Press, 1998.

Meek, Richard and Erin Sullivan, eds. *The Renaissance of Emotion: Understanding Affect in Shakespeare and his Contemporaries*. Manchester: Manchester UP, 2015.

Ng, Su Fang, *Literature and the Politics of Family in Seventeenth-Century England*. Cambridge: Cambridge University Press, 2007.

Norbrook, David. *Poetry and Politics in the English Renaissance*, rev. edition. Oxford: Oxford University Press, 2002.

Paster, Gail K., Katharine Rowe, and Mary Floyd-Wilson, eds. *Reading the Early Modern Passions: Essays in the Cultural History of Emotion*. Philadelphia: University of Pennsylvania Press, 2004.

Picciotto, Joanna. *Labors of Innocence in Early Modern England*. Cambridge, MA: Harvard University Press, 2010.

Pocock, J. G. A. *The Machiavellian Moment: Florentine Political Thought and the Atlantic Republican Tradition*, rev. edition. Princeton: Princeton University Press, 2016.

Rebholz, Ronald A. *The Life of Fulke Greville: First Lord Brooke*. Oxford: Clarendon Press, 1971.

Röder, Katrin. *Macht und Imagination: Fulke Grevilles Konstruktion diskreter Autorschaft*. Heidelberg: Winter, 2006.

Scott, Jonathan. *England's Troubles: Seventeenth-Century English Political Instability in European Context*. Cambridge: Cambridge University Press, 2000.

Sierhuis, Freya. "The Idol of the Heart: Liberty, Tyranny, and Idolatry in the Work of Fulke Greville." *The Modern Language Review* 106 (2011): 625–646.

Sommerville, Johann P. *Politics & Ideology in England 1603–1640*. London: Longman, 1986.

Swart, K. W. *Willem van Oranje en de Nederlandse opstand 1572–1584*. The Hague: Sdu, 1994.

Temple, William. *Miscellanea. By a Person of Honour*. London: [A.M.] and [R.R.], 1680.

Tuck, Richard. "A New Date for Filmer's *Patriarcha*." *Historical Journal* 29 (1986): 183–186.

6 "A voyce cries out; *Reuenge and Liberty*"– republicanism and gender in Fulke Greville's *Alaham*

Vassiliki Markidou

Fulke Greville's surviving dramas, *Mustapha* and *Alaham*, have, as has been noted, "unfortunately received little critical appreciation."[1] I would add that the latter has received even less than the former. Why so? To start with, while praising Greville's drama on other accounts its first literary critics found it falling short as regards its capacity to represent life-like characters. Geoffrey Bullough claimed that "the history of Greville's dramatic career is one of failure" since the writer was "[l]ess interested in men and women than ideas."[2] Along similar lines, Ivor Morris labeled Greville "the worse dramatist of all [the Elizabethans]" because he was "a playwright with the instinct of an essayist, concerned with the contemplation of human life rather than its portrayal."[3] In addition, the pioneer in critical studies of Greville's works, Morris W. Croll, singled *Alaham* as the English play that is the hardest to interpret. In his own words: "there is probably no play in the language in which it is harder to understand continuously what happens than *Alaham*."[4] This chapter aims to fill the gap in the critical appreciation of Greville's second extant drama as well as to demonstrate that it is far from either a dramatic failure or an imperceptible play. I contend that in large measure *Alaham* is shaped by as well as reflects its author's precarious political identity and equivocal stance towards early modern gender conventions; and will attempt to trace its equally ambiguous dramatization of the interrelationship between republicanism and gender. In doing so, I do not intend to read Greville's drama "as political parables" for I concur with Joan Rees that this would constitute "an oversimplification" while "to describe *Alaham* as a political play is inadequate."[5] Nonetheless, his dramatic works are to a large extent preoccupied with the pitfalls of courtly politics while his career as a courtier and holder of state offices could not but have great influence on them.

In what is perhaps his most well-known text beside *Cælica*, namely *The Life of Sidney*, which according to Brett Roscoe "functions largely as an apology for Greville's dramas," the writer points out that he "chose not to write to them on whose foot the black Oxe had not already trod, as the Proverbe is, but to those only, that are weather-beaten in the Sea of the World, such as having lost the sight of their Gardens, and groves, study to saile on a right course among Rocks, and quick-sands."[6] He thus announces his will to guide the intended readers of his drama, namely those that have been plunged into a turbulent world with no view of a safe haven, out of the *"labyrinths of error,/Shops of deceit,* and *Seas of misery"* that beside being associated with philosophical and religious issues, they are part and parcel of the highly corrupt and dangerous world of courtly politics, especially in the last anxiety-ridden decade of the Elizabethan reign when according to critical consensus Greville began to pen *Alaham.*[7]

In the 1590s when the ageing English monarch forbade discussion concerning the thorny issue of succession, failed in curbing mounting factionalism, and turned towards an increasingly absolutist mode of sovereignty, republican ideas gained wide currency. If we are to take Patrick Collinson at face value, in "Elizabeth's monarchical republic"—a term he coined to present the mixed constitutional form of government in England—"citizens were concealed within subjects."[8] Collinson's claim highlighted the self-governing abilities of early modern Englishmen, whether members of the Privy Council or local officeholders. However, as Markku Peltonen has aptly noted in his examination of "the centrality of eloquence in the Elizabethan notion of citizenship," this concept was highly contested since some desired to see it extended to a large body of people while others wanted it restricted to "a more exclusive body of councillors and nobles."[9] Along similar lines, Ethan Shagan points out that even as early as in the reign of Elizabeth I's father a great degree of friction existed between royal and local administration while the humanists, though well educated in republican ideas, were not in favor of "participatory local self-government."[10] Hence, as Andrew Hadfield argues:

> If republicanism stood for any clear and coherent doctrine in late sixteenth-century England, it was the intellectual conviction that it was necessary to control the powers of the crown by establishing a means of ensuring that a coterie of virtuous advisers and servants would always have the constitutional right to counsel the monarch, and so influence and control his or her actions within the limits of the law.[11]

Crucially then, as underlined by Blair Worden, "in pre-civil-war England it was the abuse of monarchy, not the principle, which attracted complaint."[12] That is to say, even in the seemingly most apolitical texts of that era there is a republican substratum registered in the use of "ideologically freighted words" that are relevant to issues such as liberty, absolutism, equity, the popular, and the populace.[13] This employment of humanist republican discourse however, while aiming to limit the absolute power of the monarch, was far from a sustained effort to establish a republican constitution.

Moreover, as Hadfield points out, "republicanism was a literary phenomenon, as well as a matter of constitutional belief and doctrine, because it consisted of a series of stories" which "were easy to narrate, repeat, retell and refigure, signaling a republican subject matter, or area, without *necessarily* entailing a commitment to any programme."[14] Central among these stories were those of the birth of the Roman Republic following Lucrece's rape by Tarquin and the fall of the Republic and concomitant establishment of the Roman Empire by Octavius Caesar.[15] The key characteristics of literary republicanism were the following:

> concern for the establishment and maintenance of a civic culture; hatred of tyrannical rule; suspicion of hereditary succession; belief that the ruler is really a servant of the people, whatever he or she might think; interest in political assassination; an awareness of the key features of the history of the Roman republic and a desire to show that they have widespread significance and application.[16]

Although *Alaham* is set very far from Rome since it presents a corrupt empire in the Persian Gulf, it nonetheless displays most of these republican traits.[17] This combination might seem an odd choice by its author, yet it provided him with a means of covertly exposing the exigencies of his era with a(n) (at least) one step removed content (i.e., its oriental setting which conveniently smoothens the ideological freight of its humanist republican discursive substratum). Such a realization sheds more light into Greville's "confession" in his *Life of Sidney* that he chose to destroy his Roman drama (on Antony and Cleopatra) for fear that the latter would make him suffer great political danger, while keeping his two oriental ones (*Mustapha* and *Alaham*). As David Norbrook has brilliantly noted, Greville "kept touching on ideas more radical than those to which he was officially committed."[18] His extant dramas display precisely this thin line by having dramatic personas employ the classical republican language in settings safely remote from actual historical republics.

To trace *Alaham*'s equivocal treatment of republican ideas, let us begin with its outset. "[T]he speach of a Ghost, one of the old Kings of Ormus" unsettles the boundaries between the world of the living and the dead.[19] Even more importantly, the deceased sovereign's discontented specter unearths past narratives of weak rule, courtly factionalism, and regicide ("by my trusted *Basshas* was I slaine"—Prologue, 56) and blurs them unsettlingly with the present and the future as he prophesizes the regicide/patricide of the old, also weak, current King of Ormus by his ruthlessly ambitious second male offspring, Alaham. Appropriating the "news from Hell" convention with a twist, the beginning of this drama plunges its readers into the dark depths of Hades ("*Pluto* the king, the Kingdome, miserie"—Prologue, 18) in order to present them with a starkly dystopian orient that functions as a seabed of corruption and sin.

Within this highly unsettling political context, *Alaham*'s engagement with republican discourse is clear from its onset. The Prologue's discourse is deeply humanistic, resting as it does on the pillars of classical mythology (ex. *"Acheron," "Lethe," "Pluto"*—8, 10, 18) and the Scriptures (ex. *"sinnes"* such as *"Atheisme," "Pride,"* and *"Hypocri[cy]"*—33, 34, 35, 37). The specter also articulates its suffering in distinctly religious terms that interestingly cut across denominational lines ("Here rackt, torne, and exil'd from vnitie"-31) and presents its tormentors as dead tyrants who translate into furies that plague him:

> Here Tyrants that corrupt authoritie,
> Councell'd out of the feares of wickednesse,
> Cunning in mischiefe, prowd in crueltie,
> Are furies made, to plague the weaker ghosts,
> Whose soules, entising pleasure only lost;
> The weaker Kings, whose more vnconstant vice
> Their States vnto their humors made a prey;
> For suffering more then Kings to Tyrannise,
> Are damn'd; though here to be, yet not to stay:
> For backe they goe, to tempt with every sinne,
> As easiest it the world may enter in.
>
> (40–50)

Tyranny appears as the utmost "cardinall" sin, which renders even the speaking dead sources of corruption rather than conveyors of moral exempla and dicta to the living as was culturally expected. In mapping this heinous distortion, the ghost ironically launches an attack against tyranny (given his participation in it), draws heavily on republican language ("Tyrants," "corrupt," "authoritie," "Councell'd," "weaker Kings," "Tyrannise," "Subjects growing full is Princes wane"—Prologue, 40, 41, 45, 47, 54) and prophesizes an endless cycle of tyranny and violence.

A strong attack against and/or abhorrence of tyrannical rule is articulated by diverse characters such as the Prologue and the messenger (Nuntius) as well as by the Choruses of the Good Spirits and of the People, not to mention (at times) even Alaham and Hala themselves. Moreover, the Chorus to Act 4, namely a chorus "Of People," warns Alaham that he should not ignore the state for a king without the people's support is like a head without a heart: "Yet if Kings be the *head*, we be the *heart;*/And know *we loue no soule, that doth not loue vs.*" (15–16). The message is loud and clear: the sovereign should cater to the needs and desires of his subjects. Even more significantly, they call themselves "the glasse of Power" and proclaim that "the *Peoples* standard is the warrant/What man ought not to doe, and what he should./Of words we are the Grammar, and of deeds/The harvest both is ours, and eke the seeds" (39–43). The people, rather than their monarch, have the last word while their will reflects lucidly the ideals of civic awareness, political participation, and consensual government. Most crucially, they strike a blow against absolutist ideology by reminding the monarch of his fallibility, sinfulness, and mortality. For as they exclaim, first: "*Nor can the throne, which Monarchs doe liue in,/ Shaddow Kings faults, or santyfye their sinne*"; and second, "while Kings fashion God in humane light,/Men see, and skorne what is not *Infinite*" (53–55). The Basha Mahomet also voices a deep suspicion of hereditary monarchy: "Kings children are no Kings; Authority/Goes not by blood; she sets another rate:/Vse, is her kinne; Grace, her affinity" (1.2. 99–101). Within this radical political context that gives rise to a surplus of republican discourse, a number of political assassinations take place, the most crucial ones being those of the old king, Zophi, Alaham, and Alaham's sons. Last but not least, although the drama does not engage directly with key features of the history of the Roman republic, its shadow looms large over the play's oriental empire as will shortly be demonstrated.

To return to the beginning of the drama, the specter that fills the role of the Prologue chillingly foreshadows Alaham and Hala's crimes—including the multiple deaths they will bring about—and highlights their shared tyrannical attitude-to-be. Indeed, Alaham, "fond of the fathers Throne," will render "[d]esire his idol; libertie his might" (Prologue, 89–90) and commit regicide, patricide, fratricide, and usurpation. Along similar lines, Hala, "strong in lust,/Liberall out of selfe-loue, of error proud" (Prologue, 95–96), will murder both sovereign/husband and son—ironically, the one fathered by her lover, Caine, under the false impression that he is the offspring that Alaham begot with her—in her attempt to avenge her lover's assassination at Alaham's command and, even more crucially, to supplant her illegitimate offspring on the throne. Thus, from its onset Greville's drama fashions its two main characters as alarmingly alike, that is to say, as sinful, tyrannical figures. It also underscores early on that paradoxically they will eventually either appropriate or unsettle the politically inflected trope of martyr-like figures. For though Alaham will refashion himself as a sacrificial victim in the midst of his suffering in excruciating pain from a poison administered by Hala, she "i[]n prides vainglorious martyrdome shall burne" (Prologue, 98).

Alaham's protean qualities are evident from his first appearance. He initially fashions himself as a divided self: he accuses himself of being a "coward soule" that "standst" "doubting now," moving "to and fro" (1.1.1–2), thus highlighting his oscillation between good and evil. Fittingly, he evokes "good, and euill spirits"; yet, before long, he announces that he is "forc'd" "these strange pathes [to] walke of vglinesse" by "threatning gulfes of treacherie" (1.1.10; 1.1.12–13). As he moves from this brief *psychomachia* to creating justification for committing regicide/patricide, he delineates the tyrannical traits of the old king. He points out that his sovereign/father has transgressed divine will by deciding together with his bashas to exile the heir to the throne, Zophi, rather than render him "a sacrifice for this Estate" (1.1.31) as the oracle decreed; moreover, he is "passion-ledd" and displays favoritism, hence neglecting his political duties and turning "the

Court [into] a farme" (1.1.62; 1.1.58). Therefore, king and court are ruled by insatiable will and appetite rather than by reason and virtue. Bringing these tyrannical attributes to their logical endpoint, Greville's drama has the old king ironically as well as tragically deliver the following self-cancelling speech that unmoors his sovereign status: "Treason against me cannot treason be:/All laws haue lost authority in me." (4.1.112–113). His statement echoes the radical republican argument that if the monarch has transgressed the (divine and natural) law, it is legitimate to depose or even kill him.

Among the aforementioned reprehensible traits of the old king, his and his bashas' refusal to submit to divine will and render the heir to the throne a sacrificial scapegoat verifies that the state's corruption remains uncleansed. Hence, a vicious circle of mimetic violence erupts, in which murder after murder takes place and the "sacrifice" of "scapegoat" after "scapegoat" (such as the old King, Cælica, Zophi, Alaham, and Alaham's sons) fails to do away with the empire's "pollution" by tyranny and its evils. The drama's entrapment in this incessant circle of violence, presented as both a product and an instigator of tyranny, testifies to its considerable political charge. In other words, *Alaham* articulates a strong critique of tyranny while encouraging critical evaluation of the idea of overthrowing a tyrannical monarch. This pivotal ambiguity is obvious, for example, in the fact that the first dramatic persona who engages in dialogue with Alaham, namely the priest, Heli, is critical to the legitimization of tyrannicide yet highly corrupt hence the validity of his advice is highly questionable. The religious representative warns Alaham: "Reuenge falls heauie, when God doth fobeare." (1.1.218). Nonetheless, as the Prologue has already mentioned, Heli is "teaching from without, /Corrupted faith, bound vnder laws of might" (Prologue, 126–127). Thus, when he asks Alaham to "Let father moue thee: Pittie thou the State," the transgressor-to-be responds cynically: "Our State is there, where our well-being lies" (1.1.210, 1.1.212). While the former pleads with the affective capacities of his interlocutor and underscores the stock early modern interrelationship between family and state, the latter redefines the state's contours by linking it solely with personal profit. Alaham not only refuses to take counsel but also unashamedly puts private before public interests. He also proclaims himself "Gods Champion" who will his "father for a while depose,/Lest he the Kingdome, we the Church doe lose" (1.1.224–226). In his effort to deal with the multiple ramifications of what he is planning to commit, namely what was widely deemed a crime against God, sovereign, and father, Alaham appropriates histrionically the traditional religiously militant imagery. In other words, he announces that he will put on the garb of God's soldier who will defend both state and church by cleansing heavy corruption and sin. In short, Alaham attempts to fashion the forthcoming regicide/patricide as divinely sanctioned. Fittingly, Heli modifies his strong objection to Alaham's determination to "alter Monarchie" (1.1.224) to a hesitant acknowledgement of the great difficulty, if not impossibility, of achieving such a goal. Undoubt-edly, Greville's drama showcases the radical instability and malleability of identity, whether monarchical, familial, or religious.

Alaham's equivocal stance towards the idea of doing away with a tyran-nical sovereign is stressed precisely by means of this instability, more par-ticularly by the irony of two such dramatic agents turning themselves into tyrannical figures. If Alaham eliminates his tyrannical father/monarch only to become a worse one, Hala follows a similar path as she murders Alaham and turns into an even more "monstrous" tyrant than him. For although she is not literally a ruler, she is unmistakably associated with unnatural female rule. In particular, after making up his mind to commit regicide/patricide, Alaham evokes the evil spirits to help him "plucke downe King, with king's authority,/And make men slaues, with show of liberty" (1.1.322–323); clearly, his sole aim is to gain and abuse power with the guise of freedom. Subsequently, he turns a central republican ideal, that of liberty, into a theatrical performance that will serve his devious aspirations. Indeed, as the First Chorus of Good Spirits inform us, he decides to "vnder-take/The ruine of his King, and father, for ambition's sake" (53–54) rather than in the interest of the people.[20] Even worse, as they also point out, "Vice still makes example her owne fate;/For with like mischiefe *Hala* shakes both him [Alaham], and his Estate" (57–58). Mirroring Alaham, Hala proclaims her own "inward warre" between "sense" and "duties Tyr-annie" (2.1.2, 2.1.3); announces sooner than later her "resolve/To study spite, and practice cruelty"; and displays the trappings of monarchy as the-atrical props employed to further her dark goals: "Purple shall hide my lust, a Crowne my shame" (2.1.24, 2.1.40). She thus displays the stock conflation of sovereignty, theatricality, and lust that, as Rebecca Bushnell has shown, was deemed a central tyrannical trait in Western treatises (such as those penned by Desiderius Erasmus and Sir Thomas Elyot).[21]

The strong similarities between the two main characters of Greville's drama are hard to miss. Both Alaham and Hala experience supernatural visitations and evoke evil spirits; display extreme inward wickedness and are determined to do great harm; bring about disaster; constitute highly deceptive, histrionic characters; transgress both divine and natural law; lust for power and/or sexual gratification; and overrule a tyrant only to turn into worse tyrannical figures. Through these similarities, *Alaham* not only highlights the limits of republican thought but also appears to undermine the traditional polarities of gendered identity on which early modern patri-archy depended. Yet, it moves on to present Alaham, the murderous tyrant, re-fashioning himself both as a tormented sinner whose "remorse" and pangs of "Conscience" his "entrailes teare" (5.2.82, 5.2.87), and as a sup-plicant to Hala, begging her as he does to spare their son's life. He also casts himself as a fallen, shamed, and penitent male tyrant who dramatic-ally exclaims: "It was my sinne alone,/That gloried many ways to tyran-nize:/For all the doomes of ill let me suffice" (5.3.23–25), thus inviting our sympathy. Clearly, in its last Act Greville's drama exenorates, even if partially so, Alaham and even more crucially, it achieves this atonement at the expense of dramatizing as well as condemning Hala as the quintessence of tyranny. In striking contrast to his refashioned identity, she keeps firm to evil to the very end through her final summoning of the Furies of Hell to "[e]nter vpon this large infernall wombe" and "leade the way" (5.3.134). By means of this horrid invocation, Hala casts herself as the archetypal tyrant whose reign will be in Hell. Her devilishness and deviousness are also obvious in that while scheming for Alaham's destruction she was histrionically assuming the role of obedient wife and confidante hence fully concealing her murderous intentions. Therefore, she ironically outdoes Alaham by turning into an emblem of what were held to be the main qualities of the tyrant and, according to early modern anti-theatricalists, of the actor: heavy role-playing, shifting from one identity to another, refusing to demonstrate "a 'real' or single self, on which moral or political character can be grounded."[22] Hala also becomes the par excellence tyrannical figure of the play, "literally" encapsulating the effeminacy, insatiable sexual appetite, intemperate vice, and excessive theatricality stereotypically deemed attributes of the tyrant.[23] As Alaham tells himself right before his death: "you haue seene that before you die,/Which no age will beleeue; *One worse than I.*" (5.3.88–89). Clearly, despite the earlier disruption of gendered binary oppositions, in the final Act of the drama penitent consciousness appears as masculine while monstrous subjectivity as feminine. Such a gender-inflected dramatization is in full alignment with the writer's aim. In *The Life of Sidney*, Greville notes that he has created his female characters along the following lines:

> But as Poets figured the vertues to be women, and all Nations call them by Feminine names, so have I described malice, craft, and such like vices in the persons of Shrews, to shew that many of them are of that nature, *even as we are*, I meane strong in weaknesse; and consequently in these Orbs of Passion, *the weaker Sexe commonly the most predominant* (emphases mine).[24]

The writer's argument oscillates between upholding traditional misogyny and unhinging it by underscoring the (negative) similarities between the sexes, yet the conceptualization of the female sex as the quintessence of human failings is unshakable. Along similar lines, in *Alaham* Hala functions as an effective vehicle for both undermining and imposing the validity of early modern gender stereotypes as well as for exemplifying humanity's tragic experience of the fall. For although as stated earlier she outdoes Alaham on many accounts, she also appears as a monstrous, witch-like, whorish female that thirsts for lust, power, and revenge and has no qualms about murdering her close family members and ending up in hell while her final image is undoubtedly the darkest one.

True to Greville's upholding of unresolved dualities (which, as Robert Appelbaum astutely analyzes in this volume, constitutes precisely what enables him to write) his second extant drama reaches its closure by presenting Alaham and Hala as yet again converging rather than diverging, even if in a highly ambiguous manner. Hala's last words ("With *Alaham* his father he must dwell:/I will go downe, and change this Ghost with hell"—5.3.145–146) which mark the drama's *denouement* echo strongly Alaham's earlier invocation:

> You wandring spirits frame in me your Hell;
> I feele my brother, and my sister there.
> Where is my wife? There lacks no more but shee:
> Let all my owne together dwell with me.
>
> (5.2.88–91)

Correspondingly, Alaham's dramatic invocation to the "Infernall wombe" to "receive thy right," that is, himself, as he is dying, poignantly foreshadows Hala's summons of the Furies of Hell to "[e]nter vpon this large infernall wombe" and "[l]eade the way" (5.3.134, 5.3.136) to her final descent there. Beyond a shred of doubt, in Grevillian drama the family unit exemplifies fallen humanity and its concomitant entrance to hell, yet the female sex constitutes the quintessence of that sorrowful decline.

Besides filling this dramatic role, Hala also constitutes the key to unraveling the play's dramatization of a highly ambiguous interrelationship between republicanism and gender. To grasp this realization, it would be helpful to compare/contrast her to the epitomic female figure associated with republicanism. Both the Roman Lucrece and the oriental consort to the Persian King Alaham, Hala, turn their speech as well as their bodies into weapons against their marginalization and disempowerment by the male sex while they also bring about the overthrow and elimination of the male tyrant. Nonetheless, unlike the virtuous Lucrece who calls upon patriarchal agents to avenge her rape after her imminent self-inflicted violence, Hala wreaks revenge on the one who has wronged her by having killed her lover and defiantly announces that she will commit suicide and enter hell. In doing so, not only does she rise as a strikingly subversive gendered figure, she also becomes both a powerful mouthpiece for the articulation of republican ideas and a means of challenging them. On the one hand, she attacks ferociously Alaham's tyranny; articulates her opposition to hereditary succession; attempts to supplant her illegitimate son on the throne; and orchestrates as well as carries out political assassinations. On the other, she undermines both republican and proto-feminist discourse by towering as a female tyrant that enacts "barbaric" violence. In *Alaham*'s climax of dramatic violence, she poisons her husband; watches him die and derives pleasure in witnessing his torture; ignores his pleas to spare their offspring; and kills the fruit of her bond with her lover, Caine, under the impression that she has killed the son fathered by Alaham because as she tells her husband: "in him thou art" (5.3.68).

Although both Alaham and Hala's crimes illustrate in a highly dramatic manner the interrelationship between the familial and the political, the latter's are even more striking as they include the par excellence taboo murder, namely that of offspring by mother, steeped as they are in Medean overtones.[25] Hala outdoes Alaham in rage, revenge, and sinfulness and in doing so, she strips him of his authority and masculinity, hence of his (politically and socially constructed) identity. As he retorts in horror: "I have no being, while she there doth sit,/Subiect in sexe, but King, in rage of wit." (5.3.36–37). Since any kind of surrender of male to female rule was viewed a stock trait of male tyranny, the oriental despot's wife leads him not only to articulate his inability to uphold proper patriarchal order but also to ironically acknowledge himself as a tyrant.

Hala also enacts a "linguistic divorce from her sexual identity" and undergoes "a ritual disengendering" so as to gain "some transitional not-woman/not-man state" which will enable her to murder both king/husband and (as she first erroneously thinks) legitimate heir/son.[26] Thus, to return to the Roman republican overtones of the drama, while Lucrece's raped body allegorizes the ravaged body politic, Hala's choice of having poison permeate slowly yet steadily Alaham's body renders it a porous, hence effeminized one which in turn allegorizes the (already) diseased body politic that perversely feeds upon itself. "*Hala*'s Present [to Alaham], this Triumphant Robe/[which] Shewes all Estates, things reall, humors, lawes" (5.1.8–9) is in fact embalmed in "the poyson that [she] deuis'd" and on which he "do'st feed" (5.3.11, 5.3.10). As the crown and the robe's poison seeps through Alaham's body, the trappings of (his tyrannical) monarchy dramatically expose their deceptive and corrupting effect. It is worth noting that although both Lucrece and Hala are associated with the uprooting of their abusers' genealogical and monarchical lines, Lucrece's call for avenging brings about the foundation of the Roman Republic while Hala's revenge refuels an incessant cycle of violence that sheds light on the limits of republicanism. Greville's choice of drawing such an emphasis is also registered in "A Treatise of Monarchy," which, like *Alaham*, he began to compose in the 1590s. As Hadfield points out, in this verse treatise, the frequent degeneration of monarchy into tyranny is highlighted and the story of the end of the Roman republic is told with a twist: while Caesar is presented "as usual in work written in the 1590s" as a tyrant, Brutus and Cassius are cast as "equally ambitious and self-serving, tyrants who never got to rule."[27] The strong link between Greville's plays and treatises, which the writer testified to in his *Life of Sidney*, is made particularly evident here. In his own words: "The treatises, to speak truly of them, were first intended to be for every act a chorus" but they "did easily wonder beyond proportion" so they were turned into separate works.[28] The aforementioned part of "A Treatise of Monarchy" and *Alaham* forge a formidable warning to Greville's contemporaries on the ills of both degenerate monarchy and illegitimate resistance.

Alaham comes full circle since it begins and ends with the themes of political upheaval, moral corruption, and excessive violence. In doing so, it refuses to support fully either monarchism or republicanism and provide its readers with a clear political program. Instead, it presents the dangers and pitfalls of royal absolutism while, to an extent, tapping into the foundational myth of republicanism in order to underscore the failure of political violence to contain state crisis and cleanse a corrupt body politic. Greville's drama see-saws between criticism and conservatism, dissidence and conformity, while it also reflects its author's deep pessimism concerning the nature of (human) government and highly ambivalent stance towards early modern gender stereotypes. More than anything else though, *Alaham* dwells heavily on the precarious making and unmaking of identities as well as on the gains and losses that such a process entails.

Notes

1 Brett Roscoe, "On Reading Renaissance Closet Drama: A Reconsideration of the Chorus in Fulke Greville's *Alaham* and *Mustapha*," *Studies in Philology* 110, no. 4 (2013): 762–788, 774. In *The Life of Sidney*, Greville discloses to his reader that apart from *Mustapha* and *Alaham* there was also a third tragedy entitled *Antonie and Cleopatra*, which he set on fire in fear that (given the fall of Essex to whose Tacitean circle he belonged) it could bring him trouble with "the present Governors, and government." See Fulke Greville, *The Life of the Renowned Sir Philip Sidney* (1652; reproduced by Delmar: Scholars' Fascimiles and Reprints, 1984), 150.

2 See *Poems and Dramas of Fulke Greville, first Lord Brooke*, ed. Geoffrey Bullough, vol. 2 (New York: Oxford UP, 1945), 58.

3 Ivor Morris, "The Tragic Vision of Fulke Greville," *Shakespeare Survey* 14 (1961): 66–75, 66. Both Bullough and Morris have given credit to Greville's dramas on other accounts: the former for their bold experimentation, the latter for their "imaginative integrity, and their latent power." See Bullough, 4 and Morris, 66. Karen Raber has underscored the unfairness of negative assessments of Greville's closet drama by the criteria of early modern public theatre; and pointed out that unlike drama meant to be staged and thus having to go through intense state censorship Greville's closet tragedies were circulated to a very select elite, courtly coterie readership, was precisely what made them all the more dangerous since they were "meant to be instantly apprehended *as* political commentary." Lucas Erne though, following Mary Ellen Lamb's refutation of T. S. Eliot's claim that the Countess of Pembroke intended to reform the English stage by having gathered around her a group of writers that wrote plays which opposed popular theatre, has argued that "closet" dramas and popular ones should be viewed as "complementary rather than antagonistic in the influence they exerted." Moreover, Coburn Freer; Alison Findlay, Stephanie Hodgson-Wright, and Gweno-Williams; and Daniel Cadman have argued that the term "closet drama" is an inaccurate one for plays labeled as such. See Karen Raber, *Dramatic Difference: Gender, Class and Genre in the Early Modern Closet Drama* (Newark and London: University of Delaware Press and Associated UPress, 2001), 115; Mary Ellen Lamb, "The Myth of the Countess

of Pembroke: The Dramatic Circle," *The Yearbook of English Studies* 11 (1981): 194–202, 196; Lucas Erne, *Beyond "The Spanish Tragedy": A Study of the Works of Thomas Kyd* (Manchester: Manchester UP, 2001), 212; Coburn Freer, "Mary Sidney: Countess of Pembroke" in *Women Writers of the Renaissance and Reformation*, ed. Katharina Wilson (Athens: University of Georgia Press, 1987), 481–521, esp. 484; *Women and Dramatic Production, 1550–1700*, eds. Alison Findlay, Stephanie Hodgson-Wright, and Gweno-Williams (London: Longman, 2000); Daniel Cadman, *Sovereigns and Subjects in Early Modern Neo-Senecan Drama: Republicanism, Stoicism and Authority* (London and New York: Routledge, 2016), 5–6.

4 Morris W. Croll, *The Works of Fulke Greville: A Thesis* (Philadelphia: J.B. Lippincott, 1903), 40. Cited in Roscoe, "On Reading Renaissance Closet Drama," 774–775. Ironically, in contrast to Croll, Morris claims that Greville "cannot write a play without making clear its significance in the light of his own opinions" and views this as a crucial factor that renders him the greatest failure in Elizabethan drama. See Morris, "The Tragic Vision of Fulke Greville," 66.

5 Joan Rees, *Fulke Greville, Lord Brooke, 1554–1628: A Critical Biography* (London: Routledge & Kegan Paul, 1971), 139, 159.

6 Greville, *The Life of the Renowned Sir Philip Sidney*, 134–135.

7 Fulke Greville, *An Inquisition upon Fame and Honour*, in *Poems and Dramas of Fulke Greville First Lord Brooke*, ed. Geoffrey Bullough (New York: Oxford UP, 1945), vol. 1, stanza 1, 1–2. As Joan Rees has noted, Greville's reference to his *Antonie and Cleopatra* confirms that his three tragedies "were in existence before 1600–01"; hence, "we have a time range in which we can fairly confidently put the inception and perhaps the first completion of a work, but the only *terminus ad quem* which is certain is Greville's death in 1628," given the fact that he kept revising his works as is evident in the various manuscripts that have survived. See Rees, *Fulke Greville, Lord* Brooke, 143. Greville's biographer, Ronald A. Rebholz, contends that Greville began to compose Alaham "in 1599 or 1600." See Ronald A. Rebholz, *The Life of Fulke Greville, First Lord Brooke* (Oxford: Oxford UP, 1971), 331.

8 Patrick Collinson, "The Monarchical Republic of Queen Elizabeth I," in *Elizabethan Essays*, ed. Patrick Collinson (London: Hambledon Press, 1994), 31–57, 19. For both endorsing and critical responses to Collinson's coinage, see *The Monarchical Republic of Early Modern England: Essays in Response to Patrick Collinson*, ed. John F. McDiarmid (Aldershot: Ashgate, 2007). On the issue of early modern republicanism, see also, for example, Quentin Skinner, *The Foundations of Modern Political Thought*, 2 vols (Cambridge: Cambridge UP, 1978); Blair Worden, "Classical Republicanism and the English Revolution," in *History and Imagination: Essays in Honour of Hugh Trevor-Roper*, ed. Hugh Lloyd-Jones, Valerie Pearl and Blair Worden (London: Duckworth, 1981), 182–200; Blair Worden, "English Republicanism," in *The Cambridge History of Renaissance Political Thought*, ed. J. H. Burns and Mark Goldie (Cambridge: Cambridge UP, 1991); Jonathan Scott, "The English Republican Imagination," in *Revolution and Restoration: England in the 1650s*, ed. John Morrill (London: Collins and Brown, 1992), 35–54; *Republicanism, Liberty, and Commercial Society, 1649–1776*, ed. David Wootton (Stanford: Stanford UP, 1994); and Markku Peltonen, *Classical Humanism and Republicanism in Early Political Thought, 1570–1640* (Cambridge: Cambridge UP, 1995). For a useful introduction to republicanism and republican exchanges from the sixteenth to the nineteenth century, see Rachel Hammersley, "Introduction: The Historiography of Republicanism and Republican Exchanges," *Special Issue: Republican Exchanges, c.1550-c.1580*, *History of European Ideas* 38, no. 3 (2012): 323–327.

9   Markku Peltonen, "Rhetoric and Citizenship in the Monarchical Republic of Elizabeth I," in *The Monarchical Republic of Early Modern England*, ed. John F. McDiarmid(Aldershot: Ashgate, 2007), 109–128, 110, 111.

10 Ethan H. Shagan, "The Two Republics: Conflicting Views of Participatory Local Government in Early Tudor England," in *The Monarchical Republic of Early Modern England*, ed John F. McDiarmid (Aldershot: Ashgate, 2007), 19–36, 19.

11 Andrew Hadfield, *Shakespeare and Republicanism* (Cambridge: Cambridge UP, 2005), 17.

12 Blair Worden, "Republicanism, Regicide, and Republic: The English Experience," in *Republicanism: A Shared European Heritage*, ed. Martin van Gelderen and Quentin Skinner (Cambridge: Cambridge UP, 2002), vol. 1, 307–327, 311.

13 Annabel Patterson, *Reading Between the Lines* (London: Routledge, 1993), 221.

14 Hadfield, *Shakespeare and Republicanism*, 54.

15 Ibid.

16 Hadfield, *Shakespeare and Republicanism*, 73.

17 The link between classical republican discourse and oriental tyranny is also reflected in the fact that when in the 1620s Greville invited the Leiden scholar Isaac Dorislaus to his own university, Cambridge, to offer a series of lectures on Tacitus, the latter "made his subject [for his first lecture] the contrast between legal and tyrannical, what he calls 'Asiatic,' monarchy." See Rolland Mellor, "Tacitus, Academic Politics, and Regicide in the Reign of Charles I: The Tragedy of Dr. Isaac Dorislaus," *International Journal of the Classical Tradition*, 11, no. 2 (Fall 2004): 153–193, 176.

18 David Norbrook, *Poetry and Politics in the English Renaissance*, revised edition (Oxford: Oxford UP, 2002), 150.

19 *Poems and Dramas of Fulke Greville*, ed. Bullough, vol. 2, 138. According to Rebholz, Greville "probably composed at least four versions of *Alaham*, only one of which is extant," 329.

20 Fittingly, when he ascends the throne, Alaham's triumph over his newly-won sovereignty is fissured by lamentations and the messenger's (Nuntius's) disturbing news on how the danger of a civil discord has been provoked by the deaths of Alaham's father, brother and sister and the concomitant cry for "*Reuenge, and Liberty*" (4.2.72).

21 See Rebecca Bushnell, *Tragedies of Tyrants: Political Thought and Theater in the English Renaissance* (Ithaca: Cornell UP, 1990), 61.

22 Ibid.

23 Bushnell, *Tragedies of Tyrants*, 20–25 and 56–59.

24 Greville, *The Life of Sidney*, 222.

25 For the links between *Alaham* and the Medean myth, see Rees, *Fulke Greville, Lord* Brooke, 114; *Poems and Dramas of Fulke Greville*, vol. 2, ed. Bullough, 258; Peter Ure, *Elizabethan and Jacobean Drama: Critical Essays*, vol. 2, ed. J. C. Maxwell (Liverpool: Liverpool UP, 1974), 116; Matthew C. Hansen, "Gender, Power and Play: Fulke Greville's *Mustapha* and *Alaham*," *Sidney Journal* 19, nos. 1–2 (2001): 125–142, 132–138. [*Fulke Greville: A Double Special Issue*, ed. Matthew C. Hansen and Matthew Woodcock].

26 Hansen, "Gender Power, and Play," 133, 138, 137.

27 Hadfield, *Shakespeare and* Republicanism, 94.

28 Greville, *The Life of the Renowned Sir Philip Sidney*, 90.

Bibliography

Bushnell, Rebecca. *Tragedies of Tyrants: Political Thought and Theater in the English Renaissance*. Ithaca: Cornell University Press, 1990.

Cadman, Daniel. *Sovereign and Subjects in Early Modern Neo-Senecan Drama: Republicanism, Stoicism and Authority.* London and New York: Routledge, 2016.

Collinson, Patrick. "The Monarchical Republic of Queen Elizabeth I." In *Elizabethan Essays.* Edited by Patrick Collinson, 31–57. London: Hambledon Press, 1994.

Croll, Morris W. *The Works of Fulke Greville: A Thesis.* Philadelphia: J.B. Lippincott, 1903.

Erne, Lucas. *Beyond "The Spanish Tragedy": A Study of the Works of Thomas Kyd.* Manchester: Manchester University Press, 2001.

Findlay, Alison, Stephanie Hodgson-Wright, and Gweno-Williams, eds. *Women and Dramatic Production, 1550–1700.* London: Longman, 2000.

Freer, Coburn. "Mary Sidney: Countess of Pembroke." In *Women Writers of the Renaissance and Reformation.* Edited by Katharina Wilson. Athens: University of Georgia Press, 1987.

Greville, Fulke. *An Inquisition upon Fame and Honour.* In *Poems and Dramas of Fulke Greville First Lord Brooke.* Edited by Geoffrey Bullough. New York: Oxford University Press, 1945.

Greville, Fulke. *Poems and Dramas of Fulke Greville, first Lord Brooke.* Edited by Geoffrey Bullough. New York: Oxford University Press, 1945.

Greville, Fulke. *The Life of the Renowned Sir Philip Sidney.* 1652; reproduced by Delmar: Scholars' Fascimiles and Reprints, 1984.

Hadfield, Andrew. *Shakespeare and Republicanism.* Cambridge: Cambridge University Press, 2005.

Hammersley, Rachel. "Introduction: The Historiography of Republicanism and Republican Exchanges." *Special Issue: Republican Exchanges, c.1550–c.1580, History of European Ideas* 38, no. 3 (2012): 323–327.

Hansen, Matthew C. "Gender, Power and Play: Fulke Greville's *Mustapha* and *Alaham.*" *Sidney Journal* 19, nos. 1–2 (2001): 125–142.

Hansen, Matthew C. and Matthew Woodcock, eds. *Sidney Journal* 19, nos. 1–2 (2001): 125–142 [*Fulke Greville: A Double Special Issue*].

Lamb, Mary Ellen. "The Myth of the Countess of Pembroke: The Dramatic Circle." *The Yearbook of English Studies* 11 (1981): 194–202.

McDiarmid, John F., ed. *The Monarchical Republic of Early Modern England: Essays in Response to Patrick Collinson.* Aldershot: Ashgate, 2007.

Mellor, Rolland. "Tacitus, Academic Politics, and Regicide in the Reign of Charles I: The Tragedy of Dr. Isaac Dorislaus." *International Journal of the Classical Tradition,* 11, no. 2 (Fall 2004): 153–193.

Morris, Ivor. "The Tragic Vision of Fulke Greville." *Shakespeare Survey* 14 (1961): 66–75.

Norbrook, David. *Poetry and Politics in the English Renaissance,* rev. edition. Oxford: Oxford University Press, 2002.

Patterson, Annabel. *Reading Between the Lines.* London: Routledge, 1993.

Peltonen, Markku. *Classical Humanism and Republicanism in Early Political Thought, 1570–1640.* Cambridge: Cambridge University Press, 1995.

Peltonen, Markku. "Rhetoric and Citizenship in the Monarchical Republic of Elizabeth I." In *The Monarchical Republic of Early Modern England: Essays in Response to Patrick Collinson.* Edited by John F. McDiarmid, 109–128. Aldershot: Ashgate, 2007.

Raber, Karen. *Dramatic Difference: Gender, Class and Genre in the Early Modern Closet Drama*. Newark and London: University of Delaware Press and Associated University Presses, 2001.

Rebholz, Ronald A. *The Life of Fulke Greville, First Lord Brooke*. Oxford: The Clarendon Press, 1971.

Rees, Joan. *Fulke Greville, Lord Brooke, 1554–1628: A Critical Biography*. London: Routledge & Kegan Paul, 1971.

Roscoe, Brett. "On Reading Renaissance Closet Drama: A Reconsideration of the Chorus in Fulke Greville's *Alaham* and *Mustapha*." *Studies in Philology* 110, no. 4 (2013): 762–788.

Scott, Jonathan. "The English Republican Imagination." In *Revolution and Restoration: England in the 1650s*. Edited by John Morrill, 35–54. London: Collins and Brown, 1992.

Shagan, Ethan H. "The Two Republics: Conflicting Views of Participatory Local Government in Early Tudor England." In *The Monarchical Republic of Early Modern England: Essays in Response to Patrick Collinson*. Edited by John F. McDiarmid, 19–36. Aldershot: Ashgate, 2007.

Skinner, Quentin, ed. *The Foundations of Modern Political Thought*, 2 vols. Cambridge: Cambridge University Press, 1978.

Ure, Peter. *Elizabethan and Jacobean Drama: Critical Essays*. Edited by J. C. Maxwell. Liverpool: Liverpool University Press, 1974.

Worden, Blair. "Classical Republicanism and the English Revolution." In *History and Imagination: Essays in Honour of Hugh Trevor-Roper*. Edited by Hugh Lloyd-Jones, Valerie Pearl, and Blair Worden, 182–200. London: Duckworth, 1981.

Worden, Blair. "English Republicanism." In *The Cambridge History of Renaissance Political Thought*. Edited by J. H. Burns and Mark Goldie, 443–478. Cambridge: Cambridge University Press, 1991.

Worden, Blair. "Republicanism, Regicide, and Republic: The English Experience." In *Republicanism: A Shared European Heritage*. Edited by Martin van Gelderen and Quentin Skinner. 2 vols., vol. 2, 307–320. Cambridge: Cambridge University Press, 2002.

Wooton, David, ed. *Republicanism, Liberty, and Commercial Society, 1649–1776*. Stanford: Stanford University Press, 1994.

Part II

Robert Southwell
(1561–1595)

7 "This pompe is prizèd there"

Southwell's challenge to courtly identities in "New Prince, New Pompe"

Theresa Kenney

Southwell's Nativity poems: their importance in his oeuvre

Several of Southwell's Nativity lyrics are heard around the world at Christmas time, over 400 years after their composition, when sixteenth and seventeenth-century poems better known to scholars lie closed in their book covers, opened only by literature students. This makes Southwell arguably the most heard poet from the late sixteenth century in England, thanks to Benjamin Britten's beautiful *Ceremony of Carols*, wherein the composer enshrined two of the poems from his Nativity Group, as Frank Brownlow has called it.[1] It is a curious twist of literary historical fate, and one wonders what audiences who are not scholars get from listening to these distinctly un-modern poems.[2] Twenty-first century listeners are probably not as alert as his contemporaries would have been to language that clearly aims at correcting false ideas about proper courtly conduct, the specific arena Southwell chooses for his introduction of one poem's subject: "New Prince, New Pompe." My argument in this chapter is that in this Nativity poem, Southwell is not only praising and meditating on the newborn Christ Child, but is also presenting the antitheses at the heart of the Incarnation as a castigation of the Elizabethan court. Although it is a castigation, the poem expresses a hope that the fragile Christian identity his educated audience shares but has forgotten can be something it re-adopts in beholding the Christ Child in the stable. Greenblatt has said in *Hamlet in Purgatory* that ghosts are "good for thinking about theater's capacity to fashion realities, to call realities into question, to tell compelling stories, to puncture the illusions that these stories generate and to salvage something on the other side of disillusionment."[3] Southwell clearly felt that the Christ Child was good for puncturing illusions as well, and that there was nothing so salutary for confounding the "discourse" of power in human enterprises as meditating on the Word come down from Heaven. In inviting readers to adopt the role of courtiers, Southwell allows for self-fashioning in both those who inhabit the earthly court and those who do not, and by aiming to underscore the weaknesses of the Elizabethan court, Southwell models internal change that can be effected through the reader's imaginative participation in the events in the courtly stable. Between the poem's opening word, "Behould," and its final invitation, "With joy approch, O Christian wighte," Southwell teaches a lesson in the kind of vision necessary to rescue a corrupted Christian identity from the false joys of wealth and political power.

Of course, unlike Greenblatt, he would not have thought that his words about the Word were "desperate explanatory hypotheses," grasping after meaning in a meaningless world. Christ's Incarnation was for Southwell the nexus of all meaning on earth, and the very act that enabled human beings to escape from their own meaningless self-created cultures. Gary Kuchar's discussion of Southwell's poems within the Lacanian psycho-analytical frame that views individual identity as a construct formed after the self encounters its own failure to live up to its ideal self will also leap to mind when we think about the problem of a courtly identity that obstructs the formation of a true Christian identity.[4] Kuchar explains that "a loss of a past that could never have been present as such" is precisely what allows for the formation of a self-perceiving subject. We could say that Southwell similarly perceives—and hopes—that the reminder of Christ's birth in Bethlehem will inspire self-perception in his listener as well as in his own soul. However, this poem certainly presumes, *contra* Lacan, that healthy self-perception can be gained or restored through remembrance of the event of the Nativity, an event that reverses worldly values in order to restore in human beings the image of God. In this case, the lost past *was* "present as such."

In his Nativity poems, Southwell reminds his listeners (who in the 1590s would not have counted his reminders as inventions) that Christ divests himself of the attributes of heavenly power but does not assume the attributes of earthly power. He does this not to lose power—as St. Augustine maintained, Christ cannot stop being God just because he has become human—but to demonstrate how people on earth can become true Kings and Queens.[5] Not investiture but divestiture is the key. Humans put on disguises and arm themselves with stage props; God discards them. In "New Prince, New Pompe," we see that Southwell hoped his poems would enable his readers to invert their earthly values and adopt the values of Bethlehem, the true court, the court of the King of Heaven.

> BEHOULD, a sely tender Babe,
>   In freezing winter nighte,
> In homely manger trembling lies;
>   Alas, a piteous sighte!
> The inns are full, no man will yelde
>   This little pilgrime bedd;
> But forc'd He is with sely beastes
>   In cribb to shroude His headd.
> Despise not Him for lyinge there,

First what He is enquire;
An orient perle is often founde
  In depth of dirty mire.
Waye not His cribb, His wodden dishe,
  Nor beastes that by Him feede;
Way not His mother's poore attire,
  Nor Josephe's simple weede.
This stable is a Prince's courte,
  The cribb His chaire of State;
The beastes are parcell of His pompe,
  The wodden dishe His plate.
The parsons in that poore attire
  His royall liveries weare;
The Prince Himself is come from heaven,
  This pompe is prizèd there.
With joy approch, O Christian wighte!
  Do homage to thy Kinge;
And highly prize His humble pompe
  Which He from heaven doth bringe.
                    (From *St. Peter's Complaint*, newly augmented, [*c.*1605][6])

If "the Prince himself is come from heaven" and "this pompe"—the glorious humility and poverty of the stable of Bethlehem—"is prizèd there," then the pomp of Queen and court is indicted as false, and in fact opposed to true Christian pomp. Southwell emphasizes the challenge that Christ's choice, as King, to be born in poverty poses to humanity, whose values are inverted. Of course, Southwell is far from unique among Christian writers in imagining the birth of Christ as initiating the world's redemption not just from sin but also from a false idea of what is valuable or worthy of the human person's energies and desires. One thing that is interesting and perhaps unique about Southwell's poems is the situation in which they were written, and the hope for reform they seem to express. He is instructing the court, almost certainly the rich and powerful of his own day as his imagined audience, consciously striving to re-orient the queen and her followers towards poverty and simplicity as right expressions of magisterial authority. If he imagines the monarch and her courtiers reading his poems, and this one in particular, Southwell requires of them a profound re-examination of their own way of expressing their identity as persons in power. Given his concern with rectifying the course of poetry expressed in his letter to his "worthy good cosen Maister W.S.," it is certainly not beyond possibility that he imagines his poems being read by those in power in court.

This interpretation may seem to fly in the face of Scott Pilarz's irenic view of Southwell's stance towards sectarian discord in *Writing Reconciliation*.[7] Pilarz demonstrates that Southwell was opposed to such subversive acts as the Babington Plot and indeed, that he himself argued in his *Humble*

Supplication that a Catholic might be true to his faith and to his Queen, and not be a traitor to the crown.[8] The *Humble Supplication* itself is proof that Southwell imagined his audience as including Elizabeth and her court.[9] I do not intend to construe Southwell's poems as anti-Protestant, however. Southwell's poems are indeed controversial and revolutionary, but they are so in the same way that Dante's ratification of poverty as the only remedy for both a sick church and a sick state is in *The Divine Comedy*. That is, the spiritual illness that sees grandeur and glittering pomp as the natural accoutrements of authority always afflicts humanity, and its exposure will always seem revolutionary. Aside from acquainting listeners with the pathos and gravity of the imagery of the Proleptic Passion (that is, the Passion anticipated in the suffering and humiliation of Christ's infancy) and the gratitude-inspiring surprise at God's own prizing of the earth, Southwell reminds his audience that we still prize people for their possessions and riches, their polished trappings. This is the persistent error of mankind faced with the allurements of power and wealth, and Southwell wants to train his readers to remove the veil, as St. Lucia does in Dante's *Purgatorio* during the Dream of the Siren.[10] Southwell's approach of reinterpreting almost every object associated with the Nativity is a lesson in right seeing. He touches with his magician's wand each item and error falls away. That is the function of the lists of antitheses in several of these poems, but for our present purposes, we will focus on "New Prince, New Pompe."

Interpretation of signs: the antitheses

In "New Prince, New Pompe," Southwell turns to this favorite theme, the reversal of worldly values brought about by the advent of Christ at Christmastime. In this lyric, Southwell is concerned to demonstrate the physical reality of Christ's infancy and his poverty, and he insists that this is the pomp of heaven—not a deficiency, but a glory. The corrected heavenly court of Bethlehem in this poem is the court where what is "silly," or weak, is "sely," holy, as the continued knowledge of the word's original derivation would indicate to sixteenth-century readers.[11]

The development of the conceit in these poems tends to be a decoding of what the unconverted listener sees, so that he or she can see through appearances and comprehend the regal reality of lowly things. Southwell's use of antithesis is much noted and often discussed as an element of his euphuistic style, but for him it conveys meaning and is not just a structural tool. Following Grosart, Louis Martz charged Southwell with using "excessive parallelism and antithesis," but saw the scheme mostly in the light of artistic taste.[12] Joseph Nolan, a nineteenth century writer, said,

> The faults of Southwell's style were the faults of his time – obscuring inversions, too frequent use of antithesis.... A frequent use of antithesis usually shows more care for the manner than for the matter of

an expression; but it is to be remembered that Southwell's long scho-
lastic training made him quick at nice distinctions, and that, in the
antithesis, as he uses it, the contrast is truly in the ideas and does not
depend on any trick of similarity of verbal arrangement. Its use makes
his verse occasionally monotonous; but the verse does not seem
forced, for the use of the figure was quite natural to the man as a
trained reasoner.[13]

Nolan's anxious defense of Southwell gets in a general way at the specific
point I am making here: Southwell's antithetical style is at its most pur-
poseful when he is redefining things misunderstood. He expects us to see
everything in the world differently because of the birth of Jesus, as his
balanced antitheses work to re-transform all things into their opposites:

> This stable is a Prince's courte,
> This cribb His chaire of State;
> The beastes are parcell of His pompe,
> The wodden dishe His plate.

Southwell sees the Son of God's choice to enter the world in poverty and
obscurity as a reproach to the rich and powerful, and to all who worship
them and their accoutrements. Like the long line of Christian poets before
him, his view of the court is a revolutionary one, opposed to worldly
values, though he does not advise political rebellion. The overthrow he has
in mind is much more radical than any replacement of one earthly power
by another. As much as he might have preferred a Catholic monarch on the
throne, he would have given the same advice to a Mary Tudor or a Mary
Stuart as he gives to the educated readers of 1590's England. Indeed, if his
advice were taken, who would paint Elizabeth in her pearls and jewels?
Why would satins and magnificent wigs and other regalia ever appear? The
sumptuary laws of the period were in force to maintain the rhetoric of
power and Elizabeth seriously reiterated old standards and in fact lamented
their desuetude.

The simplicity of royalty

The classical world had its own heroic poverty, or august plainness, but
there is no doubt that from its beginnings, Christianity valued poverty and
simplicity, and not just for ethical reasons. Christ's kenosis, his emptying of
himself, is what the Incarnation actually is. The term kenosis comes from St.
Paul, ἐκένωσεν (*ekénōsen*), which conveys the concept "emptying":

> [5] For let this mind be in you, which was also in Christ Jesus:
> [6] Who being in the form of God, thought it not robbery to be equal
> with God:

> [7] But emptied himself, taking the form of a servant, being made in the likeness of men, and in habit found as a man.
>
> [8] He humbled himself, becoming obedient unto death, even to the death of the cross.
>
> [9] For which cause God also hath exalted him, and hath given him a name which is above all names:
>
> [10] That in the name of Jesus every knee should bow, of those that are in heaven, on earth, and under the earth:
>
> [11] And that every tongue should confess that the Lord Jesus Christ is in the glory of God the Father.
>
> (Philippians 2:5–11)

When Southwell contemplates Christ's self-emptying, he does not imagine, as many a modern theologian might, any loss of godhead. As Guy Jobin has argued, kenotic theology, with its belief in Christ's actual loss of some elements of his divinity in the process of the Incarnation, did not really come into fashion until the nineteenth century.[14] However, it is clear it was in the air as early as the 1640s, for in 1641 the poet Richard Crashaw brought evidence against a Reverend Ellis that he had publicly stated that in his "inanition," Christ had become personally limited.[15] This was a step too far for Protestants of the time; no Jesuit priest of the 1590s would have held this view. The idea of the Son of God's kenosis is instead for Southwell a manifestation of divine power through precisely the human weakness the Son takes on. Christ wins victories with unexpected weapons, as St. Ephrem points out in his *Sermo de domino nostro* or "Sermon on Our Lord": "Death could not devour our Lord unless he possessed a body, neither could hell swallow him up unless he bore our flesh; and so he came in search of a chariot in which to ride to the underworld. This chariot was the body which he received from the Virgin; in it he invaded death's fortress, broke upon its strongroom and scattered all its treasure."[16]

Southwell is always thinking about how Christ expresses his royalty. However, Christ's taking on the garment of man's flesh is not a role but a reality. Looking back to St. Bernard, in *An Epistle of Comfort*, Third Cause, he contrasts the arrogance of Haman and of the court in general with the humility of Christ:

> Aman, a most ambitious and haughty-minded man, thought the greatest honour that a prince could do his subject was to make him ride on his palfrey, attired in his most royal and stately robes (Esther 6). If therefore, tribulation be the most precious garment that Christ did wear, and the Cross his palfrey, we are greatly honoured when he advanceth us the same prerogative.... *Christ's garments* comfort not those that walk in robes, saith St Bernard, *the stable* and *the manger* comfort not those that love the highest rooms in the synagogues.... Let us look on the sacred coat, not of our son, but of our Father and Redeemer, of whose

humanity it is said: *Why is thy* garment red and thy apparel like theirs
that tread in the wine press? and who *is* this that cometh from Edom
with stained attire (Isaiah 63:2)? Let us cast our eyes upon this coat,
dyed in his own innocent blood.[17]

Southwell here refers to the traditional identification of Christ's knightly
regalia or his clothing as his human flesh.[18] Rosemary Woolf says that in
the tradition of Christ as the lover–knight, his "aketoun," or battle-tunic,
was "the human flesh which the virgin gave him in her womb."[19] In
becoming incarnate, Christ the word takes on his bloody garment of the
body in preparation for his war on sin and death. Southwell repeats the
idea in his poem on the Virgin Mary, "Her Nativity": For God on earth
she is the royall throne, /The chosen cloth to make his mortall weede."[20]
This is real self-fashioning, next to which the persistent, pejorative sense of
self-disguise that permeates Greenblatt's seminal work on *Renaissance Self-
Fashioning* pales. Southwell's heroic Christ has little time for anxiety over
what image he is projecting, for his is a rhetoric of action rather than
speech, and the *Epistle of Comfort* enjoins the same confidence upon his
followers, who must recognize their suffering as advancement in the court
of Heaven. If Southwell's rhetoric is verbal, the effect of the rhetoric is
envisioned as behavioral. Alison Shell argues that we should "understand
Southwell as the nexus of much of the most profound thought of his
age."[21] One reason this is true is that Southwell enjoins an imaginative
identity on his audience that permits real self-transformation. Southwell
creates the space in the courtly stable as a locus into which the meditative
reader can enter, following him, if he includes himself in the invitation in
the final stanza, "With joy approch, O Christian wighte." However,
because of the brevity of lyric poetry, the stability of the new identity
depends entirely on the perseverance of the "Christian wighte" outside the
confines of the poem: the identity can only be stable if they "flit not from
this heavenly boy," as he enjoins in "New Heaven, New Warre."[22] But, as
Southwell himself says, it is possible for the new identity to remain
unchanged over time.[23]

Christ's royal simplicity is a repeated focus of all of Southwell's meditations on the Christ Child and the Incarnation itself. Regarding simplicity in
this way should remind us of Dante's extended dialogue with his ancestor
Cacciaguida in the *Paradiso*: here Dante creates an image of an idyllic
Florence, where the flaunting of silks and satins and jewels and the deceptive practice of wearing cosmetics are all unknown.[24] Or we might think of
St. Louis of France, who, according to his biographer, Jean de Joinville,
was a pattern of self-effacing simplicity in dress.[25]

Shakespeare's Richard II, on the other hand, is a paradigm of the kind
of aristocrat Southwell has in mind in "New Heaven, New Warre," and
"New Prince, New Pompe." Shakespeare is thinking of the royal problem
with Christian simplicity in *Richard II*. As Isabel Karreman points out, in

Act III scene iii, Richard reinvests himself with the image of a martyr, but destabilizes all images of himself by forbidding those present to read the record of his sins, a book meant only for the eyes of the divine Judge, and even further by breaking the looking glass he asks to be brought to him so that its manifold shattered images reflect the multiplicity of faces or selves he might now be able to assume. But Karreman is even at this point talking about Richard's own self-fashioning or images in the eyes of the audience.[26] Richard's divestiture nonetheless means something different for Shakespeare as playwright than it does for the ceaselessly talking King. For the playwright, the robbing of the King's rightful if abused clothing, in particular the crown, opens a door for him to be a man.

John Donne spoke of exactly this subject before a royal congregation some decades after Southwell's death. He reminded them sternly, after a flattering exordium, of Christ's "glorious Palace," where there is "no passing of guards, nor ushers. No examination of thy degree or habit. The Prince is not asleep, nor private, nor weary of giving, nor refers to others."[27] His noble congregation, accustomed to the flattery of attendants, the number of servants, the exhibition of affluence and rank might well have taken offense if they attended to him seriously at all. But Donne's most daring stroke is the picture of a prince who, unlike an earthly monarch, does not take naps, does not exclude visitors, withholds no act of generosity, and never "passes the buck." It is not a direct attack on James, but it is unlikely the king could have exonerated himself from this list of a ruler's weaknesses or faults. The ideal being offered him is an ideal of simplicity and availability, with the only regard for rank being mindfulness of responsibility.

The seventeenth century thus continued the castigation of the pomp and wealth of court; perhaps most memorable of all is Milton's defense of the regal simplicity of the unclothed Adam and Eve in *Paradise Lost*. Clothes are accessories of the Fall. Crashaw similarly agrees in his poem on the Epiphany[28] in imagining the queen and the royal children casting their crowns before the manger that their magnificence and integrity come from divesting themselves of royal accoutrements in a way reminiscent of Southwell's own poem on the execution of Mary Queen of Scots, wherein he imagines her mounting to her true princely state by bending before the executioner's weapon: "By death from prisoner to a prince enhaunc'd/ From crosse to crown, from thrall to throne againe ..."[29]

Sumptuary laws

Southwell clearly has in mind the sumptuary laws that assigned as rightful prerogative the wearing of silks and velvets, ermine, and so forth to the monarch. Station was indicated by dress almost to the exclusion of all other signs. The sumptuary laws Elizabeth promulgated during her reign continue the medieval legal and social tradition of clearly segregating the ranks of society in this way. In her case, Elizabeth is to a certain extent

merely reiterating the decrees of her father and her sister, rather than inno-
vating in any way, as she herself mentions. Here, her enjoining of plainer
dress on aristocrats and particularly those beneath them has nothing to do
with a severe puritanism, but rather with promoting a sense of restraint,
loyalty to the goods of the realm, and financial responsibility.

[Greenwich, 15 June 1574, 16 Elizabeth I]

None shall wear in his apparel:

> Any silk of the color of purple, cloth of gold tissued, nor fur of sables,
> but only the King, Queen, King's mother, children, brethren, and
> sisters, uncles, and aunts; and except dukes, marquises, and earls, who
> may wear the same in doublets, jerkins, linings of cloaks, gowns, and
> hose; and those of the Garter, purple in mantles only.
> ... Satin, damask, silk, camlet, or taffeta in gown, coat, hose, or
> uppermost garments; fur whereof the kind groweth not in the Queen's
> dominions, ... except the degrees and persons above mentioned, and
> men that may dispend £100 by the year, and so valued in the subsidy
> book."[30]

The laws aim to reinforce the status of the royal family and upper aristo-
cracy, and betray not a hint of Christian preference for poverty or recognition of Christ's choice of poverty over wealth. Southwell is right to believe
that the view of his almost entirely Christian audience could use some correction. However, in no wise does he consider the outward dress an
indication of inner royalty. Robing himself for battle in man's flesh does
not decrease Christ's royal status.

Defamiliarization and refamiliarization

That status is something the poet believes right-seeing eyes should be able
to perceive. In "Lewd Love Is Losse," Southwell begins by castigating the
false-judging view of lovers of worldly things: "Misdeeming eye! That
stoopest to the lure/Of Mortall worthes, not worth so worthy love."[31] In
several of his poems on the Christ Child, Southwell uses a technique often
found in Nativity lyrics, both medieval and early modern: defamiliarization.
Probably borrowed from folk poetry or the riddles of folklore, this traditional element makes the reader guess at the identity of the mysterious child
without naming him. In poems on Christ's birth, the effect is to train the
audience to recognize by signs rather than by name, a kind of extended par-
aphrastic depiction of him. Modern readers are still familiar with the topos
of defamiliarizing the Christ Child to require the audience to acknowledge
him through signs that definitively identify him. Although we are not conscious that this is a tradition we are partaking in, no one finds the beginning

of "What Child Is This?" in the least bit strange. We know the question prepares us for the triumphant revelation of the chorus: "This, this is Christ the King." The Christ Child in these lyrics is often any baby at the beginning, or just a child in his mother's arms, until the poem progresses onward to give us more and more of his identifying marks. For instance, in "Somer is comen & winter gon," a thirteenth-century lyric, the poem gives the audience increasingly obvious identifying marks of Christ in his passion, until it reveals his identity: "Ihesu is Þe childes name,/King of al londe."[32] This is just one of many similar examples. Whether we are aware of its reverend ancestry or not, the riddling nature of the Nativity lyric is a persistent element that Southwell uses to develop his theme of true identity. However, in this poem, Southwell tells his audience that they should not be baffled; they should see the true princeliness of the child's surroundings and accoutrements. In effect, he reverses the tradition he knows well to produce refamiliarization in the reader. The child is not disguised, but you, the reader, are used to disguises, and so you find it hard to perceive what is being shown openly.

The mentions of the Proleptic Passion and implications of the Eucharist in stanzas one and two already begin to identify the child as Christ:

> In homely manger trembling [he] lies;
> Alas! a pitious sighte!
> The inns are full, no man will yelde
> This little Pilgrime bedd;
> But forc'd He is with sely beastes
> In cribb to shroude His headd.

Christ's experience of physical suffering in the Nativity is obliquely tied in to the Passion in the description of his resting in the manger as "shrouding his head." Southwell dwells on the beginning of Christ's salvific sufferings by imagining the cold of winter and the reaction of the tender newborn's little body to it: he describes his body "trembling." Of course, the Babe in the first stanza could be any child—a poor baby shivering in the winter cold is unfortunately not an unusual thing in this world. But this baby is "sely," and as I have mentioned above, for Southwell and his readers, the word meant "holy" as well as "simple," weak," or "vulnerable" (as he no doubts means when he applies the same term to the beasts in the stable). The very word that allows Southwell to emphasize the child's ordinariness and weakness is the one that first alerts us to the presence of the Divinity.

The mighty babe: power in weakness

Although the child is and appears vulnerable, he is, after all, a Prince. In other lyrics such as "New Heaven, New Warre," and "A childe my Choyce," Southwell perhaps emphasizes Jesus's might more, but he still insists on it here.[33] The image of the Mighty Babe is an ancient one, and Southwell's variations on it in his Nativity series call to mind its appearance in patristic and popular sources.[34] That the Child Jesus had suffered and labored as part and parcel of his salvific mission to take on himself the punishment of humanity for its evildoings was a traditional concept, although theological movements in the sixteenth and seventeenth century were changing the way at least Protestant Christians thought about the duration of Christ's suffering and the relative importance of the modern believer's access to it. But in the traditional understanding of the Incarnation and the Nativity, the baby's privations and indignities were thought to have been prophesied in the Psalms. In Southwell's generation, the Flemish artist very popular among the Jesuits, Hieronymous Wierix (1551–1619), created a print of the Christ Child carrying the instruments of the Passion, or the *arma Christi*, in a basket while also carrying the cross. The print is garnished with the quotation from Psalm 87:16, "In laboribus a iuventute mea," "In labors from my youth," a biblical passage that was often seen as prophesying Jesus' lifelong sufferings.[35]

The quotation on the Wierix print is one that St. John of the Cross treated in his *Subida del Monte Carmelo* when discussing Christ's choice to come into the world in poverty.[36] This is probably why the image came to be more widespread during the Counter Reformation. But even if Southwell did not know the Carmelite source, he would have been familiar with St. Augustine's commentaries on the psalms; Augustine is one of the earliest to assert the psalm's Christological valence.[37] He interprets it as meaning "from the youth of the body of Christ," and he includes in the definition of Christ's body both his actual earthly body and the Church on earth, which constitutes the suffering members of that body. Cassiodorus restates Augustine's equation of the speaker with the Church, but also very clearly in his "Conclusion drawn from the psalm" says, "this is Christ's chorus ... for the faithful people, following [h]is most holy passion, gave answer with a most splendid imitation," and he goes on to speak of the pains Christ himself bore.[38] For Southwell, the suffering of the Christ Child created a union between God and humanity and allowed the faithful to contemplate their role in the body of the Church, and to consider who Christ was and what he knew as an infant. It provides a way of knowing him; it allows him to be recognized for who he is. Again, for Southwell, identity is not a mask put on but one put off, not an assumption but a renunciation. His kenotic theology, based in the self-emptying of Christ which is the Incarnation, should make perfect sense to his audience, but the sad truth is that it does not.

Up to this point I have been writing around the poem, and to move beyond background to the poem itself, the great craftsmanship of the lyric reveals at every turn Southwell's strategy. Modern readers who are tempted to discount Southwell's poetic abilities because his thesis/antithesis structures and his moralizing seem too heavy handed should observe the facility and dexterity he demonstrates here. The homely "manger" where the infant lies is the bed of the little Pilgrim, where he "shrouds his head." In this set of lines, whose language could not be more simple and clear, Southwell packs a myriad of integrated references, saturating the stanza with implications of Christ's intentionality, his preference for poverty, his mission to die on the cross, his veiling of the glory of his godhead, the hiddenness of his presence in the Eucharist, and more. Like Herbert after him, Southwell is able to merge simplicity of language with polysemous imagery deftly and almost unnoticeably. This satisfies the intellectual desire for difficulty, a problem to solve, and one of the aesthetic norms for beauty, *claritas*, as Thomas Aquinas defines it. Southwell devotes the meat of the poem to what I would call a prolonged *correctio*: each redefinition is intended to unveil the truth to the reader who is convinced of the opposite. A prince's court is a prince's court, correct? No, the stable is the prince's court, the *real* way real, *heavenly* courts look. Plate is plate? No, the wooden dish is plate. Who would want plate? It is not the dinnerware of a real King. The crux, I believe, is in the line about the "chair of State." Who has a chair of State? Southwell is clearly thinking of the difference between the King or Queen's throne and Christ's manger, thus addressing the true nature of magisterial authority. All other kinds of performances of authority are false; they are masks, disguises, and fronts. Jesus, who could choose anything, chooses the "crib [as] His chair of State," and this is the kind of chair someone who is really king (or queen) should desire. Thus Southwell's poem acts as a kind of *Mirror for Magistrates*. It painstakingly teaches what true authority and power look like to an audience whose eyes are accustomed to a glamor, a false image, something we might say an Archimago has conjured up to deceive them, while the poet undeceives them like Prince Arthur's diamond mirror of truth in *The Faerie Queene* (which was written at about the same time).[39]

It is possible also that Southwell imagines himself in the evanescent moment of the poetic tableau in which the reader is invited to be a courtier; he could be addressing himself as well as other "Christian wight[s]" in the final stanza. If so, Southwell is making present to his own eyes the "humble pompe" and himself approaching to "give homage" where it is due. The "applicatio" section of the lyric, where the meditation reaches fruition in action, is, as always, open ended: does he, do the readers, approach with joy? Do they come near and behold the traveler who has come from heaven? The imperative verb only orders; it cannot assert. But it does point to a different monarch than the one the political world offers.

The little pilgrim transforms before our eyes into the King as Southwell closes on the paradox of "humble pompe."[40] This is the thing Christ brings from Heaven, ratifying its normative value by the authority of its origin. The dignity, and even glory, of poverty displaces the shams of court and state: "this pompe is prizèd there." Southwell's lyric makes a radical statement about human values, correcting a false impression that the surrender of earthly riches is a temporary sacrifice, to be recompensed by their acquisition in heaven. Southwell asserts that the opposite is true, and that the stable and manger reveal the very nature of Heaven. The Christ Child's pilgrimage to earth is intended to transform it, rather than to transform him. There is no place on earth more like paradise than the stable of Bethlehem, but he has come to transform the whole earth as Southwell invites the reader: "With joy approch, O Christian wighte!/Do homage to thy Kinge;/And highly prize His humble pompe,/Which He from heaven doth bringe."

Like the Puritans of the day, Southwell points to the heavenly King as a solution to the problems that always plague the human court. Christ has already given an example of the correct way of ruling and the correct way of showing one's nobility. To accept this apparent antithesis as truth, those in power would have to renounce power, or at least its usual trappings. To be a proper Christian courtier one must be prepared to follow this Prince, as Southwell is. To do that is to be prepared to die, and Southwell is so prepared. But human frailty always poses a threat to the adoption of a desired identity, as permanent as Southwell wishes that identity to be. The reason the courtly identity Southwell proposes to himself as much as to his audience could be precarious is because it is easier for the human being to flee discomfort and trial than to embrace them.

When he was on his way to England and his mission, Southwell admitted to human fear of the punishment that awaited him if discovered, as Jessie Childs has shown.[41] "It is true that the flesh is weak and can do nothing and even now revolts from that which is proposed," Southwell wrote before embarking. Here we might again invoke that ideal mirror image Kuchar explores in "A Vale of Tears"; the would-be heavenly courtier might indeed despair of ever attaining such simplicity and bravery. However, Kuchar also agrees with Elaine Scarry, that "the act of perceiving ... beauty has a built-in liability to self-correction and self-adjustment, so much so that it appears to be a key element in whatever beauty is."[42] The revelation of the real beauty of the Child and his court within the stable beauty allows the "Christian wighte" to "approch" "with joy." For Southwell also says, "Rather than shrink from them as torturers, I call to them to bring my crown." It is that antithetical habit of mind that later will reinterpret the items in the stable at Bethlehem so that we can see them aright, as accoutrements of Christ's royal dignity. This is the view of the true Christian, as St. Paul says in his Epistle to the Philippians (1:11): "For to me, to live is Christ, and to die is gain." Southwell always maintains that Christ is the center of meaning, and the conveyer of identity. To know the meaning of a word, one should as it were look it up in the dictionary that is Christ. If Queen and court had valued Christ's poverty and humility as he imagines they might possibly do, however, perhaps he would not have had to die on Tyburn Hill. For the age was not yet tired of the old princes and the old pomp.

Notes

1 Frank W. Brownlow, *Robert Southwell* (New York: Twayne, 1996), 115–121.
2 Other poems have not been so lucky—think of the Nativity lyrics of Donne, Jonson, Herbert, and Milton, for example!
3 Stephen Greenblatt, *Hamlet in Purgatory* (Princeton: Princeton UP, 2001), 200.
4 Gary Kuchar, "Southwell's 'A Vale of Tears': A Psychoanalysis of Form," *Mosaic: An Interdisciplinary Critical Journal*, 34, no. 1 (2001): 107–108.
5 Augustine, *De Trinitate* Book I.75. PL 42. See also Basil Studer, *Trinity and Incarnation: The Faith of the Early Church*, ed. Andrew Louth (Edinburgh, Scotland: T & T Clark Ltd., 1993), 122.
6 Robert Southwell, "New Prince, New Pompe," in *The Poems of Robert Southwell, S. J.*, ed. Nancy P. Brown and James H. McDonald (Oxford: Clarendon, 1967), 17–18. See also Alexander Grosart, *The Complete Poems of Robert Southwell, S. J.*, (London: Greenwood Press, 1941), 107–108.
7 Scott R. Pilarz, S. J. *Robert Southwell and the Mission of Literature, 1561–1595: Writing Reconciliation.* (Aldershot: Ashgate, 2004).
8 Robert Southwell, *An Humble Supplication to her Maiestie*, ed. R. C. Bald (Cambridge: Cambridge UP, 2011).
9 Afroditi-Maria Panaghis discusses the various identities Southwell takes on in his "Humble Supplication to Her Majestie": "He expresses a political stance which professes loyalty to Queen Elizabeth, states that he is capable of 'annihilating the subject if need be as well as separate commitments,' and asserts that he sees no conflict between his religious and political self." A.-M. Panaghis, "Robert Southwell's Articulation of Self-Fashioning," in this volume. Panaghis cites Ronald Corthell, "The Secrecy of Man: Recusant Discourse and the Elizabethan Subject," *English Literary Renaissance* 19, no. 3 (1989): 289. Panaghis herself suggested in thinking about this poem that Southwell imagines himself as a pilgrim to the court, hoping to change the political landscape. Though he does not state that explicitly, I think it is very possible he fashioned the poem with that intention in mind, given his adoption of the roles of subject, courtier, and advisor to the Queen in the *Supplication*.
10 Dante, *The Divine Comedy: Purgatorio*, trans. Robert and Jean Hollander (New York: Random House, 2004).
11 The OED says, "In the 16th and 17th centuries *silly* was very extensively used in senses A. 2 – A. 5 [worthy, good, pious, holy auspicious, fortunate, helpless, weak, etc.], and in a number of examples it is difficult to decide which shade of meaning was intended by the writer."
12 Louis Martz, *The Poetry of Meditation* (New Haven: Yale UP, 1954), 193. See also Brian Cummings, *The Literary Culture of the Reformation: Grammar and Grace* (Oxford: Oxford UP, 2001), 350.
13 Joseph A. Nolan, "Robert Southwell," *The American Catholic Quarterly Review*, 7 (1882): 454.
14 Guy Jobin, "Instituer l'évidement? Heuristique kénotique et positivité éthique," *Laval théologique et philosophique*, 67, no. 1 (2011): 75. See also Edward T. Oakes, S. J., "Kenotic Christology: Thomasius, Gess, Mackintosh" in his *Infinity Dwindled to Infancy: A Catholic and Evangelical Christology* (Grand Rapids: Eerdmans, 2011), 319–330, esp. 321.
15 Hilton Kelliher, "Crashaw at Cambridge," in *New Perspectives on the Life and Art of Richard Crashaw*, ed. John R. Roberts (Columbia: University of Missouri Press, 1990), 212.
16 St. Ephrem the Syrian, *Sermo de Domino nostro*, 3–4.9, in Lamy, *Opera*, 1: 152–158, 166–168.

17 Robert Southwell, *Epistle of Comfort*, ed. Margaret Waugh (London: Burns & Oates, 1966), 103.

18 Theresa Coletti has traced the image of Christ making for himself his own body as his making a tunic for himself from the Virgin Mary through the Holy Spirit to, among others, the sermons of St. Anthony of Padua, the *Stanzaic Life of Christ*, and the Towneley Cycle's *Crucifixion*. Coletti explains that the image of the Virgin Mary weaving is an image of both the Incarnation and the Passion because it suggests both the swaddling clothes of the infant Christ and the *tunica inconsutilis*, the seamless garment for which the Roman soldiers cast lots. See Theresa Coletti, "Devotional Iconography in the N-Town Marian Plays," *Comparative Drama*, 11 (1977–1978): 25–26. See also Mary Dzon, "Birgitta of Sweden and Christ's Clothing," in *The Christ Child in Medieval Culture" Alpha es et O!*, eds. Mary Dzon and Theresa Kenney (Toronto: University of Toronto Press, 2012). Leo Steinberg has also referred to the idea of Christ's body as clothing; he cites a homily by Photius, the ninth-century bishop of Constantinople, but of course Photius was deriving it from much older authors. Leo Steinberg notes an analog of this image in Homily 7, "The Annunciation," from *The Homilies of Photius, Patriarch of Constantinople*, trans. Cyril Mango (Cambridge: Harvard UP, 1958), 148. See his note in a discussion of Christ's wounded body in *The Sexuality of Christ in Renaissance Art and Modern Oblivion* (Chicago: Pantheon Books, 1983), 375, n. 15.

19 Rosemary Woolf, *The English Mystery Plays* (Berkeley: U of California P, 1972), 267. Gail McMurray Gibson, "The Thread of Life in the Hand of the Virgin," in *Equally in God's Image: Women in the Middle Ages*, eds. Julia Bolton Holloway, Constance S. Wright, and Joan Bechtold (New York: Peter Lang, 1990), 50ff. The paragraphs notes 16 and 17 refer to appeared in similar form in my essay, "The Christ Child on Fire: Southwell's Mighty Babe," *English Literary Review*, 43, no. 3 (Autumn 2013): 415–445.

20 Southwell, "Her Nativity," in Nancy P. Brown and James H. McDonald, *The Poems of Robert Southwell, S. J.* (Oxford: Clarendon Press): 3–4.

21 Alison Shell, *Catholicism, Controversy and the English Literary Imagination, 1558–1660* (Cambridge: Cambridge UP, 1999), 285. Gary Bouchard has argued for Southwell's extensive influence on a range of writers from Spenser in the 1590s to the metaphysical poets and other religious poets of the ensuing century. "Who Knows Not Colin's Clout? Assessing the Impact of Southwell's Literary Success upon Spenser" *LATCH* 3 (2010): 151–163. He advances his fully developed argument in his book, *Southwell's Sphere: The Influence of England's Secret Poet* (South Bend: St. Augustine Press, 2018).

22 Southwell, "New Heaven New Warre," in Brown and McDonald, *The Poems of Robert* Southwell, 13–15. Southwell seems to imagine a stable reaction to the summons to poverty on the part of the magi in "The Epiphanie":

> Heaven at her light, earth blusheth at her pride,
> And of their pompe these peeres ashamed be,
> Their crowns, their robes, their traine they set aside
> When Gods poore cottage, clouts, and crew they see,
> All glorious things their glory now despise
>
> Sith God Contempt doth more then Glory prise.
> ... And with their gifts the givers hearts do stay,
> Their mind from Christ no parting can remove,
> His humble state, his stall, his poore retinew
> They fancy more then all their rich revenew.
>
> (Brown and McDonald, 8)

23 As Afroditi-Maria Panaghis mentions in Chapter 9 in this collection, Southwell when talking about his shifting roles says he can be, like St. Paul, "all things to all men, and to God ever one and the same." Robert Southwell, *Spiritual Exercises and Devotions of Blessed Robert Southwell, S J.*, ed. J.-M.de Buck, S J. London: Sheed and Ward, 1931. 59–60. See A.-M. Panaghis, "Robert Southwell's Articulation of Self-fashioning" in this volume.

24 Dante, *Paradiso*, trans. Robert and Jean Hollander (New York: Doubleday, 2007), 363.

> I saw Bellincion Berti wear a belt of leather
> and plain bone, and saw his lady step back
> from the glass, her face untouched by paint.
> And I saw one of the Nerli and a del Vecchio
> both content with wearing simple, unlined skins,
> their ladies busy with their spindles and their flax.
>
> (*Para.* XV. 106–117)

The retrospective, at first unimpressive, blazon of the nobles' typical garb becomes a song of praise for the abstemious and honest men and women of the past, who needed no disguises to convince others of their importance or their status.

25 Jean de Joinville, *The Memoirs of the Lord of Joinville*, trans. Ethel Wedgwood (Kessinger Publishing, 2004). Reprint. The king would sit under a tree to render judgment in clothing so simple (though the cap of black peacock feathers Joinville describes might not exactly appear to modern audiences as the garb of poverty) that his wife Marguerite would beg him to dress appropriately for his role as king. Louis agreed on one condition: that she should wear the clothes he picked out for her in return. Marguerite quickly demurred and allowed Louis his unkingly garments. Louis's simplicity is one of the first things Joinville speaks of in his biography of the king and saint:

> He used to say: That we ought so to clothe and care for our bodies that sober men of the world might not deem us over-nice, nor young men deem us slovens. And this reminds me of the father of the present king [NB: Joinville means Louis's son Philippe le Bel; the present king for whose wife he is writing the biography is Louis's grandson] and the embroidered coats-of-arms that they make nowadays. For I told him, that never in my travels over seas did I see embroidered coats, neither belonging to the king nor to anyone else. And he told me, that he had garments embroidered with his arms such as had cost him eight hundred pounds parisis. And I told him that he would have employed them better, had he given them to God, and had made his clothes of good taffety as his father was wont to do.

26 Isabel Karreman, *The Drama of Memory in Shakespeare's History Plays* (Cambridge: Cambridge UP, 2015), 73. Karreman writes of the king's abdication in *Richard II*, "[W]hile Richard does indeed divest himself of his royal prerogatives, he does so through a ritual performance that in effect reinvests his person and his story with new authority.... The ritual discarding of one set of symbols or props and substituting it for another, is enacted in [this scene]."

27 See Barry Spurr, "The Analogy of Faith: The Anglican Character of Donne's Sermons," *Arts: The Journal of the Sydney University Arts Association*, 14 (1989): 13–21. Spurr cites Evelyn Simpson and George Potter, *The Sermons of John Donne* (Berkeley: University of California Press, 1958), 118.

28 L. C. Martin, ed., *The Poems English Latin and Greek of Richard Crashaw* (Oxford: Clarendon Press, 1927), 47.

29 "Decease, Release: Dum Morior, Orior." Brown and McDonald, *The Poems of Robert Southwell, S. J.*, 47.
30 Elizabeth I, "Proclamation against Excess," 1577, Print, British Library (www.bl.uk/learning/timeline/item126628.html). See also Liza Picard, *Elizabeth's London: Everyday Life in Elizabethan England*, (London: St. Martin's Press, 2003), 134–135.
31 Brown and McDonald, *The Poems of Robert Southwell, S. J.*, 62.
32 Anonymous, collected in Carleton Brown, *English Lyrics of the Thirteenth Century* (Oxford: Clarendon Press, 1924), 108–111.
33 For example, think of the closure of the latter poem: "Almighty Babe, whose tender arms can force all foes to fly,/Correct my faults, protect my life, direct me when I die." Brown and McDonald, *The Poems of Robert Southwell, S. J.*, 13.
34 Kenney, "The Christ Child on Fire," 415–445.
35 Hieronymous Wierix, Département des Estampes et Photographie, Bibliothèque nationale de France, fol. 162, 17th c.
36 See San Juan de la Cruz, *Obras Completas*, ed. Lucinio Ruano de la Iglesia (Madrid: Biblioteca de Autores Cristianos, 1982), 96.
37 St. Augustine, "In Psalmum LXXXVII Enarratio," PL 37.1119.
38 Patrick Gerard Walsh, ed., *Cassiodorus: Explanation of the Psalms* (New York: The Newman Press, 1991), 350.
39 Edmund Spenser, *The Faerie Queene* I.8.19, ed. Thomas P. Roche, Jr. (New Haven: Yale UP, 1956).
40 Southwell also insists on a heavenly pomp that differs from earthly pomp in "The Visitation." Speaking of Mary, he says, "A prince she is, and mightier prince doth beare,/Yet pompe of princely traine she would not have,/But doubtles heavenly Quires attendant were...." In Brown and McDonald, *The Poems of Robert Southwell, S. J.*, 5–6.
41 Jessie Childs, *God's Traitors: Terror & Faith in Elizabethan England* (Oxford: Oxford UP, 2014), 134–135.
42 Elaine Scarry, *On Beauty and Being Just* (Princeton: Princeton UP, 2001), 29. Cited in Gary Kuchar, "A Greek in the Temple: Pseudo-Dionysius and Negative Theology in Richard Crashaw's 'Hymn in the Glorious Epiphany'," *Studies in Philology*, 108, no. 2 (Spring 2011): 261–299.

Bibliography

St. Augustine. *De Trinitate* Book I.75. PL 42.
St. Augustine. "In Psalmum LXXXVII Enarratio." PL 37.1119.
Bouchard, Gary. *Southwell's Sphere: The Influence of England's Secret Poet*. South Bend: St. Augustine Press, 2018.
Bouchard, Gary. "Who Knows Not Colin's Clout? Assessing the Impact of Southwell's Literary Success upon Spenser." *LATCH* 3 (2010): 151–163.
Brown, Carleton. *English Lyrics of the Thirteenth Century*. Oxford: Clarendon Press, 1924.
Brown, Nancy P. and James H. McDonald, eds. *The Poems of Robert Southwell, S. J.* Oxford: Clarendon, 1967.
Brownlow, Frank W. *Robert Southwell*. New York: Twayne, 1996.
Childs, Jessie. *God's Traitors: Terror and Faith in Elizabethan England*. Oxford: Oxford University Press, 2014.
Coletti, Theresa. "Devotional Iconography in the N-Town Marian Plays." *Comparative Drama* 11 (1977–1978): 25–26.

Corthell, Ronald. "The Secrecy of Man: Recusant Discourse and the Elizabethan Subject." *English Literary Renaissance* 19, no. 3 (1989): 289.

Cummings, Brian. *The Literary Culture of the Reformation: Grammar and Grace.* Oxford: Oxford University Press, 2001.

Dante. *Paradiso.* Translated by Robert and Jean Hollander. New York: Doubleday, 2007.

Dante. *The Divine Comedy: Purgatorio.* Translated by Robert and Jean Hollander. New York: Random House, 2004.

Dzon, Mary. "Birgitta of Sweden and Christ's Clothing." In *The Christ Child in Medieval Culture" Alpha es et O!* Edited by Mary Dzon and Theresa Kenney. Toronto: University of Toronto Press, 2012.

Elizabeth I. "Proclamation against Excess." 1577. Print, British Library www.bl.uk/learning/timeline/item126628.html.

St. Ephrem the Syrian. *Sermo de Domino nostro*, 3–4.9. In Lamy, *Opera* 1: 152–158. 166–168.

Gibson, Gail McMurray. "The Thread of Life in the Hand of the Virgin." In *Equally in God's Image: Women in the Middle Ages.* Edited by Julia Bolton Holloway, Constance S. Wright, and Joan Bechtold. New York: Peter Lang, 1990.

Greenblatt, Stephen. *Hamlet in Purgatory.* Princeton: Princeton University Press, 2001.

Grosart, Alexander. *The Complete Poems of Robert Southwell, S. J.* London: Greenwood Press, 1941, 107–108.

Jean de Joinville. *The Memoirs of the Lord of Joinville.* Translated by Ethel Wedgwood. Kessinger Publishing, 2004. Reprint.

Jobin, Guy. "Instituer l'évidement? Heuristique kénotique et positivité éthique." *Laval théologique et philosophique* 67, no. 1 (2011): 75.

Juan de la Cruz, San. *Obras Completas.* Edited by Lucinio Ruano de la Iglesia. Madrid: Biblioteca de Autores Cristianos, 1982.

Karreman, Isabel. *The Drama of Memory in Shakespeare's History Plays.* Cambridge: Cambridge University Press, 2015.

Kelliher, Hilton. "Crashaw at Cambridge." In *New Perspectives on the Life and Art of Richard Crashaw.* Edited by John R. Roberts. Columbia: University of Missouri Press, 1990.

Kenney, Theresa M. "The Christ Child on Fire: Southwell's Mighty Babe." *English Literary Renaissance* 43, no. 3 (Autumn 2013): 415–445.

Kuchar, Gary. "A Greek in the Temple: Pseudo-Dionysius and Negative Theology in Richard Crashaw's 'Hymn in the Glorious Epiphany'." *Studies in Philology* 108, no. 2 (Spring 2011): 261–299.

Kuchar, Gary. "Southwell's 'A Vale of Tears': A Psychoanalysis of Form." *Mosaic: An Interdisciplinary Critical Journal* 34, no. 1 (2001): 107–108.

Martin, L. C., ed. *The Poems English Latin and Greek of Richard Crashaw.* Oxford: Clarendon Press, 1927.

Martz, Louis. *The Poetry of Meditation.* New Haven: Yale University Press, 1954.

Nolan, Joseph A. "Robert Southwell." *The American Catholic Quarterly Review* 7 (1882): 454.

Oakes, Edward T., S. J. "Kenotic Christology: Thomasius, Gess, Mackintosh." In his *Infinity Dwindled to Infancy: A Catholic and Evangelical Christology.* Grand Rapids: Eerdmans, 2011.

Panaghis, Afroditi-Maria. "Robert Southwell's Articulation of Self-Fashioning," *Precarious Identities: The Works of Fulke Greville and Robert Southwell*. New York: Routledge, 2020.

Photius. Homily 7, "The Annunciation." From *The Homilies of Photius, Patriarch of Constantinople*. Translated by Cyril Mango. Cambridge: Harvard University Press, 1958.

Picard, Liza. *Elizabeth's London: Everyday Life in Elizabethan England*. London: St. Martin's Press, 2003.

Pilarz, Scott R., S. J. *Robert Southwell and the Mission of Literature, 1561–1595: Writing Reconciliation*. Aldershot: Ashgate, 2004.

Scarry, Elaine. *On Beauty and Being Just*. Princeton: Princeton UP, 2001.

Shell, Allison. *Catholicism, Controversy and the English Literary Imagination, 1558–1660*. Cambridge: Cambridge University Press, 1999.

Simpson, Evelyn and George Potter, eds. *The Sermons of John Donne*. Berkeley: University of California Press, 1958.

Southwell, Robert. *An Epistle of Comfort*. Edited by Margaret Waugh. London: Burns & Oates, 1966.

Southwell, Robert. *An Humble Supplication to her Maiestie*. Edited by R. C. Bald. Cambridge: Cambridge University Press, 2011.

Southwell, Robert. "New Prince, New Pompe." In *The Poems of Robert Southwell, S. J.* Edited by Nancy P. Brown and James H. McDonald, 17–18. Oxford: Clarendon, 1967.

Southwell, Robert. *Spiritual Exercises and Devotions of Blessed Robert Southwell, SJ.*, ed. J.-M. de Buck, SJ, 59–60. London: Sheed and Ward, 1931.

Spenser, Edmund. *The Faerie Queene*. Edited by Thomas P. Roche, Jr. New Haven: Yale University Press, 1956.

Spurr, Barry "The Analogy of Faith: The Anglican Character of Donne's Sermons." *Arts: The Journal of the Sydney University Arts Association* 14 (1989): 13–21.

Steinberg, Leo. *The Sexuality of Christ in Renaissance Art and Modern Oblivion*. Chicago: Pantheon Books, 1983.

Studer, Basil. *Trinity and Incarnation: The Faith of the Early Church*. Edited by Andrew Louth. Edinburgh, Scotland: T & T Clark Ltd., 1993.

Walsh, Patrick Gerard, ed. *Cassiodorus: Explanation of the Psalms*. New York: The Newman Press, 1991.

Wierix, Hieronymus. Département des Estampes et Photographie, Bibliothèque nationale de France, fol. 162, 17th c.

Woolf, Rosemary. *The English Mystery Plays*. Berkeley: University of California Press, 1972.

8 Complaint as reconciliation in the literary mission of Robert Southwell

Emily A. Ransom

Among the precious few traces of Robert Southwell's Jesuit formation in Rome (1580–1586), the most celebrated is the Autograph Manuscript held at Stonyhurst College in rural Lancashire.[1] A composite notebook made up of gatherings of at least seven various sizes, many of which obviously incomplete, this relic offers a window into Southwell's theological, pastoral, and literary formation as he prepared for ministry and martyrdom from the safety of the continent. There are notes of a Latin treatise on dogmatic theology, Latin meditations and prayers, ten Latin poems, two incomplete English translations of a sermon on Mary Magdalene that would inspire *Marie Magdalens funeral teares*, and two incomplete English poems: the seven-line emblem poem "Amenomon" about a ship tossed in a storm and a tree beside a menacing axe, and "[The] Peeter Playnt," an incomplete English translation of the Italian *Le Lagrime di San Pietro* that would inspire *Saint Peters complaint*. These fragmentary notebooks contain Southwell's only English works we can say definitively were written in Rome, before his vernacular London publications began appearing in 1587, 1591, and 1595.[2] For a poet who would become a posthumous best-seller on the English press, this record of his vernacular self-fashioning is tantalizingly incomplete. All four English works are left unfinished, and furthermore are contained in gatherings that were apparently parts of larger manuscripts now lost.[3] Even in their paucity, however, they provide a valuable perspective of Southwell's cultivation of his native tongue from abroad, his developing skills as a translator and adaptor, his inspirational models, and his two-way appropriation of English and continental literature.

For the purposes of this chapter, the most crucial insight is found in "[The] Peeter Playnt," an unfinished translation of Luigi Tansillo's *Le Lagrime di San Pietro* which was undergoing widespread revival, expansion, and imitation during Southwell's Jesuit formation.[4] The original Italian poem consists of forty eight-line stanzas printed in 1560 and 1576 and included in at least four collections in the first fourteen years after the poet's death.[5] A much expanded version of the poem was published in 1585 and reprinted over a dozen times in the next three decades,[6] while the earlier version was put to music by the Flemish composer Orlande de Lassus (Orlando di Lasso) in 1595 and subsequently translated into French by François de Malherbe (Paris, 1587, 1596, 1598) and Robert Estienne (Paris, 1595, 1606) and into Spanish by Luis Galvez de Montalvo (Toledo, 1598).[7] But before it became a European fascination, an exemplary model of baroque penitential poetry, what Pierre Janelle describes as a " 'cycle of remorse,' which had its birth in Italy and spread to the whole of Western Europe," a Jesuit student in Rome had already begun translating it into English sometime before returning to England in 1586.[8] In Southwell's case, however, the half-hearted translation indicates a wider reaching project of appropriation and self-fashioning developed in his later poetry. The working title of his translation of *Le Legrime*, which would have been most accurately rendered "the tears of Saint Peter," begins with an excised definite article. Though one cannot say for sure, the most obvious explanation is that he began to write a literal translation of the title before reconsidering. Not "the tears," he decided, but rather "Peeter Playnt," or as it would later become in his much expanded and entirely transformed version, *Saint Peters complaint*.[9] Even while translating a baroque tears poem into English, Southwell was not merely infiltrating Italian styles into English poetry; he was consciously recasting continental devotion in an English style, specifically the popular English mode of complaint. A large part of his success on the Protestant press can be traced to this literary strategy already forming during his years abroad: adapting tears into complaint.

This chapter argues for the importance of the English complaint mode in Southwell's literary mission, both in terms of his poetic theory and his strategic success among Protestant readers for whom he fashioned himself as an English complaint poet. As I will demonstrate, complaint was among the most popular modes of English poetry, an affective and combative style characterized not only by lamentation but also by a cry for justice generally left in suspense. It permeated lyric poetry of the Henrician, Elizabethan, and Jacobean reigns as it had medieval literature, and before the publication of *Saint Peters complaint* it was generally identified with secular poems of fallen princes, forlorn shepherds, abandoned women, and world-weary sages. While Southwell has been rightly credited for (or accused of) bringing Italian baroque styles into English poetry, particularly the flourishing tears poetry that ventriloquized laments of St. Peter, St. Mary Magdalene, and the Virgin Mary, his method was a self-conscious adaptation of this continental Catholic *devotional* mode into an English secular *poetic* mode.[10] From the early translation abandoned before it was half-finished, Southwell was translating tears into complaint in more ways than one, not only in the words of the title but also in the poetic mode and devotional approach. Though complaint is ubiquitous across his poetic oeuvre, I will focus specifically on the ways he uses it affectively to draw the reader into the fraught trials of three of the most vehement biblical lovers, by Southwell's portrayal: Peter, Mary Magdalene, and Joseph. Without directly triggering theologically contentious topics, the characteristic affectivity and suspension of complaint invites the reader into an Ignatian approach to human passion radically different from the neo-Stoic moderation popular in contemporaneous consolation literature and indicative of Calvin's commentaries of the biblical texts. The strategic success of this literary mission that continued decades after Southwell's pastoral mission had ended is apparent not only in the dozens of editions and imitations that appeared until the civil wars of the 1640s but also in the combative piety of the devotional complaints of his Protestant successors. Though the mode is indeed combative, the strategy is conciliatory, particularly in the way the suspension eschews simplistic solutions of popular polemic. When George Herbert later asserted to his "deare angrie Lord" that he would respond to divine paradoxes with one of his own—"I will complain, yet praise"—it was Southwell who had taught him how.[11]

Southwell's strategy: complaint as reconciliation

Southwell's appropriation of literary complaint into meditation and prayer was a bold strategy for both literary and theological reasons. In fact, while scholars have long identified incisive applications of his poetry to the Catholic recusant community, this particular strategy was more missional than pastoral, aimed at the broader literary community of English poets and readers in a forcefully Protestant culture. To demonstrate this, in this section I will sketch a working definition of English complaint that his contemporaries deployed extensively, especially in terms of the affectivity and suspense that Southwell assimilated into his poetic persona. Then I will incorporate this definition into Southwell's own description of his poetic theory described in the opening epistles of his two most popular works: his theoretical justification for appropriating literary complaint in the epistle to *Saint Peters complaint* and his theological justification for appropriating affective complaint in the epistle to *Marie Magdalens funeral teares*. While the former point caters to his English Protestant readers, I will show that the latter point creates a subtle theological tension specifically in the nature and practical treatment of human passion, thus allowing Southwell to provoke and engage his Protestant readers without directly triggering the prevalent theological hot-button issues like justification, sacraments, papacy, liturgical prayer, or veneration of saints and images. With this background set, the majority of this chapter demonstrates this strategy in Southwell's treatment of Peter, Mary Magdalene, and Joseph in which he strikingly redirects the devotional emphasis from sin to love, justifies excess of passion, and allows for irresolution and suspense. The poetic convention was almost hackneyed to the point of being unidentifiable, allowing the devotional posture space to provoke and compel with the characteristic tension of complaint. Southwell strategically fashioned himself as an English complainant in order to subtly provoke his readers to reimagine their theological expectations about human passions by redirecting them.

For the purpose of this study, I will characterize the complaint as a poetic mode primarily centered on an affective and stylized account of a grievance or affliction and an unresolved pathetic appeal to justice or pity. Common categories include *de casibus* complaints of fallen prices, pastoral complaints of forlorn shepherds, female complaints of abandoned or betrayed women, Petrarchan complaints of scorned lovers, and *contemptus mundi* complaints of the vanities of the world. As an almost ubiquitous literary mode, the complaint has had the unusual fortune of being far more deployed among poets than commented upon by scholars, and this chapter does not have space to compensate fully for that neglect. Early modern rhetoricians themselves were hit-or-miss in considering the complaint among poetic genres: William Webbe's *Discourse of English Poetrie* (1586) includes it within the category of tragical poetry, George Puttenham's *Arte of English Poesie* (1588) and Francis Meres's *Palladis tamia* (1598) describe it as a category of elegy, E. K.'s commentary on Spenser's *Shepheardes calender* (1579) treats it as a category of pastoral, and Philip Sidney's *Defence of Poesy* (c.1582) does not mention it at all.[12] Two book-length studies have treated specific groupings of complaint, and various shorter studies of complaint have observed it through the lens of a particular author or persona (women, shepherds, lovers, princes).[13] Scholarly interest in complaint is growing, however, and as recently as 2018 it was included among essays on genre in the Wiley *Companion to Renaissance Poetry*, which describes it as "an unusually permeable mode, open to generic mixing."[14] Perhaps because of the promiscuity of its boundaries, medieval and early modern authors liberally use "complaint" with at least as much frequency as "ode" or "ballad," and for modern readers it is best understood not as a genre but a literary mode that triggered certain expectations for the readers.[15] At least four dozen books of poems printed during the reigns of Elizabeth I and James I advertised themselves as complaints on the title pages (see Figure 8.1), and beyond these self-advertised complaints, we can include among the motley crew a host of other bestsellers such as the many renditions of *A Mirror for Magistrates*, *Tottel's Miscellany*, *England's Helicon*, or the plethora of Petrarchan sonnet sequences. Complaints tend to feature a forlorn figure, from a historical or mythical personage to an abstract figure such as old age, who bewails the cause of his or her downfall. There is often an appeal for justice or at least to pity, hearkening to a legal suit, and in this way the common features of complaint are not formal but affective. In its Latinate sense, *affectus* is the poem's capacity to exert force upon its reader, and perhaps for this reason complaints tend to end with irresolution. They end in suspense because they are meant to move the reader: to action, to pity, to reflection, to conversion, to caution.[16] The final action of poem is the reader's.

Advertised complaint poems
during the reigns of Elizabeth I and James I

1558, 59	John Bradford, *The complaynt of veritie*
1558	David Lindsay, *Complaynt of our souveraine Lordis Papyngo*
1563	William Birch, *The complaint of a sinner*
1564	Anon., *A complaynt agaynst the wicked enemies of Christ*
1567	Robert Sempill, *The Kingis complaint*
1570	Robert Sempill, *The complaint of Scotland*
1573	John Carr, *A pitifull complaint of the penitente synner*
1576, 87	George Gascoigne, *The complainte of Phylomene*
1581	Robert Sempill, *Ane complaint upon fortoun*
1584	Thomas Lodge, *The Lamentable complaint of truth over England*
1585	Anon., *Londons complaint*
1590	Thomas Nelson, *Lamentable complaint of the people of England*
1591	Edmund Spenser, *Complaints.*
1592	Samuel Daniel, *The complaynt of Rosamond*
1593	Thomas Lodge, *The tragicall complaynt of Elstred*
1594	Richard Barnfield, *The complaint of Daphnis for Ganymede*
1595	William Hunnis, *The complaint of old age*
1595, etc.	Robert Southwell, *Saint Peters complaint*
1596	Peter Colse, *Penelopes complaint: or, mirrour for wanton minions*
1596	John Dickenson, *The sepheardes complaint*
1596	Francis Sabie, *Adams complaint*
1596	William Smith, *The Complaint of the passionate despised shepheard*
1600	Anon., *Holy churches complaint, for her childrens disobedience*
1600	Anon., *The poor peoples complaint*
1600	John Lane, *Tom Tel-Troths message, and his pens complaint*
1601	Robert Chester, *Loves martyr: or, Rosalins complaint*
1603	Richard Mulcaster, *A comforting complaint*
1605	Richard Barnfield, *Complaint of poetry for the death of liberality*
1609	Gervase Markham, *The lamentable complaint of Paulina*
1609	William Rowley, *Lamentable complaint for the losse of the wandring knight*
1610	George Muschet, *The complaint of a Christian soule*
1610	George Webbe, *Times complaint*
1611	Jean Loiseau de Tourval, *Three precious teares of... complaint*
1612, 14	John Taylor, *Pastorall equivocques or the complaint of a shepheard*
1613	John Taylor, *Odcombs complaint: or Coriats funerall epicedium*
1614	Samuel Rowlands, *Sir Thomas Overbury, or, The poysoned knights complaint*
1615, 25	Anon., *A Louers complaint being forsaken of his loue*
1615	Thomas Collins, *The complaint of the sorrowfull shepheardesse*
1615	Richard Niccols, *Monodia or Walthams complaint*
1616	Henry Farley, *The complaint of Paules to all Christian soules*
1619	Arthur Newman, *Pleasures vision with deserts complaint*
1620, 25	Anon., *The maidens complaint of her loves inconstancie*
1620	Anon., *The Popes complaint to his minion cardinals*
1622	William Crashaw, *The complaint or dialogue, betwixt the soule and the bodie*
1622	Edward Cutler, *The backes complaint, for bellies wrong*
1622	John Taylor, *Water-cormorant his complaint against a brood of land-cormorants*
1625	Anon., *The wofull complaint, and lamentable death of a forsaken louer*
1625	John Davies, *Papers complaint... against the paper-spoylers of these times*
1625	Sir David Murray, *The complaint of the shepheard Harpalus*
1625	David Primrose, *Scotlands complaint. Upon the death of our late soueraigne*

Figure 8.1 Advertised complaint poems during the reigns of Elizabeth I and James. I.

The affective and suspended characteristics of complaint make it use-fully suited for Southwell's Ignatian mission, on both literary and pastoral levels. On the literary level, the Jesuit had a freedom to order the things of the world for the greater glory of God (*ad maiorem dei gloriam*) and saw literature as the handmaid of religion toward that end.[17] For Southwell, this mission extended beyond the individual soul reading the text and was

not even confined to the ecclesial structures of the country for whose conversion the English Jesuits were willing to sacrifice their lives. It was also a
thorough-going cultural mission that employed literary tastes in order to
transform them, an aesthetic conversion with profound theological roots
in its approach to the human soul, desire, and passion. The epistle to *Saint
Peters complaint* explicitly identifies his target audience as his contemporary poets who "by abusing their talent, and making the follies and
fayninges of love, the customary subject of their base endevours" had dis-
credited the craft to the point that "a Poet, a Lover, and a Liar, are by
many reckoned but three wordes of one signification."[18] The goal of his
poetry was thus "to let them see the errour of their workes" by "weav[ing]
a new webbe in their owne loome" in order to show "how well verse and
vertue sute together."[19] Because of both the popularity and the frequent
perceived abuse of complaint, it was an ideal candidate for the poetic loom
for Southwell's weaving in his mission to redeem literature.

Complaint was also fitting for its affect, which connects the Jesuit's literary objective to his Ignatian training and his pastoral mission. Southwell
describes his contemporary Petrarchan poets who "busy themselves in
expressing such passions, as onely serve for testimonies to how unwoorthy
affections they have wedded their wils," identifying the problem in the faculties of the soul that his Ignatian training taught him to direct.[20] Connecting affection with the will comes directly from Ignatius of Loyola, the
founder of the Jesuits, who followed in the tradition of Augustine in seeing
affections as movements of the will which could be praiseworthy or blame-
worthy depending on how they were directed.[21] In these terms the will
(*voluntas*) is understood not only as a cognitive choice but also as the
faculty of desire, coming from the Latin *volo* (to wish, want, intend). For
Ignatius in fact, the final stage of meditation involves a movement of the
will that might be mostly affect—love, gratitude, sorrow—and he tends to
describe the actions of the will with its Latin root verb *afficio*.[22] In this
way, Southwell's literary ambition was not only to write poems with holier
themes but also to direct the reader to worthier affections. Thus by fashioning himself as an English complaint poet, Southwell had the affective
capacity to redirect, even to refashion, his readers' passions. The affective
function of literature is more explicit in his epistle to *Marie Magdalens
funeral teares* in which he describes the ailing literary climate as one in
which "passion, and especially this of loue, is in these daies the chiefe com-
maunder of moste mens actions, & the Idol to which both tongues and
pennes doe sacrifice their will bestowed labours." But rather than suppressing passion or love in particular, Southwell insists that "there is
nothing nowe more needefull to bee intreated, then how to direct these
humors vnto their due courses, and to draw this floud of affections into
the right chanel."[23] Again, since "the finest wits are now giuen to write
passionat discourses," he concludes, "I would wish them to make choise of
such passions, as it neither should be shame to vtter, nor sinne to feele."[24]

Southwell's literary mission was pastoral even as it went beyond the recusant community with whom he celebrated sacraments; he had a pastoral mission to English literary culture to redirect and heal human passion.

This attempt to redirect passion rather than to moderate it is a radical departure from the approaches found in contemporaneous consolation literature, and it carries profound theological implications. Studies of early modern consolation literature generally describe some form of neo-Stoic moderation in its approach to the passions, or alternatively an "emotional intelligence" to cure "diseased passions" like anger, melancholy, and fear.[25] Renaissance authors such as Petrarch and Rabelais attempted to combine the Stoic condemnation of the passions with an Augustinian and Thomistic submission of passion to the rule of reason.[26] Restraint was not only a matter of Aristotelian moderation; it was also a sign of physical health, and numerous studies have tracked medical treatments of extreme passions associated with humoral imbalance.[27] Somewhat ironically, the rise of the secular complaint is often explained as a cathartic remedy for the very unhealthy passions it arouses, emerging from a psychological need for consolation after the loss of the sacrament of confession, as if without sacramental satisfaction the only consolation for grief is grief itself (*dolor est medicina e dolori*).[28] George Puttenham, for example, described the poet as a "Phisitian" who makes "the very greef it selfe (in part) cure of the disease."[29] But both Puttenham's defense of the medicinal qualities of poetic grief and scholarly psychological explanations for its appeal are indicative of the obvious tension between what is depicted in poetic complaint and the ostensible better judgment of its authors and readers. With regard to the passion of sorrow, at least, English sermons and consolation works took their cue from Paul's letter to the Corinthians that distinguished between the worldly sorrow that leads to death and the godly sorrow that leads to repentance, specifically the sorrow for sin which certainly may involve tears but not the ostentatious expressions of penitence of the papists.[30] Even sorrow for the death of loved ones should be moderated, bearing in mind Paul's exhortation to the Thessalonians to "sorowe not euen as other[s] which haue no hope."[31] Whether excessive passions were indicative of disordered affections or lack of faith, Aristotle's golden mean was a sign of Christian maturity.

While acknowledging the merits of Aristotelean moderation and Augustinian rule of reason, however, Southwell provides an alternative approach that uses poetic affect to redirect affections, validating superabundant passion by repairing it. "Passions I allow, and loues I approue," he goes on in his epistle to the *funeral teares*, "onely I would wishe that men would alter their obiect and better their intent." He uses the medieval commonplace that passions are "allotted vnto vs as the handmaides of reason" to validate each of Aquinas's eleven passions—in Southwell's translation, love, hatred, anger, desire, hope, fear, dislike, audacity, sorrow, despair, and joy—but he goes beyond the moderation that his sources recommend.[32] With a somewhat idiosyncratic application of his source material, Southwell combines Aquinas's discussion of love as a passion with that of love as a theological virtue, bringing it from the list of passions that should serve as handmaids of reason to a potential mistress of reason itself.[33] Aquinas acknowledges in his section on the theological virtues (faith, hope, and love) that there is no golden mean, no moderation, no possibility for excess in the love of God.[34] Likewise, Southwell claims that the Magdalen's love "could neuer exceede, because the thing loued was of infinite perfection." He describes her seeming excess of passion in a way that could be applied in different ways to the other biblical complainants in his poetry, with "her will so setled in a most sincere and perfect loue, that it ledde all her passions with the same bias,"[35] teaching readers who might not be able "to temper passion in the meane" at least "to giue the bridle onely where the excesse cannot be faultie."[36] Later in the text, love guides not only the other passions but even reason itself, as his narrator gives up reasoning against the Magdalene because her "reason is altered into loue," and later explains that "Loue is not ruled with reason, but with loue."[37] Southwell ultimately deploys the affective capacities of complaint to direct his readers to this place where "excesse cannot be faultie," not fighting against the passionate excess of his contemporary poets and their readers with rational arguments for moderation but rather creating a venue in which passion could be unleashed and refashioned into an encounter with divine love.[38] Love that could control reason could serve as guide to all the other passions, and thus there was a possibility for redemption not from passion but through it. Southwell appeals to secular tastes and puts pressure on theological tidiness, opening a literary space to reconcile passion and piety even as he opens a devotional space for his Protestant readers to be reconciled subconsciously to a Catholic poet.

Southwell's Peter: from penitent to lover

Since sorrow for sin was championed as godly sorrow, it is no surprise that the long titular *Saint Peters complaint* was popular among both Protestant and Catholic readers. While mainstream and recusant editions of Southwell's poems make different choices about inclusions and ordering, the anomalously long poem is in first position in all fifteen collections of his poetry that broadcast its name on the title pages.[39] Although Tansillo's *Lagrime* was a smashing hit on the continent, an illustration of lavish and wholehearted penitence characteristic of the literature of the Catholic Reformation, Southwell departed from it drastically to make penitence more palatable to Protestant readers while subtly subverting their expectations, and its popularity inspired immediate cross-confessional imitation, appropriation, and devotion.[40] Tansillo's original 320-line, third-person short epic of Peter's imagined penitence between his third denial on the night of Holy Thursday and the resurrection on Easter Sunday barely resembles Southwell's 792-line, first-person complaint narrated by the protagonist.[41] By eliminating the narrative of the Italian poem that depicted Peter as a tragically fallen hero—"Il magnanimo Pietro, che giurato/Hauea tra mille lancie, e mille spade/Al suo caro Signor morir à lato" (F4ʳ)[42]—Southwell removed the risk that his Protestant readers would see it as an ostentatious display of exterior penitence and would instead see it as an individualized account of interior conversion and true repentance. More subtly, amid the hypnotic length and the tapestry of conceits, paradoxes, and allusions, he shifts the weight of the sorrow from repentance to love. Without providing his readers the resolution of forgiveness nor even a complete model of contrition, Southwell guides them through the experience of finding love in the midst of the torment of self-reproaching shame. In the center of the complaint, the fallen hero and failed lover encounters the memory of the one he betrayed and is refashioned through the erotic language of Petrarchan complaint. Repentance eventually comes as a result, but it is relatively short and notably incomplete; Southwell's Peter is saved through love.

The length and apparent disorganization of the complaint, while not a point of favor among its earliest critics, supplies it with a sonorous tone and sedative effect; like many other protracted complaints, it must be entered into rather than viewed as it were from without.[43] The progression of the 132 six-line stanzas is an interior journey that roughly translates the stages of an Ignatian meditation from the first week of the *Spiritual Exercises*, the Jesuit guide for spiritual retreats, into the language of complaint.[44] The first eight stanzas (ll. 1–48) serve as a poetic invocation that could almost be a prelude, Ignatius's opening request for what the complainant-turned-retreatant desires (*id quod volo*): in Peter's case, for better or worse, he desires tears, care, sighs, remorse, and torment. The next forty-six stanzas (ll. 49–324) go through the Ignatian stage of memory (*memoria*) as Peter recalls the events of the night in a catalogue of complaint styles: *de casibus* as he is a fallen hero, Petrarchan as he is a failed lover, and *contemptus mundi* as life is reduced to vanity. At the center of the complaint, the next thirty-three stanzas (ll. 325–522) are Southwell's greatest departure from Tansillo and from the tears poetry of his contemporaries as the memory of Christ's eyes move Peter to the next stage of meditation, understanding (*intellectus*), and take the focus off of the penitent and onto love. Finally in the last forty-seven stanzas (ll. 511–792) Peter comes to an incomplete repentance that is at least an affective movement of the will (*voluntas*), unable to resolve to change but desiring it nonetheless. His passionate grief and self-shaming have led him not to complete contrition but to love, which ultimately reconciles him to his own unresolved sorrow.

The early part of the complaint, relating to the stage of memory, is probably the least appealing section for modern readers with its tirade of blame and shame, but by Ignatian standards even compunction is an encounter with love. The first meditation Ignatius prescribes involves the exercitant comparing his or her many sins to the sin of the fallen angels or Adam and Eve. Similarly, the second meditation includes a reflection on one's smallness in relation to other human beings, to angels and saints, and to God, and asking oneself in response, "what now can I alone be, little man that I am?"[45] In the same way, Peter's self-complaint begins with his realization of the magnitude of his own sin compared to so many apparently greater sins. He is lower than Judas and Caiaphas who at least esteemed Christ's life worth thirty pieces of silver: "I, worse then both, for nought denied him thrise" (102). He demonstrated "more hatefull tyrannies" than the Jews who spit at Christ because he "spit thy poyson in [his] makers face" (129–130) rather than mere spittle. But an awareness of Christ's love is a key element of the Jesuit conception of compunction; indeed, the final colloquy for the first meditation on sin in the *Spiritual Exercises* involves "imagining Jesus Christ approaching me fastened to the cross," conversing with him "as friends speak to friends, or servants to masters."[46] For Ignatius, the ultimate goal of a reflection on sin is not the feelings of fear and shame, though they are steps along the way; it is wonder at Christ's love, amazement that the world and all its creatures have been given to enliven and preserve so base a sinner.[47] Likewise, in this section Peter is conscious not only of a sin of commission but of omission, his failure to love, his "luke-warme desires in crasie love" (199).[48] This emphasis on love is a prominent feature of early modern Jesuit meditations on sin; for example, in his meditation on the tears of Peter in the *Meditationes de praecipuis fidei nostrae mysteriis* (1605), Southwell's Spanish contemporary Luis de la Puente says:

> Consider ... the bitter teares of saint Peter, which did not proceed from a feare of punishment, but from a love vnto his Master; For calling to mynd the fauors and benefitts he had receaued of him, togeather with the ingratitude he had shewed in denying him in such an occasion, his eyes did conuert themselues into two fountaynes of teares, with an extreame bitternes and greefe of hart.[49]

Notably, sin is only seen as such in the context of the rich love of Christ, the life one has received from him, and thus the very acknowledgment of one's fault includes the hope of its amendment. By a Jesuit understanding of compunction, sorrow and love are opposite sides of the same coin.

Ultimately, Peter's extremities of grief and shame direct him to love. The centerpiece of the complaint is the meditation on Christ's eyes, the moment Peter recalls an intimate detail recorded only in Luke's account of the passion. Immediately after Peter's third denial, as Luke records, "our Lord turning looked on Peter. And Peter remembered the vvord of our Lord, as he had said, That before the cocke crovv, thou shalt thrise denie me. And peter going forth a doores, vvept bitterly."[50] Tansillo makes a brief glance at the intimacy of this memory in his 1560 version that Southwell translated, but the Italian notably removes the potential eroticism of lovers' eyes in the expanded version printed in 1585.[51] Southwell on the other hand amplifies the Italian couplet into 200 lines of amorous encomia.[52] Christ's eyes are a "spotlesse Sunne" (336), "flames devine" (349), "graceful quivers of loves dearest darts" (352), "liquid pearle" (357), and "blasing comets, lightning flames of love" that warm his frozen heart (361).[53] Southwell combines these erotic metaphors with more devout comparisons, such as "registers of truth" (344), "nectared Aubryes of soule feeding meats" (351), and "living mirrours" (367). The metaphors become extended metaphysical conceits, especially in the case of the "gracious spheres" (403), "little worldes" (409), and "mixtures" of "sweet elements" (415), and they evoke biblical images such as the "Pooles of Hesebon" (379), "Bethelem cisternes" (427), "Turtle twins all bath'd in virgins milke" (433), and the rod with which Moses struck "the Horebb rocke" (439).[54] The eyes become an "endlesse ... labyrinth of blisse,/Where to be lost the sweetest finding is," the "Sweet volumes ... Where blisfull quires imparadize" the minds of the Saints (337–342), situating the lost soul within the one who finds her.[55] They "did vouchsafe to warme, to wound, to feast/My cold, my stony, my now famishde breast" (353–354), enacting sensual affect, penetration, and consummation all at once. Indeed, the more concretely we imagine his stony breast being wounded by the eyes, the more it aligns with *compunctio* in its etymological sense: a prick or puncture. Christ's eyes wound like those of the Petrarchan lady, but Christ's vision is one that "By seeing things ... make[s] things worth the sight,/You seeing, salve, and being seene, delight" (377–378). It is a wound that heals.

In the final section of the poem as Peter moves to his affective movement of the will, his repentance does not get beyond the desire to repent, but the encounter with love has reconciled him to the sorrow from which the poem has not freed him, refashioning him through it. He finally summons the tears that Tansillo began with, which are importantly not the bitter tears of remorse that we see in the Italian; they are the sweet relief to his bitter self-condemnation. They are the "ofspring of my griefe" that bring "needfull aide" and "wishde relief" to their languishing parent (463–465), the "good effectes of ill deserving cause" that are "Ill gotten impes, yet vertuously brought forth" (469–470). Thus this movement of the will, the calling forth of his affective response—"Come sorrowing teares" (463), "Come good effectes of ill deserving cause" (469), "Come shame, the lincea of offending mind" (517)—is not a punishment for his sin but is actually a relief. In the poignant climax of the poem, Peter becomes reconciled to sorrow in an oddly intimate bit of allegory.

> At sorrowes dore I knockt, they crav'de my name;
> I aunswered one, unworthy to be knowne:

What one? say they, one worthiest of blame.
But who? a wretch, not Gods, nor yet his owne.
A man? O no, a beast? much worse, what creature?
A rocke: how cald? the rocke of scandale, Peter.

From whence? from Caiphas howse, ah dwell you there?
Sinnes farme I rented, there, but now would leave it:
What rent? my soule: what gaine? unrest, and feare,
Deare purchase. Ah too deare. Will you receive it?
What shall we give? fit teares, and time, to plaine me,
Come in, say they; thus griefes did entertaine me.

(703–714)

It is a strangely tender scene, somewhat of a benign precursor to the House of Care in Spenser's 1596 *Faerie Queene* (4.5), as if Spenser's Care spoke in the voice of Herbert's "Love" [III]. Like the forlorn lover Scudamour in Spenser's allegory, Peter passes his "nightes without repose" (719), but the sorrow that welcomes him is an oddly gracious host, inviting his lowly guest inside, sympathetic to the dear price he paid for his unrest, offering the requested entertainment. This willing suspension of relief in the house of sorrow is the natural progression from the encounter with Christ's love; his later rather incomplete repentance is a briefly glimpsed consequence. In nearly 800 lines, the closest Peter ever gets to the resolve never to sin again, specified in the Council of Trent as a necessary element of true contrition, is his "poore desire … to mend my ill," but despite the desire he can only assert, "I should, I would, I dare not say, I will. // I dare not say, I will; but wish, I may" (761–764).[56] Instead of drafting an illustration of full contrition, Southwell's complaint shows sorrow as the place of encounter with love. Peter encounters the memory of the eyes that love him through the very mechanics of complaint and thereby encounters the love itself. In the midst of Reformation controversies about salvation, justification, repentance, and the like, the poem does not define Peter's sorrow according to the doctrine of penance; it depicts it as a complaint that is itself an encounter with love. Peter is refashioned from a sinner into a lover, his sorrow is refashioned from penitence into intimacy, and the reader is affectively provoked into the same transformation.

Southwell's Magdalene: faultless excess[57]

If Southwell's transformation of tears poetry from penitence into a lover's complaint is evident even in his depiction of Peter's sorrow after denying Christ, it is especially apparent in his refashioning of Mary Magdalene. In the sixteenth century the penitent Magdalene was an increasingly popular model of devotion for both Protestant and Catholic authors. The medieval tradition merged potentially three or four different biblical women to create a full biography for her: the sinful woman of Luke 7 who washes Christ's feet with her tears; Mary of Bethany who falls at Jesus's feet weeping after the death of her brother Lazarus in John 11 and later sits at his feet and anoints them with perfume while Martha serves the meal in Luke 10 and John 12; another unnamed woman who anoints Jesus's head in the home of Simon the leper right before the passion in Matthew 26 and Mark 14; and Mary Magdalene who follows Jesus in his ministry after being released from seven demons in Luke 8 and who is mentioned in the passion and resurrection accounts in all four gospels, most notably when she weeps at the sepulcher on Easter morning in John 20.[58] The scene in which Christ defends the sinful woman who weeps onto his feet and dries them with her hair out of loving gratitude for the forgiveness of her many sins was by far the most popular in the Middle Ages, often combined with the incidents of perfume, and it translated easily into varying Protestant and Catholic reformation emphases on repentance and conversion.[59] Furthermore, in the wake of controversies surrounding medieval doctrine and devotion of the Virgin Mary, the Magdalene was becoming a popular female model of devotion in England, conveniently more developed in scripture than the Virgin.[60] Patricia Badir identifies more than 100 English poems, biographies, homilies, sermons, and plays devoted to the Magdalen's tears between 1550 and 1700.[61] In fact, while Southwell was certainly influenced by the Italian fascination on the tears of the Magdalene during his years in Rome—generally in the form of extended, third-person, narrative poetic encomia of her tears from her conversion to her legendary penitence in the wilderness after Christ's ascension—he demoted repentance to a marginal topic in his works and put the tears of superabundant love at the center.[62] In addition to his prose meditation *Marie Magdalens funeral teares* that was printed in six editions of its own and another five combined editions with his poetry, Southwell wrote two short lyrics that emphasized passionate complaint: "Mary Magdalens blush" and "Marie Magdalens complaint at Christs death." Even the former which is about her compunction for her sins concludes by validating her sensuous passions as the avenue for the redemption, and the latter is situated fully in the realm of a lover's complaint with no mention of sin. In this way Southwell uses English complaint to validate not only the godly sorrow for sin, but even the seemingly excessive passions of secular love poetry. Suddenly godly sorrow could look quite a bit like the sorrow of "other[s] which haue no hope"; poetically at least, it could imitate it.[63]

Southwell's literary celebration of the Magdalene's superabundant sorrow as a lover of Christ rather than a penitent had medieval precedent in England even as it put pressure on some theological assumptions in the contemporary English church. Easily his celebration of the Magdalene's sorrow took inspiration from a prolific tradition of complaints of the Virgin Mary by the cross of her son, the *planctus Mariae* lyrics that were almost as numerous as the parallel tradition of *planctus Christi*, complaints of Christ from the cross.[64] More directly, it connected to two works attributed to Chaucer in the early modern period, the Latin pseudo-Origen sermon that Chaucer claimed to have translated in his *Legend of Good Women* and that Southwell definitively did in Rome, and a rather erotic late medieval *Complaynte of the louer of Cryst Saynt Mary Magdaleyn* included in early modern editions of Chaucer's works.[65] With the reformations, however, came suspicion of ostentatious, showy spirituality associated with papists, and scholars have described a general Protestant aversion to ritualized mourning for the dead, seeing it "as effeminate, barbaric, and contrary to faith."[66] John Calvin, for example, who was the most influential early reformer for the Elizabethan church, had criticized the Magdalene's tears by Christ's tomb in John 20 as "idle and useless weeping" that emerged from her "superstition" and "carnal feelings."[67] Weeping for Calvin was important as a sign of repentance from sin, but not the grief of loss, even in the Magdalene's case when it was Christ's own death that she mourned. Southwell's lyrics thus capitalized on contemporary secular tastes of the female complaint and on native English medieval literary traditions in order to put pressure on the theological assumptions of his English contemporaries. Excessive passion, even when it was sensuous and feminine, could also be redemptive.

From its title to its peculiar end, "Mary Magdalens blush" is a curious deflection from repentance to passion, blurring the lines between love as a sensual passion and as a theological virtue. Continental poetry emphasized the Magdalene's tears and conversion almost exclusively.[68] Southwell's title redirected the emphasis to her "blush," her shame or modesty, and by the end of the poem the source of her blush is especially ambiguous.[69] The Magdalene begins by describing the "raving fits" that have produced "The signes of shame that staine my blushing face" (1–2), reflecting on her past sins, traditionally prostitution, and "How cheape I sould, that Christ so dearely bought" (10). Again the sin is only distinguished in the context of love, and Christ's love is understood in the same language as her sensual sins: with the image of Cupid. She had hardened herself like rock against the "ghostly dynts that grace at me did dart" (13), aiming her heart instead to the wounds of other flights. By halfway through the poem when she describes her "Woe worth the bow, woe worth the archers might,/That drave such arrowes to the marke so right" (17–18), it is unclear which arrows have wounded her—the arrows of shame, the arrows of lust, or the arrows of grace—and in any case she must remain wounded because "To pull them out, to leave them in, is death:/One, to this world: one, to the world to come" (19–20). Though initially the arrows were her sensuous desires, now they are the arrows of compunction. Ultimately, the ambiguity between grace's arrows and Cupid's, between the sensual wounds of shame and love, becomes nearly irrelevant. In the penultimate stanza, her sense—passions, affect, emotion—seems to be a clear enemy of the soul as she exclaims, "O sence, O soule, O had, O hoped blisse,/You wooe, you weane; you draw, you drive me back" (25–26). But the wooing and drawing of the sense's past bliss, rather than the weaning and driving back of the soul's future bliss, becomes strangely redemptive by the end. The Magdalene ultimately exonerates her passions when she declares that "sense doth scarse deserve these hard complaints,/Love is the theife, sense but the entring place" (33–34), harkening to Jesus's defense of her actions before the condemning Pharisee: "Many sinnes are forgiuen her, because she hath loued much."[70] Again, Southwell confuses any potential distinction between love as a theological virtue or as a passion which resides in the sensual (rather than intellective) part of the soul. After originally deflecting grace's darts, her lustful senses welcomed the arrow wounds of love. Lustful passion itself is refashioned into an opening for divine love. In this case she does not actually repent (in the sense of *metanoia*, a turning away) of her human passion but finds it transfigured and redeemed.

In "Marie Magdalens complaint at Christs death," sin is taken out of the equation altogether, and passions dominate the poem from beginning to end: the passions of sorrow, despair, anger, and overshadowing love. Most of the stanzas turn around a longing for death, the certainty that life holds no hope of good or even that it is merely a living death, a typical line of argument in complaint poetry. Like the Virgin in medieval *planctus* lyrics, like the Magdalene in the pseudo-Chaucerian *Complaynte of the louer of Cryst Saynt Mary Magdaleyn*, like the countless women in secular female complaints, Southwell's Magdalene declares that "my life from life is parted" and thus her only desire is for "Death [to] come take thy portion" (1–2).[71] Through love her life is united with that of her lover, and "One that lives by others breath,/Dieth also by his death" (11–12). Scholars have often noted the special relevance the Magdalene's position had for the recusant Catholic community separated from what they believed to be the Real Presence of Christ's body and blood in the Catholic Eucharist, allowed only the "Shaddowes," "Paynted meate," and "Signes, not salves of miserie"(20–23) in the English church; but the rejection of false consolation is also typical of complaint, and Southwell's Protestant readers could have connected those words to their own rejection of false human invention over the truth of the gospel.[72] But once again, her various passions—sorrow, suicidal despair, and anger at the "Spitefull speare, that breakst this prison" (37) of Christ's heart where her life was formerly nestled—are ruled by the passion of love.[73] In seemingly suicidal despair she begs, "let love my life remove,/Sith I live not where I love" (29–30), and it is love that she retains in the final lines after the spear has worked the "double treason" of "Loves and lifes delieverie" (39–40), a dark parody of childbirth. Love has united her so closely to the object of her love that "love" and "life" interchangeably become metonyms for Christ and for her; at one point she bemoans that "From my love, my life is wrested" (27) (thus "love" is Christ and "life" is what remains for her), but in the end she insists to the spear that "Though my life thou drav'st away,/Maugre thee my love shall stay" (41–42) (thus "life" is Christ and "love" is what remains for her). As her love and her life have been torn away from each other, their meanings have been confused and strangely merged, and thus offer a shred of hope or at least agency in her suffering. Her life without her love is a living death since he is her life, but she has agency to hold onto the love that temporally gives her only suffering with a hint of the future resurrection. It is the extremity of her love that generates both her helplessness and her agency, that engenders both despair and the possibility of resurrection. For Southwell's Magdalene, love as a passion opens the way for love as a theological virtue, and thus the "excesse cannot be faultie." By fashioning himself as an English complaint poet, Southwell affectively draws the reader to a place where even the most censured and sensuous human passions can be redeemed.

Southwell's Joseph: reconciling irresolution

When excess is not faulty, when the fires of love can lead all other passions and even guide reason itself, the impassioned sorrows of complaint do not require resolution. In addition to leaving Peter and Mary without the consolation of the resurrection, ultimately possessing only love that fuels their sorrows while reconciling the complainants to them, Southwell leaves a betrayed Joseph suspended between love and hate, suggesting in fact that the irresolution is necessary. "Josephs Amazement" is perhaps the most Petrarchan of Southwell's poems, portraying the betrothed husband of Mary with all the anger, jealousy, despair, sorrow, and disgust of a betrayed lover. The poem depicts his interior torment when his betrothed is found to be with child and "for that he vvas a iust man, & vvould not put her to open shame: vvas minded secretely to dismisse her."[74] In Southwell's version the decision Matthew records is hardly made, and his Joseph wrestles mostly between the options of abandoning her and staying with her, with a brief consideration that he legally could have her killed. Thus "wrought" as he is "with divers fits of feare and love" (5), he is "daunted with a deadly wound" (13), desires death, and spends most of the eighty-four lines trying to fight against his own love in order to abandon her. Whenever he sets his foot to the door, "Love winneth time, till all conclude in no" (24) and "She whom he flies doth winne him home againe" (30), and thus Joseph continues "warring with himselfe" and fighting a battle "Where every wound upon the giver lights" (35–36). Clearly in this poem, "amazement" refers to his "maze of doubtfull ende" (79), the condition the OED defines as mental paralysis and stupefaction, a new meaning for the relatively new word.[75] Joseph is in a mental maze he would rather leave, and it is love that keeps him there.

Typical of complaint, the tension of the poem is left unresolved, particularly because any satisfactory resolution would either require the initiative of the angel that Joseph cannot produce or a final rejection of Mary that his love will not allow. The closest Joseph comes to resolve is in fact in his decision to keep loving.

> But Josephs word shall never worke her woe,
> I wish her leave to live, not doome to die;
> Though fortune mine, yet am I not her foe,
> She to her selfe lesse loving is then I.
>
> (55–58)

It is love, not reason, that keeps his other passions in check, even as it is love that keeps him in torment. With every reason to believe he has been betrayed and without having received the consolation of the angel to explain the cause of her pregnancy ("The Holy Spirit did it!"), Joseph's only recourse to the pain of betrayed love is to keep loving, to be more loving to his treacherous beloved than she is to herself, to desire her good even at the heavy cost of his agony. He eventually realizes that his desire to flee the anguished perplexity is futile, for after all, "who can flie from that his hart doth feele?/What change of place can change implanted paine?" (73–74), and thus the poem ends with the speaker in this haunting "amazement."

> Yet still I tread a maze of doubtfull end;
> I goe, I come, she drawes, she drives away,
> She wounds, she heales, she doth both marre and mende,
> She makes me seeke, and shunne, depart, and stay:
> She is a friend to love, a foe to loth,
> And in suspence I hang betwene them both.
>
> (79–84)

The complaint leaves him there, suspended between going and coming, being drawn and driven away, being wounded and healed, his love marred and mended, seeking and shunning, departing and staying, loving and loathing. He is resolved to his irresolution, and Southwell's reader who presumably is glad that the pregnant Virgin Mary was not killed or abandoned may feel pity for him but still must be glad to see him willing to suffer the agony of suspense.

Joseph's final suspense, typical of Southwellian complaint, is essential to the poem's affective strength and connects to the Jesuit's mission: not only to reconcile verse and virtue, passion and piety, but also to reconcile Protestant readers to the faith and devotion of a Catholic poet. The reader is meant to feel the dramatic irony of the scene, knowing all the while as the Joseph of the poem never does that Mary's virginity is unstained, because the reader must ultimately make a choice to face or flee uncertainty. In this case, much more starkly than in the poems of Peter and the Magdalene that put pressure on approaches to repentance and passion, this uncertainty reflects one of many suspicions his Protestant readers might have felt toward the Roman church. Though no Protestants doubted the virgin birth, explicit as it is in scripture, many criticized Marian devotion for its lavish praise and potential idolatry, especially as the reformations progressed. Early on, Luther did not protest the invocation of saints, Mary's perpetual virginity, or her title of Queen of Heaven, though he tempered these with an emphasis on her "nothingness" and utter lack of merit for the graces she received.[76] Later reformers such as Calvin disallowed her intercession and asserted that any request made to her for grace is an "execrable blasphemy," even if she was, in Bullinger's words, "the most unique and the noblest member" of the church.[77] In England, Hugh Latimer went so far as to attack her sinlessness, interpreting her interruption of Jesus's teaching in Luke 8 as evidence "that we gave her too much, thinking her to be without any sparkle of sin," though he was somewhat radical among his contemporary reformers for taking that view.[78] Marian invocations and feasts disappeared and occasionally reemerged in the established prayer books and calendars, and the Thirty-Nine Articles of 1563 completely forbade any invocations of the saints as "a fond thing vainly invented and ... repugnant to the Word of God" (20), which included Mary by default.[79] After six decades of reformation whiplash, the certainty of the average Englishman could hardly match the vehemence of the printed polemic, and with regard to Marian piety as many other ambiguously debated devotions, there was much room for anxiety and doubt.

In complaint, Southwell affectively invited the reader into the uncertainties of human passion as much as the uncertainties of doubt and ambiguity. Because complaint operated on this "suspence," it invited conversation. As Southwell's wide reception, importance, and influence in English literature has been increasingly acknowledged over the past few decades, this strategy in part explains his appeal in a country that had executed him as a religious traitor. Furthermore, it suggests a greater thumbprint on the development of English literature in the following generation, not only over those who directly imitated him but also those who accepted his challenge to see "how well verse and vertue sute together" more broadly, particularly in the rise of devotional lyric during the Stuart reigns.[80] As Southwell's popularity continued with twenty-five London editions of his various works, from the 1591 edition of *Marie Magdalens funeral teares* the year before his arrest all the way until the 1636 edition of *Saint Peters complaint* on the eve of the civil wars, English readers were compelled by the combative piety of his devotional complaints.[81] When the young recusant John Donne was flexing his poetic muscles in verse translation, for example, he chose the biblical model for the complaint mode, Lamentations, for his project, and its devotional anxiety can be seen throughout his *Holy Sonnets*.[82] George Herbert's *The Temple* in fact opens with a complaint, a *planctus Christi* lyric that depicts the crucified Jesus asking repeatedly "Was ever grief like mine?" to introduce a volume of lyrics with a poet who often attempts to "meet arms" with God, groaning in affliction with hope that God is "in the grief."[83] In its "maze," the complaint held together passion and piety, doubt and devotion, desire and disgust, hatred and love, hope and despair, agency and helplessness, masculinity and femininity. For this reason, it also held together Catholic and Protestant devotion, and "in suspence" the poets could "hang betwene them both."

Notes

1 Stonyhurst College MS. A. v. 4.

2 Southwell's first print editions were the prose *Epistle of Comfort* likely printed by secret press in Arundel House in 1587, the prose *Marie Magdalens funeral teares* printed by John Wolfe for Gabriel Cawood in 1591 a year before the author's arrest and reprinted twice before his death, five posthumous collections of poems that appeared the year of his execution in 1595 (two editions of *Saint Peters complaint with other poemes* printed by John Wolfe, one of the same printed by Gabriel Cawood, and two editions of the supplementary *Moeniae* printed by John Busbie), and the prose *The triumphs over death* printed by John Busbie also in 1595.

3 "[The] Peeter Playnt" is in the sixth notebook (f50–f55) whose first three sheets are numbered 29–31; the longer translation of the Magdalene sermon is in the seventh notebook (f56–f64) with sheets numbered 249–256; the emblem poem and the shorter translation are on recto and verso sides of a page inserted toward the end of the seventh notebook (f61).

4 The *Lagrime* itself has a fascinating an underexplored history. Erika Milburn has written on Tansillo's literary career before being placed on Paul IV's 1559 Index, and the introduction to Luca Torre's edition describes the relationship between the ban and the subsequent composition of the *Lagrime* as a personal penance to regain the favor of the Pope. As Alexander J. Fisher argues, particularly in connection to Orlando di Lasso's 1595 musical setting of the poem dedicated to Peter's "vero e legitimo successore" (true and legitimate successor) Pope Clement VIII, the subsequent vogue of the poem across the continent for decades seems to be connected to the redemption of the papacy in post-Tridentine Europe.

5 Agostino Ferentilli's *Primo volume della Scelta di stanze di diversi autori toscani* (Venice, 1571, 1579, 1584); Francesco Turchi da Trivigi's *Salmi penitenziali di diversi eccellenti autori con alcune rime spirituali di diversi* (1572); Zabata's *Nuova scelta di rime di diversi begli ingegni* (Genoa, 1573); and *Prima parte della scelta di rime di diversi autori* (Genoa, 1582). I am indebted to Mario Praz for these citations. See "Robert Southwell's 'Saint Peter's Complaint' and Its Italian Source," *The Modern Language Review*, 19 (1924): 273.

6 Genoa, 1587; Carmagnola, 1588; Venice, 1589; Venice, 1592; Venice, 1598; Venice, 1599; Venice, 1601; Venice, 1605; Venice, 1606; Venice, 1608; Venice, 1611; Naples, 1613; Venice, 1618.

7 Pierre Janelle, *Robert Southwell the Writer: A Study in Religious Inspiration* (New York: Sheed & Ward, 1935), 205. Joseph G. Fucilla also identifies Spanish and Portugese versions by Marqués de Berlanga, Jerónimo de Cobos, Diego d'Avalos y Figueroa, Fray Damián Alvarez, Juan Sedeño, Hurtado de Mendoza, Jerónimo de Heredia, Martín de Bolea, Luis Martín de la Plaza, and Jacinto de S. Francisco; in addition to resonances within poems of Lope de Vega, José de Valdivieso, Rodrigo Fernández de Ribera, Pedro de Jesús, and Quevodo; and a translation within an octave of Cervantes's *Don Quixote*. See "On the Vogue of

Tansillo's 'Lagrime di San Pietro' in Spain and Portugal," *Rinascita*, 2 (1939): 74–75.

8 Pierre Janelle, *The Catholic Reformation* (Milwaukee: The Bruce Publishing Company, 1949), 175.

9 This departure was not shared by continental imitators of Tansillo, nor even by all English imitators of Southwell: the French adaptations by Estienne and Malherbe were both literally translated as *Les Larmes de S. Pierre*, and the Spanish adaptation by Montalvo, *El Llanto de San Pedro*, replaced tears with the broader term for weeping. Likewise, an anonymous *Saint Peters Ten Teares* appeared two years after Southwell's poems.

10 Most notably, Louis Martz promoted this thesis in his seminal 1954 *Poetry of Meditation: A Study in English Religious Literature of the Seventeenth Century*, which provided the foundations for later studies by R. V. Young and Anthony Raspa to explore the formative role of Southwell's Ignatian aesthetic in shaping English devotional poetry.

11 "Bitter-sweet" (1, 5), in *The English Poems of George Herbert*, ed. Helen Wilcox (Cambridge: Cambridge University Press, 2007), 587.

12 While E. K. does not explain the classification of complaint for some of the eclogues of Spenser's *Shepheardes Calender*, Hallett Smith attempts to explain how these classifications function in the poems. The case is unwieldy, as fitting for Spenser.

13 John Peter looks specifically at *contemptus mundi* complaints, and Wendy Scase looks at those that express political grievance demanding litigation. In shorter studies, Jennifer Bryan looks at Hoccleve's *planctus Mariae* poem, John Kerrigan explores female complaint in relation to Shakespeare, Lauren Berlant has written on medieval female complaint, Richard Danson Brown and Hugh Maclean have written multiple articles on Spenserian complaint, and Robert Miller, Nancy Dean and William Davenport have explored the complaint in relation to Chaucer.

14 Rosalind Smith, Michelle O'Callaghan, and Sarah C. E. Ross, "Complaint," in *A Companion to Renaissance Poetry*, ed. Catherine Bates, Blackwell Companions to Literature (Hoboken, NJ: Wiley, 2018), 339.

15 Renaissance understanding of genre was in fact generally much more amorphous than that of the classical authors they imitated. Alastair Fowler describes the approach to form in the Renaissance as neither formation nor formalism of genres, but rather one of "adapting old forms or imparting to them a new spirit," combining both formal and substantive features: topics, moods, diction, figures, meters, subjects, themes. Heather Dubrow describes genre as a "code of behavior established between the author and his reader," a "subtle amalgamation of qualities" like a human personality. Alastair Fowler, "The Formation of Genres in the Renaissance and After," *New Literary History*, 34 (2003): 185, 190; Heather Dubrow, *Genre* (London: Methuen, 1982), 2.

16 Though Southwell was a pioneer of devotional complaint poetry, Catholic and Protestant theologians alike highlighted the fundamental power of the Christian rhetor to move his or her listeners affectively, and Philip Sidney's *Defense of Poesy* argued for poetry's unique capacity to do so. For more on the importance of affect in Christian rhetoric across the Renaissance period, see Debora Kuller Shuger's extensive and learned studies on what she terms "sacred rhetoric." *Sacred Rhetoric: The Christian Grand Style in the English Renaissance* (Princeton, NJ: Princeton University Press, 1987); "The Philosophical Foundations of Sacred Rhetoric," in *Religion and Emotion: Approaches and Interpretations*, ed. John Corrigan (Oxford: Oxford University Press, 2004): 115–132.

17 Janelle's encyclopedic *Robert Southwell the Writer* reflects on various ways Southwell expresses and diverges from his Jesuit education, and Scott Pilarz, S. J. reflects on that mission in his literature, both in a focused essay on his pastoral ministry ("'To Help Souls': Recovering the Purpose of Southwell's Poetry and Prose," in *Discovering and (Re)Covering the Seventeenth Century Religious Lyric*, ed. Eugene R. Cunnar and Jeffrey Johnson (Pittsburgh: Duquesne University Press, 2001), 41–61), and a larger literary biography (*Robert Southwell and the Mission of Literature, 1561–1595: Writing Reconciliation* (Aldershot: Ashgate, 2004)).

18 Because of the significance of this letter "to his loving Cosin" for Southwell's poetic theory, scholars have suggested addressees among his popular contemporaries. Christopher Devlin, Peter Milward, and Richard Wilson argue that the prefatory letter is covertly addressed to Southwell's distant cousin Shakespeare, to whom the 1609 edition of his sonnets attributed "A Lover's Complaint," in part because of the proximity of the composition of the *Saint Peters complaint* and the publication of *Venus and Adonis*, though they disagree about the lines of influence between the two. In the 1616 Jesuit printing of Southwell's poetry the prefatory letter was addressed "To my worthy good cousin, Master W. S." and signed "Your loving cousin, R. S.," and if W. S. is indeed Shakespeare then there is a pun in the prefatory poem that concludes his suit for heavenly poetry with the admission that "the Graunt restes in your will." Gary Bouchard, on the other hand, provides the most recent discussion of the letter's affect on Spenser in his publication of the *Fowre Hymnes*.

19 "The Author to his loving Cosen," in *The Poems of Robert Southwell, S. J.*, edited by James H. McDonald and Nancy Pollard Brown (Oxford: Clarendon Press, 1967), 1.

20 Ibid.

21 See for example *City of God*, 14.6. Ignatius likewise draws his benchmarks stages of meditation—memory (*memoria*), understanding (*intellectus*), and will (*voluntas*)—from Augustine's tripartite division of the soul that reflects the Trinity.

22 Alexandre Brou, S. J., *Ignatian Methods of Prayer* (Milwaukee: Bruce Publishing Company, 1949), 117.

23 *Marie Magdalens funeral teares* (London, 1591), A3v.

24 Ibid., A6r.

25 Wendy Olmsted, *The Imperfect Friend: Emotion and Rhetoric in Sidney, Milton, and Their Contexts* (Toronto: University of Toronto Press, 2008), 4. Studies by Reid Barbour, Andrew Shifflett, George W. McClure, and G. W. Pigman III among others also demonstrate the prevalence of stoic moderation in Renaissance philosophy and consolation. Notably, however, the view of Aristotelian moderation has itself been usefully moderated. Lange's study on tears in the Renaissance combines the growing rationalization of tears within medical writing and sermons with lyric poetry's more passionate approaches to grief, Joshua Scodel traces a shifting relationship between excess and the mean especially in erotic and political writing, and Richard Strier argues against the universality of the principle.

26 See *City of God* XIV.9 and *Summa Theologiae* 1a.2ae.24, 2. Coluccio Salutati notably argued against Stoic apathy, but still on Augustinian terms. Jill Kraye has written more on this Renaissance attempt to combine Stoic and Augustinian thought. Jill Kraye, "Moral Philosophy," in *The Cambridge History of Renaissance Philosophy*, ed. Quentin Skinner, Eckhard Kessler, and Jill Kraye (Cambridge: Cambridge University Press, 1988), 367–368; Thomas Dixon, *From Passions to Emotions: The Creation of a Secular Psychological Category* (Cambridge: Cambridge University Press, 2003), 22.

27 For example, Elena Carrera, ed., *Emotions and Health, 1200–1700* (Leiden: Brill, 2013); Gail Kern Paster, *Humoring the Body: Emotions and the Shakespearean Stage* (Chicago: University of Chicago Press, 2004); Marjory E. Lange, "Humourous Grief: Donne and Burton Read Melancholy," in *Speaking Grief in English Literary Culture: Shakespeare to Milton*, ed. Margo Swiss and David A. Kent (Pittsburgh: Duquesne University Press, 2002), 69–97.

28 Joanne Diaz, "Grief as Medicine for Grief: Complaint Poetry in Early Modern England, 1559–1609" (PhD diss., Northwestern University, 2008), 8–9. Diaz finds the Latin proverb in a late sixteenth-century portrait of an unnamed woman by Marcus Gheeraert the Younger. The supplementary sacramental function of secular complaint is especially depicted in Thomas N. Tentler's *Sin and Confession on the Eve of the Reformation* (233–245), and John Kerrigan's *Motives of Woe* more recently continues that argument (25).

29 Puttenham, 1.47. See also P. G. Stanwood, "Consolatory Grief in the Funeral Sermons of Donne and Taylor," in *Speaking Grief in English Literary Culture: Shakespeare to Milton*, ed. Margo Swiss and David A. Kent (Pittsburgh: Duquesne University Press, 2002), 197–216.

30 "For godlie sorowe causeth repentance vnto saluacion, not to be repented of: but the worldie sorowe causeth death" (2 Cor. 7:10, Geneva). For the importance of this notion of godly sorrow in early modern poetry, see the introduction to Gary Kuchar's *The Poetry of Religious Sorrow in Early Modern England* (Cambridge: Cambridge University Press, 2008), particularly 4–11; for the importance of this distinction for Protestant theologians, see Peter Iver Kaufman, *Prayer, Despair, and Drama: Elizabethan Introspection* (Urbana: University of Illinois Press, 1996), 15–40.

31 I Thes. 4:13, Geneva.

32 *Marie Magdalens funeral teares*, A3v. Aquinas's eleven passions are *amor, odium, desiderium/concupiscentia, fuga/abominatio, delectatio/gaudium/laetitia, dolor/tristitia, spes, desperatio, timor, audacia,* and *ira.* (*Summa Theologiae* Ia.IIae. quest. 23, art. 4). Southwell's translations are mostly good, though *fuga/abominatio* is often translated as "disgust" today, and it should be noted that Southwell's use of "dislike" to mean "aversion" or "repugnance" is earlier than the first recorded in the OED.

33 Aquinas quotes the language of passion serving as reason's handmaid (*ancilla*) rather than its mistress (*domina*) from Gregory the Great (*ST* II–II 158.1.ad2), but the concept goes as far back as Plato's image of the passions being horses in the soul's chariot with reason as charioteer (*Phaedrus* 246a–254e).

34 The discussion of the impossibility of excess in love of God does not come into Aquinas's discussion of love as a passion as Southwell does, only in his discussion of it as a theological virtue (*ST* I–II 64.4).

35 *Marie Magdalens funeral teares*, A6r.

36 Ibid., A8v.

37 Ibid., B6v, H4r.

38 Gary Kuchar's *Divine Subjection* usefully elaborates on the function of Southwell's poetics of excess especially for his recusant readers, in addition to the potential discomfort his readers might have had with stereotypically feminine excess. *Divine Subjection: The Rhetoric of Sacramental Devotion in Early Modern England* (Pittsburgh: Duquesne UP, 2005).

39 The only editions of his poetry in which it is not included are obviously the three editions of *Mœoniæ*, which were printed as a supplement to *Saint Peters complaint* before eventually being included within the editions of *Saint Peters complaint* from 1620 onwards. Robert Miola has written usefully on the significance of the various orderings of the poems among different confessional communities, but this uniformity seems just as significant.

40 On the heels of the 1595 publication of Southwell's *Saint Peters complaint*, an anonymous *Saint Peters Ten Teares* appeared in 1597, William Broxup's *Saint Peters Path to the Joyes of Heauen* and Samuel Rowlands's *The Betraying of Christ* appeared in 1598, and Richard Verstegan's *Saint Peeters Comfort* appeared in 1601. Beyond these direct imitations, stanzas appeared in Elizabeth Grymeston's 1604 *Miscelanea. Meditations. Memoratives* under the subheading of "sixteene sobs of a sorowfull spirit" which the author "usually sung and played on the winde instrument," and Susanne Woods has argued that Aemilia Lanyer's 1611 *Salve Deus Rex Judaeorum* can be read as a response to Southwell. John Klause has traced many connections between Southwell and his distant cousin Shakespeare, Gary Kuchar in *The Poetry of Religious Sorrow*, has argued for Protestant parodies and responses from Shakespeare to Milton and Alison Shell's magisterial *Catholicism, Controversy and the English Literary Imagination* has made Southwell's influence on seventeenth century devotional poetry a scholarly commonplace.

41 This count does not include its own 24-line verse epistle and makes the poem over five times as a long as Southwell's second longest poem "A Phansie turned to a sinners complaint," which reaches only 152 lines.

42 Even Southwell's translation of these lines is not as grand. The final reading of the draft of "[The] Peeter Playnt" reads, "That sturdy peer which with an othe did boaste/Amyds a thousand pyckes and blody blades/At his deare masters syde to yeld the ghoast" (1–3).

43 The poem's first modern editor Alexander B. Grosart assessed that despite its thematic "thread of unity," the poem as a whole "really is rather a succession of separate studies" on Peter's sorrow (lxxxiv). For all his admiration of Southwell, Martz likewise judges the poem to be an "unwieldy collection of 132 stanzas" and finds it an "often tedious work," and his treatment of it is thereby sparse (194). James Russell Lowell criticized the poem as Peter's "drawl[ing] through thirty pages of maudlin repentance, in which the distinctions between the north and northeast sides of sentimentality are worthy of Duns Scotus" (1:253). Pierre Janelle, one of the scholars who argues that Southwell lost dexterity with his native tongue and contemporary English poetic movements during his education in Rome, considers the poem initially "disappointing" because of its "overlying crust of conceits and oratory," an example of the writer's "juvenile partiality for literary 'elegance'" and "veil of artificiality" that he learned on the continent and would later abandon as he matured as an author (205, 223). Even in recent scholarship, Anne Sweeney describes the poem as being "constructed along more typically baroque rhetorical lines" characterized by "a quivering extravaganza of repetitions on an emotional theme perhaps too hectic for English literary tastes" (11–12).

44 While the Ignatian structure is evident in the stages of the interior process, the length and repetitiveness prevent a strict mapping of this process. Alternatively, Kuchar argues provocatively that the imagery of the poem follows the alchemical process of transformation of a base stone into a refined substance. "Alchemy, Repentance, and Recusant Allegory in Robert Southwell's *Saint Peters complaint*," in *Redrawing the Map of Early Modern Catholicism*, ed. Lowell Gallagher (Toronto: University of Toronto Press: 2012), 159–184.

45 *iam quid homuncio ego unus esse possum?* (58). Quotations from the *Spiritual Exercises* are translated from the Vulgata version in Ignatius of Loyola and cited parenthetically by paragraph number.

46 *imaginando Iesum Christum coram me adesse in cruce fixum … sicut amici sermo ad amicum, vel servi ad dominum* (53).

47 In his commentary on this section of the *Exercises*, Gilles Cusson explains that

> the awareness of sin does not aim at the annihilation of the sinner, but at the
> true discovery of God's love for him.... In this sense, the experience of the first
> week is something uniquely positive. Not only does it unfold in the presence
> of the Savior, but the abyss of sin is meditated upon only to allow us to
> sound the immense length and the breadth of the divine love for man.

(161–162)

For more on the Christology of the first week, see Hugo Rahner, *Ignatius the
Theologian*, 53–93.

48 "Craze" initially enters the English language as a verb for Chaucer, meaning to
break or shatter, and thus "crazy" in the early modern period can mean either
cracked or sickly. The adjectival form was fairly new when Southwell composed
Saint Peters complaint. The OED first records its literal meaning of "cracked"
or "shaky" in Philip Stubbs's 1583 *Anatomie of abuses*, and the second in
Spenser's 1595 pastoral complaint *Colin Clouts come Home Againe*.

49 Luis de la Puente, S. J. *Meditations upon the Mysteries of our Holie Faith*,
trans. John Heigham (St. Omer: 1619), 2:186. La Puente goes on to describe
the lament in which Peter asks, "how canne I liue, having renownced the
author of life?" and Anne Sweeney identifies the parallel moment in Southwell's
poem when Peter asks "How can I live, that have my life deny'de?" (55) as an
employment of the rhetorical self-questioning in the *Spiritual Exercises*.
Sweeney, *Snow in Arcadia*, 28.

50 Luke 22:61–62 (Rheims, 1582).

51 Even in the earlier version, for Tansillo, the "wordes of wrath of loue full" (68)
from Christ's eyes contain wrath almost exclusively, accusing the penitent of
being a "frende disloyall ... discyple fierce" (32) and being "faythless and
vngratefull aboue all other" (62). Thus when Tansillo compares Peter's vision
of the gaze of Christ to the moment when a "youthful dame her beautuoise face
in glasse/of Christall bryghtnes did so well discrye" (33–34), the mirror reveals
only Peter's fault. ("parole di sdegno e d'amor piene" [F4v]; "Amico disleal,
discepol fiero" [F3v]; "Perfido e ingrato soura ogn'altro sei" [F4r]; "Giouane
donna il suo bel uolto in specchio ... uide ... di lucido cristallo" [F3v].)

52 Notably, there is no transition to this sudden turn to extended encomia, which
comes directly after Peter has spiraled from self-accusation into a tirade of blame
against the other actors of the evening: he includes complaints against the soldiers
who did not kill him in the garden (151–156), against the portress to whom he
had made his first denial (211–216), against John for bringing him in to the high
priest's courtyard (229–234), against the fire for whose temporary warmth he had
sold his soul (253–258), against the cock who announced his fall (259–276), and
against women in general who instigate the falls of great men (301–324). There is
no transition from this unbecoming tirade to the intimate memory.

53 "Liquid pearle" as a metaphor for tears or dew would later become a common-
place in English literature. Among dozens of other examples, it appears in
Christopher Marlowe's *Hero and Leander* (1598, l. 297), William Shakespeare's *A Midsummer Night's Dream* (1600, 1.1.216), and John Milton's
Paradise Lost (1667, 3.519). Other than William Byrd's translation of Luca
Marenzio's madrigal in 1588 ("Liquid and watry pearles, Loue weept full
kindely"), Southwell's is the first printed example of the metaphor in English.
Southwell likely first heard it from Marenzio ("Liquide perle Amor da gli'occhi
sparse/In premio del mio ardore," (26)), whose years in Rome overlap exactly
with his (1578–1586), and whose *Primo libro di madrigali a cinque voci* (1580)
was published during that period.

54 Cf. Sg. 7:4; 2 Sam. 23:13–17; Sg. 5:12; Exod. 17:1–7; cf. Num. 20:1–13. Notably, the reference to Bethlehem's cisterns compares Christ's tears to the water David longed to drink, remarkable in an ostensibly penitential poem that says nearly nothing about the penitent's tears until the end. Luis de Granada, a favorite among the English recusant community, similarly claimed that "the eies of our Sauiour Christe doe not onelie speake, but also worke, as it plainlie appeared by the teares of Peter, which albeit they gushed from the eies of Peter, yet did they much more proceide from the looke and eies of Christe." *Of prayer and meditation*, trans. Richard Hopkins (Paris, 1582), 70v–71r.

55 The OED records the first use of the verb *imparadise* in Samuel Daniel's *Delia* (1592), and the adjectival form *imparadised* in the 1590 *Arcadia*. Depending on the date of composition of *Saint Peters complaint*, this use was roughly contemporaneous.

56 The elements of true contrition involve both "sorrow and detestation of mind for sin committed" and "the resolution of not sinning again" (*animi dolor ac detestatio … de peccato commisso, cum proposito non peccandi de cetero*, 14.4.16).

57 Some of the material for this section is being published in a more extended form in "Passions and the Passion: Robert Southwell's Mary Magdalene," in *Id Quod Volo: The Dynamics of Desire in the* Spiritual Exercises *and Postmodernity*, ed. James Hanvey, S. J. and Travis La Couter (Leiden: Brill, 2020 (projected)).

58 Early in the Renaissance, humanist scholarship began to point out the potential distinction between these women, but the image of the rounded, developing woman remained firmly rooted in literature. For the early debate, see especially the controversy between Jacques Lefèvre d'Etaples and John Fisher in the early sixteenth century, well recounted in Sheila M. Porrer, *Jacques Lefèvre d'Etaples and the Three Maries Debates* (Geneva: Droz, 2009); and Anselm Hufstader, "Lefèvre d'Etaples and the Magdalen," *Studies in the Renaissance*, 16 (1969): 31–60. For the medieval tradition of the Magdalene, see Helen Meredith Garth's *Saint Mary Magdalene in Mediaeval Literature* (Baltimore: The Johns Hopkins Press, 1950).

59 In Joseph Szövérffy's extensive survey of medieval Magdalene hymns, a large majority treat her conversion and the anointing in the home of Simon, and there are less than half as many that refer to her scenes by cross or sepulcher. Similarly, he finds that the Magdalene is referred to as *Peccatrix* roughly three times more frequently than as *Apostola*, and finds only one hymn that refers to her as *Testis crucis Christi*. Among the dozens of hymns surveyed, he finds only two ("Flere libet" and "Maria collaudemus") with distant echoes of the *planctus* motif. See " 'Peccatrix quondam femina': A Survey of the Mary Magdalene Hymns," *Traditio*, 19 (1963): 102.

60 Diarmaid MacCulloch has identified a general silence in Protestant theology over the topic of the Virgin, though Arthur Marotti argues for her vestiges remaining deeply entrenched in English poetry. Gary Waller and Barry Spurr, among others, have traced these vestiges in English poetry and drama, and scholars have long connected the cult of the Virgin Queen to the lost cult of the Virgin Mother (e.g., Elkin Calhoun Wilson, Roy Strong, Helen Hackett). Hilda Graef has written helpfully on the various approaches to Marian theology among early reformers, and Paul Williams has written more specifically on the Marian devotion among the Tudor reformations in particular.

61 Patricia Badir, *The Maudlin Impression: English Literary Images of Mary Magdalene, 1550–1700* (Notre Dame, IN: University of Notre Dame Press, 2009), 3; Paul Williams, "The Virgin Mary in Anglican Tradition," in *Mary: The Complete Resource*, ed. Sarah Jane Boss (London: Continuum, 2007), 319–324.

62 Elizabeth Davis has written on the significance of the Magdalene in the Spanish Golden Age, and recent articles by Jordi Aladro and Alicia Colombí de

Monguió, and Maria del Pilar Chouza-Calo demonstrate a growing interest in this European fascination.

63 I Thes. 4:13, Geneva.

64 Sandro Sticca, Filippo Ermini, and F. J. Tanquerey have written historical studies of the continental analogues and historical roots of this tradition, including hymns and lyrics by Jacopone da Todi, John XXII, Bernard of Clairvaux, Bonaventure, Innocent III, Gregory XI, and Gregory I.

65 In England the pseudo-Origen sermon was first printed in Latin in 1505 and printed in English translation in 1555 and 1565. Margaret Jennings has written an analysis on the rhetorical techniques of the Latin text, and Karen Gross and John McCall have written on its potential influence on Chaucer. The poem, on the other hand, was initially printed anonymously in 1520 and spuriously attributed to England's great poet in an anthology six years later, and it appeared in all subsequent early modern editions of his works. Bertha Skeat closely examines the language and style of the poem in the introduction to her 1897 edition, and Debora Shuger explores its eroticism in "Saints and Lovers."

66 Katharine Goodland, *Female Mourning in Medieval and Renaissance English Drama: From the Raising of Lazarus to King Lear* (Aldershot: Ashgate 2005), 4.

67 Jean Calvin, *Commentary on the Gospel according to John*, tr. William Pringle (Edinburgh: Calvin Translation Society, 1847), 2:254.

68 E.g., Erasmo da Valvasone's *Le Lagrime della Maddalena* (1579), Camillo Camilli's *Le Lagrime di Santa Maria Maddelena* (1583), Pedro Malón de Echaide's *La Conversión de la Magdalena* (1588), Lope de Vega's "Las lágrimas de la Magdalena" (1614), and Diogo Mendez Quintella's *Conversam e Lagrimas da gloriosa Sancta Maria Magdalena* (1615).

69 The OED attributes the first printed use of "blush" as a noun referring to facial reddening as Shakespeare's 1595 *Henry VI, Pt. 3*, the same year this poem was first printed in March. The composition of the poem was certainly not after his arrest in 1592 and potentially several years before since it is often judged to come earlier in his poetic development, though composition dates can only be speculative.

70 Luke 7:47 (Rheims, 1582). The translators of the English College at Rheims, to whom Southwell had been connected during his formation, noted on this passage that "Not only faith (as you may perceiue) but loue or charitie obtaineth remission of sinnes."

71 For example, after bewailing "Alas to this wo that euer I was bore," the *Complaynte of the louer of Cryst* shows the abandoned lover dictating her tombstone: "Here within resteth a gostely creature/Crystes true louer mary Magdeleyn/ Whose herte for loue brast in peces tweyn" (B5r).

72 Indeed, even the late medieval pseudo-Chaucerian poem, first printed before the Henrician reformation and the eventual suspicion of the doctrine of the Real Presence, the Magdalene was already depicted nostalgically bemoaning that she had "loste his presence/Whiche in this worlde was all my sustenaunce" (A3v).

73 For Southwell's Magdalene, her soul's "prison, was his hart" (36) that has now been pierced through his chest. This slightly softens but still employs the eroticism of the pseudo-Chaucerian complaint in which the Magdalene requests that after the bursting of her heart her survivors may "Take out my herte the very rote and all/And close it within this boxe of oyntment" and thus "To my dere loue make theof a presente" (B5v) in the tomb of the lover who left her.

74 Mt. 1:19 (Rheims).

75 The OED gives the first use of that definition in Shakespeare's 1609 *Troilus & Cressida*, and lists the 1590 *Faerie Queene* as the first use of the more common meaning of fear or apprehension. Though like all of Southwell's poems this one was written before 1592, it was not printed until the expanded 1602 edition.

76 In his 1521 *Exposition of the Magnificat*, Luther insisted that the greatest honor we can do to her is to pray,

> O blessed Virgin and Mother of God, how utterly nothing and despised you have been, and yet God has looked upon you so graciously and abundantly and has done great things in you. You have not been worthy of any of these, and the superabundant grace of God is in you far above your merit.

In his 1522 *Sermon on Mary's Nativity* he insisted that since her special grace as the Mother of God is not due to her own merit, "we are just as holy as she," and in a 1527 sermon on the Annunciation he added among the possible meanings of her name "a little drop of water" to emphasize her nothingness. Quoted in Hilda Graef, *Mary: A History of Doctrine and Devotion*, vol. 2, *From the Reformation to the Present Day* (New York: Sheed and Ward, 1965), 8–11.

77 Quoted in Graef, *Mary*, 12–15.

78 Quoted in Paul Williams, "The Virgin Mary in Anglican Tradition," in *Mary: The Complete Resource*, ed. Sarah Jane Boss (London: Continuum, 2007), 319.

79 Quoted in Graef, *Mary*, 16. While the 1544 Litany included an invocation to the Virgin, it was removed in the Prayer Book together with other invocations to the saints and the commemoration of the Virgin in the Eucharistic Prayer. The extrabiblical Marian feasts disappeared in 1549 and 1552, which commemorated only the explicitly biblical feasts of the Annunciation and Purification; while the Calendar of 1561 restored the feasts of Mary's Conception, Nativity, and Visitation, the feast of her Assumption would not return to Anglican calendars until the twentieth century. Williams "Virgin Mary," 322. See also his "The English Reformers and the Blessed Virgin Mary," in *Mary*, ed. Boss, 238–255.

80 Scholars have suggested influence on canonical authors such as William Shakespeare, Edmund Spenser, Aemilia Lanyer, John Donne, George Herbert, Robert Herrick, and Richard Crashaw, in addition to identifying many direct imitations and appropriations from a range of others such as Sir John Davies, Thomas Nashe, Nicholas Breton, Thomas Lodge, Elizabeth Grymeston, Richard Verstegan, Henry Constable, William Alabaster, Gervase Markham, Thomas Robinson, William Broxup, Samuel Rowlands, Thomas Jordan, and Henry Vaughan.

81 This count does not include the Edinburgh edition of his poems, the eleven recusant editions of various works, or the twelve editions of/with the letter to his father between 1632 and 1675 that was attributed to Sir Walter Raleigh. Nine of them are collections of *Saint Peters complaint, with other poems* (original and expanded versions), three are the supplemental *Moeoniae*, six are *Marie Magdalens funeral teares*, three are *The Triumphs Over Death*, one is *A Short Rule of Good Life*, and three are complete collections that include all of the above.

82 While dating the composition of Donne's poems and his conversion from Roman Catholicism to the established church is difficult, Southwell's 1592 arrest happened the year before a priest was found in John's nineteen-year-old brother Henry Donne's chambers. Henry died of plague in Newgate Prison after undergoing torture in 1593, and the priest William Harrington was hung, drawn, and quartered in 1594, one year before Southwell suffered the same fate after his prolonged torture. The twenty-three-year-old Donne would certainly have felt a personal connection to the unfolding drama that led to the publication of Southwell's poems. For the early modern references to Lamentations as a biblical complaint, see Barbara Kiefer Lewalski, *Milton's Brief Epic: The Genre, Meaning, and Art of Paradise Regained* (Providence: Brown UP, 1966).

83 "The Sacrifice" (refrain), "The Temper" [1] (13), "Affliction" [III] (2).

Bibliography

Aladro, Jordi, and Alicia Colombí de Monguió. "Antecedentes e Influencias Literarias en la Obra Lírica de Lope en Torno a la Magdalena." In *Eros Divino: Estudios Sobre la Poesīa Religiosa Iberoamericana de Siglo XVII.* Edited by Julián Olivares, 99–134. Zaragoza, Spain: Prensas Universitarias de Zaragoza, 2010.

Anonymous. *The complaynte of the louer of Cryst Saynt Mary Magdaleyn.* London: 1520.

Aquinas, Thomas, OP. *Summa Theologiae: Latin Text and English Translation, Introductions, Notes, Appendices, and Glossaries.* Edited by Thomas Gilby *et al.* 61 vols. Cambridge: Blackfriars, 1964–1981.

Augustine. *City of God.* Edited by David Knowles. Translated by Henry Bettenson. Harmondsworth: Penguin Books, 1977.

Badir, Patricia. *The Maudlin Impression: English Literary Images of Mary Magdalene, 1550–1700.* Notre Dame, IN: University of Notre Dame Press, 2009.

Barbour, Reid. *English Epicures and Stoics: Ancient Legacies in Early Stuart Culture.* Amherst: University of Massachusetts Press, 1998.

Berlant, Lauren. "The Female Complaint." *Social Text* 19/20 (1988): 237–259.

Bible and Holy Scriptures conteyned in the Olde and Newe Testament. Translated according to the Ebrue and Greke, and conferred with the best translations in diuers languges. With moste profitable annotations vpon all the hard places, and other things of great importance as may appeare in the epistle to the reader. Geneva: 1560.

[Bible] *New Testament of Iesus Christ, translated faithfully into English, out of the authentical Latin, according to the best corrected copies of the same, diligently conferred vvith the Greeke and other editions in diuers languages.* Rheims: 1582.

Bouchard, Gary M. "*Who Knows Not Southwell's Clout?* Assessing the Impact of Robert Southwell's Literary Success upon Spenser." *LATCH* 3 (2010): 151–163.

Brou, Alexandre, S. J. *Ignatian Methods of Prayer.* Milwaukee: The Bruce Publishing Company, 1949.

Brown, Richard Danson. "A 'goodlie bridge' Between the Old and the New: The Transformation of Complaint in Spenser's *The Ruines of Time.*" *Renaissance Forum: An Electronic Journal of Early Modern Literary and Historical Studies* 2, no. 1 (1997): 64 paragraphs.

Brown, Richard Danson. "'A Talkatiue Wench (Whose Words a World Hath Delighted in)': Mistress Shore and Elizabethan Complaint." *Review of English Studies* 49 (1998): 395–415.

Bryan, Jennifer E. "Hoccleve, the Virgin, and the Politics of Complaint." *PMLA* 117 (2002): 1172–1187.

Byrd, William. *Musica transalpina Madrigales translated of foure, fiue and sixe partes, chosen out of diuers excellent authors.* London: 1588.

Calvin, Jean. *Commentary on the Gospel according to John.* Translated by William Pringle. Edinburgh: Calvin Translation Society, 1847.

Canons and Decrees of the Council of Trent: Original Text with English Translation. Edited by H. J. Schroeder, OP. St. Louis: B. Herder Book Co., 1941.

Carrera, Elena, ed. *Emotions and Health, 1200–1700.* Leiden: Brill, 2013.

Chouza-Calo, Maria del Pilar. "Lope de Vega and 'Las lágrimas de la Magdalena': An Erotic Conversion." In *El Siglo de Oro antes y después de El arte nuevo.* Edited by Oana Andreia Sâmbrian-Toma, 49–58. Craiova, Romania: SITECH, 2009.

Cusson, Gilles. *Biblical Theology and the Spiritual Exercises: A Method Toward a Personal Experience of God as Accomplishing Within Us His Plan of Salvation.* St. Louis: The Institute of Jesuit Sources, 1988.

Davenport, William Anthony. *Chaucer: Complaint and Narrative.* Woodbridge: D.·S. Brewer, 1988.

Davis, Elizabeth B. " 'Woman, Why Weepest Thou?': Re-visioning the Golden Age Magdalene." *Hispania* 76 (1993): 38–48.

Dean, Nancy. "Chaucer's Complaint, a Genre Descended From the *Heroides*." *Comparative Literature* 19 (1967): 1–27.

Devlin, Christopher. *The Life of Robert Southwell, Poet and Martyr.* New York: Farrar, Straus and Cudahy, 1956.

Diaz, Joanne. "Grief as Medicine for Grief: Complaint Poetry in Early Modern England, 1559–1609." PhD diss., Northwestern University, 2008.

Dixon, Thomas. *From Passions to Emotions: The Creation of a Secular Psychological Category.* Cambridge: Cambridge University Press, 2003.

Dubrow, Heather. *Genre.* London: Methuen, 1982.

Ermini, Filippo. *Lo Stabat Mater e I Pianti della Vergine nella Lirica del Medio Evo.* Città di Castello: Casa Editrice S. Lapi, 1916.

Fisher, Alexander J. " 'Per mia particolare devotione': Orlando di Lasso's *Lagrime di San Pietro* and Catholic Spirituality in Counter-Reformation Munich." *Journal of the Royal Musical Association* 132 (2007): 167–220.

Fisher, John. *De unica Magdalena.* Paris: 1519.

Fowler, Alastair. "The Formation of Genres in the Renaissance and After." *New Literary History* 34 (2003): 185–200.

Fucilla, Joseph G. "On the Vogue of Tansillo's 'Lagrime di San Pietro' in Spain and Portugal." *Rinascita* 2 (1939): 73–85.

Garth, Helen Meredith. *Saint Mary Magdalene in Mediaeval Literature.* Baltimore: The Johns Hopkins Press, 1950.

Goodland, Katharine. *Female Mourning in Medieval and Renaissance English Drama: From the Raising of Lazarus to King Lear.* Aldershot: Ashgate, 2005.

Graef, Hilda. *Mary: A History of Doctrine and Devotion*, vol. 2, *From the Reformation to the Present Day.* New York: Sheed and Ward, 1965.

Granada, Luis de, OP. *Of prayer and meditation.* Translated by Richard Hopkins. Paris: 1582.

Gross, Karen Elizabeth. "Chaucer, Mary Magdalene, and the Consolation of Love." *Chaucer Review* 41 (2006): 1–37.

Hackett, Helen. *Virgin Mother, Maiden Queen: Elizabeth I and the Cult of the Virgin Mary.* New York: St. Martin's Press, 1995.

Herbert, George. *The English Poems of George Herbert.* Edited by Helen Wilcox. Cambridge: Cambridge University Press, 2007.

Hufstader, Anselm. "Lefèvre d'Etaples and the Magdalen." *Studies in the Renaissance* 16 (1969): 31–60.

Ignatius of Loyola, S. J. *Exercitia spiritualia S. Ignatii de Loyola et eorum directoria.* Edited by José Calveras and Cándido de Dalmases, vol. 100 of *Monumenta Ignatiana.* Rome: Institutum Historicum Societatis Iesu, 1969.

Janelle, Pierre. *Robert Southwell the Writer: A Study in Religious Inspiration.* New York: Sheed & Ward, 1935.

Janelle, Pierre. *The Catholic Reformation.* Milwaukee: The Bruce Publishing Company, 1949.

Jennings, Margaret. "The Art of the Pseudo-Origen Homily *De Maria Magdalena*." *Medievalia et Humanistica* 5 (1974): 139–152.

Kaufman, Peter Iver. *Prayer Despair, and Drama: Elizabethan Introspection*. Urbana: University of Illinois Press, 1996.

Kerrigan, John. *Motives of Woe: Shakespeare and "Female Complaint": A Critical Anthology*. Oxford: Clarendon Press, 1991.

Klause, John. *Shakespeare, the Earl, and the Jesuit*. Madison, NJ: Fairleigh Dickinson University Press, 2008.

Kraye, Jill. "Moral Philosophy." In *The Cambridge History of Renaissance Philosophy*. Edited by Quentin Skinner, Eckhard Kessler, and Jill Kraye, 303–386. Cambridge: Cambridge University Press, 1988.

Kuchar, Gary. "Alchemy, Repentance, and Recusant Allegory in Robert Southwell's *Saint Peters complaint*." In *Redrawing the Map of Early Modern Catholicism*. Edited by Lowell Gallagher, 159–184. Toronto: University of Toronto Press: 2012.

Kuchar, Gary. *Divine Subjection: The Rhetoric of Sacramental Devotion in Early Modern England*. Pittsburgh: Duquesne University Press, 2005.

Kuchar, Gary. *The Poetry of Religious Sorrow in Early Modern England*. Cambridge: Cambridge University Press, 2008.

Lange, Marjory E. "Humourous Grief: Donne and Burton Read Melancholy." In *Speaking Grief in English Literary Culture: Shakespeare to Milton*. Edited by Margo Swiss and David A. Kent, 69–97. Pittsburgh: Duquesne University Press, 2002.

Lefèvre d'Étaples, Jacques. *De Maria Magdalena, triduo christi, et vna ex tribus Maria, disceptatio*. 1518.

Lewalski, Barbara Kiefer. *Milton's Brief Epic: The Genre, Meaning, and Art of Paradise Regained*. Providence: Brown University Press, 1966.

Lowell, James Russell. "Library of Old Authors." In *Literary Essays*, 1:247–348. Boston: Houghton, Mifflin, 1899.

MacCulloch, Diarmaid. "Mary and Sixteenth-Century Protestants." In *The Church and Mary*. Edited by R. N. Swanson, 190–217. Rochester: Boydell Press, 2004.

MacLean, Hugh. "'Restlesse anguish and unquiet paine': Spenser and the Complaint, 1579–1590." In *The Practical Vision: Essays in English Literature in Honour of Flora Roy*. Edited by Jane Campbell and James Doyle, 29–47. Waterloo: Wilfred Laurier University Press, 1978.

Marenzio, Luca. *Il primo libro de madrigali a cinque voci novamente*. Venice: 1580.

Marotti, Arthur F. "Forward." In *Marian Moments in Early Modern British Drama*. Edited by Regina Buccola and Lisa Hopkins, xiii–xx. Aldershot: Ashgate, 2007.

Martz, Louis L. *The Poetry of Meditation: A Study in English Religious Literature of the Seventeenth Century*. New Haven: Yale University Press, 1954.

McCall, John P. "Chaucer and the Pseudo-Origen *De Maria Magdalena*: A Preliminary Study." *Speculum* 46 (1971): 491–509.

McClure, George W. *Sorrow and Consolation in Italian Humanism*. Princeton, NJ: Princeton University Press, 1991.

Milburn, Erika. *Luigi Tansillo and Lyric Poetry in Sixteenth-Century Naples*. Leeds: Maney Publishing, 2003.

Miller, Robert P. "The *Miller's Tale* as Complaint." *The Chaucer Review* 5 (1970): 147–160.

Milward, Peter. *Shakespeare's Religious Background*. Bloomington: Indiana University Press, 1973.

Miola, Robert S. "Publishing the Word: Robert Southwell's Sacred Poetry." *Review of English Studies* 64 (2013): 410–432.

Olmsted, Wendy. *The Imperfect Friend: Emotion and Rhetoric in Sidney, Milton, and Their Contexts.* Toronto: University of Toronto Press, 2008.

Origen (pseudo). *An homelie of Marye Magdalene declaring her ferue[n]t loue and zele towards Christ. Newly translated.* London: 1555.

Origen (pseudo). *Omelia orige[n]is De beata maria magdalena.* London: 1505.

Paster, Gail Kern. *Humoring the Body: Emotions and the Shakespearean Stage.* Chicago: University of Chicago Press, 2004.

Peter, John. *Complaint and Satire in Early English Literature.* Oxford: Clarendon Press, 1956.

Pigman, G. W., III. *Grief and English Renaissance Elegy.* Cambridge: Cambridge University Press, 1985.

Pilarz, Scott, S. J. *Robert Southwell and the Mission of Literature, 1561–1595: Writing Reconciliation.* Aldershot: Ashgate, 2004.

Pilarz, Scott, S. J. " 'To Help Souls': Recovering the Purpose of Southwell's Poetry and Prose." In *Discovering and (Re)Covering the Seventeenth Century Religious Lyric.* Edited by Eugene R. Cunnar and Jeffrey Johnson, 41–61. Pittsburgh: Duquesne University Press, 2001.

Plato. *Euthyphro, Apology, Crito, Phaedo, Phaedrus.* Translated by Harold North Fowler. The Loeb Classical Library. Cambridge, MA: Harvard University Press, 1953.

Porrer, Sheila M. *Jacques Lefèvre d'Etaples and the Three Maries Debates.* Genève: Droz, 2009.

Praz, Mario. "Robert Southwell's 'Saint Peter's Complaint' and Its Italian Source." *The Modern Language Review* 19 (1924): 273–290.

Puente, Luis de la, S. J. *Meditations upon the Mysteries of our Holie Faith.* Translated by John Heigham. St. Omer: 1619.

Puttenham, George. *The Art of English Poesy.* Edited by Frank Whigham and Wayne A. Rebhorn. Ithaca: Cornell University Press, 2007.

Rahner, Hugo, S. J. *Ignatius the Theologian.* Translated by Michael Barry. New York: Herder and Herder, 1968.

Ransom, Emily A. "Passions and the Passion: Robert Southwell's Mary Magdalene." In *Id Quod Volo: The Dynamics of Desire in the* Spiritual Exercises *and Postmodernity.* Edited by James Hanvey, S. J. and Travis La Couter. Leiden: Brill, forthcoming.

Raspa, Anthony. *The Emotive Image: Jesuit Poetics in the English Renaissance.* Fort Worth: Texas Christian University Press, 1983.

Scase, Wendy. *Literature and Complaint in England, 1272–1553.* Oxford: Oxford University Press, 2007.

Scodel, Joshua. *Excess and the Mean in Early Modern English Literature.* Princeton, NJ: Princeton University Press, 2002.

Shell, Alison. *Catholicism, Controversy and the English Literary Imagination, 1558–1660.* Cambridge: Cambridge University Press, 1999.

Shifflett, Andrew. *Stoicism, Politics, and Literature in the Age of Milton.* Cambridge: Cambridge University Press, 1998.

Shuger, Debora Kuller. *Sacred Rhetoric: The Christian Grand Style in the English Renaissance.* Princeton, NJ: Princeton University Press, 1987.

Shuger, Debora Kuller. "Saints and Lovers: Mary Magdalene and the Ovidian Evangel." *The Bucknell Review* 35 (1992): 150–171.

Shuger, Debora Kuller. "The Philosophical Foundations of Sacred Rhetoric." In *Religion and Emotion: Approaches and Interpretations*. Edited by John Corrigan, 115–132. Oxford: Oxford University Press, 2004.

Skeat, Bertha M., ed. *The Lamentation of Mary Magdalene*. Cambridge: Fabb and Tyler, 1897.

Smith, Hallett. *Elizabethan Poetry: A Study in Conventions, Meaning, and Expression*. Cambridge, MA: Harvard University Press, 1952.

Smith, Rosalind, Michelle O'Callaghan, and Sarah C. E. Ross. "Complaint." In *A Companion to Renaissance Poetry*. Edited by Catherine Bates, 339–352. Blackwell Companions to Literature. Hoboken, NJ: Wiley, 2018.

Southwell, Robert, S. J. Autograph Manuscript. Stonyhurst College MS. A. v. 4.

Southwell, Robert, S. J. *Marie Magdalens funeral teares*. London: 1591.

Southwell, Robert, S. J. *The Poems of Robert Southwell, S. J.* Edited by James H. McDonald and Nancy Pollard Brown. Oxford: Clarendon Press, 1967.

Spurr, Barry. *See the Virgin Blest: The Virgin Mary in English Poetry*. New York: Palgrave Macmillan, 2007.

Stanwood, P. G. "Consolatory Grief in the Funeral Sermons of Donne and Taylor." In *Speaking Grief in English Literary Culture: Shakespeare to Milton*. Edited by Margo Swiss and David A. Kent, 197–216. Pittsburgh: Duquesne University Press, 2002.

Sticca, Sandro. *The Planctus Mariae in the Dramatic Tradition of the Middle Ages*. Translated by Joseph R. Berrigan. Athens: University of Georgia Press, 1988.

Strier, Richard. *The Unrepentant Renaissance: From Petrarch to Shakespeare to Milton*. Chicago: University of Chicago Press, 2011.

Strong, Roy. *Gloriana: The Portraits of Queen Elizabeth I*. London: Thames & Hudson, 1987.

Sweeney, Anne. *Robert Southwell: Snow in Arcadia: Redrawing the English Lyric Landscape, 1586–1595*. Manchester: Manchester University Press, 2006.

Szövérffy, Joseph. " 'Peccatrix quondam femina': A Survey of the Mary Magdalene Hymns." *Traditio* 19 (1963): 79–146.

Tanquerey, F. J. *Plaintes de la Vierge en Anglo-Français (XIIe et XIVe Siècles)*. Paris: Édouard Champion, 1921.

Tansillo, Luigi. *Le Lagrime di S. Pietro*. In *Il secondo libro dell' Eneida di Virgilio dove si contiene la distruttione dell' antichissimo imperio d'Asia*. Edited by Giovanni Mario Verdizotti. Venice: 1560.

Tentler, Thomas N. *Sin and Confession on the Eve of the Reformation*. Princeton: Princeton University Press, 1977.

Torre, Luca. "La doppia edizione de *Le lagrime di San Pietro* di Luigi Tansillo tra censura e manipolazione." PhD diss., Università degli Studi di Napoli Federico II, 2010.

Waller, Gary. *The Virgin Mary in Late Medieval and Early Modern English Literature and Popular Culture*. Cambridge: Cambridge University Press, 2011.

Williams, Paul. "The Virgin Mary in Anglican Tradition." In *Mary: The Complete Resource*. Edited by Sarah Jane Boss, 314–39. London: Continuum, 2007.

Wilson, Elkin Calhoun. *England's Eliza*. Harvard Studies in English, vol. 20. New York: Octagon, 1966.

Wilson, Richard. "A Bloody Question: The Politics of *Venus and Adonis*." *Religion and the Arts* 5, no. 3 (2001): 297–316.

Woods, Susanne. "Lanyer and Southwell: A Protestant Woman's Re-Vision of St. Peter." In *Centered on the Word: Literature, Scripture, and the Tudor-Stuart Middle Way*. Edited by Daniel W. Doerksen and Christopher Hodgkins, 73–86. Newark: University of Delaware Press, 2004.

Young, R. V. *Doctrine and Devotion in Seventeenth-Century Poetry: Studies in Donne, Herbert, Crashaw, and Vaughan*. Cambridge: D. S. Brewer, 2000.

9 Robert Southwell's articulation of self-fashioning

Afroditi-Maria Panaghis

Robert Southwell articulated the process of his self-fashioning, the configuration and restoration to wholeness through suffering, scourging, self-annihilation, death, and dismemberment in *A Humble Supplication to her Maiestie, A Short Rule of Good Life, Fourfold Meditation: Of the Foure Last Things,* and *Spiritual Exercises and Devotions.* The works outline the manner by which the *numinous* conflates feelings of spiritual transcendence and the oscillations between states of pleasure and pain once the awakening of the self to the consciousness of divine reality, and the potential union with the One, the daunting "wholly other," is realized.[1] They register elements of the *numinous* both positive, *mysterium fascinans,* such as sublimity and entrancement on the one hand; and negative, *mysterium tremendum,* self-abasement, horror, and repulsion on the other.[2] They also depict the torment and triumph of the Christian self, mark the progress of the soul from earthly life to judgment day, juxtapose virtuous to sinful life as well as concretize the notions of sin and salvation. Besides defining the experience of a transcendental reality and the rapture at the vision of heavenly joy; Southwell expresses sympathy for sinners, comfort for the persecuted Catholics, and describes suffering and martyrdom "as a price to be paid to redeem the country from heresy."[3] Finally, by commenting on the politico-religious events of his time Southwell unravels the precarious interplay of his multiple selves.

Although both the self and the soul form the total being the latter is for a religious the only aspect that matters. The self suggests awareness of accepted values while the soul one's spiritual existence and preoccupation with the divine.[4] The tendency of religion to divide as well as integrate the worldly self and the God-orientated soul, began during the renaissance.[5] Numerous debates evidence "a concept of the self in the late sixteenth and early seventeenth-century England as not merely volatile but paradoxically affirmed in its moments of self-cancelling or shattering."[6] Although during the reformation the notion of the self stressed spiritual life, both Protestants and Catholics encouraged individuals to submit to authority, and assimilate within the community.[7] Cynthia Marshall contends that "the violence accompanying the establishment of new forms of religious and state authority gives vivid testimony to the uneasiness or even terror with which many people in the early modern era confronted their autonomous existence."[8] After all, "a focus on the individual self was morally suspect within a Christian ideology that encouraged selflessness and humility."[9] Similarly, Jonathan Sawday argues that the self was regarded negatively in the early modern era because selfhood was considered a sign of spiritual degeneracy.[10] Thus "the idea of dissolving or annihilating selfhood was a desirable goal within orthodox religious discourses";[11] since "dissolving the self through submission to God is actually constitutive of identity."[12] It is against this backdrop that Catholics experienced subjectivity in Elizabethan England. Scott R. Pilarz for instance, claims that religious identity in Southwell's England was fluid;[13] while Ronald Corthell points out the difficulties Catholics encountered in their effort to possess a subject position within "the Elizabethan picture."[14] Although I agree with both, I postulate that self-fashioning demanded an ever-ending process of depreciation and deconstruction followed by re-evaluation and reconstruction as the works under review attest. I also maintain that Southwell allows the fabrication of new selves within the bounds of God's word and universe, and by debating the politico-religious events of his time, emphasizes that both self and soul should unite to serve God. Furthermore, by taking on "different subject roles at different times and perhaps, even different roles at the same time";[15] Southwell reflects the tribulations and persecution he underwent, and underlines the idea that this process is "personal" as well as "psychological."[16] Consequently, his works are enhanced with an undercurrent text that presents one or more self out of the many (the defender, the reconciliator, the sinner, the preacher, the prisoner, the contemplative, the sacrifice, or the martyr) that appear in his ouevre. However, cognizant that his self as a writer along with all the rest of his selves, would soon vanish, with the exception of that of the martyr; he tried to preserve them in his writings. Thus his texts should be viewed as imaginative reconstructions of the self with polysemous meanings instead of simple records of religious discussions or political events.

The self as defender and reconciliator: *A Humble Supplication to her Maiestie* (1595)

While the Elizabethan government was determined to build a Protestant nation and reformers hoped that the old religion would fade away, Catholicism persisted with the aid of clergy and laity who remained devoted to the old religion, and the missionary priests who returned to England from the continent throughout the second half of its reign. The plan for the conversion of England gradually evolved as Catholics suffered hardships and exile and anticipated the return of the old status quo.[17] When Queen Elizabeth ascended to the throne her country was in a state of religious upheaval, but once the Act of Supremacy named her Supreme Governor of the Church of

England, and the Act of Uniformity required that all her subjects attend Protestant services adopting *The Book of Common Prayer* her position was consolidated and the bond between England and the Papacy was severed, the administration began persecuting and outlawing Catholicism with the aim to eradicate it. With the conversion of Elizabeth's court to Protestantism, a large number of Catholics refused to join the established church and continued instead to conform to their faith in secret.[18] The penalties for this offense included heavy fines, forfeiture of goods and land, imprisonment, and execution for treason.[19] Clearly, Catholicism was in danger of dying out completely especially after legislation was passed to criminalize holding Mass, administering the sacraments, criticizing state religion as well as possessing or printing Catholic writings.[20] Meanwhile William Allen visited England and entreated Catholics to remain steadfast in their allegiance[21] otherwise, with the passage of time they would either become "indifferent" or show readiness "to compromise with their persecutors," or "become used to the situation," or "resort to all sorts of subterfuges, even going to Protestant churches to conceal their faith."[22] Thus many Catholics challenged state authority by proclaiming their beliefs and embracing martyrdom willingly. Southwell for instance, invests his works with extraordinary poignancy and drama to encourage them to follow Christ through sacrifice and martyrdom modeled on the Passion. He also evokes the memory of England's glorious past to solicit English Catholics to resist the government's unjust laws. As a result "Catholicism survived in England in an attenuated, underground form, despite the institutional overlay of the Church of England."[23]

As numerous bills were passed with the aim to maintain domestic stability, eliminate the policies of the Marian regime and most importantly, continue the reformation, English Catholics, and particularly seminary priests, "found that masking their belief and position offered a potentially lifesaving response to their uncertain if not illegal and treasonous position."[24] A study of the history of that period, and the State Papers in the Public Record Offices, both in England and on the Continent, show that "the brute force of faithless men, combined to destroy and crush, root and branch out of the land, the ancient faith … by means of a series of savage enactments."[25] Meantime, "every record of the heroic lives or virtuous deeds of Catholics was studiously suppressed, or maliciously misrepresented, in order to justify, by a gigantic falsehood, the most atrocious cruelties and injustice," and conceal the fact that they were "sanctioning a persecution of Christians as barbarous and inhuman as any that was ever inflicted in Pagan times."[26] Matters worsened for Catholics when Francis Walsingham was appointed secretary in 1573. With the intention to uproot Catholicism from England, he masterminded a spy network both at home and abroad and succeeded in infiltrating Catholic communities, bringing about the execution of many prominent men and women, including Mary Queen of Scots, and thwarting, allegedly, numerous plots against

Elizabeth's life. In addition, during the 1580s and 1590s, times of religious and political turmoil, the arrival of the Jesuit missionaries was considered "a prelude to invasion and assassination" and that prompted harsh measures against them.[27] While stressing the plight of his co-religionists Southwell's reconciliator self advises not only the Catholics, but all of his compatriots to choose tolerance and peaceful coexistence.

Within this politico-religious context Southwell contested Allen who upheld that one could not have two masters, and claims that the Catholic subject could exist within the Protestant Elizabethan order. Obviously, he remained in an eternal state of paradox divided between his personal self devoted to God, and his public one loyal to the queen. He expresses a political stance which professes loyalty to queen Elizabeth, states that he is capable of "annihilating the subject if need be as well as separate commitments," and asserts that he sees no conflict between his religious and political self.[28] Coincidently, the state "declared and denied at the same time the split between the public subject, that of the missionary that was regarded as a threat to the government, and the private one."[29] Furthermore, before his execution Southwell confirmed this duality when he admits that as a private subject he is "a priest of the Catholic church, and of the Society of Jesus"; but as a public subject, "solemnly denie[s] that he had ever attempted, contrived, or imagined any evil against the queen."[30] When the public self addresses the queen exclaiming "what armie soeuer shoulde come against you, we will rather yield our breastes to bee broached by our enimies swords, than vse our swords to the effusion of our Country bloud, as we would for God" the writer suggests reconciliation between the two communities.[31] He also declares that he always prayed for her, recommended his country to the mercy of God, and concludes with the hope that his death "may be for [his] own and for [his] country's good, and the comfort of the Catholics [his] brethren."[32] But the private self is not ignored as his words "of which most clement God and Father of Mercies, through the blood of Jesus Christ, I in the first place crave forgiveness for all things wherein I may have offended since my infancy" illustrate.[33] Southwell adds:

> I deliver my soul into the hands of God my Creator, earnestly beseeching Him that He may preserve and strengthen it with His grace, and grant it to continue faithful in this final conflict. For what may be done to my body I have no care. But since death, in the admitted cause for which I die, cannot be otherwise than most happy and desirable, I pray the God of all comfort that it may be to me the complete cleansing of my sins and a real solace and increase of faith and constancy to others.[34]

Hence *Supplication*, besides being a masterwork in controversy, is an example of martyrological literature that depicts the recusants' ordeal, proposes conciliation, and outlines the process of self-fashioning.

Since national identity in the sixteenth and seventeenth century was mainly Protestant, Catholics were not only marginalized, they were also considered enemies of both queen and state. Therefore "with religious belief now an aspect of nationhood, the self-construction of the English Catholic should be placed within the context of their physical exclusion from England."[35] Actually, the long exile of Catholics, their education in "the Low Countries, France, and Rome, and their reliance upon the hospitality and financial support of foreign princes" was enough to arouse the suspicion of the state as to their intentions.[36] For instance, Jesuit missionaries were closely watched, and were accused of being linked to Spanish expansionist dreams by using the sacraments to "mooue, stirre up, perswade to renounce their naturall allegiance," from the queen of England.[37] Southwell refutes these allegations and protests against the accusation that the Catholic priests were "unnatural subjects, baseborn, dissolute agents of Spain, and criminal ruffians."[38] He rejects the charge of treachery because, according to him, they were penalized and executed for their religious beliefs and not their politics.[39] He also concurs with Allen about "the futility of Lord Burghley's plea that martyrs were put to death not for their religion, but for high treason."[40] He explains that although "treason requires betrayal of one's compatriots," it would be a "greater betrayal to let [their] souls be lost" therefore shifting the stress from politics to religion.[41] Thus *Supplication* should also be considered a historical document wherein the defender self is compelled to justify the actions of the Catholic priests as entirely spiritual since they labored "for the saluation of soules, and in peaceable and quiet sort, to confirme them in the ancient Catholike faith, in which theyr forefathers liued & died, these thousand foure hundred yeares, out of which we vndoubtedly beleeue it is impossible that any soule should be saued."[42] Obviously, Southwell longs to reunite the English with Catholicism and their national past, and postulates that "England's break from the Church of Rome separated it from salvation history."[43] He believes that its return would re-establish its connection not only with its "national past," but also with the future.[44]

Supplication not only rebuts the 1591 *Proclamation* and offers Southwell's "discourse as a substitute," it also pleads for tolerance for the Catholic minority on grounds of equity and justice.[45] He employs rhetoric and imagination, and blends the political with the religious self to create an argumentative ploy so as to engage in an ideological dialogue with the government. Moreover, *Supplication* presents a well-informed discussion of the Babington plot and a description of the atrocities committed to all those who were arrested. Southwell exhibits an additional self, that of the reconciliator when, unlike many of his co-religionists, he opposed the plot because he believed that such conspiracies only aggravated the predicament of the Catholics. He also invites the queen to embrace the old faith so that the blood that had been spilled would not go to waste. Coincidently, Pilarz claims that Southwell was motivated by an impulse of reconciliation and that he tried to settle the dispute between extremists on both sides of the confessional divide as regards the issue of loyalty and belief.[46] Of course the government rebuffed Southwell's appeal because accepting it would mean admitting the torture and cruelties committed against Catholics, and treachery if England were to reconcile with the Church of Rome. Furthermore, I would like to add that Southwell's call for peaceful coexistence springs basically from his belief in "the doctrine of reconciliation" that refers to the barrier created between God and the individual as a result of transgression.[47] The doctrine presupposes union with the divine following confession, repentance, and return to Jesus who personally suffered in order to offer redemption to sinners, sanctification, and a perfect standing before God. Adopting the role of the spokesman for the victimized community, Southwell also maintained that the queen "seldom or never heareth the truth of our persecutions," and acknowledged that her "lenity and tenderness being knowne to soe professed an enemy of these Cruelties ... would never permit their continuance if they were expressed to [her] Highness as they are practiced upon us."[48] Thus the defender self absolves the queen of any wrongdoing and condemns her advisors for intentionally misinforming her about the Catholics' condition, creating fictitious charges, and issuing tough measures against them. He reckons that they would not dare deliver such "a discourse so full farced with contumelious tearmes as better suted a declamorous tongue, than your Highness's penne."[49] Moreover, it should also be noted that the state referred to the Jesuits as diabolical liars and charged them with employing equivocation to persuade Catholics to commit treasonous acts. According to the *Treatise of Equivocation*, a seminary priest could resort to any method to baffle his audience. He could use words with multiple meanings, give only one of several possible answers to a question, or exploit ambiguities.[50] Thomas Morton contends that "the equivocating priest [had to] confront a potentially divided self, one in which the very act of mental reservation (the indirect intent) conflicts with the core dictates and understanding of one's conscience (the direct intent)."[51] He also points out that in "temporizing or obscuring, words become lies and selves become split" hence suggesting the precarity of the self.[52] The Jesuit missionaries were not only engaged in the practice of equivocation, so vitipurated by Sir Edward Coke, but also with disguise. Although equivocation intended to evade the state, it could also, "in its undecidability and resistance to ideological closure, decenter the subject." It was equally dangerous as disguise that could "absorb the personality."[53] Southwell too, beside using equivocation during his trial, like many others, risked losing himself "in the act of impersonation," when he adopted disguise and an alias, Cotton, to blur his true identity, as a means of survival, evading pursuivants, mingling in government circles, and for as long as he was free, carrying out his mission and performing his religious duties.[54] He also defends disguise when he states that "sith we cannot reforme the Inconvenience till your Maiestie think it good to license vs without danger to exercise our

Functions."[55] However, disguise has a dual function since it combines simultaneously self-cancellation and self-construction and as such concretizes the precarity of the process of self-fashioning. The next section presents the self as sinner and preacher often co-existing with the defender self.

The self as sinner and preacher: *A Short Rule of a Good Life* (1596) and *Fourfold Meditation: Of the Foure Last Things* (1606)

As "the bondsman of God and of His vicars,"[56] Southwell's defender self had to deal with, besides the political situation, the ecclesiastical disputes, and "the great harm [that had] come to the Christian Commonwealth through the unworthiness and quarrelsomeness and the obstinacy of religions."[57] At the same time, during the six years of his underground ministry his preacher self evangelized and wrote in order to convert as many as possible to the old faith as well as inspire the faithful. John Gerard claims that Southwell "excel[ed] in the art of helping and gaining souls ... being at once prudent, pious, meek, and exceedingly winning."[58] The preacher self proved "a fisher of souls, a model of life to seculars, and a mirror of virtues; a labourer in the harvest of Christ, an inseparable servant of Him, a declared and public enemy of the devil, the world, and the flesh."[59] He wrote about the shortness of life, the need for timely repentance, and juxtaposed heavenly joys to earthly pleasures so as to exhort sinners to change their ways. It is to this end that *Short Rule*, printed shortly after his martyrdom, was written, and dedicated to the Countess of Arundel who risked her life offering protection and money to Catholic priests. It is a directive for a life spent in a worldly context but with the mind and heart fixed upon the life beyond; in other words, the aim was to teach the earnest faithful to live an upright life, and restore their soul to virtue. Following Ignatius Loyola's *Spiritual Exercises*, the preacher self depicts the anguish as well as the victory of the Christian soul, and encourages the reader to identify with the narrator who attempts to reconcile man to God, and help the devout live according to the rules of a "goodlie life & in so doing ... hapilie attaine the crowne of glorie."[60] To be a good Catholic suggests aiding others, giving up all possessions, and even leaving loved ones behind. Lastly, he addresses the relationship between subjects and secular rulers, God's "viceregents and substitutes," as well as religious superiors, and neighbors, a matter that interested his readership.[61]

When the narrator states that he could not "serue God in this world, nor go about to enjoye [Him] in the next," because His three enemies "the Worlde, the Flesh, and the Deuill will repine and seeke to hinder" him, not only does he infer to the bleak condition of the Catholics and the necessity for political survival but also personal salvation.[62] As a result he "must neuer looke to haue one hower secure from their assaultes," and his "whole life must be a continuall combate with these aduersaries" whose "malice is

so vnplacabble, and their hatred against [him] so rooted in them."[63] Besides
disputing with the authorities to protect Catholics, Southwell also posits as
a layman who struggles to resist temptation; therefore religion and politics
coincide and the sinner self unites with that of the preacher and defender
self. Furthermore, because he is "apte to fall, [he] must often renue [his]
good purposes, which for that it is a materiall point, it will be good to sette
downe with [him] selfe these rules."[64] Subsequently, Southwell's sinner self
is expected to undergo a ceaseless process of becoming, keeping it in this
way in constant peripeteia. He is convinced that no matter the tribulations
that the faithful were called upon to endure there was comfort in persecution, imprisonment, suffering, even in violent death and martyrdom; for
"without continuall violence & force, [the soul] cannot attaine to vertu, or
leaue vice, whereunto it is much inclined, [he] must assure [himself] that
care & watchfulness is euer necessary."[65] He agrees with Loyola that the
Divine permits violence to be done to the flesh for the sole purpose of
repressing passions, an experience which he describes as one of pain and
pleasure, of jouissance, so as to achieve heavenly bliss.[66] Southwell also
asserts that God loves His creatures and if He "allows hazards to overtake
them, it proceeds of love and is for [their] greater good and that having laid
a heavy burden upon weak forces will by His grace supply all [their] fears,
wants, and frailties."[67] Christians have to give themselves "up to God …
become His perpetual bond-slaves and servants, as to be no longer able to
will or not to will anything of [themselves]; therefore know for certain that
whatever may befall [them] happens by His peculiar providence."[68] The
writer contends that a good Christian should consider "for what end and
purpose [he] was created, and what Gods designement was, why he
redeemed [him] with his owne bloud, bestowed no infinite benefites vppon
[him] and still continueth his mercy towards [him]."[69] In addition, he
reminds the devout of the moment when life on earth will expire and they
will be "summoned by Death to appeare before [their] Landlorde, who
with most rigorous iustice will demaunde account of euery thing" and that
"discharg[ing their] account [will] be either crowned in eternall ioy, or condemned to perpetuall damnation."[70] He proposes spiritual growth while
withstanding temptation, and advises that all should turn to God, the
father, and the Catholic Church, the mother, for strength.[71]

Southwell also concedes that he had to pose questions such as "what
was I O Lord? What am I? What shall I be?" to which he responds, "I was
nothing, I am now nothing worth & am in hazard to be worse than
nothing I was conceiued to originall sinne, I may hereafter feele the eternall
smart of sinne"; and "I was in my mother, a loathsome substance I am in
the world, a sacke of corruption, I shall be in my graue, a prey of vermine"
hence suggesting the need for contemplation and self-knowledge but also
self-fashioning.[72] He points out that Christians should not only consider
the power of the self, but also its abasement and the fact that it is nothing
more than dust and nothingness. After all, the notion of self-depreciation

and dissipation, according to Rudolph Otto, is an act of religious humility that leads to the annihilation of the self and the transcendence of the soul.[73] Finally, Southwell advises that abandoning the material world and following the guidelines delineated in *Short Rule* will ultimately lead to spiritual transcendence, and "God's glory in this world and His reward in the next."[74]

The preacher self together with the sinner self is also present in *Fourfold Meditation: Of the Foure Last Things* (1606), which depicts and traces the progression of the soul to either heaven or hell. Southwell recurs to the numinous which considers God as an "other," the dependency on some-thing objective and outside the self, a transcendent reality as well as the perception of awe-inspiring mystery that captivates and pervades the mind with tranquility.[75] Otto describes the feeling of the "wholly other," sweep-ing like "a gentle tide, pervading the mind," or "erupt[ing] from the depths of the soul with spasms and convulsions leading to the strangest excitement and intoxicated frenzy and ecstasy."[76] He affirms that the divine is indeed the strongest, loveliest, and dearest, and our encounter with Him is "the alluring moment of the *numinous*, schematized by means of the ideas of goodness, mercy, and love."[77] I contend that Southwell invites his readers to join him in experiencing the *numinous*, this "over-whelming religious experience," the manifestation of the "wholly other, the heavenly, that which is beyond the intelligible and familiar, that effaces the self and fills the individual with excessive joy."[78]

Fourfold Meditation portrays the sinner self on its deathbed terrorized at the thought of having to present itself before the Lord. The persona declares that humans have inherited not only sin and death through Adam's fall but also hope of salvation through Christ's sacrifice.[79] When God spoke, says the persona, the sinner self "semedst deafe and dombe," and although He "gave [it] all [it] didst detest [Him]," while the devil who "gave [him] naught wholie [him] posest" (stanzas 31, 34).[80] Southwell also describes Judgment Day and the appearance of the sinner self before the High Judge to receive recompense or retribution. God reminds the sinner self that did not walk the righteous path and disdained heavenly joys of Christ's sacrifice. Hoping to help individuals discern good from evil, the persona reports God and Satan as active players in the world and man's soul. He warns those who disobey divine law with hell and everlasting torture, while those who sin but confess and repent he promises redemp-tion after a period of atonement. Clearly, the persona alludes to the wrath of God, the manifestation of the *mysterium tremendum* which signifies a holy fear of the Lord.

Short Rule focuses on the sinner self in a world besieged with tempta-tions while *Fourfold Meditation* begins with the moment of death in order to elicit fear in all those who are interested in short-lived delights. Southwell states that the transgressor's material possessions that evoke pleasure will be inherited by those who remain behind, and that his body "shall serve for maggots, for a praye,/The body must tranceformed be to claye./For whose delight such costilie clothes were bought," and "crawling wormes to feed on thee doth waite" (stanzas 17, 26–27). He underlines the significance of the soul when he exclaims "what is the body without the soule but a corrupt carcase? & what the soule without God but a sepulcher of sinne?"[81] He also draws upon Loyola to advocate that death has great power "to withdraw the soul from an inordinate love of the visible things of the world" and help "conceive a holy fear of the Lord."[82] He confirms that "the ioyes are past on which [he] seteth [his] herte," his "former faultes are sett before [his] eyes," and "despaire in secret lies/And all [his] senses with terror appall." Once earthly joys vanish, an eternal life of darkness in a loathsome place begins (stanza 27). Similarly, in the third section of the poem, "Of Paines of Hell," the persona refers to the Judge's words of condemnation and the eternal damnation of the offender, thus reflecting the notion of *mysterium tremendum* through the ghastly dungeon, the huge gulf of hell and its monsters, the rigor of the pain, and the eternity of the punishment. In horror and despair the transgressor self tries unsuccessfully to escape the infernal place "wher hope is past and damned foules lament,/Wher wormes doe crawle and uglie serpents creepe,/Wher paines abound and sorrowes make [him] weepe" (stanza 74). But according to Southwell, there is also hope as the "Ioyes of Heaven" affirms. Consequently, the paradoxical notion of the *numinous* also encompasses fascination and rapture for the "goodlie place [where] all beautie doth surmount, [and] glorie dost excel," and where "none doth suffer wrack," hell, or God's wrath (stanzas 90,120). As in *Short Rule*, the preacher self addresses the faithful with the hope that all "the ioyes and paines which [they] see may move [their] mind to leade [their] life upright," so that one day they may enjoy contemplating God (stanza 125).

The self as contemplative: *The Spiritual Exercises and Devotions* (1578)

The preacher self withdraws as the sinner self lingers and the contemplative self forges ahead. In *Exercises and Devotions*, Southwell borrows from Loyola's *Spiritual Exercises* practices to discipline the body, the emotions, and the mind, as well as the process of self-introspection, the method of narration, colloquial speech, and conceits to fuse abstract theological ideas with the concreteness of real life. The text provides a glimpse into the inner life of the young novice through contemplation, prayer, dialogues with God, and reflections. The Jesuits "formalized the process of meditation" wherein "the soul or mind engages in acts of interior dramatization. The speaker blames himself for the transgressions he committed; converses with God; and approaches His love through memory, understanding, and will."[83] When the preacher self prompts his readers to turn their eyes toward Jesus's Passion in order to derive courage, and describes the experience of sickness, death, and regeneration at a higher level, he implies the idea of being made whole through sacrifice. Although this experience seems to be the prerogative of the preacher self, through identification the readers may participate and thus realize their self's finiteness, imperfection, the manifold illusions in which it has been immersed, and the distance that separates it from the One. Plotinus claimed that the soul's goal is to transcend from the sensible to the intellect, and eventually unite with the One.[84] Evelyn Underhill defined this union as "the expression of the innate tendency of the human spirit toward complete harmony with the transcendental order, with God, which is truly entrancing but also confounding, captivating, and transporting."[85] Yet the union of the soul with transcendent reality necessitates purgation of the sinner self which permits "sinful flesh to be torn by penance in this life," while healing will occur "in the happiness of the life to come."[86]

In *Exercises and Devotions*, Southwell reveals that he decided to join the Society of Jesus so that "by constant mortification of the self, by sincere contempt of the world ... by a perfect observance of [his] rule and [his] vows [he] may become, as far as [he] can, like unto Christ who was crucified for [him]," but at the same time, "strive with all [his] heart to love Him do penance in this life for the numberless sins committed against God."[87] He also announces his determination to "commit [himself to] the authority of His ministers and representatives, and entrust to them the entire care of [his] soul and body," remain faithful to his vocation, and by following Christ, prepare to sacrifice himself and "with all [his] energies devote [himself] to the salvation of [his] neighbour."[88] Like in *Short Rule*, he recommends the devout to espouse virtues such as kindness, modesty, love, charity as well as live like beggars in order to obtain redemption. Once again, he advises sinners who shut their ears to God's words, barred their heart from His entry, abandoned their faith, transferred their loyalty to the devil, and neglected the voice of Christ, to amend. Thus *mysterium tremendum*, "the daunting and repelling moment of the *numinous*, schematized by means of the rational ideas of justice, and moral will becomes the holy wrath of God" that prevents humans from sinning.[89] Southwell also declares that offendors should never forget that they were captive in their sins until Christ was "tortured and scourged and put to a shameful death" so that they may go free and eventually unite with the divine.[90] By identifying with Christ, he predicts that he too will be sacrificed, thus reflecting his impending death, yet his preacher self will continue to save souls through conversion to the old faith, and confirms that God will bestow a crown of glory once they take up their cross to tread the path of tribulation. Lastly, the contemplative self insists on the meditation of the mysteries of Christ which enflame the heart, excite the mind, and enable the faithful to detect the deceit and dangers that beset them.

Southwell confesses that his soul was "espoused to the crucified one," that he became a son to the Virgin, "a companion of Saints, a dweller in the house of God, a captain in the army of Christ, a foundation stone in the Church appointed by God Himself to strengthen its foundations."[91] He grew into "a fisher of men's souls, to those in the world an example of life and a mirror of virtue, a worker in Christ's harvest, His perpetual bondman."[92] Finally, he admits that he "belong[s] to God and His vicars in such a way that they have full power over [him], but never again shalt [he] have it over [himself]."[93] Thus he emerges as "a leader to the blind and a staff to the lame, all things to all men, and to God ever one and the same."[94] Likewise, Southwell foreshadows what was bound to befall him as a missionary since he could be imprisoned, maltreated, wasted by hunger and thirst, mutilated, scourged, and slain. All the same, he should be ready to fight without heeding the wounds, toil without seeking rest, do God's will, root out passions, and for the kingdom of heaven suffer violence. After all, for him, it did not matter if martyrdom was the only way since death was bound to come for him any day. Southwell "consider[s] that the very law of nature demand[s] that [he] give [himself] wholly to God and serve Him with [his] whole heart and mind."[95] He promises to carry out his duties as a priest, obtain self-knowledge as well as determine the reason why patience, humility, meekness, obedience, and other virtues that characterize Christ are non-existent in him. After all, self-scrutiny is one of the principal exercises that leads to insight and the discovery of the negative tendencies that control our acts and hinder our growth and improvement. Even the mind can suppress counter-productive attitudes and allow spiritual advancement. Lastly, it is necessary to understand and live the relationship with God in the real world, in Southwell's case, this occurs in prison, and not in the setting of a secluded retreat.

The self as prisoner, sacrifice, and martyr

Imprisoning Southwell, as others before him, intended to contain the "basic threat of Catholic resistance" which "involved a determination to affirm their status as men of conscience punished for their religious convictions, against the equally determined efforts of the authorities to type them as traitors."[96] According to Louis Montrose, "by trying and executing Roman Catholics on political rather than on religious grounds the Elizabethan regime sought not only to manifest its power but also to legitimate that power in the face of the fundamental ideological challenge posed by its papist opponents."[97] In 1592 Southwell was betrayed and arrested at Jerome Bellamy's home, a staunch Catholic that had befriended many underground priests.[98] It is noteworthy that through the mapping of biblical spaces such as heaven and hell in *Fourfold Meditation* and geographic ones, such as the Arundel and Bellamy homes, the Tower, Newgate, and Tyburn, places that feature in Southwell's life, religion is linked to politics.[99]

Thus the preacher self joins the prisoner self to underscore the violence and atrocities that befell the Catholics and their missionaries under Elizabeth I. Once Southwell was incarcerated and his active life and contact with the outside world were terminated, the prisoner self displaces that of the preacher. Although prison was the locus where state presence dominated, paradoxically it was totally detached from the world thus it offered the opportunity for prayer, self-denial, and contemplation necessary for the numinous experience, and the establishment of a new self. I agree with Frank W. Brownlow who postulates that Southwell's writings reflect his life and that he did not only "write about sacrifice, but wrote himself as sacrifice and lived what he had written."[100] The prisoner self that was to be tormented for three years, brought to trial, sentenced for treason, and executed at Tyburn on February 21, 1595 solely for being a Catholic priest, prepares for sacrifice.[101] Southwell avows that he will die because he is a Catholic priest of the Society of Jesus with no other charge brought against him.[102] To the accusation of treason he pleaded not guilty, yet he admitted that he returned to his country simply to administer the Sacraments and perform the ordinary duties of a clergyman of the Church of Rome. Henry Foley claims that Southwell was "conscious of suffering in the supposed best causes, he seems to have met death without terror, and to have received the crown of martyrdom not with resignation but with joy."[103] In *Supplication*, the defender self pointed out that the Catholic priests faced fierce oppression although they were only "descending upon the country full of zeal for the preservation of the older order in religion," and to "safeguard the faith of those who still believed, and to dissipate the errors and the prejudices of those who had been misled."[104] He refutes that Catholics were not persecuted as his words "all waies vver watched, infinite houses searched, hewes & cries raised, frights bruted in the peoples eares, and all mens eies filled with a smoke, as though the whole Realme have beene on fire" attest.[105] He also affirms that although the missionaries were "vnmercifully tormented," their deaths "though as full of pangs as hanging, drawing, and vnbowelling vs quicke can make them," were considered "remedies ... more releasing then increasing [their] miseries."[106] When the sacrificial self addresses the multitude, before his execution, saying "whether we live, we live unto the Lord; or whether we die we die unto the Lord. Therefore, whether we live or whether we die, we are the Lord's";[107] Southwell encourages Catholics to resist "the authorities' attempts to break their spirit."[108] Gradually, the prisoner self transforms into the sacrificial one which, once death occurs, the martyr self takes over linking in this manner, the precarious process of self-fashioning to martyrdom. As a result, the image of the martyr does not possess only a political meaning but a religious one as well, since Southwell's self-affirmation as a sacrifice should be viewed as an imitation of Christ. Actually, he asks readers to identify with martyrs "in their acts of personal dissolution as a strategic means to redefine identity in terms of religious devotion."[109]

Such sacrifice is only possible, he states, because "God [gave] us His life, enflames us with His love-a love manifest in the Crucifixion, in the Incarnation, in the very fact of our Creation. God [gave] us ourselves in Creation, yet we deform that gift in false love; thus, that we may be restored, He offers us the gift of Himself."[110]

In conclusion, Southwell's articulation of the precarious process of self-fashioning that is his configuration and restoration to wholeness through affliction, self-annihilation, imprisonment, and death has been demonstrated. His public self that was persecuted and eventually executed is presented alongside his private self that struggled for salvation, martyrdom, union with the divine, and glorification; that is, "grief and pain are transformed into glory, and the martyr achieves his identity."[111] Throughout he underscores the self, the worldly aspect, that remained loyal to the monarch while his soul to his superiors and God. In addition, within the context of his works, not only did Southwell "construct the authorial persona as a pious and forceful Catholic preacher" he also presents a political subject and advocate, and stresses his "personal history as Jesuit martyr and his transfigured identity as a Saint."[112] His oeuvre records shifting subject-positions that entail the self in a response mode of change and adaptation. Hence subjectivity involves movement from defender to conciliator, to sinner, to preacher, to contemplative, to prisoner, to sacrifice, and finally, to martyr and saint. Therefore "the disparities," that Corthell outlines between "a transcendent subject on the one hand and a historically produced subject on the other seem bound up with the highly paradoxical character of martyrdom, a social action at once self-consuming and self-dramatizing."[113] Robert S. Miola also points out that

> the manuscript and print publications of Southwell's poetry assume and construct different identities for the author, variously defining the relations between poet and sacred text. Sometimes the Catholic manuscript miscellanies feature Southwell unidentified ... thus his personal identity becomes subsumed into his larger function as liturgist, as one teacher of Catholic doctrine among others, as one of several agents of commemoration and ritual.[114]

In a nutshell, the discussion of the four texts delineates not only the continuous process of self-fashioning, and Southwell's effort to immortalize his multiple selves, but also demonstrates his ardor to succor co-religionists, advance Catholicism, and rescue his country from Protestantism.

Notes

1 Rudolph Otto, *An Inquiry into the Non-Rational Factor of the Idea of the Divine and the Relation to the Rational*, trans, John W. Harvey (Oxford: Oxford UP, 1936), 49.

2 Ibid, 42.
3 Anne Dillon, *The Construction of Martyrdom in the English Catholic Community* (London and Burlington: Ashgate 2002), 372.
4 W. W. Meissner, *Life, and Faith: Psychological Perspectives on Religious Experience* (Washington: Georgetown UP, 1987), 54.
5 Peter Burke, "Representation of the Self from Petrarch to Descartes," in *Rewriting the Self: Histories from the Renaissance to the Present*, ed. Roy Porter (London and New York: Routledge, 1997), 17.
6 Cynthia Marshall, *The Shattering of the Self: Violence, Subjectivity, and Early Modern Texts* (Baltimore: Johns Hopkins UP, 2002), 14.
7 Ibid., 20.
8 Ibid., 14.
9 Ibid.
10 Jonathan Sawday's "Self and Selfhood in the Seventeenth Century" in *Rewriting the Self: Histories from the Renaissance to the Present*. ed. Roy Porter (London and New York: Routledge, 1997), 20.
11 Ibid.
12 Marshall, *The Shattering of Self*, 20.
13 Scott Pilarz, *Robert Southwell: Missions of Literature 1561–1595* (London and Burlington: Ashgate, 2004), 28.
14 Ronald Corthell, "The Secrecy of Man: Recusant Discourse and the Elizabethan Subject," *English Literary Renaissance*, 19, no. 3 (1989): 272.
15 Matthew Clark, *Narrative Structures and the Language of the Self* (Columbus: Ohio State UP, 2010), 3. See also Irving Howe, "The Self in Literature," in *Constructions of the Self*, ed. George Levine (New Brunswick: Rutgers UP, 1992), 249–266.
16 Anne Sweeney, *Robert Southwell: Snow in Arcadia Redrawing the English Lyric Landscape* (Manchester: Manchester UP, 2013), 50–51,18.
17 Louis Montrose, *The Subject of Elizabeth: Authority, Gender, and Representation* (Chicago: Chicago UP, 2006), 193.
18 Some prominent members of the English gentry, including Countess Anne Howard, held clandestine private masses in their homes and even harbored Jesuit priests.
19 Robert S. Miola, "Catholic Writings," Chapter 31 in *A New Companion to English Renaissance and Culture*, ed. Michael Hattaway (Oxford: Wiley Blackwell, 2010), 2 vols. In addition, "Catholics practiced their religion in private and public prayer and protest, in words meditated, whispered, spoken, sung, written and printed. Such words of course, were forbidden and felonious yet Catholics still spoke the words of either faith in prayer. They regularly braved persecution to attend Mass in the homes of the faithful, as is abundantly clear from the surviving records of Jesuit missionaries – Edmund Campion, Robert Southwell, John Gerard, Henry Garnet, and William Weston, for example – as well as from many state records of arrest and trial." 449.
20 "By torture, Elizabeth sought to learn the plans of her enemies, and, by executions, to uproot suspected sympathy with the cause of Philip II. For the Catholics, it was a time of bloody persecution: to be a Catholic was a crime; to be a priest was high-treason; and to be a Jesuit was to be hunted as a wild beast." Moreover, "the Jesuits went to England as apostles of God, not as plotters against Elizabeth. As priests, they sought to keep alive the ancient faith." See Joseph Nolan, "Robert Southwell," *American Catholic Quarterly Review* 7 (1882): 426, 432.
21 William Allen declares that the Catholics struggled to keep the flame of faith ablaze, and asserts that "the people were not Protestants by choice," and that

there was need for "an organized body of trained men to look after their spiritual needs, to comfort them in their trials, and to keep them well-instructed in their religion." See Thomas J. Campbell S. J., *The Jesuits 1534–1921* (New York: The Encyclopedia Press, 1921), 134.

22 Ibid.

23 David Cressy and Lori Anne Farrell, *Religion and Society in Early Modern England* (New York & London: Routledge, 2005), 7.

24 Montrose, *The Subject of* Elizabeth, 74.

25 Written by a member of the Society of Jesus, Preface to *Jesuits in Conflict: or Historic Facts* (London: Burns and Oates, 1873), vi.

26 Ibid.

27 Arthur F. Marotti, *Religious Ideology and Cultural Fantasy: Catholic and Anti-Catholic Discourses in Early Modern England* (Indiana: Notre Dame UP, 2005), 32. See also Dillon, *The Construction of* Martyrdom, 276.

28 Corthell, The Secrecy of Man," 289. In addition, Allen urged separation between political and religious allegiances and argued that the English mission was only concerned with reconciling Catholics to the official church. See William Allen, *A True, Sincere, and Modest Defense of English Catholics*, I (London: 1584), 80–83. Marotti also contends that "once the monarch was designated the head of the English church religious conformity and political loyalty were inextricably bound." See *Catholicism, and Anti-Catholicism in Early Modern English Texts* (New York: St. Martin's Press, 1999), 1.

29 Corthell, "The Secrecy of Man," 275.

30 Archbishop Richard Challoner, *Memoirs of Missionary Priests and other Catholics of other Sexes, have suffered death in England on Religious account from the year 1577 to 1684*, vol. 1 (Manchester: Mark Wardle, 1803), 177. See Robert Southwell, *A Humble Supplication to her Maiestie*, ed. R. C. Bald (Cambridge: Cambridge UP, 1956), 40–41; and Henry Foley, "The Life and Martyrdom of Father Robert Southwell," in vol. I of *Records of the English Province of the Society of Jesus* (London: Burns and Oates, 1877), 374 where Southwell is quoted saying: "I do acknowledge and confess that I am a priest of the Catholic and Roman Church I thank God most highly for it, and of the Society of Jesus."

31 Southwell, *A Humble Supplication*, 35.

32 Ibid. Southwell declares "I commend into the hands of Almighty God my poor country, desiring Him for His infinite mercy's sake to reduce it to such perfect insight, knowledge, and understanding of His truth, that thereby they may learn to praise and glorify God, and gain to their souls' health and eternal salvation" Foley, ("The Life and Martyrdom," 374.

33 Challoner, *Memoirs of Missionary Priests*, 177; and "Memoir" in *The Poetical Works of Reverend Robert Southwell*, ed. William B. Turnball (London: John Russell Smith, 1856), xxix.

34 Challoner refers to Southwell's last words "Into thy hands, Lord, I commend my spirit; thou hast redeemed me, O Lord God of truth, my God and all; God be merciful to me a sinner" 177; see "Memoir" xxx; and Foley who quotes Southwell stating: "I commend into the hands of Almighty God my poor soul, that it would please Him for His great mercy's sake to confirm and strengthen it with perseverance unto the end of this my last conflict; and this poor body of mine, as it shall please her Majesty to dispose thereof," 374.

35 Dillon, *The Construction of* Martyrdom, 337. See also Marotti, *Religious Ideology*. 16.

36 Dillon, *The Construction of* Martyrdom, 337.

37 Southwell, *A Humble Supplication*, 63.

38 Southwell, *A Humble Supplication*, Appendix I, 59.

39 See Wallace McCaffey, *Queen Elizabeth and the Making of Policy 1572–1588* (Princeton: Princeton UP, 1981); and Marotti, *Religious Ideology*. Finally, Louis Montrose declares that "the Catholic missionary priests and their abettors made up a special category of deviant Elizabethan subjects for while the state deemed them to be traitors and prosecuted them, as such they proclaimed themselves to be prisoners of conscience, loyal subjects who were being persecuted for their faith alone." See Montrose, *The Subject of Elizabeth*, 187.

40 Allen, states that "the execution of justice, the whole object of which was to show that those who were suffering were traitors to their Sovereign," *A True, Sincere, and Modest Defense of English Catholicism*, 6. Lord Burghley also declares that "men were executed not for religious beliefs but for their political aspirations, and that reconciliation to the spiritual authority of Rome was in fact a political act while it remained resolutely silent about those statutes of the last 20 years which had revolutionized the religious order of England; thereby ignoring the linkage of doctrine and policy in the English Church." See William Cecil, *The Execution of Justice, A True, Sincere, and Modest Defense of English Catholics*, ed. Robert M. Kingdon (Ithaca: New York, Cornell UP, 1965), 9–10. According to Thomas Campion, "if the Catholic is to be a traitor, then English history is a history of traitors." See Peter McGrath, *Papists and Puritans under Elizabeth I* (London: Bladford Press, 1967), 73; and Wallace McCaffey, 455. When the presiding judge asked the accused if they had anything to say, Campion replied: "The only thing that we have now to say is that if our religion makes us traitors we are worthy to be condemned, but otherwise we are and have been as true subjects as ever the queen had. In condemning us, you condemn all your own ancestors, all that was once the glory of England, the Island of Saints, and the most devoted child of the See of St. Peter." See Campbell, *The English Mission* 143. Years later, Bishop Richard Challoner writing about Southwell declared that "the several plots against the life and regal dignity of Elizabeth were, for the most part, the work of foreign associations hostile to the queen on political grounds, or the phantom conspiracies of Walsingham and Burghley for the purpose of casting odium on the Catholic cause." See Challoner, *Memoirs of Missionary Priests*, 10, 78.

41 Sadia Abbas, "Polemic and Paradox in Robert Southwell's Lyric Poems," *Criticism*, 45, no. 4, (Fall 2003): 455. Southwell also states "For I die because I am a Catholic priest elected into the Society of Jesus in my youth; nor has any other thing, during the last three years in which I have been imprisoned, been charged against me." See Robert Southwell, *The Complete Works of Robert Southwell with Life and Death* (London: D. Stewart, Warwick Chambers, Paternoster Row, E.C. 1876), 21.

42 Southwell, *A Humble Supplication*, 1.

43 Paul D. Stegner, "Treasonous Reconciliations: Robert Southwell Religious Polemic and the Criminalization of Confession," *Reformation*, 16 (2011): 24.

44 Ibid.

45 Corthell, "The Secrecy of Man," 286. Stegner also notes that "against government's accusations, Catholic writers professed political loyalty to the queen and spiritual submission to papal authority," "Treasonous Reconciliations," 15.

46 Pilarz, *Robert Southwell*, states that "*Supplication* was suppressed by Jesuits who did not agree with Southwell because they considered it too conciliatory, while the government printed it at first, because they agreed with the writer, and later suppressed it because it exposed the cruelties committed against Catholics, and exposed the intentions of the queen's councillors," xiii. See also Stegner, "Treasonous Reconciliations," 16.

47 James Denny, *The Christian Doctrine of Reconciliation* (London: Quinta Press, 2012). Denny postulates that there is "a personal God and personal relation between Him and man. When this relation is interrupted or changed by man's action, he feels himself alienated or estranged from God, and the need for reconciliation emerges." He adds that "the heart of the reconciliation like in the readjustment or restoration of the personal relation between God and the creature which has lapsied by its own act into alienation from Him, in other words, it consists in the forgiveness of sins" 5–6. See also *The Bible*, Col. 1: 20–22.

48 Southwell, *A Humble Supplication*, 44.

49 Ibid., 2. Pilarz states that Southwell "pursued a two-pronged approach throughout the *Supplication*, insisting on the loyalty of misrepresented Catholics to a misinformed Elizabeth, and pleading the case of a persecuted population that has been denied a voice," *Robert Southwell*, 235.

50 Janet Halley, "Equivocation and the Legal Conflict over Religious Identity in Early Modern England," *Yale Journal of Law and Humanities*, 3, no. 33 (1991): 34. Coke states that "their perfidious and perjurious equivocationg, abetted, allowed and justified by the Jesuites, not only to conceale or denie an open trueth, but religiously to averre – to protest upon salvation – to swear that which themselves know to be most false – and all this by reserving a secret and private sense inwardly to themselves, whereby they are by their ghostly fathers perswaded, that they may safely and lawfully delude any question whatever." See Edward Coke, *Treatise of Equivocation*, ed. David Jardine (London: Longman, Brown, Green, and Longmans, 1851), 3.

51 Ibid.

52 Ibid.

53 John Bossy, *The English Catholic Community 1570–1850* (London: Darton, Longman & Todd, 1975), 51–52.

54 Ibid. See also Christopher Devlin, *Life of Robert Southwell: Poet and Martyr* (New York: Farrar, Straus & Cudahy, 1956), 182.

55 Southwell, *A Humble Supplication*, 8–9.

56 Robert Southwell, *Spiritual Exercises & Devotions*, trans. P. E. Hallett (New York: Benziger Brothers, 1931), 61. Southwell believed that he could "raise the lowered prestige of the Catholic Church, and build up again the ruins that others by their vices [had] caused." He was convinced that he had to "strive with all [his] strength to cleanse the [Catholic Church] from its ignominy and to restore it to its pristine glory," 34. For more information on the subject see Bossy, *The English Catholic Community*, 7, and Arnold Pritchard's *Catholic Loyalism in Elizabethan England* (Chapel Hill: North Carolina UP, 1978).

57 Southwell, *Spiritual Exercises and Devotions*, 197. Similarly, Loyola contended that the unity of the Church had been shattered by heresy and that its survival was in danger from the widespread corruption of its spiritual leaders and the ignorance and indifference of the people. Only a revitalization of the spiritual life, and a fresh kindling of thought by the creation of a new consciousness would prevent disaster. See Ignatius Loyola, *The Spiritual Exercises of St Ignatius*, trans. Elder Mullan S. J. (New York: P. J. Kenedy, 1941).

58 John Gerard, *The Condition of Catholics under James I* (London: Longmans, Green & Co., 1871), 20; and Gerard's *Autobiography of a Hunted Priest*, trans. Philip Caraman (San Francisco: Saint Ignatius Press, 2012). Foley also states that "in the performance of his sacerdotal functions Southwell likewise inspired general confidence. With much assiduity he applied himself to the conversion of his father and brother, and he was apparently rewarded by success." Foley, *Records of the English Province of the Society of Jesus*, 339–347.

59 Southwell, *Spiritual Exercises and Devotions*, 60.

60 Robert Southwell, *A Short Rule of Good Life* (London: G. Eld. 1606), chapter 2:35.

61 Ibid., 9. In the Preface to *A Short Rule*, Allen states that "Southwell had designed to publish vnto the world, the description of this most gainefull voyage in heauen; be-decked with the most precious ornaments of all Christian vertues, and with the most pleasant and comfortable brightnesse of notable rules of spirituall life; euery one of which, may be as it were a Lanterne vnto thy feete, and a continuall Light vnto thy steppes," 7. See also Marotti, *Catholicism, and Anti-Catholicism*, 17.

62 Southwell, *Short Rule*, chapter 3: 46.

63 Ibid., chapter 1: 20.

64 Ibid., chapter 1: 21.

65 Ibid., chapter 5: 65.

66 Loyola, *The Spiritual Exercises*, 32.

67 Southwell, *Short Rule*, chapter 1:16.

68 Ibid., chapter 1:25.

69 Ibid., chapter 1:16.

70 Ibid., chapter1:26.

71 Robert Southwell, "Epistle to his Father," in *A Short Rule of Good Life* (London: G. Eld, 1606), 232; and Turnball, xliii–lxi.

72 Southwell states "I was nothing, I am nothing, and I may be perhaps worse than nothing I was conceived in original sin; I am full of actual sin. Miserable was I in my entrance, more miserable am I in my passage; I shall perchance be more miserable in my exit. When I was nothing, I was in no peril of damnation, but without hope of salvation, Now am I in doubtful hope and grave peril; I shall either be blessed by gaining what I hope for or most unhappy be inheriting what is now my danger. As I was, damnation was impossible; as I am, salvation is scarcely possible; so shall I be either condemned for evermore of saved for evermore. What I have been I know, for I was the worst, what I may be I know not, because uncertain of grace I what I shall be I cannot tell, because doubtful of salvation. What I was O Lord, forgive I what I am, correct; what I shall be, direct from past evils to present good, and to future rewards. Amen," *Short Rule*, chapter 11:180. See also Southwell's *Spiritual Exercises and Devotions* where he states "never forget that thou art dust and ashes and therefore most liable to dissolution and dissipation," 84; and Foley's "The Life and Martyrdom of Father Robert Southwell," 310.

73 Otto, *An Inquiry*, 20.

74 Southwell, *Short Rule*, chapter 2:42.

75 William James, *The Varieties of Religious Experience: A Study in Human Nature* (New York: Longmans, 1917), 380. See Jordan Paper, *The Mystic Experience: A Descriptive and Comparative Analysis* (New York: State University of New York Press, 2004), 31; and Helen C. White, *Tudor Books of Private Devotion and English Devotional Literature* (Madison: Wisconsin UP, 1963), 112; and Otto, *An Inquiry*, 145.

76 Otto, *An Inquiry*, 12–13.

77 Otto, *An Inquiry*, 145. While mysticism focuses on the believer's union with the Absolute, the transcendent, the cosmos, and fills the soul with bliss in the Bridegroom's embrace; the numinous considers God as an other, beyond the individual.

78 Otto, *An Inquiry*, 10, 26.

79 Gordon D. Kaufman, "The *Imago Dei* as Man's Historicity," *The Journal of Religion*, 36, no. 3, (July 1956):157.

80 Robert Southwell, *Fourfold Meditation: Of the Foure Last Things*, ed. Charlie Edmonds (London: Elkin Mathews,1895).

81 Southwell, "Epistle to his Father," 202.

82 Loyola, *The Spiritual Exercises*, 306–207.

83 Louis Martz, "Introduction," in *The Poetry of Meditation* (New Haven: Yale UP, 1962), 1–2.

84 Plotinus, The Fifth Ennead, Eighth Tractate, "On Intellectual Beauty," in *The Enneads*, trans. Stephen MacKenna (New York: Larson Publications, 1992), 485–597.

85 Evelyn Underhill, *Mysticism: A Study in the Nature and Development of Man's Spiritual Consciousness* (New York: Meridian Books, 1955), 168.

86 Southwell, *Spiritual Exercises and Devotions* 31, 38.

87 Ibid., 33.

88 Ibid., 3.

89 Otto, *An Inquiry*, 144.

90 Southwell, *Spiritual Exercises and Devotions*, 47. Ibid.

91 Ibid., 60.

92 Ibid., 48, 81.

93 Ibid., 60.

94 Ibid., 59–60.

95 Ibid., 89.

96 Peter Lake and Micheal Questier, *The Anti-Christ's Lewd Hat: Protestants, Papists, and Players in Post-Reformation England* (New Haven: Yale UP, 2002), 243. See also William Allen, *An Apologie and True Declaration* (London: 1581), 19.

97 Montrose, *The Subject of Elizabethan Authority*, 187.

98 Devlin states that "Anne Bellamy in her misery was to be offered the hope of saving her family from all future vexation by enticing Southwell to spend one night under their roof, informing Topcliffe meanwhile of the time and hiding-place." He adds, that in early 1580 "Richard Topcliffe had become active in this campaign; by the early 1590's he was established as the most assiduous and most notorious agent of the regime's concerted campaign against papistry. He was tireless in the pursuit and apprehension of clandestine priests and appallingly zealous in interrogating them, giving evidence against them at trial, and supervising their public executions," 276. See also Montrose, *The Subject of Elizabethan Authority*, 190.

99 Will Coster and Andrew Spicer, "Introduction: The Dimensions of Sacred Space in Reformation Europe," in *Sacred Space in Early Modern Europe*, ed. Will Coster and Andrew Spicer (Cambridge: Cambridge UP, 2005), 9.

100 Frank W. Brownlow, *Robert Southwell* (Boston: Twayne Publishers, 1996), 100.

101 Sweeney declares that "most probably the Queen appears to have given Topcliffe permission to torture using a new method guaranteed to get results while leaving no incriminating marks, known as stress posture," 258.

102 Challoner, *Memoirs of Missionary Priests*, 177.

103 Foley, "The Life and Martyrdom of Father Robert Southwell," 376. Montrose also states that "by choosing to perform the execution at the scene of the crime, the state was framing punishment to expiation, thus conferring upon it the status of a ritual occasion and not merely a theatrical one. The public spectacle of corporal punishment intended to assert the authority of the state and to admonish its subjects could just as easily become the instrument of a fundamental challenge to the state own spiritual legitimacy." He adds that "if execution were to succeed in transforming a spectacle of cruelty into a penitential theater of God's judgments both the active cooperation of the condemned and ecclesiastical agents were required. Public performances of

confession and contrition upon the gallows would validate the justice of the punishment, solve the soul of the condemned and powerfully impress upon the crowd an admonition to cure obedience and religious conformity," 188, 197, 209. Similarly, Elizabeth Hanson states that "interrogation by torture, followed by public trial and execution was the sequential means by which such 'secret intentions' could be probed, unmasked, published, and punished." *Discovering the Subject in Renaissance England* (Cambridge: Cambridge UP, 1998), 25–26. Finally, James Heath claims that "under the direction of Lord Burghley and Secretary Walsingham the use of torture in the interrogation of captured missionary priests and various others deemed traitors became a policy vigorously pursued by the Elizabethan government" *Torture and English Law: An Administrative and Legal History From the Plantagenets and the Stuarts* (Westport: Praeger, 1982), 93–147.

104 Allen, *A True, Sincere, and Modest Defense of English Catholicism*, 6.
105 Southwell, *Supplication*, 40–41.
106 Southwell describes the torment that Catholics experienced as follows:

> some are hanged by the hands eight or nine hours, yea twelve hours together, till not only their wits, but euen their senses fayle them, & when the soule weary of so painefull an harbor, is ready to depart, then apply the cruell comforts & reuiue vs, only to martyr vs with more deaths ... some are whipped naked so long, and with such execesse, that our enimies vnwilling to giue constancy the right name, said that no man without the helpe of the diuell, coulde with such undauntednesse suffer so much. Some besides their tormentes haue beene forced to be continually bound & clothed many weekes together, pyned to their yet, consumed with varmine, and almost stifeled with stench, and kept from sleepe, till they were past the use of reason, and then examined vppon the aduantage, when they coulde scarce giue an account of their owne names.
>
> *Supplication*, 64–66

107 Romans xiv:7–9.
108 Questier, 243. Stegner also states that "against government's accusations, Catholic writers professed political loyalty to the queen and spiritual submission to papal authority," "Treasonous Reconciliations," 15. In *Supplication* Southwell depicts the conditions of the Catholic prisoners as follows:

> divers have bene throwne into unsavourie and darke dungeons, and brought soe neere starvinge, that some for famine have licked the very moisture of the wall; some have soe far bene consumed that they were hardly recovered to life. What unsufferable Agonies we have bene put to upon the Rack, it is not possible to expresse the feeling soe farr exceedeth all speech. Some with instruments have bene rowled on together like a ball, and soe Crushed, that the bloud sprowted out at diverse parts of their bodies.
>
> 64–66

109 Marshall, *The Shattering of the Self*, 21. John Foxe declares that the work of martyrs was "to glorify God by their death, to subscribe and bear witness unto the truth by their blood, and by the contempt of their present life, to witness that they do seek after a better life by their constancy and steadfastness, to confirm and establish the faith of the Church, and to subdue and vanquish their enemy," Montrose, *The Subject of Elizabethan Authority*, 198.
110 Sister Diana Marie Shaw, "Such Fire is Love: The Bernardine Poetry of Robert Southwell S. J." *Christianity and Literature*, 62, no. 3 (Spring 2013): 348.
111 Marshall, *The Shattering of the Self*, 20.

112 Robert S. Miola, "Publishing the Word: Robert Southwell's Sacred Poetry,"
    The Review of English Studies, (2012): 432. Susannah Monta also argues that
    Southwell's *A Short Rule* "managed to bring together Catholics and Protest-
    ants through devotional guidelines hence the work was published many times
    by Protestants." See "Uncommon Prayer? Robert Southwell's *A Short Rule of
    a Good life* and Catholic Domestic Devotion in Post-Reformation England," in
    Redrawing the Map of Early Modern English Catholics, ed. Lowell Gallagher
    (Toronto: Toronto UP, 2012), 237.
113 Corthell, "The Secrecy of Man," 279.
114 Miola, "Publishing the Word: Robert Southwell's Sacred Poetry," 431.

Bibliography

Abbas, Sadia. "Polemic and Paradox in Robert Southwell's Lyric Poems." *Criti-
    cism*, 45, no. 4 (Fall 2003): 453–482.
Allen, William. *A True, Sincere, and Modest Defense of English Catholics*, vol. I.
    London: 1584.
Allen, William. *An Apologie and True Declaration*. London: 1581.
Bossy, John. *The English Catholic Community 1570–1850*. London: Darton,
    Longman & Todd, 1975.
Brownlow, Frank W. *Robert Southwell*. Boston: Twayne Publishers, 1996.
Burke, Peter. "Representations of the Self from Petrarch to Descartes." In *Rewrit-
    ing the Self: Histories from the Renaissance to the Present*. Edited by Roy Porter.
    London and New York: Routledge, 1997.
Campbell, Thomas J. S. J. *The Jesuits, 1534–1921*. In Vol. 1 of *A History of the
    Society of Jesus from Its Foundation to the Present Time*. New York: The Ency-
    clopedia Press, 1921.
Cecil, William. *The Execution of Justice in England, A True, Sincere, and Modest
    Defense of English Catholics*. Edited by Robert M. Kingdon. Ithaca: Cornell
    University Press, 1965.
Challoner, Richard. *Memoirs of Missionary Priests and other Catholics of other
    Sexes, have suffered death in England on Religious account from the year 1577
    to 1684*, vol. 1. London: Mark Wardle, 1803.
Clark, Matthew. *Narrative Structures and the Language of the Self*. Columbus:
    Ohio State University Press, 2010.
Coke, Edward. *Treatise of Equivocation*. Edited by David Jardine, 3. London:
    Longman, Brown, Green, and Longmans, 1851, 3.
Corthell, Ronald. "The Secrecy of Man: Recusant Discourse and the Elizabethan
    Subject." *English Literary Renaissance*, 19, no. 3 (1989): 272–290.
Coster, Will and Spicer, Andrew. "Introduction: The Dimensions of Sacred Space
    in Reformation Europe." In *Sacred Space in Early Modern Europe*. Edited by
    Will Coster and Andrew Spicer. Cambridge: Cambridge University Press, 2005.
Cressy, David and Lori Anne Farrell. *Religion and Society in Early Modern
    England*. New York and London: Routledge, 2005.
Denny, James. *The Christian Doctrine of Reconciliation*. London: Quinta Press, 2012.
Devlin, Christopher. *Life of Robert Southwell: Poet and Martyr*. New York:
    Farrar, Straus & Cudahy, 1956.
Dillon, Anne. *The Construction of Martyrdom in the English Catholic Com-
    munity*. London and Burlington: Ashgate 2002.

Foley, Henry. "The Life and Martyrdom of Father Robert Southwell." In Vol. I of *Records of the English Province of the Society of Jesus*. London: Burns and Oates, 1877.

Gerard, John. *Autobiography of a Hunted Priest*. Translated by Philip Caraman. San Francisco: Saint Ignatius Press, 2012.

Gerard, John. *The Condition of Catholics under James I*. London: Longmans, Green & Co., 1871.

Halley, Janet. "Equivocation and the Legal Conflict over Religious Identity in Early Modern England." *Yale Journal of Law and Humanities*, 3, no. 33 (1991): 33–52.

Hanson, Elizabeth. *Discovering the Subject in Renaissance England*. Cambridge: Cambridge University Press, 1998.

Hattaway. Michael, ed. *A New Companion to English Renaissance and Culture*. 2 vols. Oxford: Wiley Blackwell, 2010.

Heath, James. *Torture and English Law: An Administrative and Legal History From the Plantagnets and the Stuarts*. Westport: Praeger, 1982.

Howe, Irving. "The Self in Literature." In *Constructions of the Self*. Edited by George Levine. New Brunswick: Rutgers University Press, 1992.

James, William. *The Varieties of Religious Experience: A Study in Human Nature*. New York: Longmans, 1917.

Jardine, David, ed. *Henry Garnet*. London: Longman, Brown, Green, and Longmans, 1851.

Kaufman, Gordon D. "The *Imago Dei* as Man's Historicity." *The Journal of Religion*, 36, no. 3 (July 1956): 157–168.

Lake, Peter and Michael Questier. *The Anti-Christ's Lewd Hat: Protestants, Papists and Players in Post-Reformation England* (New Haven: Yale University Press, 2002).

Loyola, Ignatius. *The Spiritual Exercises of St Ignatius*. Translated by Elder Mullan S. J. New York: P. J. Kenedy, 1941.

McCaffey, Wallace. *Queen Elizabeth and the Making of Policy 1572–1588*. Princeton: Princeton University Press, 1981.

McGrath, Peter. *Papists and Puritans under Elizabeth I*. London: Bladford Press, 1967.

Marotti, Arthur F. *Catholicism and Anti-Catholicism in Early Modern English Texts*. New York: St Martin's Press, 1999.

Marotti, Arthur F. *Religious Ideology and Cultural Fantasy: Catholic and Anti-Catholic Discourses in Early Modern England*. Indiana: Notre Dame University Press, 2005.

Marshall, Cynthia. *The Shattering of the Self: Violence, Subjectivity, and Early Modern Texts*. Baltimore: Johns Hopkins University Press, 2002.

Martz, Louis. "Introduction." In *The Poetry of Meditation*. New Haven: Yale University Press, 1962.

Meissner, W. W. *Life, and Faith: Psychological Perspectives on Religions Experience*. Washington: Georgetown University Press, 1987.

Miola, Robert S. "Catholic Writings." In *A New Companion to English Renaissance and Culture*. Edited by Michael Hattaway, 2 vols. Oxford: Wiley Blackwell, 2010.

Miola, Robert S. "Publishing the Word: Robert Southwell's Sacred Poetry." *The Review of English Studies*, 64 (2012): 410–432.

Monta, Susannah. "Uncommon Prayer? Robert Southwell's *Short Rule of a Good life* and Catholic Domestic Devotion in Post-Reformation England." In *Redrawing* the *Map of Early Modern English Catholics*. Edited by Lowell Gallagher. Toronto: Toronto University Press, 2012.

Montrose, Louis. *The Subject of Elizabeth Authority, Gender, and Representation*. Chicago and London: University of Chicago Press, 2006.

Nolan, Joseph. "Robert Southwell." *American Catholic Quarterly Review*, 7 (1882): 426, 432.

Otto, Rudolph. *An Inquiry into the Non-Rational Factor of the Idea of the Divine and the Relation to the Rational*. Translated by John W. Harvey. Oxford: Oxford University Press, 1936.

Paper, Jordan. *The Mystic Experience: A Descriptive and Comparative Analysis*. New York: State University of New York Press, 2004.

Pilarz, Scott. *Robert Southwell: Missions of Literature 1561–1595*. London and Burlington: Ashgate, 2004.

Plotinus. The Fifth Ennead, Eighth Tractate, "On Intellectual Beauty." In *The Enneads*. Translated by Stephen MacKenna. New York: Larson Publications, 1992.

Pritchard, Arnold. *Catholic Loyalism in Elizabethan England*. Chapel Hill: University of North Carolina Press, 1978.

Sawday, Jonathan. "Self and Selfhood in the Seventeenth Century." In *Rewriting the Self: Histories from the Renaissance to the Present*. Edited by Roy Porter. London and New York: Routledge, 1997.

Shaw, Sister Diana Marie, "Such Fire is Love: The Bernardine Poetry of Robert Southwell S.J." *Christianity and Literature*, 62, no. 3 (Spring 2013): 333–353.

Society of Jesus. Preface to *Jesuits in Conflict: or Historic Facts*. London: Burns and Oates, 1873.

Southwell, Robert. *A Humble Supplication to her Maiestie*. Edited by R. C. Bald. Cambridge: Cambridge University Press, 1956.

Southwell, Robert. *A Short Rule of Good Life*. London: G. Eld. 1606.

Southwell, Robert. "Epistle to his Father." In *A Short Rule of Good Life*. London: G. Eld. 1606.

Southwell, Robert. *Fourfold Meditation: Of the Foure Last Things*. Edited by Charlie Edmonds. London: Elkin Mathews, 1895.

Southwell, Robert. *Spiritual Exercises & Devotions*. Translated by P. E. Hallett. New York: Benziger Brothers, 1931.

Southwell, Robert. *The Complete Works of Robert Southwell with Life and Death*. London: D. Stewart, Warwick Chambers, Paternoster Row, E.C. 1876.

Stegner, Paul D. "Treasonous Reconciliations: Robert Southwell Religious Polemic and the Criminalization of Confession." *Reformation*, 16 (2011): 5–35.

Sweeney, Anne. *Robert Southwell: Snow in Arcadia Redrawing the English Lyric Landscape*. Manchester: Manchester University Press, 2002.

Turnball, William B., ed. "Memoir." In *The Poetical Works of Reverend Robert Southwell*. London: John Russell Smith, 1856.

Underhill, Evelyn. *Mysticism: A Study in the Nature and Development of Man's Spiritual Consciousness*. New York: Meridian Books, 1955.

White, Helen C. *Tudor Books of Private Devotion and English Devotional Literature*. Madison: Wisconsin University Press, 1963.

10 Southwell's influence

Imitations, appropriations, reactions[1]

Alison Shell

The blood of martyrs can germinate unpredictably. When the Elizabethan Jesuit priest Robert Southwell was put to death in 1595, he could have had little idea that his literary remains would have a seminal influence on both the sacred and the secular verse of his time. *Saint Peters complaint* and *Mœoniæ*, volumes of his verse printed after his execution in 1595, became best-sellers for several years; his poems were also copied widely in manuscript inside and outside the recusant culture he knew.[2] The popularity of his writing, especially his tears poetry, helped to initiate a turn to religion in late Elizabethan literature, and fellow Catholics were not alone in finding his work inspirational.[3]

But he posed a problematic legacy to his literary successors, not least because it could be hard to call him an exemplar.[4] Many comparably influential poets – Sir Philip Sidney and Edmund Spenser among them – are respectfully invoked in this period, but Southwell is rarely credited by name: which is not surprising, given his adherence to an outlawed religious denomination and his traitor's death. Acknowledgements of his influence sometimes take the form of an *hommage*, where his characteristic subject-matter and style are tacitly appropriated in the expectation that the audience will recognise the allusion. At other times his influence is subsumed, fought against or both, as part of the ongoing Protestant mission to make over Catholic writing.[5] Within the devotional activity Southwell inspired, he becomes anonymous for different reasons, largely out of his success at enabling his readers' self-transcendence and spiritual heightening. The writers considered below – Elizabeth Grymeston, William Evans, Richard Verstegan, Michael Drayton, George Herbert – demonstrate the range of reactions that Southwell elicited.

Stephen Greenblatt's influential discussion of another Reformation-era saint, Thomas More, posits an opposition between self-fashioning and self-cancellation.[6] Though Greenblatt does not discuss devotional writing at length, the latter coinage seems apt for a genre which typically points towards God and away from the self, aiming to reform both writer and reader along exemplary Christian lines. Whether devotional writers draw on Scripture, on named predecessors or on a general stock of pious tropes,

they foreground *imitatio* and reassortment. Originality is never straightfor-
wardly desirable during the early modern period, and devotional writing is
a genre where explicit claims to authorial originality may seem especially
inappropriate. Characteristically, the self-effacing author foregrounds
Christian precedent, offering work up to the reader for the betterment of
his or her spiritual condition, and the reader customises accordingly.[7] In
keeping with Southwell's missionary agenda, his verse is unusually suscep-
tible to this type of appropriation: powerful because of, not in spite of, its
reliance on homiletic exhortation and didactic commonplace. As animated
by the reading habits of the time and Southwell's personal example, this
makes strenuous religious and ethical demands upon well-affected readers.

The Catholic writer Elizabeth Grymeston, who remodelled Southwell's
verse for use in her own prayer life, illustrates the kind of religious self-
fashioning his writing inspired.[8] From her posthumously published advice
book *Miscelanea*, we learn that she reassorted stanzas from "Saint Peter's
Complaint" and intermingled them with devotional reflection, "usually
sung and played" on "the winde instrument" – seemingly an organ, the only
wind instrument which allows one to sing and play simultaneously.[9] The
following extract illustrates how Southwell's verse was embedded in her
devotional programme.

Happie is the man whose life is a continuall prayer

> O God to whom nothing is so great as can resist, nothing so little as is
> contemptible: O Christ the guide of those that seeke thee, the light of
> those that finde thee: O Holy Ghost that both fillest and includest all
> things; I am ashamed to be seene of thee, because I am not assured to be
> received by thee, having neither deserued pardon for my faults, nor
> participation of thy glorie: yet sweet Jesu, supply my defects, that by thy
> mercie I may obtaine remission, and by thy merits deserue saluation.
> Let thy passion worke compassion for me
>
> A sorie wight the obiect of disgrace,
> The monument of feare, the map of shame,
> The mirror of mishap, the staine of place,
> The scorne of time, the infamie of fame,
> An excrement of earth to heauen hatefull,
> Iniurious to man, to God ungratefull.

(D4b)[10]

As adopted by Grymeston, this stanza becomes an extension of her own
prayer: so much so that her sentence runs on into Southwell's prosopopoeia.
In fact, she goes some way beyond what Southwell intends – his preface to
the poem urges the reader, "Learne by [saints'] faultes, what in thine owne
to mend," recommending a combination of empathy with St. Peter and

interpretive distance from him.[11] By aligning herself with St. Peter so fully, Grymeston is metamorphosing into him, to the extent that she prays as a man by taking on his voice. As the heading to the passage reminds us, it was the convention – in Grymeston's era, and till recently – to use the male gender when referring to humanity in general, and the timid audacities of a female author could align well with the continual repentance for which Southwell's St. Peter provides a model.[12] As the choice of this passage illustrates, describing oneself in the harshest epithets was central to early modern spirituality: which, at first sight, runs strikingly counter to the hierarchies implicit in a mother's advice book such as this.[13] So far from passing on maternal counsel *de haut en bas*, Grymeston uses Southwell's verse to self-flagellate in front of her offspring. Yet to call oneself the worst of sinners was exemplary, even if one was a mother addressing a child, and adopting the voice of Southwell's St. Peter is a way for Grymeston to deploy this back-handed devotional stratagem. The very act of borrowing from Southwell becomes part of Grymeston's abjection; as she writes, deploying an image often used to justify literary appropriation: "the spiders webbe is neither the better because wouen out of his owne brest, nor the bees hony the woorse, for that gathered out of many flowers; neither could I euer brooke to set downe that haltingly in my broken stile, which I found better expressed by a grauer author" (A3b).

Another Catholic writer of this period, writing on the topic of repentance in a very different context, also borrows from Southwell. The manuscript play "The History of Purgatory," written as part of Christmas-tide festivities in the early seventeenth century, centres on a soul facing trial after death.[14] Satan puts the case for hell, and Michael joins in the condemnation with the following speech:

> If wiles of witt, had ouer raught thy will
> thy foyle had founde, excuse, in want of skill
> Or sutle traynes, misled thy steeps awrye
> yll deeds thou might, though not yll doome denye
> But witt and will, must now confesse with shame
> both deede and dome, to haue deserued blame
> Thy ffancie deem'd, fit guyde to leade thy way
> witt lost his ayme, and will was ffanses pray
> But, now sith ffansye, did with ffollye ende
> now after death, to late it is to mende
> But, now thou hast, a loade so heauie founde
> that makes thee boow, yea full flat to the grounde ...[15]

This adapts two stanzas from Southwell's "Davids Peccavi".

> If wiles of witt had overwrought my will
> Or sutle traynes misledd my steppes awrye

My foyle had founde excuse in want of skill
Ill deede I might though not ill dome denye
But witt and will muste now confesse with shame
Both deede and dome to have deserved blame

I phansy deem'd fitt guide to leade my waie
And as I deem'd I did pursue her track
Witt lost his ayme and will was phancies pray
The rebell wonne the ruler went to wracke
But now sith phansye did with follye end
Wit bought with losse will taught by wit will mend.

(19–30)

Like "Saint Peter's Complaint," "David's Peccavi" is a prosopopoeia. In it, the king and psalmist acknowledges wrongdoing, both over his affair with Bathsheba and in sending Bathsheba's husband Uriah to his death. In the dramatic reworking of these stanzas, much of Southwell survives, but there are suggestive changes in line-order and content. Most obviously, the dramatist shifts the speech from the first to the second person, deletes the references about the rebel and the ruler – less relevant to the soul than to David – and completely rewrites the subsequent lines. If "after death, to late it is to mende," Southwell's cautious evocation of repentance would be inappropriate.

The idea of bowing "flat to the grounde" is suitable enough for a drama in which the action takes place after death, but it is also – quite literally – bathetic. Here, as occasionally elsewhere in this play, the juxtaposition of Southwell's lines to those of its dramatist painfully illustrates the limited poetical abilities of the latter: which, in turn, begs the question of whether Southwell's verse is just being used to patch the later writer's deficiencies. Yet the play is a recusant production, outspokenly advocating prayer for the dead and lamenting the decay of hospitality after the Reformation; its readers and audience members would have been very likely to pick up on allusions to Southwell's verse, making it probable that the author intended these to be noticed. Besides, in the prologue to the play, the dramatist sets out an agenda not dissimilar to Grymeston's, in which borrowing or "gleeninge" from other writers becomes an expression of personal humility.

When as diuine matters, declare we
An Angels voice, ys fitter to declare
With reuerence, diligence, and great care
Then seculer men, as gleenes here and their
Our Authour, ys but a seculer man[16]
gleeninge flowers of inspiration
ffrom learned men, that are his conductour
the holie Ghost, their guyde and protectour …

(2)

The play exhibits another extended borrowing from Southwell. When Mercy speaks in defence of the soul, she compares it to "other brittle moulds, that now are Saints" and continues:

> Ly[c]ense my single selfe, to seeke a phere [companion]
> Cloude not with mistie loves, your Orient cleere
> You heavenlye sparkes of wytt, shew native light
> sweete flightes you shoote, to this Soule levell right ...
> ffavor my wish, wellwishinge, workes no yll
> I move the suyte, the graunt stands in your will

(46)

These lines are adapted from "The Author to the Reader" at the beginning of "Saint Peter's Complaint." The first part is taken from the point where, in relation to St. Peter, Southwell exhorts his reader "Muse not to see some mud in cleerest brooke,/They once were brittle mould, that now are Saintes," while the second rewrites Southwell's concluding stanza:

> License my single penne to seeke a phere,
> You heavenly sparkes of wit, show native light:
> Cloude not with mistie loves your Orient cleere,
> Sweete flightes you shoote; learne once to levell right.
> Favour my wish, well wishing workes no ill:
> I moove the Suite, the Graunt restes in your will.[17]

In the original poem, Southwell is pleading with other poets to turn from amorous verse to religious; as rewritten and reassigned to Mercy, the lines advocate the soul's salvation. As a transfer, it does not quite work, since Southwell's injunction that his fellow writers should not obscure their perception with "mistie loves" becomes redundant. Nevertheless, the alteration from "my single penne" to "my single selfe" might, for anyone picking up on the reference, have added to the poignancy of the plea: Mercy is not even buttressed by authorial identity as Southwell was. Her relative isolation – at this point in the drama she is the only character to be defending the soul – also resonates with Southwell's own prophetic stance, and her address to fellow heavenly beings would surely have gained emotional efficacy from the belief, shared by author and audience, that Southwell himself was now a saint in heaven.

Some poets responded more directly to Southwell's call to arms. Among them was William Evans, whose *Pietatis lachrymae* was published in 1602, at the height of the Southwellian-influenced fashion for tears poetry. Print would have inhibited any declaration of allegiance to Southwell's faith, but what little is known about Evans would not be incompatible with a pro-Catholic writer, and the volume was dedicated to two patrons with Catholic sympathies: Sir Thomas Kitson and his "staunchly recusant" wife Elizabeth.[18] Quotations from and allusions to Southwell permeate both *Pietatis lachrymae* and its paratextual matter. Philemon Holland, speculating about the possible reception of the volume in a dedicatory verse, quotes from Southwell's couplet "In paynim toyes the sweetest vaines are spent:/To Christian workes, few have their tallents lent":

With some fantasticke foolish braine or other,
(Causles) thy weeping lines may be disgraced
While wisdomes wit their folly doth discouer,
And thou thereby in better thoughts be placed.
Thy lynes (no Panimne toyes) thy Text deuine,
Exhales such darkning clouds that Sun may shine.[19]

Evans's own introduction, sarcastically enjoining profane poets to "Deuote thy wits to loue and venery, /... Be-witch mens soules with beauties fopperie,/By Uenus forged-Goddesse praise to winne" quotes Southwell's "Ambitious heades dreame you of fortunes pride:/Fill volumes with your forged Goddesse prayse."[20] Elsewhere, he responds to Southwell's mournful reflection on contemporary poetics, "Christs Thorne is sharp, no head his Garland weares," by entitling one of his holy sonnets "Christes Crowne is sharpe."[21] One early modern meaning of "garland" is a verse-anthology or miscellany, so this expands upon Southwell's original double meaning.[22]

However, Evans is not an entirely uncritical disciple of Southwell. "A passion of an afflicted soule," an early item in his collection, appears at first sight to be simply a reworking of "Saint Peter's Complaint": it begins in a pastoral setting, where a young man laments how his sinfulness surpasses even that of St. Peter. The following stanzas contain many recollections of Southwell's poem: for instance, the lines "Earths excrement, (alas) of all men hatefull;/vnkinde vnto my selfe, to God vngratefull," a couplet which Evans barely rewrites, and Grymeston also selected.[23] Yet the ending takes a different turn from the original. An aesthetically challenging feature of "Saint Peter's Complaint" is its recapitulation of woe; mimicking the thought-processes of a depressive in the way it circles back on itself, it gives us no obvious trajectory towards divine comfort.[24] Though Christ's mercy is edged up to more than once, the speaker sinks again into a state where it is hard to distinguish contrition from despair. In this context, the poem's ending, tentative in any case – "Tender my suite, clense this defiled denne,/Cancell my debtes, sweete *Jesu*, say Amen" (791–792) – becomes especially inconclusive. The last words of Evans's abject speaker are not dissimilar: "Mercy sweet Iesu mercy let me win,/Since now I hate my selfe, & loath my sin" (B5b). But as rewritten and repositioned, they have a very different effect from St. Peter's unanswered plea: the speaker ends on a note of explicit self-alienation in declaring "I hate my selfe," which, in turn, is framed within a broader first-person narrative. As the complaint dies away, this earlier voice takes up the tale:

This he no sooner said, but I might see
A man well seeming Angell-Saint to be;
Of comely hue of golde his pleated hayres,
More graue in Wisdoms booke, then aged yeares.
His feete insteed of sandals troade the ayre,
And windes for wings, did this Cælestiall beare. ...

Doe not dispaire (quoth he) thou wofull man,
Doubt not, but he that made all, all things can;
Thinke not that he that breath'd into thee breath,
Will ought reioyce in thy soules fearefull death.
No wretched man thy God willes thee to know,
Sinnes red as scarlet, he makes white as snow.[25]

Seale this (O Lord) cleare my sinne-spotted-Den,
Teares beg the warrant, Iesu say Amen.

(B5b–6a)

This concluding couplet is potentially attributable either to the narrator or the complainant, and also voices the aspirations of a well-affected reader. In it, Evans does revert to and rewrite the ending of Southwell's poem, but the visitation of the "Angell-Saint" has lifted the mood, with its external assurance that the petition will be answered.

On one level, this interprets Southwell as Southwell must have intended, given his pastoral duty to communicate the Christian message of salvation. Yet Evans's rewrite only illustrates how radically Southwell's original minimises hope: dramatising St. Peter in his darkest hour, forgoing anticipation of the Resurrection and leaving any sustained confidence in divine grace up to the reader to supply. Southwell has no more fervent literary admirer than Evans, but even Evans shies away from Southwell's darkest intuitions; his reworking, emphasising God's grace to the penitent, has a normative effect and can be seen as correcting Southwell.[26] Something similar is true of the Catholic author Richard Verstegan, whose *Odes* (1601) include a pastiche of "Saint Peter's Complaint" entitled "St Peters Comfort." Like the original, this begins in despondent mode, but – as the title indicates – the tone progressively lightens. Around the middle of the poem, St. Peter can declare: "The wound is heal'd, yet must the skar remaine,/The skar my stil remembrance of the sore,/For which, kynde grief stil wil I entertaine,/That neuer may sufficiently deplore" (82). But by its end, the mood has modulated to one of thankfulness:

O endlesse comfort ending thus my care,
Vn-ending thankes must therefore bee my parte,
VVhich for thy due, I duly wil prepare,
To offer on the Alter of my hart,

VVhereas the fyre of loue for euer lies,
To serue for my eternal sacrifise.

(84)

A more thoroughgoing critique of Southwell's agenda shapes an early version of a poem by Michael Drayton. Like "A passion of an afflicted soule," this features a sinner complaining in a rural setting, capitalising on the period's fashion for Spenserian pastoral. The first of a collection of eclogues which initially appeared in 1593 in the collection *Idea: The shepheardes garland*, it was republished in 1606, heavily revised, and appeared for a third time in 1619.[27] The differences between the first version and the later two are considerable, not just from the stylistic point of view but in their moral focus. The first version shows Rowland – Drayton's pastoral name – sunk in a melancholy partly occasioned by sin, partly by lack of preferment; he pours out his complaint to a deity successively imaged as Pan, Jove and the Christian God, and asks that his contrition should win forgiveness.[28] As first recognised by Bernard H. Newdigate, the poem pastiches Southwell.[29] Drayton had experimented with religious verse earlier in his career with *The harmonie of the church* (1591), a versification of the Song of Songs and other portions of the Bible, and he may have been especially interested in Southwell's work for that reason. But his agenda in this poem, marked as it is by worldly disappointment and imaginative syncretism, seems far removed from Southwell's, suggesting that his engagement with Southwell's work may primarily show eagerness to be *au fait* with the latest literary productions.[30] If so, the knowingness of alluding to Southwell at all would have been accentuated by the overt parody of him at the end of the poem.

O shepheards soveraigne, yea receive in gree,[31]
The gushing teares, from never-resting eyes,
And let those prayers which I shall make to thee,
Be in thy sight perfumed sacrifice:
Let smokie sighes be pledges of contrition,
For follies past to make my soules submission.

Submission makes amends for all my misse,
Contrition a refined life begins,
Then sacred sighes, what thing more precious is?
And prayers be oblations for my sinnes,
Repentant teares, from heaven-beholding eyes,
Ascend the ayre, and penetrate the skies.

My sorowes waxe, my joyes are in the wayning,
My hope decayes, and my despayre is springing,
My love hath losse, and my disgrace hath gayning,
Wrong rules, desert with teares her hands sits wringing:

Sorrow, despayre, disgrace, and wrong, doe thwart
My Joy, my love, my hope, and my desert. ...

Thus breathing from the Center of his soule,
The tragick accents of his extasie,
His sun-set eyes gan here and there to roule,
Like one surprisde with sodaine lunacie:
And being rouzde out of melancholly,
Flye whirle-winde thoughts unto the heavens quoth he.[32]

Like Evans, Drayton deploys a poetic observer to provide an external perspective on the complainant's emotional turbulence. But in place of
Evans's gentle amelioration of Southwell, we are given a caricature of a
sinner's spiritual disquiet. Even the speaker recognises his own "lunacie"
when he signs off on his deranged prayer: "Flye whirle-winde thoughts
unto the heavens." Yet, if anything, his return to composure leaves him in
a worse state. As night falls, "*Rowland* from this time-consumed stock,/
With stone-colde hart now stalketh towards his flock" (83–84). His
chronic *accidia* has not been allayed by hyperbolic complaint, which suggests its lack of spiritual efficacy.[33] In the two subsequent versions of the
poem, the religious language remains to some extent, but the theme of
religious contrition almost disappears; the sole reference to "sinnes" is
calculatedly ambiguous, perhaps referring to the speaker, perhaps to the
sinfulness of the world.[34]

Shepheards great Soveraigne, graciously receive,
Those thoughts to thee continually erected,
Nor let the World of Comfort me bereave,
Whilst I before it sadly lye dejected,
Whose sinnes, like fogs that over-cloud the Aire,
Darken those beames which promis'd me so faire.

In addition, the final stanza goes completely, displaced by Rowland's complaint at his lack of recognition and preferment:

My hopes are fruitlesse, and my faith is vaine,
And but meere shewes, disposed me to mocke,
Such are exalted basely that can faine,
And none regards just ROWLAND *of the Rocke.*
To those fat Pastures, which Flocks healthfull keepe,
Malice denyes me entrance with my Sheepe.

Yet nill I Nature enviously accuse,
Nor blame the Heavens thus haplesse me to make,
What they impose, but vainly we refuse,
When not our power their punishment can slake.

> Fortune the World, that towzes to and fro,
> Fickle to all, is constant in my wo.[35]

In both incarnations, Drayton's rewritten eclogue is – as so often with this genre – a debate about the poet's role more than anything else. Though Rowland is Drayton's alter ego, he should not be wholly identified with Drayton, author of the finished product. Rather, he stands for the poet at the point of decision and experimentation, within a pastoral landscape which enables the trial, endorsement and rejection of various poetic personae: which is how Drayton is able to present Rowland speaking like Southwell, even though he has reservations about Southwell's poetry. Perhaps we are meant to read this autobiographically, as an admission of Drayton's temporary penchant for Southwell's verse and its attendant mental attitudes; perhaps he is simply trying the Southwellian persona on for size and discarding it. Either way, it is striking that the parody vanishes from the later reworkings: perhaps it felt dated or – given that Southwell had been executed by then – in bad taste. If Drayton's poetic persona "Rowland of the Rocke" can be read as retaining a suggestion of Southwell's St. Peter – the rock on whom the church was built – it would surely suggest the saint's later integrity rather than his contrition at having denied Christ.[36]

George Herbert, also writing after the initial vogue for Southwell's work had passed, manifests a similarly ambivalent relationship with his predecessor, despite – or because of – the fact that the two poets have much in common. What Herbert borrows from Southwell is, most of all, a poetic attitude: a commitment to devotional writing, coexisting with a certain intolerance of secular literature. What are probably Herbert's first surviving English poems set the tone for what is to follow: two sonnets sent to his mother in 1610, his first year of undergraduate study, which lament the dominance of love-poetry and ask for God to be more celebrated by poets. In them, Herbert asks God, "Doth Poetry/Wear *Venus* Livery? only serve her turn?/Why are not *Sonnets* made of thee?" and again, "Why should I *Womens eyes* for Chrystal take? /Such poor invention burns in their low mind/Whose fire is wild, and doth not upward go/To praise and on thee Lord, some *Ink* bestow."[37]

These are stirring words, but also deeply disingenuous. It is not to downplay Herbert's religious fervour to remark that these sonnets show the agonistic restlessness of a new literary generation. Written around the same time as Shakespeare's were published, they reflect, like them, the sense that straightforward amatory sonnets were *passé*. But where Shakespeare consciously parodies the tradition – most famously in Sonnet 130, "My mistress' eyes are nothing like the sun" – Herbert sets off towards God in a direction that he claims has hardly been travelled.[38] As a well-read undergraduate, he would have known he was exaggerating. Though the after-effects of the English Reformation certainly had a withering effect on non-biblical religious verse, instilling widespread uneasiness about imaginative additions to Scripture and prompting a move towards secular topics, several other English poets had written religious verse in the recent past.[39] The very poetic genre Herbert chooses, that of the sonnet, may be paying homage to previous efforts in that vein by Donne and others.[40] Yet Southwell provides the most obvious antecedent for two distinctive features of Herbert's poetic practice: his advocacy of a plain style which is nevertheless consciously artful, and his avowed distance from secular verse.[41] Herbert almost certainly knew Southwell's rebuke several years earlier to his poetic contemporaries: "Still finest wits are culling Venus' rose./On Paynim toys the sweetest veins are spent;/To Christian works, few have their talents lent."[42] By the time Herbert was writing, Southwell was not – as illustrated by the writers discussed above – the only English poet to have taken this position, but he was the earliest, and remained the most conspicuous. Herbert ignores him as he ignores the rest.

In his mature verse, Herbert again critiques poets for bypassing religious matter. The famous rhetorical question in "Jordan I," "May no lines passe, except they do their dutie/Not to a true, but painted chair?" (4–5) recasts the Platonic prejudice against the second- or third-hand truths of creative writing, to condemn poetry which at best praises God's creation rather than God himself.[43] Again, Herbert may be harking back to a time when it was difficult for poets to write creatively about religion except at several removes, and Southwell, who did so much to counter this, would have been one model for Herbert's witty christianisation of this neoplatonic commonplace. For instance, in his lyric "Man to the wound in Christs side," Christ's wound is seen as a cave which represents not the limitation of perception, as it does in Plato's *Republic*, but the destination of choice for all seekers after heavenly bliss: "O happy soule that flies so hie,/As to attaine this sacred cave" (25–26).[44]

The aspiration to seek refuge in Christ's wounds is common within devotions on the Passion, epitomised in the medieval prayer *Anima Christi* – "O good Jesu, hear me,/Within Thy wounds hide me."[45] Herbert utilised it in one of his own poems, "The Bag," but in a manner which epitomises his distance from Southwellian devotional poetry. The poem begins in a way which appears puzzlingly gratuitous.

> Away despair; my gracious Lord doth heare.
> Though windes and waves assault my keel,
> He doth preserve it: he doth steer,
> Ev'n when the boat seems most to reel.
> Storms are the triumph of his art:
> Well may he close his eyes, but not his heart.
>
> (1–6)[46]

This refers to the occasion in the Gospels when the disciples are alarmed by a storm and wake up the sleeping Jesus, who rebukes them for their lack of faith, but quells the wind and sea.[47] It bears no direct relation to the poem's main focus, the narrative of the Incarnation and Passion developed from stanza 2 onwards – "Hast thou not heard, that my Lord JESUS di'd?/Then let me tell thee a strange storie ..." (7–8) – perhaps a reason why the poem has routinely been reckoned among Herbert's least appealing.[48] But read as Herbert's commentary on an earlier tradition exemplified by Southwell, it starts to make sense. While storms were a fairly common figure for the journey of the guilty soul towards repentance, any of Herbert's contemporaries familiar with recent religious poetry would have noticed how this opening stanza evokes the storm at the beginning of "Saint Peter's Complaint": "Launch foorth my Soule into a maine of teares,/Full fraught with griefe the traffick of thy mind:/Torne sayles will serve, thoughtes rent with guilty feares:/Give care the sterne: use sighes in lieu of wind" (1–4).[49] Southwell's St. Peter proclaims himself to be setting out on a voyage of despair; Herbert's speaker dismisses despair in the very first sentence as a way of clearing the air for genuine devotional utterance.

But is it Southwell's St. Peter who is being criticised, or Southwell himself? Peter, after all, is only a prosopopoeia, and "Saint Peter's Complaint" is not endorsing him by giving voice to him; Southwell himself – as Herbert may have known – advised emotional moderation.[50] Perhaps the best answer is to read "The Bag" as a critique not of Southwell himself, but of the devotional trends Southwell tapped into and the poetic tradition he instigated. The 1590s and early 1600s saw many writers who followed in Southwell's path while failing to pick up on his checks and balances, presenting uncontrolled transports of grief as exemplary; Grymeston's meditations, quoted earlier, illustrate this trend and suggest how it may have influenced devotional practice. Thus, in announcing "Away despair," and proclaiming his trust in God, Herbert's speaker – and thus Herbert himself – may well be dissociating himself from the perceived excesses of Southwellian tears poetry, rather than Southwell himself.

Herbert's poem is governed by the conceit that the wound in Christ's side can be seen as a carrying-pouch, or bag, for dispatching man's petitions to God. When Christ is "returning" to heaven upon the cross, "there came one/That ran upon him with a spear," and turning "to his brethren," Christ asks them:

If ye have any thing to send or write,
(I have no bag, but here is room)
Unto my fathers hands and sight
(Beleeve me) it shall safely come.
That I shall minde, what you impart;
Look, you may put it very neare my heart.

(25, 26, 30, 31–36)

On one level, the thought of thrusting something into a bleeding stomach-wound is bound to engender visceral disgust. Devout early modern readers, especially those who had practised Ignatius Loyola's Spiritual Exercises or were influenced by similar devotional traditions, would have alleviated this by meditating on the salvific quality of Christ's wounds. Southwell's "Man to the wound in Christs side" encourages this exemplary manner of reading: "Heere would I view that bloudy sore,/Which dint of spiteful speare did breed,/The bloody woundes laid there in store/Would force a stony heart to bleede" (17–20). Comparing this to Herbert's stanza forcibly presents one with a poet's main alternatives when engaging with the topic: whether he should emphasise the affective impact of the wounds, or leave this up to the reader's imagination. "The Bag" is one of the least Ignatian poems possible, with the carrying-pouch conceit steering the reader firmly away from the physicality of Christ: perhaps Herbert's attempt to create a fully thought-through Protestant poetic praxis, most at ease when picturing the divine by means of analogy.[51] At the end, Christ reiterates his intention to act as messenger between God the Father and man, returning to and confirming the injunctions at the beginning of the poem: "what he sends/I will present, and somewhat more,/Not to his hurt. Sighs will convey/Any thing to me. Heark despair, away" (39–42). Regret for sin is fitting, but Christ cares too much about man's well-being to ask for anything more than "sighs"; transports of repentance, we infer, are so nearly related to despair that they can only hinder salvation.

Some poems in *The Temple* convey a very different message about the efficacy of intense emotion within repentance.[52] But in "The Bag," Herbert's critique of the Southwellian tradition makes it necessary for him to advocate restraint, and this tells us something about the emotional register that he made his own. In "Saint Peter's Complaint," Southwell insistently pushes up against the limits of language, experience and perception. Herbert prefers litotes, conveying the ineffability of God through understatement. In retrospect, this stance has repeatedly, and not unreasonably, been co-opted into ideas of the Anglican *via media*; at the time, it would have uncoupled Herbert's poem from the Southwell-influenced hyperbolists of the previous generation. Just as the operatic *furor* of such plays as Thomas Kyd's *The Spanish Tragedy* was first widely copied and then ridiculed, Southwell's rhetorical stratagems were fertile enough to breed cliché and dissociation.

Two poets writing after Herbert's death, during the years of the Civil War, provide a coda to this discussion. In the introduction to Part 2 of *Silex scintillans* (1655), Henry Vaughan described Herbert as the first poet that "with any effectual success" stemmed the tide of profane verse.[53] Effacing Southwell along with Herbert's other predecessors in the field of divine poetry, the notion of "effectual success" may be denominationally biased. Vaughan was, after all, writing at a time when dispossessed Anglicans were much inclined to idealise their church and its great men. *Silex scintillans* is explicitly inspired by Herbert's poetic illustriousness and saintly reputation, with Vaughan constituting himself a son of George as so many did. Some years earlier, the young Catholic writer Francis Chetwinde – perhaps seeing himself as a nephew of Southwell – had cited the poet as an inspirational figure within the English Catholic literary pantheon, together with Jonson and Sir John Beaumont; the title of the poem in which he does this, *The New Hellicon*, reveals his canonising agenda.[54] While there is more work to be done on how Southwell's poetry was transmitted in manuscript, initial studies suggest that it was a staple of Catholic scribal endeavour well after his work had ceased to be printed.[55] Thus, it becomes possible to identify two main strands in the reception history of Southwell. There was an intense, appropriative, often agonistic response to him within the literary mainstream from the early 1590s, peaking in the years immediately after his death and continuing into the Jacobean era. England's Catholic community, on the other hand, not only inspired Southwell's work but was loyal to it longest. Some of its members were poets themselves, like Verstegan or Chetwinde. Others will have been more ordinary lovers of divine verse who, long after Southwell had fallen out of fashion in the literary main-stream, quietly kept reading him, copying him and, like Grymeston, using him as a starting-point for prayer.[56]

Though one of the most powerful literary and spiritual influences on late Elizabethan and Jacobean England, Southwell has always been canonically problematic. This chapter has argued that his contemporary importance can be hard to discern because he was reacted to so strongly, whether as an anonymised literary antagonist or as the provider of raw food for the devout: which raises the wider issue of how his authorial stance, effacing personal individuality and foregrounding the baroque invitation to religious emotion, has acted upon readers from the Elizabethan age onwards. In our own time a distinguished admirer of Southwell, the poet Geoffrey Hill, has identified an ecstatic strain in him, commenting: "I would ... suggest that the radical pun perceivable in 'ecstasy', in being 'beside oneself', either with a frenzy of egoistic thoughts or with a disciplined indifference to them, would not be lost on [Southwell]."[57] While Southwell's St. Peter certainly experiences "a frenzy of egoistic thoughts," the idea of "disciplined indiffer-ence" describes Southwell's own poetic persona rather well; unlike – say – Donne, Southwell leaves himself alone. His readers are not told how he stands in relation to God, but enjoined to consider how they do: an awkward question at any time, and bound to leave a secularist nonplussed. But Southwell's particularity intrudes in other ways, since he writes as one preparing for martyrdom, and is read as one who suffered it. Unofficially venerated from his execution onwards, he was canonised in 1970. Thanks to the pious conformations of hagiography, saints are sometimes perceived as less than individual. Yet the veneration paid by Roman Catholics to relics points in the opposite direction, suggesting a glorification of physical iden-tity through the miraculous potential of a saint's bones, possessions and scraps of clothing.[58] Southwell's verse can be seen as related to that legacy. Often enough, as this chapter has illustrated, it becomes detached from its progenitor. But when it bears his name, it can hardly be encountered without thinking of his martyrdom, and when one reads it, one reads a relic.

Notes

1 My thanks to Hannibal Hamlin for reading a draft of this chapter, and for additional help given by Peter Davidson, Arnold Hunt and the editors of this volume. Preliminary versions of it were delivered to audiences at Durham and Oxford Universities; I am grateful to them for their interest and suggestions.

2 See, most recently, Robert S. Miola, "Publishing the Word: Robert Southwell's Sacred Poetry," *Review of English Studies* 64, no. 265 (2013): 410–432.

3 On the genre of complaint, see Rosalind Smith, Michelle O'Callaghan and Sarah C. E. Ross, "Complaint and Elegy," chapter 25 in *A Companion to Renaissance Poetry*, ed. Catherine Teresa Bates (Chichester: Wiley Blackwell, 2018). On Southwell's influence on the genre, see Gary Kuchar, *The Poetry of Religious Sorrow in Early Modern England* (Cambridge: Cambridge UP, 2008), chapter 1; Arthur F. Marotti, "Southwell's Remains: Catholicism and Anti-Catholicism in Early Modern England," in *Texts and Cultural Change in Early Modern England*, ed. Cedric C. Brown and Arthur F. Marotti (Basingstoke: Macmillan, 1997), chapter 2; and my *Catholicism, Controversy and the English Literary Imagination, 1558–1660* (Cambridge: Cambridge UP, 1999), chapter 2. Recent studies of Southwell's writing include Anne Sweeney, *Robert Southwell: Snow in Arcadia: Redrawing the English Lyric Landscape, 1586–95* (Manchester: Manchester UP, 2006) and Scott R. Pilarz, *Robert Southwell and the Mission of Literature, 1561–1595: Writing Reconciliation* (Aldershot: Ashgate, 2004).

4 See Kuchar, *Poetry of Religious Sorrow*, 46–48, and Shell, op. cit. Of Gervase Markham's *Marie Magdalens lamentations* ((London: Edward White, 1601), Kuchar comments: "Southwell is everywhere and nowhere; he has become more of a ghost than a clearly avowed intertextual presence within the work" (48). A manuscript copy of Markham's poem was owned by Julian Crewe, a Catholic laywoman: see Lisa McClain, "'They have taken away my Lord': Mary Magdalene, Christ's Missing Body, and the Mass in Reformation England," *Sixteenth-Century Journal* 38, no. 1 (2007), 77–96, at 77. In "Reforming St Peter: Protestant Constrictions of St Peter the Apostle in Early Modern England," *Sixteenth-Century Journal* 33, no. 1 (2002): 33–49, Karen Bruhn examines William Broxup's *Saint Peters path* (1598), a Protestantised rewriting of "Saint Peter's Complaint" which fails to credit Southwell.

5 On the idea of agonistic response to strong poetic inspiration, see Harold Bloom, *The Anxiety of Influence: A Theory of Poetry*, 1st edition. (New York: Oxford UP, 1973).

6 Stephen Greenblatt, *Renaissance Self-Fashioning from More to Shakespeare*, 1st edition. (Chicago: Chicago UP, 1980), index under More's name.

7 For the self-reflexivity generated by soteriological thought-processes, see Claire McEachern, *Believing in Shakespeare: Studies in Longing* (Cambridge: Cambridge UP, 2018).

8 Betty S. Travitsky's *Oxford Dictionary of National Biography* article on Grymeston calls Southwell a "kinsman" of Grymeston's.

9 *Miscelanea*, 1st edition. (London: Felix Norton, 1604), D4b. All quotations are taken from this edition. Travitsky, op. cit., comments on Grymeston's literary borrowings. The chapter heading runs: "Morning Meditation, with sixteen sobs

of a sorrowful spirit, which she used for mentall praier, as also an addition of sixteen staves of verse taken out of Peters complaint, which she usually sung & plaied on the winde instrument." Household or residence organs were used for domestic music-making from the sixteenth century onwards: see Barbara Owen's entry on "residence organ," 317–319 in *Continuum Encyclopedia of Popular Music of the World: Volume II: Performance and Production*, ed. John Shepherd *et al.* (London: Continuum, 2003). In a poem about his mother's musical activities, her son Bernye Grymeston does refer to "pipes" (E4b).

10 For Southwell's original, see stanza 6 in "Saint Peter's Complaint," 64 in *St Robert Southwell: Collected Poems*, ed. Peter Davidson and Anne Sweeney (Manchester: Carcanet, 2007). All references and quotations to Southwell's verse are taken from this edition.

11 "The Author to the Reader," prefixing "Saint Peter's Complaint" line 6 (63). On interpretive distance, see Kuchar, *Poetry of Religious Sorrow*, 33–34.

12 On another female copyist and appropriator of Southwell, see Victoria E. Burke and Sarah C. E. Ross, "Elizabeth Middleton, John Bourchier, and the Compilation of 17th-Century Religious Manuscripts," *The Library* (7th series) 2, no. 2 (2001): 131–160.

13 This was a popular genre for women writers: see Patricia Demers, *Women's Writing in English: Early Modern England* (Toronto: Toronto UP, 2005), 176–180.

14 "The History of Purgatory," possibly by Robert Owen [early 1600s]: item 7 in BL Add. MS. 11427. I discuss the dating, authorship and context of this play in *Shakespeare and Religion* (London: Arden, 2010), chapter 2. The references below follow the document's contemporary pagination.

15 *The History of Purgatory*, 25.

16 "Seculer men/man" may mean that the writer is a layman, or that he considers himself more worldly than the writers from whom he borrows.

17 A borrowing from "Saint Peter's Complaint" itself occurs in the same speech: "Whose happie spirits, under the Alter slayne/Dive in sweete desiers …" (47). "Saint Peter's Complaint," stanza 64, reads "O Pooles of Hesebon, the bathes of grace,/Where happy spirits dive in sweet desires" (lines 379–380).

18 See Joy Rowe, "Kitson family (*per. c.*1520–*c.*1660)," *Oxford Dictionary of National Biography*.

19 Southwell, "The Author to the Reader" (prefixing "Saint Peter's Complaint"), 17–18; William Evans, *Pietatis lachrymae* (London: Edward Allde, 1602), A6a.

20 *Pietatis lachrymae*, A7a; "Saint Peter's Complaint," 31–32.

21 "The Author to the Reader," line 15; *Pietatis lachrymae*, D1a.

22 *Oxford English Dictionary*, "garland," *n.*, 4 (first citation from 1526). Ref to Drayton's *Idea: the shepheardes garland*, see below.

23 *Pietatis lachrymae*, A8a–B6a. See above, p. 230.

24 Nancy Pollard Brown, "The Structure of Southwell's 'Saint Peter's Complaint'," *Modern Language Review* 61, no. 1 (1966): 3–11. Cf. the interpretation of *Mary Magdalen's Funeral Tears* undertaken by Bronwyn V. Wallace, "Robert Southwell's Intimate Exegesis," chapter 10 in *Sensing the Sacred: Religion and the Senses in Medieval and Early Modern Culture*, ed. Robin Macdonald, Emilie K. M. Murphy and Elizabeth L. Swann (Abingdon: Routledge, 2018). On the place of repetition in religious writing, see Susannah Brietz Monta, "Repetition," chapter 8 in *The Cambridge Companion to Literature and Religion*, ed. Susan M. Felch (Cambridge: Cambridge UP, 2016).

25 This alludes to Isaiah 1:18.

26 See Marjory E. Lange, *Telling Tears in the English Renaissance* (Leiden: E.J. Brill, 1996), 44–45.

27 All quotations are from J. William Hebel with Kathleen Tillotson and Bernard H. Newdigate, eds. *The Works of Michael Drayton*, 5 vols (Oxford: Shakespeare Head Press/Basil Blackwell for Oxford UP, 1931–1941). *Idea: The shepheards garland* (1593) is in vol. 1, 45–94 (notes in vol. 5, 4ff.); *Pastorals. Contayning eclogues* (1619) in vol. 2, 515–573 (notes in vol. 5, 183 ff.). The text in *Pastorals*, as Hebel comments (183), is very similar to that of the intermediate edition, *Poemes lyrick and pastoral* (1606).

28 On Catholicism and pastoral, see Phebe Jensen, *Religion and Revelry in Shakespeare's Festive World* (Cambridge: Cambridge UP, 2008), chapters 3 and 5 (Drayton's revisions are discussed at 205–208).

29 Bernard H. Newdigate, *Michael Drayton and His Circle* (Oxford: Oxford UP, 1941), 215 (also discussing Drayton's allusions to lines from the Roman Catholic breviary).

30 Much of Drayton's parody would be equally applicable to Southwell's later imitators. However, the early date suggests that Southwell himself is Drayton's target; while Southwell's verses were not in print in 1593, they were almost certainly circulating in manuscript at that time. See Davidson and Sweeney in Southwell, *Robert Southwell: Collected Poems*, 145–151, and "Introduction" to Robert Southwell, *The Poems of Robert Southwell, S.J.*, ed. James H. McDonald and Nancy Pollard Brown (Oxford: Clarendon, 1967).

31 "Favour, good will," punning on "Weeping, mourning": OED, *n.*2 and *n.*3.

32 Drayton, *Idea* (1593), Eclogue 1, lines 43–60, 73–78.

33 The unease of a contemporary reader, Henry Gurney, with the register of "Saint Peter's Complaint" may be related to concerns about hyperbole: "If that ther may a fault espied be/it is in that Decorum is not kept/sith youthfull phrase & arte do disagree/from fisher man, that into age was stept/whose Stile appostolique was grave & plaine/as that wch doth worldes Curiousnes disdeyne ..." See Steven W. May, "Henry Gurney, A Norfolk Farmer, Reads Spenser and Others," *Spenser Studies* 20 (2005), 183–223 (quotation 208–209).

34 On the downplaying of religious language, see Drayton, *The Works of Michael Drayton*, vol. 5, 183, vol. 5, 183. Cf. Curtis Perry, *The Making of Jacobean Culture: James I and the Renegotiation of Elizabethan Literary Practice* (Cambridge: Cambridge UP, 1997), 70–71.

35 Drayton, *Pastorals*, Eclogue 1, lines 43–60.

36 I am grateful to Vassiliki Markidou for this suggestion.

37 "New Year Sonnets": Sonnet 1, lines 3–5; Sonnet 2, lines 8–11. All quotations are from George Herbert, *George Herbert: The Complete English Poems*, ed. Helen Wilcox (Cambridge: Cambridge UP, 2007).

38 See the introduction to William Shakespeare, *Shakespeare's Sonnets*, ed. Katherine Duncan-Jones (London: Arden, 1997).

39 I make this argument more fully in *Catholicism, Controversy and the English Literary Imagination*, chapter 2.

40 See William L. Stull, " 'Why Are Not "Sonnets" Made of Thee?' A New Context for the 'Holy Sonnets' of Donne, Herbert, and Milton," *Modern Philology* 80, no. 2 (1982): 129–135.

41 Gary Kuchar, *George Herbert and the Mystery of the Word: Poetry and Scripture in Seventeenth-Century England* (Cham: Springer/Palgrave Macmillan, 2017), chapter 7, discusses the relationship between the "New Year Sonnets" and Southwell's work in terms of alchemical poetics. See also Gary M. Bouchard, "The Roman Steps to the Temple: An Examination of the Influence of Robert Southwell, SJ, upon George Herbert," *Logos: A Journal of Catholic Thought and Culture* 10, no. 3 (2007), 131–150; and Hannibal Hamlin, "George Herbert Plays Host to Robert Southwell: Allusions in 'Love' (III)," in *New Ways of*

Looking at Old Texts, VI: Papers of the Renaissance English Text Society, 2011–2016, ed. Arthur Marotti (Tempe: Medieval & Renaissance Texts & Studies/Renaissance English Text Society), forthcoming in 2019). I am grateful to Professor Hamlin for letting me see a copy of this article before publication.

42 See above, p. 234.
43 Cf. Herbert, *George Herbert*, 202.
44 For another storm-metaphor, cf. "The prodigall chyldes soule wracke" (38–39).
45 See the entry for "Anima Christi" in the online *Catholic Encyclopaedia*.
46 On negative critical reactions to the poem, see Wilcox's preface, 518–519.
47 See Mark 4:37–41; Luke 8:22–25.
48 See Wilcox's commentary in Herbert, *George Herbert*.
49 On the literary representation of storms in this era, see Gwilym Jones, *Shakespeare's Storms* (Manchester: Manchester UP, 2015).
50 See Lange, *Telling Tears*, and my *Catholicism, Controversy*, chapter 2.
51 Though, if so, it would pose an interesting tension with Herbert's evocation of a bloody Crucifixion in a poem like "The Agony," and his declared preference for religious straightforwardness in "Jordan (I)."
52 E.g., "Sighs and Grones" (Herbert, *George Herbert*, 297–300).
53 "The Author's Preface to the Following Hymns": quoted from Henry Vaughan, *Henry Vaughan: The Complete Poems*, ed. Alan Rudrum (Harmondsworth: Penguin, 1976), 142.
54 In classical mythology Mount Helicon was considered a source of poetic inspiration; Chetwinde may also be referring to the anthology *Englands Helicon* (1600). See my "Divine Muses, Catholic Poets and Pilgrims to St Winifred's Well: Literary Communities in Francis Chetwinde's 'New Hellicon' (1642)," in *Writing and Religion in England, 1558–1689: Studies in Community-Making and Cultural Memory*, eds. Roger Sell and Anthony Johnson (Farnham: Ashgate, 2009), 273–288.
55 The last seventeenth-century printing of Southwell's verse was in 1636 (STC 22968).
56 Folger Shakespeare Library, MS V a 126 [dated to ca. 1625 on the online catalogue], juxtaposes Southwell's poems with prayers. On mid-seventeenth-century Catholic copyists of Southwell, see Helen Hackett, "Women and Catholic Manuscript Networks in Seventeenth-Century England: New Research on Constance Aston Fowler's Miscellany of Sacred and Secular Verse," *Renaissance Quarterly* 65, no. 4 (2012): 1094–1124; and Cedric C. Brown, "Recusant Community and Jesuit Mission in Parliament Days: Bodleian MS Eng. poet. b. 5," *Yearbook of English Studies*, 23 (2003): 290–315. See also the items listed for Southwell in the *Census of English Literary Manuscripts (CELM)*.
57 Geoffrey Hill, "The Absolute Reasonableness of Robert Southwell," chapter 2 in *Collected Critical Writings*, ed. Kenneth Haynes (Oxford: Oxford UP, 2008), quotation at 37. This essay was originally published in *The Lords of Limit* (1984).
58 A relic of Southwell is kept at the Jesuits in Britain Archives, Mount Street, ref. R/132; my thanks to the Archivist, Rebecca Somerset. On the notion of Southwell's literary remains as relics, see Bouchard, "The Roman Steps" and Marotti, "Southwell's Remains," op. cit., and Sean Ross, "Robert Southwell: Sacrament and Self," *English Literary Renaissance* 47, no. 1 (2017): 73–109.

Bibliography

Manuscripts

Folger Shakespeare Library, MS V a 126: manuscript including copies of Southwell's verse.

British Library Add. MS. 11427, item 7: Owen, Robert (?). "The History of Purgatory."

Printed primary sources

Broxup, William. *Saint Peters path*. London: Felix Kingston, 1598.
Drayton, Michael. *The Works of Michael Drayton*. Edited by J. William Hebel with Kathleen Tillotson and Bernard H. Newdigate. 5 vols. Oxford: Shakespeare Head Press/Basil Blackwell for Oxford University Press, 1931–1941.
Evans, William. *Pietatis lachrymae*. London: Edward Allde, 1602.
Grymeston, Elizabeth. *Miscelanea*. 1st edition. London: Felix Norton, 1604.
Herbert, George. *George Herbert: The Complete English Poems*. Edited by Helen Wilcox. Cambridge: Cambridge University Press, 2007.
Markham, Gervase. *Marie Magdalens lamentations*. London: Edward White, 1601.
Shakespeare, William. *Shakespeare's Sonnets*. Edited by Katherine Duncan-Jones. London: Arden, 1997.
Southwell, Robert, Saint. *St Robert Southwell: Collected Poems*. Edited by Peter Davidson and Anne Sweeney. Manchester: Carcanet, 2007.
Southwell, Robert, *The Poems of Robert Southwell, S. J.* Edited by James H. McDonald and Nancy Pollard Brown. Oxford: Clarendon Press, 1967.
Vaughan, Henry. *Henry Vaughan: The Complete Poems*. Edited by Alan Rudrum. Harmondsworth: Penguin, 1976.
Verstegan, Richard. *Odes*. Antwerp: A. Conincx, 1601.

Secondary sources

Bloom, Harold. *The Anxiety of Influence: A Theory of Poetry*, 1st edition. New York: Oxford University Press, 1973.
Bouchard, Gary M. "The Roman Steps to the Temple: An Examination of the Influence of Robert Southwell, SJ, upon George Herbert." *Logos: A Journal of Catholic Thought and Culture* 10, no. 3 (2007): 131–150.
Brown, Cedric C. "Recusant Community and Jesuit Mission in Parliament Days: Bodleian MS Eng. poet. b. 5." *Yearbook of English Studies*, 23 (2003): 290–315.
Bruhn, Karen. "Reforming St Peter: Protestant Constrictions of St Peter the Apostle in Early Modern England." *Sixteenth-Century Journal*, 33, no. 1 (2002): 33–49.
Burke, Victoria E., and Sarah C. E. Ross. "Elizabeth Middleton, John Bourchier, and the Compilation of 17th-Century Religious Manuscripts." *The Library* (7th series) 2, no. 2 (2001): 131–160.
Demers, Patricia. *Women's Writing in English: Early Modern England*. Toronto: Toronto University Press, 2005.
Greenblatt, Stephen. *Renaissance Self-Fashioning from More to Shakespeare*, 1st edition. Chicago: Chicago University Press, 1980.
Hackett, Helen. "Women and Catholic Manuscript Networks in Seventeenth-Century England: New Research on Constance Aston Fowler's Miscellany of Sacred and Secular Verse." *Renaissance Quarterly*, 65, no. 4 (2012): 1094–1124.
Hamlin, Hannibal. "George Herbert Plays Host to Robert Southwell: Allusions in 'Love' (III)." In *New Ways of Looking at Old Texts, VI: Papers of the Renaissance English Text Society, 2011–2016*. Edited by Arthur Marotti. Tempe:

Medieval & Renaissance Texts & Studies/Renaissance English Text Society, forthcoming in 2019.

Hill, Geoffrey. "The Absolute Reasonableness of Robert Southwell." In *Collected Critical Writings*. Edited by Kenneth Haynes. Oxford: Oxford University Press, 2008.

Jensen, Phebe. *Religion and Revelry in Shakespeare's Festive World*. Cambridge: Cambridge University Press, 2008.

Jones, Gwilym. *Shakespeare's Storms*. Manchester: Manchester University Press, 2015.

Kuchar, Gary. *George Herbert and the Mystery of the Word: Poetry and Scripture in Seventeenth-Century England* (Cham: Springer/Palgrave Macmillan, 2017),

Kuchar, Gary. *The Poetry of Religious Sorrow in Early Modern England*. Cambridge: Cambridge University Press, 2008.

Lange, Marjory E. *Telling Tears in the English Renaissance*. Leiden: E. J. Brill, 1996.

Marotti, Arthur F. "Southwell's Remains: Catholicism and Anti-Catholicism in Early Modern England." In *Texts and Cultural Change in Early Modern England*. Edited by Cedric C. Brown and Arthur F. Marotti. Basingstoke: Macmillan, 1997.

May, Steven W. "Henry Gurney, A Norfolk Farmer, Reads Spenser and Others." *Spenser Studies*, 20 (2005), 183–223.

McClain, Lisa. "'They have taken away my Lord': Mary Magdalene, Christ's Missing Body, and the Mass in Reformation England." *Sixteenth-Century Journal*, 38, no. 1 (2007): 77–96.

McEachern, Claire. *Believing in Shakespeare: Studies in Longing*. Cambridge: Cambridge University Press, 2018.

Miola, Robert S. "Publishing the Word: Robert Southwell's Sacred Poetry." *Review of English Studies*, 64, no. 265 (2013): 410–432.

Monta, Susannah Brietz. "Repetition." In *The Cambridge Companion to Literature and Religion*. Edited by Susan M. Felch. Cambridge: Cambridge University Press, 2016.

Newdigate, Bernard H. *Michael Drayton and his Circle*. Oxford: Oxford University Press, 1941.

Perry, Curtis. *The Making of Jacobean Culture: James I and the Renegotiation of Elizabethan Literary Practice*. Cambridge: Cambridge University Press, 1997.

Pilarz, Scott R. *Robert Southwell and the Mission of Literature, 1561–1595: Writing Reconciliation*. Aldershot: Ashgate, 2004.

Pollard Brown, Nancy. "The Structure of Saint Peter's Complaint." *Modern Language Review*, 61, no. 1 (1966): 3–11.

Ross, Sean. "Robert Southwell: Sacrament and Self." *English Literary Renaissance*, 47, no. 1 (2017): 73–109.

Shell, Alison. *Catholicism, Controversy and the English Literary Imagination, 1558–1660*. Cambridge: Cambridge University Press, 1999.

Shell, Alison. "Divine Muses, Catholic Poets and Pilgrims to St Winifred's Well: Literary Communities in Francis Chetwinde's 'New Hellicon' (1642)." In *Writing and Religion in England, 1558–1689: Studies in Community-Making and Cultural Memory*. Edited by Roger Sell and Anthony Johnson. Farnham: Ashgate, 2009.

Shell, Alison. *Shakespeare and Religion*. London: Arden, 2010.

Smith, Rosalind, Michelle O'Callaghan and Sarah C. E. Ross. "Complaint and Elegy." In *A Companion to Renaissance Poetry*. Edited by Catherine Teresa Bates. Chichester: Wiley Blackwell, 2018.

Stull, William L. " 'Why Are Not "Sonnets" Made of Thee?' A New Context for the 'Holy Sonnets' of Donne, Herbert, and Milton." *Modern Philology* 80, no. 2 (1982): 129–135.

Sweeney, Anne. *Robert Southwell: Snow in Arcadia: Redrawing the English Lyric Landscape, 1586–95*. Manchester: Manchester University Press, 2006.

Wallace, Bronwyn V. "Robert Southwell's Intimate Exegesis." In *Sensing the Sacred: Religion and the Senses in Medieval and Early Modern Culture*. Edited by Robin Macdonald, Emilie K. M. Murphy and Elizabeth L. Swann. Abingdon: Routledge, 2018.

Conclusion

Vassiliki Markidou and Afroditi-Maria Panaghis

Precarious Identities: Studies in the Works of Fulke Greville and Robert Southwell has attempted to map the ways in which the complex early modern politico-religious context influenced the literary production of the Calvinist Greville and the Jesuit Southwell as well as to analyze how their oeuvre responded to these exigencies. The studies included in this volume have endeavored to trace the diverse and numberless constructions of the self, attested its fluidity, brittleness, and inadequacy, and show how both writers struggled to formulate their selves amid a shifting politico-religious landscape. They have affirmed how deeply intertwined religion and politics were in the renaissance, underscored points of religious and political controversy, and expressed the conceptualization of a nation characterized by violence yet struggling to avoid the eruption of civil or foreign war. The essays have also demonstrated that in the sixteenth and seventeenth century religion infiltrated the state and every aspect of life from the social and domestic relationships to the intellectual and ruling class. Lastly, they have reflected the breach from religious constraints, brought forth by humanism, rationality, and science, which eventually resulted in the distinction between the sacred and the profane as well as politics and religion.

Both Greville and Southwell exposed themselves to humanism, the former through Shrewsbury and his contact with international Protestant intellectuals and the latter at Douai and Rome. They were vitally influenced by the years they spent on the continent though in different ways. At the time of his exile during Mary I's reign Greville was influenced by Protestants in Geneva, Basel, and the Rhineland who furthered their study of biblical translations and comprehension of religious observances and church discipline as well as the doctrine of predestination and the concomitant belief in those who were elected for salvation. In this light, in his *Dedication*, he firmly holds that international Protestantism should be fully endorsed by England in order to shelter the nation from "the creeping monarchy of Rome (by her arch instruments the Jesuits)"[1] while in *Caelica*, he outlines a shift from the profane to the sacred marked by the Calvinism he acquired on the continent but which, as Brian Cummings aptly notes, he then set on a course of "colli[sion] with the certainty of its own conclusions."[2] Respectively, Southwell, during the time of his education and training at Douai and Rome, besides theology, he studied the Classics and as his poetry attests learned to practice the aesthetics of counter-reformation piety which he brought to England from Italy. An example is the complaint genre, which accommodated his Ignatian mission for both his literary and pastoral objectives and which, though a "combative" mode, he employed to evoke conciliation as well as transform and redeem sinners. Southwell believed that the reformation of English literature was a vital part of his spiritual mission hence he sought to propagate in England religious and moral topics and downplay the prevalent pagan and classical ones.

Greville and Southwell engaged in a strife between self-fashioning and self-erasure yet in the midst of this agon they presented the fragility of the self in different ways since despite the complexities and ambiguities of their religious beliefs, the former was a Calvinist courtier and the latter, a Jesuit missionary. On the one hand, Greville penned the *Life of Sidney* not only as an expression of bereavement but also as an articulation of his own precarious identity—as a courtier, statesman, writer, and biographer—within a distinctly Protestant context. Along similar lines, he postulated in *Treatise of Humane Learning* that the human being's goal is self-knowledge, which related as it is to the quest for self-fashioning, aspires to as well as entails an agonizing, and at times even desperate, effort to reconnect with the Divine and recover the pre-fallen state, even if it constantly falls short of doing so. Greville also employs the notion of self-division in *Cælica*, where for the most part duality, political and religious, of the mind and the body, the earthly and the heavenly, reflects a split self continuously in conflict which remains resolutely irresolvable. Hence, the final shift from the secular to the religious registered in his sonnet sequence cannot undo the aforementioned ambiguity that permeates the remainder of *Cælica*. Similarly in *Alaham*, Greville delineates the precarious making and unmaking of identities as well as the gains and losses that such a process involves. Southwell on the other hand forged his self-fashioning as a complainant with the aim to redeem and remold his readers' as well as his own passions, and converted saints such as Peter, Mary Magdalen, and Joseph from sinners into lovers to stress the need for transformation informed by the doctrine of *imago dei*. Southwell's self-fashioning in fact permeates his writings and registers the creation of multiple selves—preacher, sinner, and martyr among others—through recurrent self-deconstruction and self-construction that will eventually lead to the union with the Divine.

A crucial trope employed by both Greville and Southwell is that of the sinner. Both cast themselves as such and render not only the fall but also their strenuous endeavor to attain salvation in the context of the doctrine of *imago dei* while holding radically different positions on sin and redemption. In the *Treatise of Religion*, Greville reflects his deep concern with the aftermath of the fall and the idea that only the elect will be saved. He agrees with Martin Luther that "righteousness does not come from within, but is given by God. No one is just in himself, but only when his sin is taken from him by God."[3] As such, all we can hope for is some stability, "not a harmonious equilibrium but a temporary balance of forces."[4] In fact, Greville's unresolved and conflicting dualities including those related to theological issues such as sin and redemption not only persisted to the end of his life but also pervade his oeuvre. Thus on the one hand, his writings reflect poignantly the idea that the state of humankind is corrupt due to the fall hence the consequent "flaws in human nature" lead to "earthly errors,"[5] and all actions are "deeply tainted with sin."[6] On the other and despite his despair in human suffering from the negative effects of the fall, he retained a glimmer of hope, even if dim, about the prospect of achieving the prelapsarian state. This anguished, ambiguous stance is manifested in *A Treatise of Religion*, where he outlines the hardships humans face in their effort to recover the pre-fallen state, mainly their vulnerability to temptation that even reason fails to withstand. While Greville was tormented over the idea that God would choose to save some and destroy others, the Jesuit Southwell "always understood grace to make commands about human action whilst reaffirming that grace in fact obviates the need for a law of commandments."[7] Unlike Greville, Southwell advocated that all sinners, and not only the chosen few, if they have faith in Christ who sacrificed himself to save humanity, could be redeemed and that God is compassionate and would not allow its damnation. As a result, he describes a ceaseless process of transformation wherein individuals, who live in a world besieged with temptations, amend, acquire redemption, and are rewarded in the otherworld through penance, prayer, and meditation, a process that involves full acknowledgment of their sinfulness. In this context, the torture of the body purifies the soul and should be accepted without regret. In *Exercises and Devotions*, he confirms that his decision to join the Society of Jesus was motivated by his determination to continue to mortify the self by doing penance "for the numberless sins committed against God," observe Christ's rules and maybe "become, as far as [he] can, like unto Christ who was crucified for [him]."[8] In this respect, he agreed with Loyola that the Divine allows even violence to be inflicted on the flesh to suppress passions, an experience which involves both pain and pleasure in the quest for heavenly bliss. Furthermore, in considering the nativity of Christ as inaugurating the redemption of the world as well as what deserves one's energies and desires he expressed his intention to reform both individual and society. Southwell also stated that giving up mundane goods is a temporary immolation that will be rewarded in heaven. In *Fourfold Meditation* not only does he portray the sinner at the threshold of death terrified at the thought of having to appear before God he also reminds us that humans have inherited not only sin and death through Adam's fall but also the hope of salvation through Christ's sacrifice. In *Short Rule*, Southwell advises the devout to practice virtues such as kindness, modesty, love, and charity as well as adopt the life of a beggar in order to obtain redemption. He asks sinners who shut their ears to Christ's voice and turned to the devil by surrendering their faith to repent. Interestingly, in their transcendent longings, both the Calvinist statesman and the Jesuit missionary used literary conventions, statements of doubt, and reflective spiritual contemplation. Moreover, in spite of their religious divide, Greville and Southwell converged in employing themes, metaphors, *prosopopoeia*, and biblical allusions, yet unlike the former the latter did so in conjunction with Ignatian argumentative techniques to depict good and virtuous living, guide believers towards salvation, but also warn sinners that they should live by Christ's teachings if they want to escape damnation.

Undoubtedly, the religious views held by both writers affected deeply their vision of life as well as their literary production. Yet, Greville varied from Southwell in his bent to refuse satisfaction through repentance based upon salvation. In fact, Greville's Calvinism grew grimmer with the passage of time, especially as regards the notion of predestination, and his inner doubt brought him to grasp "the depth of [his] iniquity."[9] Speaking of "a God unknown," he yielded to desperation as regards society, politics, and the failure of his dreams. His *Dedication* asserts his religious uncertainty and pessimism as he questions the "secret judgments" of an impervious God who allowed Sidney's death.[10] At the same time though, his verse treatises display a rather different kind of pessimism one conjoined to idealism as well as "signs of fatalism" due to living in a world that is in continuous decline thus falling short of our "expectations and our faith." In contradistinction to Greville's highly ambiguous stance, Southwell unequivocally advocated the idea of redemption as his readiness to sacrifice himself for the cause of reclaiming the nation for Catholicism and redeeming himself, his coreligionists, and his monarch shows. The Jesuit missionary also asserted that God loves His creatures and if He "allows hazards to overtake them, it proceeds of love" and is to their benefit.[11] Christians have to give themselves "up to God ... become His perpetual bond-slaves and servants," consider the purpose for which they were created, why God decided to redeem them, and why He continues to show mercy towards them.[12]

Both Southwell and Greville, as their writings document, grappled with the meaning of heavenly life, as opposed to the earthly, and its retrieval. Since his early writings, Greville was preoccupied with the individual's relation to the Divine, nature, and the universe while he continued to question the conflict encountered by intellectual inquiry and the divinely predetermined boundaries. While Greville went on to lead a life of concession and disillusionment as well as an endless conflict between "the temporal claims of his long service and the eternal claims of his Protestant belief," Southwell assumed a stance that led to his death but won him sainthood.[13] The latter also urged his readers to participate in prayer and meditation in order to prepare for the union with the One. To him, the encounter with the Divine would result in knowledge or insight previously unavailable yet unaccountable or unforeseeable. He furthermore preached that all things temporal and material are insignificant in comparison to the purely ideal center of the spiritual and eternal world and that heavenly life is achieved by sacrificing the earthly one as illustrated by *Spiritual Exercises and Devotions*, and *Fourfold Meditation*.

As already demonstrated, not only religion but also politics impacted immensely the life and works of the two writers. Greville and Southwell were victims of state coercion exercised by William Cecil (and in the case of Greville Cecil's son, Robert, as well), hence the former's political ambitions were quelled (until the deaths of both Cecils) while the latter was executed as a traitor. Unquestionably, both took issue with the early modern political and religious authorities while none of them managed to witness either England promoting rigorously transnational Protestantism or the revival of Catholicism. Moreover, although they criticized Elizabeth's court and most particularly her counselors they remained loyal to her. Still their reaction differed. Greville, despite his deep disillusionment with the queen's court, especially after Essex's death, and his heavy critique of it especially through his drama, in the end he backed down. His ambiguous political standpoint and complex political identity are reflected in the fact that his political tracts suggest Tacitean leanings and promote the idea of opposition to tyrants, but not monarchs who implemented law and general welfare. In other words, despite his interest in Tacitus and his knowledge of continental resistance theories, Greville continued to uphold obedience to the monarch; he thus appeared to lean towards the support of a "monarchical republic" that would be ruled by virtuous "commonwealth-men." Even when in his play *Mustapha* he presented the radical alternative of rebellion through Achmat's contemplation on getting rid of tyrants in the end, as is always the case with him, he stepped back and decided that obedience to kings—the "roddes or blessings of the skye" is the lesser of two evils.[14] Thus, as has been documented, he was a "citizen concealed within [a] subject," who later in life became more conservative and "cast off the republic of his earlier longings."[15] Yet, he never refrained from highlighting the limitations and failings of human government. Greville could see neither God's presence in it nor His prescription of forming a just state, yet he saw Him intervene now and then to chastise tyranny and idolatry. He believed that government was tainted because it was disjoined from the divine order, which it was bound to emulate. Therefore, government must abide by community criteria, law, and caution and receive the weak aid of conscience and cognizance of the unavoidability of decline. Turning to Southwell, he maintained that his sovereign seldom or never heard the truth about the persecution of Catholics and argued that if she knew she would never permit such atrocities to be practiced upon them. He thus absolved the queen of any offence but condemned her advisors for deliberately misinforming her about the Catholic issue by generating false charges and producing strict measures against them. Although Southwell's view of the court was revolutionary if not radical, he never encouraged rebellion or overthrowing the monarch. When he defended himself against charges of treason, he claimed that "I testify by God, the avenger of perjury, that I have hatched neither plans nor conspiracies against the Queen or the Kingdom; I have come only to offer aid to those desiring sacraments in the Catholic rites."[16] In fact, Southwell envisioned a different kind of monarch and court that the political world was incapable of providing. He thus pointed to the heavenly King to resolve matters that afflicted the earthly court and proposed that to be a good Christian courtier one must follow "the Prince, Christ." Moreover, he promulgated a passionate conciliatory penchant without ever conceding his mission until he met his death as a traitor. It is also worth noting that although politics and religion consistently dovetail in Greville and Southwell's oeuvre, politics appears as a major topic in Greville's works with the exclusion of the *Treatise of Religion*, while Southwell's works, with the exception of *A Humble Supplication to her Maiestie*, address religious topics and "embrace a martyrdom of the spirit," even if under them a political undercurrent flows as is the case throughout his oeuvre.[17] For Greville, being a public figure, the political landscape prevails while religion forms a strong substratum; for Southwell, a missionary, religion shapes and dominates his work while politics appears as a critical subtext through which he records the suppression and persecution of Catholics as well as his desire to reform society, the court, and the ruler.

Both Greville and Southwell not only broached the complex relationship between state and church they also led a precarious life in terms of their political selves: the former, as already mentioned, was strongly interested in republicanism and displayed strong Tacitean tendencies in particular while he passed implicit, yet potentially radical critique on the Elizabethan and Jacobean courts. Greville began his career as "a deeply committed international Calvinist," he questioned the Elizabethan and all the more so the Jacobean reign, and ended his life in religious and political despondency. Similarly, his plea for divine punishment recorded repeatedly in his writings affirms his belief that both religion and politics were tarnished by tyranny and idolatry. He also maintained unresolved his conflict between belief in divine and in popular sovereignty, and between absolutism and constitutionalism. On the one hand, he called for and defended absolute monarchy, on the other he was its caustic critic, while he resented both social inequality and "faith in constitutionalism." He criticized tyranny but supported monarchy, asserted "the fruits of peace" yet made "recommendations on the conduct of war."[18] *Mustapha*, for example, constitutes to a large extent an attempt to engage with the idea of a double resistance, that is, resisting the politics of patriarchy and Calvinist defiance to the concept of fatherhood in an ideological forging of nationhood even if, as always with Greville, it cannot be sustained to the end. His dualism is exemplified in being trapped between a past he chiefly idealized and a present that he deemed putrefied. Greville's drama also reflects his deep pessimism concerning the nature of (human) government. *Alaham* starts and finishes with political agitation, moral decay, and extreme violence, dramatizes the ills of fashioning regicide and patricide as divinely sanctioned and represents a dystopia of radical instability associated with monarchical, familial, and religious identities. Coincidentally, Greville refused to support either monarchism or republicanism wholly. Instead, he presented the perils and pitfalls of monarchical absolutism as well as alluded to the foundational myth of republicanism in order to underline the inability of political violence to avert state crisis and purge a corrupt body politic. Unlike Greville's irresolute stance, Southwell, although similarly confident that the political world could not offer a good ruler, adopted the role of the Christian courtier, in order to "castigate" and "instruct" the Elizabethan court. He thus ignored Rome and William Allen's directive to all missionaries to abstain from interfering in state affairs, or referring to the Queen. He wrote "New Prince, New Pompe" to challenge the Elizabethan courtiers, employing the Incarnation and Proleptic Passion in the hope of reforming the court; and *A Humble Supplication to her Maiestie*, to refute the 1591 *Proclamation* and assert that although his coreligionists were loyal to the queen and ready to die to protect her and her kingdom they would never abandon the Church of Rome.

During the sixteenth and seventeenth centuries learning underwent dramatic change to justify the lawful quest of knowledge within the predominant religious and social culture. Whether in the fields of natural philosophy, science, or alchemy, all regarded with suspicion, exponents sought to legitimize their studies by recurring to religious rhetoric and reasoning. The writings of both Greville and Southwell reflect the radical cultural changes brought about by the advent of anthropocentric humanism, which was founded to a large extent on scientific discoveries. This revolution and intellectual revitalization that took place in the sixteenth century yielded a rational approach that intersected literary production, and introduced a new discourse that distinguished science from religion. For instance, the allegorical interpretation of the Bible was forsaken as misleading and unchristian; and reason became the alternative method that led to a more secularized explication of the hidden meanings of the text. In this light, Greville's tracts illustrate an incessant conflict between the sacred and the secular as well as between powerful feelings and reason, while Southwell, acknowledging the value of Aristotle's golden mean and Augustine's concept of reason, uses rationality to interpret theological matters that concerned the church but also employs poetic affect to re-channel affections. Moreover, both Greville and Southwell expressed strong emotions such as despair due to their deep awareness of their sinfulness and incapacity to fulfill their goals whether political or religious yet they managed to constrain and moderate them through reason.

Considering the topic of readership, Greville's stance is far more disputable than that of Southwell, who was clearly interested in conveying not only his thoughts on religious matters but also his political convictions to his readers. Unlike the Jesuit missionary, Greville never endorsed the idea of either addressing or inviting any type of wide readership of his works while alive and abstained sternly from publishing his literary products. Instead, he incessantly revised them while he set one of them—his tragedy on Antony and Cleopatra—on fire in the aftermath of Essex's execution. Nonetheless, in his *Life of Sidney*, he declared that he chose to write to those that like him were searching for a safe haven in the midst of a dangerous travail hence, setting himself in a circle of elite coterie communicants that had plunged into despair due to the ills of a corrupt, decrepit age.[19] Despite his reserved stance, and due to his anguish for the rise of Stuart absolutism, in the 1620s he founded a chair of history at Cambridge. In doing so, "he was not taking an ideological position but rather what he saw as a practical step to spare England the terrible violence that raged across Europe during the sixteenth century."[20] Greville invited the Leiden scholar Isaac Dorsilaus to give a series of lectures on Tacitus that "had become a favored preserve of Englishmen resistant to absolutism," thus reflecting his belief that "the study of ancient history might prove a check on tyranny."[21] Dorsilaus's first two lectures however, were so disturbing to William Laud that he was banned by Charles I from lecturing and forbade to do so even by Greville in spite of the fact that he continued to receive his patron's stipend for many years to come. Ironically, Dorsilaus later served as counsel for the king's persecution and was murdered by a Scot royalist. Clearly, Greville was unable to prevent the horrors of the civil war, just as he failed to forge the international Protestantism that both Sidney and he had fervently envisioned as young courtiers of the Elizabethan reign. Equally, if not even more significantly, his endowment of Tacitean lectures took unexpected turns as the near history of the civil war proved beyond any doubt. After all, John Milton was one of the Cambridge students at that time who regarded Tacitus "the greatest possible enemy of tyrants."[22]

Indeed, Greville and Southwell's works had repercussions they never intended. The former's *Dedication*, which was devoted to the life and death of his friend Sidney, was held responsible for instigating republican sentiment that would fuel the civil wars to come, none of which Greville the monarchist would have intended. Equally ironically, Southwell's work went through numerous editions and although popular, was not effective in converting Protestants into Catholicism as he had wished but instead initiated "the seventeenth-century meditative tradition of the Protestant devotional lyric." His narratives mainly intended to prepare his coreligionists for martyrdom, console and comfort them, but also persuade them that suffering was part of life and that those who endured suffering, like Christ, were ready to undergo not only persecution and imprisonment but also violent death if need be.[23] He also wrote about the bloody story of missionary priests who adopted disguise to elude the authorities, or died on the scaffold, as well as the fate of those recusant families who endangered their life to protect the leaders of the Catholic exile movement by offering them sanctuary in their homes. Clearly the printed word became a potent means that could move "the faithful to endurance and inspire the apostate to conversion."[24] Indeed, Southwell's writings were designed for proselytization yet through the publication and reprints of his work during his life he succeeded in imploding barriers between the Protestants and Catholics and presenting himself as a spiritual reconciliator, in spite of the severity of his death and sacrifice. As a peace proponent he opposed conspiracy against the Protestant state as well as ideas which inspired belligerency and divisiveness between the two communities. Instead, he was determined to find a means to terminate the strife between the Protestant state and its Catholic subjects and proposed conciliation in the hope of terminating the persecution, accusation, and execution of his coreligionists as traitors who served the King of Spain. Southwell also hoped his poems would enable his readers to reverse their earthly values and take on those of Bethlehem, the genuine court of heaven. He promulgated the need for redeeming a decayed Christian identity from materialism stressing in the meantime individual transformation. He also suggested that if the monarch and her courtiers decided to read his poems they would be resolved to appraise the manner by which they presented their identity as figures of power. In addition to political instruction, Southwell was also preoccupied with the religious teaching of the faithful. His aim was to lead readers to purer affections so by fashioning himself as an English complaint poet he attempted to redirect, even to shape, his readers' passions. Southwell linked the complaint to his mission expressing his wish to attune verse and virtue, passion and piety but also to arouse the Protestant reader's interest in his own Catholic faith. By adapting the continental Catholic devotional mode to English secular poetry, Southwell appealed to Protestant readers to harmonize passion and piety and postulated that Christ's love has the capacity to control passions as well as reason. He also invited the reader to adopt the Ignatian method to human passion that differed from the moderate neo-Stoic approach that characterized Calvin's analysis of the biblical texts. Yet Southwell has not only been praised but also blamed for importing the Italian baroque into English verse, particularly the popular tears poetry and appropriating the "continental Catholic *devotional* mode into an English secular *poetic* mode." To appeal widely to their readership the English Protestant writers, influenced by Southwell's conciliatory language, devotional verse and poetry of tears, omitted overt Catholic references and borrowed not only the profound emotional depiction of Christ's Passion but also those literary strategies discovered couched in his work.[25] Although his works were "appropriated and received variously by private circles and public audiences Catholics, Protestants and even Puritans" his "sacred poetry became a contested site of religious identity and difference."[26] However, the fact that Southwell was considered a member of a lawless religious denomination and executed as a traitor drove many writers to silently appropriate his themes and style, while at other times "his influence is subsumed, fought against or both, as part of the ongoing Protestant mission to make over Catholic writing." Furthermore, his manuscript and print publications suggested various meanings to the different communities, as for example his prose work *A Short Rule of Good Living* which presents patterns of domestic piety shared equally by Protestants and Catholics that were major to the development of religious and national identities.[27]

Concluding, *Precarious Identities* has introduced a new study to the already available scholarship by bringing Greville and Southwell together while its essays have presented original readings of their writings within the context of the shifting cultural, political, and religious context of the late sixteenth and early seventeenth century as well as laid the ground for further discussion. In other words, the volume's aim was to encourage as well as further debate in the enduring significance of the deconstruction and construction of the self, a central theme of renaissance culture, in the works of other contemporary writers divided by their religious beliefs.

Notes

1 Fulke Greville, *A Dedication to Sir Philip Sidney*, in *The Prose Works of Fulke Greville, Lord Brooke*, ed. John Gouws (Oxford: Clarendon Press, 1986), 68–69.
2 Brian Cummings, *The Literary Culture of the Reformation: Grammar and Grace* (Oxford: Oxford UP, 2009), 308.
3 Ibid., 62.
4 Freya Sierhuis, "The Idol of the Heart: Liberty, Tyranny, and Idolatry in the Work of Fulke Greville," *Modern Language Review*, 106, no. 3 (2011): 634.
5 Geoffrey Bullough, "Introduction," in *Poems and Dramas of Fulke Greville, First Lord Brooke*, ed. Geoffrey Bullough, 2 vols. (Edinburgh: Oliver & Boyd, 1939), 4.
6 Joan Rees, *Fulke Greville, Lord Brooke, 1554–1628: A Critical Biography* (London: Routledge & Kegan Paul, 1971), 6.
7 Cummings, *The Literary Culture of the Reformation*, 360.
8 Robert Southwell, *Spiritual Exercises & Devotions*, trans. P. E. Hallett (New York: Benziger Brothers, 1931), 33.
9 Fulke Greville, *Caelica*, sonnet XCIX, in *The Works in Verse and Prose Complete of the Right Honourable Fulke Greville, Lord Brooke*, vol. 3, ed. Alexander B. Grosart (St. George's, Blackburn, Lancashire, privately printed, 1870), 127.
10 Fulke Greville, *The Life of the Renowned Sir Philip Sidney* in *The Works in Verse and Prose Complete of the Right Honourable Fulke Greville, Lord Brooke*, vol. 4, ed. Alexander B. Grosart (St. George's, Blackburn, Lancashire, privately printed, 1870), 119.
11 Robert Southwell, *A Short Rule of Good Life* (London: G. Eld, 1606), chapter 1:16.
12 Ibid., chapter 1:25.
13 Kenneth Graham, *The Performance of Conviction: Plainness and Rhetoric in the Early English Renaissance* (Ithaca: Cornell UP, 1994), 97.
14 *Poems and Dramas of Fulke Greville, first Lord Brooke*, ed. Geoffrey Bullough, vol. 2 (Oxford: Oxford UP, 1945), 35.
15 Patrick Collinson, "The Monarchical Republic of Queen Elizabeth I," in *Elizabethan Essays*, ed. Patrick Collinson (London: Hambledon Press, 1994), 19.

16 Alexandra Walsham, *Church Papists: Catholicism, Conformity, and Confessional Polemic in Early Modern England* (Woodbridge, Suffolk: The Boydell Press, 1993), 14; Christopher Haigh, *English Reformations: Religion, Politics and Society under the Tudors* (Oxford: Clarendon, Press, 1993), 8.
17 Sister Diana Marie Shaw, "Such Fire is Love: The Bernadine Poetry of Robert Southwell S.J." *Christianity and Literature*, 62, no. 3 (Spring 2013): 348.
18 Sierhuis, "The Idol of the Heart," 634.
19 Greville, *The Life of the Renowned Sir Philip Sidney*, 34–35.
20 Rolland Mellor, "Tacitus, Academic Politics, and Regicide in the Reign of Charles I: The Tragedy of Dr. Isaac Dorislaus," *International Journal of the Classical Tradition*, 11, no. 2 (Fall 2004): 172.
21 Ibid.,174, 185.
22 Ibid., 181.
23 For more on the subject see Arthur Marotti, *Religious Ideology and Cultural Fantasy: Catholic and Anti-Catholic Discourses in Early Modern England.* (Indiana: Notre Dame UP, 2005), 78. Marotti also states that "religious history is an integral part of cultural history especially for an era in which people interpreted the world through religious understanding and used religious language to define most areas of individual experience and social intercourse" 206. Moreover, Peter Lake points out that "the pamphlets written during the early modern era presented the world as a battleground between the forces of good and evil. They showed a vision of an inverted and perverted social order and over against it an equally idealized view of a perfectly integrated, stable and harmonious society. The real world existed somewhere in between pushed one way or the other by the struggle that was raging between Satan and human sin on the one hand, and divine providence and justice and mercy on the other." See Peter Lake and Michael Questier, *The Anti-Christ's Lewd Hat: Protestants, Papists and Players in Post-Reformation England* (New Haven: Yale UP, 2002), 147.
24 Cummings, *The Literary Culture of the Reformation*, 329. See also Sarah Covington, "Consolation on Golgotha: Comforters and Sustainers of Dying Priests in England 1580–1625," *Journal of Ecclesiastical History*, 60, no. 2 (2009): 270–293.
25 Ibid., 332.
26 Susannah Monta, "Uncommon Prayer? Robert Southwell's *A Short Rule for a Good Life* and the Catholic Domestic Devotion in Post-Reformation England," in *Redrawing the Map of Early Modern English Catholicism*, ed. Lowell Gallagher (Toronto: Toronto UP, 2012), 248.
27 Ibid.

Bibliography

Bloom, Harold. *The Anxiety of Influence: A Theory of Poetry*. New York: Oxford UP, 1973.
Bullough, Geoffrey, ed. "Introduction." In *Poems and Dramas of Fulke Greville, First Lord Brooke*. 2 vols. Edinburgh: Oliver & Boyd, 1939.
Collinson, Patrick. "The Monarchical Republic of Queen Elizabeth I." In *Elizabethan Essays*. Edited by Patrick Collinson. London: Hambledon Press, 1994.
Covington, Sarah. "Consolation on Golgotha: Comforters and Sustainers of Dying Priests in England 1580–1625." *Journal of Ecclesiastical History*, 60, no. 2 (2009): 270–293.
Cummings, Brian. *The Literary Culture of the Reformation: Grammar and Grace*. Oxford: Oxford UP, 2009.

Graham, Kenneth. *The Performance of Conviction: Plainness and Rhetoric in the Early English Renaissance.* Ithaca: Cornell UP, 1994.

Greville, Fulke. *A Dedication to Sir Philip Sidney. In The Prose Works of Fulke Greville, Lord Brooke.* Edited by John Gouws. Oxford: Clarendon Press, 1986.

Greville, Fulke. "The Life of the Renowned Sir Philip Sidney." In *The Prose Works of Fulke Greville, Lord Brooke.* Edited by John Gouws. Oxford: Clarendon Press, 1986.

Greville, Fulke. *The Works in Verse and Prose Complete of the Right Honourable Fulke Greville, Lord Brooke, vol. 3.* Edited by Alexander B. Grosart. Lancashire, 1870.

Haigh, Christopher. *English Reformations: Religion, Politics and Society under the Tudors.* Oxford: Clarendon, Press, 1993.

Lake, Peter and Michael Questier. *The Anti-Christ's Lewd Hat: Protestants, Papists and Players in Post-Reformation England.* New Haven: Yale UP, 2002.

Marotti, Arthur. *Religious Ideology and Cultural Fantasy: Catholic and Anti-Catholic Discourses in Early Modern England.* Indiana: Notre Dame UP, 2005.

Mellor, Rolland. "Tacitus, Academic Politics, and Regicide in the Reign of Charles I: The Tragedy of Dr. Isaac Dorislaus." *International Journal of the Classical Tradition*, 11, no. 2 (Fall 2004): 153–193.

Monta, Susannah. "Uncommon Prayer? Robert Southwell's *A Short Rule for a Good Life* and the Catholic Domestic Devotion in Post-Reformation England." In *Redrawing the Map of Early Modern English Catholicism.* Edited by Lowell Gallagher. Toronto: Toronto UP, 2012.

Rees, Joan. *Fulke Greville, Lord Brooke, 1554–1628: A Critical Biography.* London: Routledge & Kegan Paul, 1971.

Shaw, Sister Diana Marie. "Such Fire is Love: The Bernadine Poetry of Robert Southwell S.J." *Christianity and Literature*, 62, no. 3 (Spring 2013): 333–353.

Sierhuis, Freya. "The Idol of the Heart: Liberty, Tyranny, and Idolatry in the Work of Fulke Greville." *Modern Language Review*, 106, no. 3 (2011): 625–646.

Southwell, Robert. *A Short Rule of Good Life.* London: G. Eld, 1606.

Southwell, Robert. *Spiritual Exercises & Devotions.* Translated by P. E. Hallett. New York: Benziger Brothers, 1931.

Walsham, Alexandra. *Church Papists: Catholicism, Conformity, and Confessional Polemic in Early Modern England.* Woodbridge, Suffolk: The Boydell Press, 1993.

Index

Page numbers in *italics* denote figures.

For Product Safety Concerns and Information please contact our EU
representative GPSR@taylorandfrancis.com
Taylor & Francis Verlag GmbH, Kaufingerstraße 24, 80331 München, Germany